BE VERY AFRAID

ROBERT WUTHNOW

BE VERY AFRAID

THE CULTURAL RESPONSE TO TERROR, PANDEMICS, ENVIRONMENTAL DEVASTATION, NUCLEAR ANNIHILATION, AND OTHER THREATS

OXFORD
UNIVERSITY PRESS
2010

OXFORD
UNIVERSITY PRESS

Oxford University Press, Inc., publishes works that further
Oxford University's objective of excellence
in research, scholarship, and education.

Oxford   New York
Auckland   Cape Town   Dar es Salaam   Hong Kong   Karachi
Kuala Lumpur   Madrid   Melbourne   Mexico City   Nairobi
New Delhi   Shanghai   Taipei   Toronto

With offices in
Argentina   Austria   Brazil   Chile   Czech Republic   France   Greece
Guatemala   Hungary   Italy   Japan   Poland   Portugal   Singapore
South Korea   Switzerland   Thailand   Turkey   Ukraine   Vietnam

Copyright © 2010 by Oxford University Press, Inc.

Published by Oxford University Press, Inc.
198 Madison Avenue, New York, NY 10016

www.oup.com

Oxford is a registered trademark of Oxford University Press

Library of Congress Cataloging-in-Publication Data
Wuthnow, Robert.
Be very afraid : the cultural response to terror, pandemics,
environmental devastation, nuclear annihilation,
and other threats / by Robert Wuthnow.
p.   cm.
Includes bibliographical references and index.
ISBN 978-0-19-973087-2
1. Emergency management. 2. Threats. I. Title.
HV551.2.W88 2010
303.48'5—dc22
2009026879

9 8 7 6 5 4 3 2 1
Printed in the United States of America
on acid-free paper

I decline to accept the end of man. It is easy enough to say that man is immortal simply because he will endure: that when the last ding-dong of doom has clanged and faded from the last worthless rock hanging tideless in the last red and dying evening, that even then there will still be one more sound: that of his puny inexhaustible voice, still talking. I refuse to accept this. I believe that man will not merely endure: he will prevail. He is immortal, not because he alone among creatures has an inexhaustible voice, but because he has a soul, a spirit capable of compassion and sacrifice and endurance. Our tragedy today is a general and universal physical fear so long sustained by now that we can even bear it. There are no longer problems of the spirit. There is only the question: When will I be blown up?

William Faulkner, Nobel Prize Acceptance Speech, 1950

CONTENTS

BE VERY AFRAID

INTRODUCTION

FOR MORE THAN SIX DECADES, humankind has lived with the knowledge that it could be the agent of its own annihilation. We are constantly reminded of crises, large and small, present and anticipated. What effect has this awareness had on us? How have we responded?

The simple answer is that we have responded quite aggressively. Faced with the possibility of nuclear annihilation, terrorism, and the prospect of pandemics, we have hardly sat back and done nothing. We have rolled up our collective sleeves and spent billions—billions waging the Cold War, billions fighting terror, and billions on vaccines and medical research.

Now that climate change is seen as a threat to our very existence, our response is the same. Plans are in the works to spend billions of dollars seeking solutions. Everything from wind power to fuel-efficient vehicles is on the table.

Critics argue that a lot of the money will be spent needlessly. Some point to preparations for the Y2K (the year 2000, or millennium bug) crisis and to pandemics that never materialized. The problem, some argue, is that big government bureaucracies have come into existence, and the bureaucrats at these agencies are promoting fear to fatten their budgets.

But of course that argument is too simple. Climate change really does threaten our existence. Millions could die from a pandemic or a dirty bomb strategically planted in a metropolitan area. We do need action to prepare for and guard against these threats.

The crux of the matter is this: We have a built-in propensity to act, but we need to engage in the *right* actions. We err so often because we are like generals fighting the last war. Terror strikes and we respond as if we are resuming the Cold War. Avian flu appears and we look to the epidemic of 1918 for guidance. Government agencies notoriously do so, but we as citizens do too. A threat appears and we buy duct tape because we did that the last time.

The complicated part is figuring out why we so often respond inappropriately. One reason why is that peril is terrifying and causes us to react with our emotions. Also, we respond less effectively than we might because it is difficult to assess risks. These are contributing factors, but they do not get at the real issue.

What has to be understood is that our responses to peril are fundamentally driven by the need to make sense of our very humanity. They are not just about solving the next crisis but about who we are as a people and as persons. How we respond tells us that we have courage, that we can overcome vulnerability, and that we can go ahead with our lives in the midst of adversity. Our responses speak to the basic fragility of the human condition.

Peril is the mirror we hold up to ourselves. It forces us to ask what it means to be human. It focuses our attention on the shortness and uncertainty of our lives. We imagine the worst—death, the death of our children, the destruction of our way of life. Would we be able to withstand the suffering? Would our cherished institutions fail? Would chaos erupt?

Living with the prospect of devastation, even annihilation, as we have for more than two generations, has shaped our entire culture. We have created and live in a culture of peril. When a major event happens and when some new threat appears on the horizon we devote an enormous amount of effort to making sense of the event—and of ourselves. And as we do that, some of what we learn is narrowly applicable to the next crisis that comes along, but much of it is not. It has to do with our sense of vulnerability and our desire to believe in our way of life. We have to sort out what is applicable and what is not.

The sorting needed is difficult because we seldom address these basic existential questions through sustained philosophical or theological reflection. Instead we affirm our humanity by convincing ourselves that engaging in practical tasks is the best approach. We assess risks and look for solutions that will get us through the next immediate crisis. The discussions become quite technical and seem very reasonable. They focus on efficiency and effectiveness. But they are also how we define ourselves. They give us meaning.

Understanding the extent of this quest for meaning takes us into realms of the social sciences that are seldom consulted when thinking about huge national and international crises. It becomes necessary to examine the psychology and the cognitive frameworks involved and to learn from the work of cultural sociologists. Our interpretive schemas become evident in the literature—the editorials and essays, fiction, poetry, personal accounts, and reports—that has been generated to make sense of peril. We need to understand both the literature and the organizations that produce this literature.

In the past, questions about responses to peril were often addressed by examining fear and the denial of fear. Grounded in Freudian psychoanalytic theories that were popular in the 1940s and 1950s, the emphasis on fear and denial became prominent in interpretations of American Cold War culture. Vestiges of this interpretive framework continue to be very much in evidence in recent treatments of the nation's response to the terrorist attacks of September 11, 2001 (abbreviated throughout this work as 9/11) and to other threats, such as global warming and pandemic influenza.

A recurrent theme in this literature is that fear results either in immobilization or in some kind of inappropriate response driven by suppressed anxiety. For example, in the 1980s it was widely argued by antinuclear activists that Americans were not doing more to mobilize against nuclear proliferation because of suppressed fear. Scholars have also argued that Americans' interest in material gratification stems from not wanting to face the fact that we could all perish or that we are permanently damaging the planet our children will inherit.

Recent scholarship, though, suggests that the emphasis on denial and immobilization is probably wrong. In reality, the more common response to crises—personal or societal—is to take action. We become mentally preoccupied with making plans and figuring out what to do. It reassures us to know that we are doing something, however tentative or ineffective it may be.

Usually this bias toward action serves us well. It encourages us to think realistically about what can and cannot be done. It results in the institutions we create to monitor and protect us from danger. The cultural response to perilous times involves a huge investment of time and resources in everything from commentary in the mass media to scholarly investigations, from scientific research to government programs.

Helpful as it is, this penchant for action sometimes gets us into trouble. Hoping that action will find solutions and make us feel better, we sometimes too easily follow the agendas set by government officials, listening to their warnings of potential threats, hoping to feel more powerful in the face of danger. The path from 9/11 to the U.S. invasion of Iraq has been a case in point.

Although the world has experienced major crises in the past, our time is unique in combining high levels of technical expertise with a continuing sense of extreme vulnerability. The more we learn about our world, the more we realize that our existence is precarious. The threat of a nuclear holocaust continues. Scientists warn of catastrophic effects on the human environment from global warming. Pandemic influenza poses recurrent danger to people everywhere. Terrorist plots have become more deadly and harder to predict. There are even threats of accidents from scientific research itself, as from a nuclear chain reaction or a supercollider experiment that spins out of control.

The fact that we have lived now for more than half a century with these potentially catastrophic threats suggests the need to step back and take stock, not of whether we have enough weapons in place or sufficient vaccines, but of what can be learned from our collective responses to these crises. Each crisis has been

different. The nuclear era dawned on the public consciousness almost instantaneously but took a long time to sink in and an even longer time for the public to
begin to assert its right to have a say in nuclear policy (weapons and power plants).
The attacks on 9/11 shocked the nation and set it on a course of action that is still
unfolding. A pandemic, some argue, could hit with little warning and with consequences far more severe than during the great influenza pandemic of 1918. The
awareness of climate change has emerged more slowly and in a bitterly contested
political context. Yet there are also common questions that arise from considering
these threats. What were the first signs of a public response to global warming?
Who was called on to provide interpretations? How did the public's faith in science
and technology come into play? Did individual citizens feel empowered or powerless? What made the difference? What kinds of emotions were monitored? How
were these understood? Did panics occur? How did policy makers respond?

IT MAY SEEM STRANGE IN RETROSPECT, but I cannot say that I grew up fearing a nuclear attack. I attended elementary school during the 1950s when children learned
to hide under their desks in case a bomb exploded overhead. I was in high school
when Kennedy and Khrushchev squared off about Soviet missiles in Cuba. I lived
close enough to a Strategic Air Command base to see the big bombers circling in
and out. A field not far away contained a missile silo with a nuclear warhead. Yet
life went on. It did so, not because we believed the world was safe, but because
there were so many practical things to think about. That was one way of responding to peril. It conditioned me to think that whatever might happen, life would go
on as usual. But was that the case? Was what I learned wrong?

Unlike authors who write about peril because they fear it has been neglected,
therefore, my interest in the topic stems from the hunch that we have actually
thought about it quite a lot—indeed, have done a lot, and have persuaded ourselves that it is manageable. In the first year after Hiroshima, the four leading
newspapers in the United States carried more than ten thousand articles about
atomic weapons, energy, and power. Nearly every major journalist, literary
figure, and theologian felt compelled to write on the topic. An effort to collect
publishable nuclear holocaust poetry by Japanese authors required fifteen volumes. A listing of films about devastating catastrophes and annihilation included more than a thousand titles. Books about impending crises, such as
Rachel Carson's *Silent Spring* and Jonathan Schell's *The Fate of the Earth*, reached
vast readerships, while such apocalyptic books as Hal Lindsey's *The Late Great
Planet Earth* and the "Left Behind" series attracted even larger audiences. One
would be hard pressed, were one broadly interested in the production of contemporary culture, to find any theme to which more cultural work has been
devoted than these extreme crises.

Of the crises that humanity currently faces or has faced in recent years, four in particular stand out—and are the ones I examine in detail. One is the threat of a nuclear holocaust. This threat or something like it had been anticipated prior to 1945 and, after rising in public consciousness on several occasions during the Cold War (such as during the Cuban missile crisis in 1962), appears to have peaked in the 1980s as evidence mounted about the irreparable global damage that would be unleashed by a nuclear war. Although discussion of nuclear war subsided after the collapse of the Soviet Union in 1989, concern about nuclear proliferation has continued. With the attacks on New York and Washington in 2001, a second threat known as weapons of mass destruction and including biological and chemical warfare came increasingly into public prominence. Since that time, terror itself has been defined as one of the great dangers facing humanity. A third has been concern about a global pandemic, most notably through the spread of avian influenza ("bird flu"). The fourth is the threat of global climate change. After long discussions of more limited effects, global warming gained increasing interest during the 1980s and acquired status as scientific fact in most quarters around 2001. Yet the debate continues about how much of a threat climate change is and how it should be confronted.[1]

These perils have generated an enormous literature telling us not only about the details of each threat but also about how to live amid peril itself. We have learned what it means to be afraid and how people typically respond when they are. We have been taught that the planet is more interconnected and complex than humans would have understood in the past. There have been lessons in all of this about personal and social responsibility. Scientists and philosophers, pundits and theologians have been called on to render interpretations.

The striking fact about this great outpouring of cultural activity is that it depicts people struggling with questions about what to do. Hardly any of it shows people paralyzed with fear, passively awaiting the end, or denying that anything is amiss. The prevailing narratives concern themselves with defining the problem, discussing possible solutions, and then calling on citizens to live up to their moral obligations to help protect the common well-being and to be good stewards of the earth. Nothing, it appears, evokes discussion of moral responsibility quite as clearly as the prospect of impending doom. The picture of humanity that emerges in this literature is one of can-do problem solvers. Doing something, almost anything, affirms our humanity.

Yet there would be danger if anyone were satisfied with the simple fact that peril prompts us to action. The major threat to our planet now posed by climate change is quite different from the possibility of a terrorist strike or an outbreak of avian flu. The responses must differ. We have been conditioned to question the effectiveness of government and to be skeptical about the value of citizens' organizations. But we know about the threats endangering our lives because of the institutions we have created to track them. The institutions sometimes fail, and yet creating them and working through them is our best hope.

The challenge is making these institutions work better for us. As we spend billions on solutions to the major perils that threaten our existence, we need to understand that more is at stake than narrow technical discussions. We have been engaged for some time now in affirming our humanity in the face of potential annihilation. We need to look carefully at what we have learned.

ONE

PERILOUS TIMES

FOR ME, IT ALL BEGAN ONE MORNING with an innocent-looking e-mail. It was from
a credible news source informing me in matter of fact language that I must be
prepared to witness the death of my children and grandchildren as a terrible virus
wreaks havoc across the globe. This warning came amid a barrage of reports from
scientists and government agencies about the expected death toll from a viral pandemic. Hundreds of millions could die. The question was not *if* but *when*. The
same day I absorbed an editorial by a former government official warning that the
threat of nuclear weapons "remains greater today" than at the height of the Cold
War. More than a dozen nations have acquired nuclear weapons. Mechanisms of
deterrence that worked when only superpowers had such weapons have weakened. Rogue dictators could trigger an international conflagration. Terrorist groups
could easily unleash a dirty bomb in any major city. The resulting chaos would be
catastrophic. That evening I watched a television program about global warming.
One of the scientists reported a consensus among the scientific community that
more harm has been done to the planet in the last half century than at any time in
human history. Unless drastic steps are taken, permanent environmental damage
resulting in famine and disease is a likely result.

How should I react to this information? The numbing banality of modern mass
communication hardly obscures the gravity of these messages. E-mail is meant to
be scanned quickly, like headlines in a newspaper, with an ominous warning of
massive danger sandwiched between cheery greetings from friends and unsolic-
ited messages from spammers. Destruction of such magnitude, I cannot help but
feel, should be announced in some other way—and it would have to be, were the
conveniences of daily life suddenly suspended. The warning nevertheless registered with me, at least momentarily. Reading a newspaper editorial and watching
a television special take a bit longer, but the fact that stories about nuclear weapons,
global warming, and pandemics appear so frequently cannot be missed. News

organizations may be hyping the story. Nevertheless, the concerns remain. Images of Dresden, Hiroshima, and Chernobyl cycle through my mind. Experts may disagree on technical details, but it is hard to escape the awareness that horrendous events are real possibilities.

The truth is that serious perils to the existence of humanity have become a fact of contemporary life. The threat of mass death, environmental devastation, and even human extinction is an alarming reality. In the past twenty-five years, more than a thousand books have been published with "Armageddon" or "apocalypse" in their titles. What was once dismissed as apocalyptic fanaticism is now the prediction of leading scientists. A large majority of the world's population has never known a time when nuclear destruction was not a possibility. Americans of my generation, now in their fifties and sixties, grew up with the nightmare of civil defense drills. Hardly a year went by without stories of narrowly averted intercontinental ballistic missile launchings. What was at first presented only as a matter of avoiding radioactive fallout (by installing shelters in our basements) proved increasingly to be a terrifying specter. The atmosphere itself would likely ignite and a global winter that no humans could survive would be the result. Because of global warming, younger generations now face a future in which entire cities, such as New Orleans, Miami, and New York may be submerged as ice caps melt and sea levels rise. Science—once considered the solution to all problems—now demonstrates the rapidity at which viruses mutate and the impossibility of guarding against them. Science further posits that human life as we know it is an infinitesimal blip in time and space.[1]

FACED WITH AN UNPRECEDENTED AWARENESS of the fragility of human life, it is almost inconceivable that we are unaffected by this knowledge. The uncertainty, the scale of the impending catastrophes, and the inability to comprehend them are surely a source of profound anxiety. To know that death awaits each of us individually is one thing. To contemplate the possibility of human extinction or death and disease on such a scale that survival itself may no longer be welcome is quite another. Those who mourn the passing of a relative or friend find comfort in considering that person's progeny and contributions and in knowing that his or her memory will live. The possibility of no progeny and no world in which the evanescent contributions of a life, or indeed of all life, would matter is nearly unthinkable. Short of such extreme scenarios, humanity now lives with the grinding impact of knowing the constant horror of terrorism, with worries about the sudden news that weapons of mass destruction have been unleashed on millions of people, and with the recurring threat of uncontrollable disease.

The world has had more than a half century to adjust to the realization that peril exists on a scale never before imagined. In that time, we might suppose, a great deal of learning—conscious or unconscious—would have taken place. Humanity may have come to a greater understanding of its fragility. Our appreciation for the uniqueness of our species may have increased. Dread could likely have turned into a pervasive anxiety, fraught with moments of hopelessness about our children's future. Or it could have been replaced by a sober awareness of what must be done to survive. Perhaps we have learned to be better prepared. The possibility exists, too, that living in constant danger has resulted in a subterranean shift in how we approach life itself. The shift could be evident in how we fill our days, in how we think about problems, and how we make plans. It may have shaped how we view the meaning of life and how we anticipate death.

Yet the psychic impact of living in profoundly perilous times has received surprisingly little attention. Perhaps the danger is too great for us to consider seriously its mental and emotional consequences. Early in the nuclear era writers applied psychoanalytic perspectives to the collective neuroses they thought surely would be observed. Clinical studies of European children traumatized during World War II served as a model. That interest waned when researchers discovered few acute symptoms from Americans' fears of a nuclear holocaust. It all but ceased as the popularity of Freudian theories declined. Polls have asked about potential crises. But polls tell us little about the existential anxieties evoked by long-term exposure to impending doom. Scientific research focuses on the technical details of how viruses are transmitted and how long it takes for a glacier to melt. It pays less attention to the public's emotional reactions. The news media are better equipped to report that a scientist has made an ominous discovery or a government official has uttered an urgent warning than to ponder the deeper meanings of being exposed for decades to ominous discoveries and urgent warnings.

The current situation is comparable to a group of campers huddled around a fire in the middle of a forest. They know a terrible threat to their very existence lurks in the forest. The threat could overtake them at any moment. It could spare some of them or it could find a way to destroy the entire forest and everything beyond. What impact does this knowledge have as they sit by the fire? Is their response conditioned only by adrenaline? Do they contemplate the end and ponder the (fleeting) significance of their lives? Or do they experience an urge for beer and hot dogs?

OUR ABILITY TO THINK, INTERPRET, QUESTION, frame, ponder, reflect, and organize—to make and appreciate art and culture—is what makes us human. Other species react instinctively. A genetically programmed signal—some mysterious, fine-tuned sensory apparatus—that a tsunami is coming tells them to flee. We alone have a capacity for abstract thought, a sense of the future, and the capacity to wonder what life means. Our adaptive faculty involves using our brains to form associations among the stimuli we receive. Were it not for this capacity, mirror neurons would prompt us to respond instinctively, harming when we witness harm, crying when we see others crying, and so on. Recent advances in cognitive neuroscience show that mental engagement blocks these reactions. The ritualistic behavior that arises in response to mourning and in times of personal crisis involves thought. It requires remembering how to properly perform the rituals, retelling the old stories, reciting texts, playing roles. We do not make up these thoughts. They are part of the repertoire that we learn from our friends and families. They reflect what we have heard in the past about crises and risks. Knowing that life can be destroyed by nuclear weapons and that the planet we inhabit can be severely damaged by carbon emissions engages our minds in the use of a cultural repertoire rich with stories, accounts, and arguments.[2]

At first blush, the response to perilous times appears to be one of not doing much. Despite the overwhelming anxieties that planetary devastation might produce, daily life is pretty much business as usual. An unthinkable tragedy, such as the attacks on September 11, 2001, occurs, and yet life goes on, barely changed from day to day. Work continues, people plan for the future, and expect to live out their days. According to a study in Israel during a period of intermittent terrorist attacks, traffic patterns demonstrated how little these attacks affected daily routines. Traffic volume dipped temporarily but returned to normal four days after each attack. Light and serious accident rates were unchanged. Fatalities rose on day three for reasons the researchers could not explain, but were at average levels a day later.[3] Writers who seek to raise consciousness about impending catastrophes nearly always begin by remarking on the public's indifference. Nobody seems to be worried about a nuclear holocaust. People are unwilling to contemplate the effects of global warming. The campers are more interested in tending the fire than in attending to the dangers lurking deeper in the woods.

The popular psychological description of this response is denial. Things that are too frightening to think about are easier to handle by denying that they could happen. Just as it is difficult to think too often about our own death, so it is hard to confront our fears about cataclysmic destruction. When "people, organizations, governments or whole societies are presented with information that is too disturbing," Stanley Cohen writes in *States of Denial*, the information is "somehow repressed."[4] Anxiety, the argument goes, is immobilizing, leading us to retreat into ourselves. It is easier to settle into the humdrum of familiar routines, imagining that these will continue against all odds.[5]

Denial, though, is not so easily accomplished. In an intriguing series of experiments, psychologist Daniel M. Wegner and his colleagues asked subjects *not* to think about a white bear—positing, as Dostoyevsky famously did in posing this challenge to his brother, that they would have difficulties. They did indeed. The more subjects tried to avoid thinking about a white bear, the more they thought of one.[6] Though hardly surprising, these results have much to say about responses to impending crises. Freud argued that denial is an act of unwilled repression, as in the case of an abused child who simply is unable to remember what happened because the memory is too painful. But denying that a city was destroyed by an atomic bomb or that a nuclear power plant could release radiation into the atmosphere is an act of conscious suppression. As with telling oneself not to think of a white bear, it requires effort. Unwilled repression would be impossible. There are too many reminders of past and impending dangers. The largest ones are impossible to forget. Events like the assassination of President Kennedy and the 9/11 attacks evoke what scientists call flashbulb memory. Every detail is etched in consciousness. Even minor threats, such as pictures of frightening faces in laboratory experiments, capture and hold attention.[7]

Denying that peril exists is something we learn, just as laboratory subjects learn not to think of white bears by training themselves to think of red Volkswagens. Thought suppression of this kind is not instinctive, but cultural. Nobody can be oblivious to discussions of nuclear annihilation, weapons of mass destruction, environmental catastrophes, and similar threats. The news media are filled with stories of these dangers. Polls show that people are in fact aware of them. Hearing of such perils, I may brush them aside almost instantaneously with the thought, "I will die sooner or later anyway," or "scientists will figure it out," or "the risks of this happening are too small to worry about." Yet these fleeting thoughts are ones I have learned. They are abbreviated scripts, slogans, and references that have been picked up from parents, friends, teachers, newspapers, television, motion pictures, and the Internet. To speak of denial is to draw on cultural categories. The psychological theory through which denial is interpreted is itself one such category. What to some appears as an irrational defense mechanism will be defined by others as simply getting on with life.

It further stands to reason that if denial is cultural, it is also social and indeed political. In the white bear experiments, subjects learned to think about red Volkswagens because an authority figure—the researcher—told them to. In real life, people think distracting thoughts and remain silent about impending danger, not because they fail to see it, but because power arrangements encourage them to talk about other things.[8] The story of the emperor's invisible new clothes nicely illustrates this point. It was the emperor's power that discouraged people from discussing the matter more candidly. An alcoholic parent, lying in a stupor on the living room floor, may not be the topic of family conversation. The reason is that confronting the problem would be more upsetting to the family's habits, its image in the community, and perhaps even its ability to put food on the table, than remaining silent. So it is with the larger perils facing humanity. The reason why people do not discuss the proverbial elephant in the room may be that their leader has brought in something much worse, such as a tyrannosaurus. They do not speak because they assume government officials must know what they are doing. The proper response, they learn, is not to ponder the fragility of life but to launch a war.

If denial is culturally conditioned, the same is true when we actively think about peril and try to understand its meanings. The short way of saying this is that peril has a history. Not so long ago, most Americans had never heard the words "global warming" or "weapons of mass destruction." But they had heard plenty about enemies, threats, and annihilation during the Cold War. When new perils arose, it was natural to respond to them in ways that had become familiar.

A SECOND WAY OF THINKING about the response to scenarios of devastation is related to the view that people simply live in denial. In this perspective, annihilation and extinction are such imponderable possibilities that it is hard to think about them, even when we try. Thus, we escape into science fiction and disaster films as an outlet for our pent-up emotions. Hundreds of such books and movies have been produced in recent decades, including *The Day the Earth Caught Fire, Dr. Strangelove or: How I Learned to Stop Worrying and Love the Bomb, Fail-Safe, War of the Worlds,* and *The Day After Tomorrow.* They describe colliding planets, scientific experiments gone awry, and nuclear wars. Literature with apocalyptic religious themes has been particularly popular. These media permit a creative response to what is impossible fully to anticipate through the thought processes we use in ordinary life. In psychological terms, what we deny is actually repressed and thus sneaks unbidden into the literary or cinematic equivalent of our nightmares and dreams. Fantasy provides a vehicle for imagining what the last humans would do before they died. It portrays how some mutated species might repopulate the earth in a future millennium. Fantasy serves as a controlled space in which to contemplate the worst, to experience the accompanying emotions, and then to return to the comforting routine of ordinary life.[9]

Fantasy, by definition, is not reality. It is easier to be entertained by it than to take it seriously. Readers rejoice when the last humans are rescued by aliens. Moviegoers revel in images of giant tidal waves and snow-covered skyscrapers. In these respects, science fiction may reveal something about the public's yearning to make sense of the worst that could happen. And yet it would be inaccurate to suggest that fantasy is the only, or even the primary, way in which people respond to the possibility of impending doom. Compared with the numbers who read science fiction novels and see scary movies, far more of us live with peril by hearing summaries of the latest scientific findings on the news and talking about potential threats with our coworkers and families.

Emphasizing denial and fantasy presupposes that the guiding response to catastrophic events, whether actual or potential, is fear. The campers focus on the fire and tell ghost stories because they are afraid of what awaits them in the woods.

A person faced with some dreadful experience, such as being maimed in a grisly accident, is likely to cope by denying that the event could happen (or, in retrospect, that it did happen). If the fear is real but cannot be confronted directly, it is likely to surface in unanticipated ways, such as in nightmares or obsessive compulsive behavior. Being unable to confront his or her fears head-on, a person finds release in fantasies about sex and violence or by retreating to an alternative view of reality. The response to perilous times is, in this view, driven principally by the stark fear that hideous scenarios evoke.[10]

Fear is very much a part of the dangerous world in which we live. Studies conducted after the September 11, 2001, attacks showed that a majority of Americans were afraid similar events would occur and a significant minority of the public reported symptoms of acute stress, depression, and anxiety. Other polls have documented fears about missile attacks, atomic bombs, radiation, pollution, and disease. None of these studies conclude that the public is overwhelmed or immobilized by fear. And yet nagging worries about large-scale death and destruction are common.[11]

The human response to fear is in the first instance physiological. Cardiovascular and respiratory responses form the familiar "fight-or-flight" syndrome. An increase in neural activity of the amygdala where fear conditioning and emotional memories are centered takes place. The physiological response leads us to think of fear as an emotion that results in irrational or instinctual behavior. However, studies show that fear also activates neural responses in the prefrontal cortex where thinking takes place. These responses process the nature and extent of the perceived threat, control emotions, define goals, compare anticipated outcomes, and determine an appropriate course of action. Except for people with acute phobias, the response to fear involves cognitive processes that organize information into patterns and enable the person to strategize about what action to take.[12]

This cognitive dimension of fear consists of basic "schemas" that enable facial recognition and language use and more complex frameworks composed of the information we glean from personal interaction, memory, reading, watching television, and so on. A person's response to fear is shaped by the society in which he or she lives. We are all influenced by family and friendship networks, schools, neighborhoods, businesses, government bureaus, religious organizations, and the mass media. How we think about terrorism and global warming is shaped by what officials and scientists tell us and by depictions of these dangers in the mass media. In most instances it is also influenced by previous encounters with peril. To help explain a potential flu epidemic, for example, journalists write about a previous one and what scientists did or did not do to prevent it. In the Middle Ages, the meanings of mass death were largely defined by religion. In our time, the meanings of peril are shaped by influential government agencies, scientists, technical experts, and journalists.

OUR INDIVIDUAL RESPONSES to small-scale crises are influenced by social arrangements. When someone dies, loved ones mourn. Their response cannot be understood only as an expression of grief. They enact the scripts they have seen others perform at wakes and funerals. Words deemed socially appropriate are spoken at a funeral or memorial service. Music is present. Other words are communicated through telephone calls, condolence cards, and in conversations. An obituary is printed in the newspaper. An inscription is placed on a grave marker. A death certificate is filed. A will is read. If an accident involves multiple deaths, additional activities are likely. A community-wide memorial service is held and an investigation may be launched. When a natural disaster destroys homes, government officials and charitable organizations are expected to respond. Donations are sent and volunteers arrive. In anticipation of a disaster, an emergency preparedness plan may be publicized. Only a fraction of this behavior can be understood as a way of dealing with the emotion of fear. All of it is a way of preparing for and making sense of an event that has the potential to disrupt ordinary life.

The activity involved in making sense of deaths, accidents, disasters, and the like serves several purposes. It keeps people busy long enough to avoid being overwhelmed by their emotions. Formulaic practices, such as funerals and readings of wills, matter most. People perform their expected roles and in so doing make sense of themselves as, say, a widow or disaster victim. These performances prepare observers for how to behave when their time comes. Sense-making also helps to repair broken relationships. When relationships are bent or shattered by death or disaster, their meanings have to be reconstructed. Conversations provide the occasion for redefining oneself. Sense-making in times of crisis also involves coming to terms with transcendence. A rupture (real or anticipated) in daily life requires people to think about their place in the cosmos.[13]

There is another important aspect of what actually happens in or in anticipation of crises. Much of what occurs focuses on accomplishing tasks. Following a death, more time is likely to be spent notifying friends and relatives, contacting a funeral home or burial service, determining who should preside at the funeral, and working on similar details than at the funeral itself. In planning a community's response to a natural disaster, residents are less likely to be preoccupied with how they will grieve, learn new roles, or relate to the transcendent than with determining what must be done. In addition, government planning will consist of determining how to warn the public, when to evacuate, if the hospital has enough beds, whether looting is likely, where families will be safe, how much food to stock, and so on. Even when planning is ineffective, it is what people think and talk about. In the hours prior to Hurricane Katrina, journalists repeatedly interviewed residents and officials to learn what preparations they were making for staying or leaving, securing their possessions, maintaining order, and assisting the elderly and the needy. These are practical considerations, but they also constitute much of the sense-making activity associated with an expected event. Besides whatever tactical value they may have in solving a crisis they give us something concrete to think about. They break the larger crisis into specific tasks and assign significance to activities and ideas according to their relevance to those tasks. They give us victims with which to identify and scapegoats to blame. In the process, the narratives occupy people's minds and involve decisions about what is happening and what should be done.[14]

The response to peril will consist in large measure of problem solving. Research demonstrates that humans are inveterate problem solvers. In laboratory experiments, human subjects faced with an utterly meaningless pattern of random numbers typically define it as a puzzle to be solved. Terminally ill cancer patients continue until their strength is all but gone seeking new treatments and possible cures. Doing so sustains hope and a sense of dignity.[15] Healthcare professionals find that one of the most common end-of-life activities is "putting one's house in order": arranging financial affairs, making a will, compiling a living will, organizing one's funeral, figuring out ways to ease loved ones' burdens.[16] What appears in some instances as a denial of death is actually a focused effort to make it through the day. Fictional portrayals of human extinction are most believable when the last people alive search for ways to extend their days. Apocalyptic scenarios focus less on cosmic wisdom than on such practical tasks as figuring out when the end will come and how best to prepare. Problem solving is equally evident in the organized responses to perils that have faced humanity in recent decades. No sooner had nuclear weapons been invented than efforts began to determine how best to control them or to better channel their destructive powers toward enemies. Going to war after the 9/11 attacks can also be seen as a form of problem solving in that it showed that the U.S. government, acting on the American public's behalf, was taking action to rid the world of evil. Responses to pandemics and environmental threats have focused largely on the search for scientific and technological solutions.

PROBLEM SOLVING SERVES A DUAL PURPOSE. It concerns the technical details of figuring out what to do. It also is one of the major ways in which humans create meaning. In his classic work on the topic, Karl Duncker described problem solving as a two-stage process. The first stage involves a holistic apprehension, an intuitive grasp that a "problem situation" exists, and an attempt to frame it in general terms as a moral issue, for instance, or as a scientific problem, and so on. Emotion is a significant part of this initial process. A person feels conflicted, troubled, or possibly afraid that something is not right. The second stage consists of penetrating more deeply into the problem, examining its underlying features, breaking it into specific parts, and mentally manipulating their arrangement to arrive at a solution.[17]

Meaning is always a function of the relationships among ideas. Problem solving locates acts and events in what Clifford Geertz called "webs of significance," which he understood to be the essence of culture. The meaning of each act and event is indicated by its relevance to the problem at hand. This is as true of cooking an ordinary meal as preparing an elaborate celebratory feast.[18] Although this is sometimes a neglected aspect of problem solving, it is confirmed in a wide variety of philosophical and experimental studies.[19] Attempting to solve a problem is not simply an effort to deal with the issue under consideration. For instance, working out an alternative energy source to reduce carbon emissions is more likely to be conceived as a technical approach to eliminating a problem than as a way to make sense of it; and yet sense-making is precisely what is involved. The search for a solution requires assumptions to be made about the nature of the problem, the likelihood that it can be solved, and who may be in the best position to tackle it. The process of identifying a problem and posing possible solutions is how a threatening situation is transformed from a threat into a reality that makes sense and can be dealt with.

Individuals facing a personal crisis respond by using the cultural scripts to which they have been exposed. The death of a loved one evokes a string of responses that people have seen modeled among their friends and family, in books and movies and songs, and through the mass media. Death was "a rather splendid event," the science writer Lewis Thomas wrote in remembering his youth, when even children "grew up knowing all about it, observing the event over and over again in the normal process of growing into maturity."[20] Children saw adults mourn and learned the etiquette of grieving. In some communities, neighbors still somberly bring casseroles; in others, the bereaved are expected to host a party. In many, it is customary to tell and retell how the loved one died; in some, conversation moves quickly to other topics.

Freedom exists to choose and tailor these scripts to personal situations. And yet the scripts are powerful, telling people what is appropriate to do and say. Making sense of how we confront the small and large perils of contemporary life requires paying close attention to these scripts and to the institutions and power relations in which they are inscribed. The scripts for dealing with personal trauma are heavily influenced by economic considerations. It is no accident that Americans spend far more on funerals than they did a few decades ago. Similarly, the task of providing acceptable interpretations of larger issues is delegated to elites who are presumed to have appropriate expert knowledge. Americans look to scientists to tell them how to think about pandemics far more than they do to writers or clergy. Government authorities exercise enormous influence in guiding public discussion about how to respond to terrorism and global warming.[21]

The making of meaning through problem solving differs only in magnitude when it concerns grave perils threatening human life itself instead of the routine challenges of managing a family or running a business. The similarity with ordinary tasks lends itself to making larger-scale problem solving an activity that confers meaning. Confronting simple tasks reinforces neural patterns. Cognitive schemata emerge early in life that tell, for instance, how to recognize faces or manipulate physical objects. Schemata organize reality into chunks of related events or stimuli and create domains that include expectations about causes and effects.[22] It becomes second nature to perceive reality in these ways and to think accordingly about how to accomplish tasks.

It is not surprising that cognition about larger and more complex problems typically involves metaphors rooted in the simplest schemata we use to organize reality. Threats come from "out there" and invade us "in here." Formulating a rational strategy of nuclear deterrence is like playing a board game such as Risk or Stratego. The good guys try to beat the bad guys. Peril is "dark." Threat levels "rise." Good plans help to "lower" risks.[23] Problem solving for large-scale dangers further resembles smaller tasks in being personified. Individual villains and heroes are sought. Stories tell what particular families have experienced and are doing to respond.

At the height of the second Sudanese civil war, from 1983 till 2005, approximately 200,000 Sudanese were living in refugee camps in Uganda, many having experienced torture and other acts of extreme violence in their homeland. Humanitarian aid workers sought to provide counseling as well as food and shelter. A study comparing several therapeutic approaches showed that one was far more effective in reducing long-term symptoms of traumatic stress. Storytelling was central to this approach. Victims told and retold their stories, incorporating traumatic events into larger narratives of themselves, their struggle for human rights, and how they planned to live after leaving the camps. Their stories established ways of making sense of what they had experienced, who they now were, and the problems they faced.[24]

The frequency with which stories occur in response to peril suggests an important connection to problem solving. Narratives are the fundamental way in which humans store and remember information. Stories work well because of their temporality. They order events in sequence, with a beginning, middle, and end.[25] Tales of how a vaccine was invented or a flood prevented organize information in this way. But that is not all they do. Narratives are fundamentally concerned with problem solving. They begin by identifying a problem, proceed with an account of the search for solutions, and culminate in the problem being solved. This is why stories are such an important part of the response to peril. Why else would books about the influenza of 1918 be so popular? They offer clues about the suddenness and scope of the outbreak, discuss the scientists and public health officials who responded, and conclude with observations about how the outbreak ended and what may have been learned in the process. There is a moral about what was effective and what was not.

This way of thinking about the response to catastrophic human events is truer to the available evidence than is an alternative perspective that often guides discussions of these events. That perspective posits a vast disjuncture between the questions raised by potential large-scale devastation and the ordinary meaning making activities of daily life, such as going to work, shopping, and watching television programs. It suggests that living in perilous times necessitates "big" answers compared with the "little" meanings that keep us going from day to day. A big question might go something like this: "If humanity is edging toward extinction, what was the purpose of human existence in the first place?" Or: "Why must we, of all generations who have ever lived, be the last, and thus have no prospect of living on through our children and grandchildren?" These questions suggest that perilous times are best understood as metaphysical conundrums. Such questions are in fact expressed by characters in apocalyptic fiction. But not often. And they seldom have as much of a place in the story as the problem solving in which characters engage.

The idea that big threats require big answers is correct, though, in a different sense. As a general rule, the bigger the danger, the bigger the scope of the effort to solve the problem. This does not imply any precise equivalence between the peril perceived and the resources devoted to confronting it. It means rather that interpretations of the scope, complexity, and possible consequences of a threat go hand in hand with discussions of what should be done to combat it. Suppose a study shows that chemical companies are discharging life-threatening substances into a lake. The response will most likely make sense of this situation by discussing specific culpability on the part of the company's management, where effective controls broke down, and what should be done to clean up the lake. In contrast, the possibility of toxins from many known and unknown sources contaminating the entire atmosphere will evoke sense making activities on a much larger scale, including discussions about the need for more scientific research, cooperation among governments, the purchasing habits of consumers, environmental protection measures, and so on.

BIG PROBLEMS THAT POSE GRAVE DANGERS to large numbers of people, including the possibility of human extinction, serve as a mirror of society. Making sense of such threats involves rendering opinions about what is wrong or could go wrong with society and about the resources society could mobilize against them. Discussions of major threats to the future of humanity are replete with ideas about who has the power to do what, where blame or responsibility should be assigned, and whether the social infrastructure is vulnerable or robust. The sense-making activity involves individuals and organizations asserting claims about what they and others have been doing and should be doing in the future. Thus, the key point is that cultural responses to the human fragility exposed by profound peril are social interpretations involving efforts to establish what should be the place of the relevant parts of society.

The problem solving that characterizes the human response to perilous times derives from a sense of moral responsibility. To do nothing in the face of danger that threatens one's family, community, nation, or world is to be morally culpable. Behaving as a morally responsible person is urgently required. And yet the nature of one's responsibility is seldom straightforward. Diagnosing a problem and figuring out what to do about it involves assumptions about the scope, effectiveness, and limits of human action. By definition, human agency is less important in explaining a natural disaster than a war, terrorist bombing, or mass killing. Natural disasters, though, pose questions about who is responsible for informing the public and devising plans to minimize loss of life. Scientists are often credited with having identified an impending peril and with being in the best position to find weapons for fighting it. Large corporations and government bureaus, but also individual leaders and rank-and-file citizens, are among those likely to be named. The naming is both self-referential, as when officials take responsibility for formulating plans, and other-directed, as when critics argue that officials should be doing more.

The cultural response to peril, then, consists fundamentally of problem solving, and problem solving necessitates arguments about who should be doing what. An e-mail about the potential loss of life from an unstoppable virus is a call to responsibility: stockpile food and water, protect one's family, avoid contact with humans who may have been exposed, and so on. A best seller about global warming is likely to outline a course of action that public officials, legislators, corporate executives, and ordinary citizens should take. In other instances, assertions about responsibility are implicit but no less present. For example, historical accounts of scientific discoveries associated with reductions (or increases) in environmental threats often describe the personal traits and moral conflicts of scientists involved. The gravity of the situation—its potential for loss of life—impels moral claims and thus holds far-reaching implications for understandings of oneself and one's society.

The problem solving associated with threats of cataclysmic destruction has special characteristics. First, the threats that give rise to problem solving activity are serious enough to affect large numbers of people, perhaps everyone in the entire world, and most certainly the whole of a given society, either directly (such as through illness and death) or indirectly (such as through economic chaos). Second, the timing and potential consequences of these threats are highly uncertain. They do not happen at regular intervals that can be predicted in advance. They could happen in an instant, develop over a period of weeks and months, occur so gradually as to be nearly imperceptible, or not happen at all. Third, these are the kind of threats that cannot be tackled only by individuals, say, though working

hard or thinking good thoughts. The problem solving required makes use of specialized knowledge and thus must be organized and is likely to necessitate a considerable investment of the society's resources. Fourth, it is nevertheless important
that individuals do their part, contributing in small ways, and in this manner take
ownership, as it were, of the problem. And fifth, whether or not the problem
solving efforts are effective cannot easily be determined and, indeed, may be impossible to ascertain. This uncertainty is associated with the fact that the threats'
timing and consequences cannot be predicted with accuracy.

WERE THE PROBLEM SOLVING INVOLVED to occur in any other era but our own, it
would be tempting to imagine that it would entail religion, magic, and ritual. The
danger facing the society would very likely be perceived as that of an angry god, the
devil, or an evil spirit. Its power to threaten the entire society with death and destruction would be understood, as would the inability to predict the timing and
consequences of its wrath. There would likely be discussions and even differences
of opinion about how to appease the gods and ward off danger. The whole society
would need to organize itself to engage in ritualistic activity, and the special knowledge of its shamans would be required. Individuals would be expected to purify
themselves, perform personal acts of ablution, and contribute to the collective
effort by playing their part in the prescribed rituals. Individuals who denied that a
problem existed, or who came up with their own solutions, might be sanctioned.
It would be difficult to determine for sure if the ceremonial activities had been
effective. And if the worst that could be imagined did actually happen, the shamans would have to provide explanations in order to maintain their credibility.

As a lens through which to understand the problem solving directed at current
global threats, the analogy with religion and magic is instructive and yet must be
regarded with caution. The language of evil and apocalypse is sometimes evident
in discussions of current dangers. Rituals of the kind practiced in premodern societies, however, are now regarded as having been misguided because the evil forces
they were meant to allay did not exist. The "enlightened" view is that people in
earlier times were deluded. A person nowadays who suggests that a natural disaster is somehow punishment by a divine or supernatural being is disputed even by
religious leaders. To liken the perils of terrorism or climate change to earlier evils
is thus to beg for a kind of critical detachment that is impossible and probably even
undesirable in considering the current fate of the world. What the analogy does
illuminate is the fact that societies facing peril do respond by investing resources
and in organized ways. The problem solving in which they engage is collectively
orchestrated. However they may have been understood, natural calamities, disease,
and enemies posed real dangers to premodern societies. The search for technical,
medical, and military solutions necessarily required an organized response.

The notable feature of the perilous times that humanity has faced over the past half century is that the response has made them seem manageable enough that we roll up our collective sleeves and work on practical solutions. There have been relatively few panics involving spontaneous outbreaks of irrational behavior. Work, family life, and other routine activities have continued. Individuals have sometimes shouldered the small tasks of learning about impending crises and pitching in to support research or protect their families. These responsibilities, though, have seldom required great sacrifices on the part of large populations, at least not in the Western world. Social movements have emerged and policies have been affected, but regimes have rarely been toppled as a result.

None of this can be understood simply as denial. Were denial the correct interpretation, billions would not have been spent on weapons, deterrence programs, research, and communication. Millions of readers and television viewers would not have paid attention to warnings and documentaries. People responded, but in ways that incorporated the problem solving into ordinary roles and competencies. Nor can the normality of the response be explained by arguing that the dangers envisioned generated little upheaval because they never happened. A nuclear holocaust did not occur, but enough destruction did take place that people could imagine the results. There were also chemical spills, accidents at nuclear plants, terrorist attacks, and natural disasters. Enough went wrong, even with well-intentioned planning, that danger could not be ignored. Indeed, it is truly surprising that more chaos, more panic, more soul searching, and more enervating fear did not ensue.

The cultural response to human fragility, judging from the horrendous threats that humanity has faced in recent decades and continues to face, consists in large measure of turning extreme danger into manageable situations—of redefining imponderable problems into smaller predicaments that we can more easily grasp. Grave danger is thus normalized, made the subject of risk assessment studies, addressed through technological innovation, turned into the banal, the familiar. There is irony in this, of course. The fact that nuclear annihilation has been averted thus far does not mean it always will be. Making death more manageable makes it no less inevitable. Even to focus obsessively on putting one's house in order can rob one of the precious time needed to ponder the larger significance (or longer-term threats) of life.

The piecemeal ways in which our individual and collective responses to peril have taken shape over the past half century and more has obscured the significant change in how peril itself is perceived. Throughout all of human history, individual persons were aware that they would die. They also knew that death could come to large numbers, here and there, either from natural disasters or from an invading army. During the twentieth century, the capacity for mass killing greatly increased, as evidenced especially in the two world wars. The invention of atomic weapons further expanded that capacity. It did so in the obvious way of making it possible to kill more people at once. The less obvious way was even more important: After 1945, it became possible for an organization somewhere in the world to wipe out a large number of people in another part of the world at any time. That organization was sometimes personified, just as the Nazi juggernaut had been. It was Stalin, Khrushchev, or Mao, for instance, who could "push the button." But personification did not obscure the fact that an organization was involved. In the United States, that organization was usually termed "the Kremlin," while in the Soviet Union, it was called "the Pentagon," or simply "Washington." Peril changed in two ways. It became constant—a danger that could happen at any moment and largely without warning, rather than only when a large army mobilized an invasion. It also came to be the product of an organization—a complex administrative structure composed of rulers, scientists, and military strategists. Writers sometimes observed that the key aspect of nuclear warfare was that humanity could now kill itself. But it wasn't humanity killing itself, exactly; rather, it became possible for organizations or groups to gain this power.

The further consequence of this change was that the manner in which peril could be averted also underwent a significant transformation. In earlier times, people looked to organizations to help them make sense of death and provide comfort. Religious organizations (often in the form of a priesthood) offered hope of an afterlife, conducted burial services, and provided incantations to ward off evil. But the church or priesthood did not also have the power to kill large numbers of people, at least not in the way that emerged during the twentieth century. Once a government bureau composed of experts and planners gained the power to push a button and instantly kill millions of people, everything changed. It then became compelling to believe that the same powerful organization that could kill could also save.

Peril has become manageable only to the extent that large-scale organizations are considered capable of managing it. Individuals may imagine that their chances of survival are greater if they have a basement bomb shelter than if they do not, but in reality, few people build such shelters because they know the effect will be minuscule compared to the ability of people in power to start or avoid a nuclear holocaust. Having come to that realization about nuclear destruction, the ordinary person adopts a similar response to other threats. Terrorism, environmental threats, mass disease—all depend on the hope that experts somewhere will provide answers.

Fear is ultimately transformed as well. It is untrue that people fear only because of fearmongers. The dangers of death and destruction are real enough. However, the extent and focus of fear is largely defined by the same institutions that can in fact kill, on the one hand, and offer protection, on the other. In democratic societies, these institutions are entrusted with the public safety. It is in the interest of the leaders of these organizations to identify possible threats to the public, to speculate enough about these threats to raise money to study them, to offer assessments of risk, to warn the public, and indeed to encourage people to take some responsibility for themselves. Fear must thus be understood as much more than an emotion. Fear is institutionalized. It reflects how society is organized. There is the specific fear of being hit by a terrorist strike or of dying from a pandemic disease. But there is also the fear that scientists may not be able to prevent an attack or that people will cease trusting in experts and then begin to panic. Peril and the perception of peril is rooted in the organization of society itself.

THAT DAY WHEN AN E-MAIL CAME about the threat of avian flu, I was in no immediate danger. The peril I faced was quite literally mediated by institutions—by an industry that has arisen to collect information about and warn against impending catastrophe. I was being informed by a news organization that in turn picked up warnings put out by the World Health Organization and Centers for Disease Control. The same was true of the other threats I came in contact with that day (and on other days). Terrorism and global warming are real dangers, but what most of us know about them is from the institutions that bear responsibility for addressing these problems. From one day to the next, the fear we experience is largely a response to what these institutions tell us. The fear is only partly about dying from a pandemic or terrorist attack. It is also about how these institutions are organized—about who is running them, whether we can or cannot trust these institutions to protect us, and what the consequences may be if these arrangements break down.

THE NUCLEAR-HAUNTED ERA

TO THE AMERICAN PUBLIC, the nuclear era began on August 6, 1945. President Harry S. Truman called news reporters to the White House that morning to announce that an atomic bomb had been dropped on Hiroshima, Japan, destroying most of the city and killing much of its population. In reality, starting dates are always ambiguous. The nuclear age could be dated from July 16, 1945, the day a successful test of an atomic bomb was conducted in the desert near Alamogordo, New Mexico. It could also be fixed in 1942, when the Manhattan Project that created the bomb was authorized, or in 1939, when a small research program began. Still earlier dates could be identified, such as Albert Einstein's theory of special relativity in 1905 or Marie and Pierre Curie's discovery of radium in 1898.

It makes equal sense to pick later dates. August 9, 1945, when U.S. forces dropped a plutonium-based bomb on Nagasaki, demonstrated that nuclear explosions were not a one-time event. Later that fall may have been when the reality of a new era began to sink in. Although news of the devastation in Japan spread quickly, it took a while for the American public to absorb its gravity. The first reports about Hiroshima said only that smoke and dust had been too thick for the crew of the B-29 bomber *Enola Gay* to assess the damage. The death toll took months to establish, as victims of radiation sickness continued to die.[1]

How did people respond? When did they come to realize that a new peril had been unleashed on the world? Immediately? Or only later? The devastation at Hiroshima and Nagasaki was an instance not only of vast physical destruction but also of what sociologist Jeffrey C. Alexander has termed *cultural trauma*—"a horrendous event that leaves indelible marks upon their group consciousness, marking their memories forever and changing their future identity in fundamental and irrevocable ways." It was like the Holocaust for European Jews or slavery for African Americans.[2]

Or was it? A woman who grew up in the Midwest was fourteen when Pearl Harbor was attacked on December 7, 1941. "We hardly ever saw an airplane. We were terrified that one might fly over at any moment and bomb us," she recalls. Two years later her brother was killed in Germany. She still reads his letters about once a month to keep his memory alive. But she has no memory of how she felt about the atomic bomb. Is she typical? Were Hiroshima and Nagasaki so far away that Americans were unaffected? Were Americans so guilty or fearful that they denied what had happened?

Journalists wrote of destructive power too great for the mind to grasp and wondered if some perilous threshold had been crossed forever. Yet it was not long until atomic bomb toys, cocktails, hamburgers, and jewelry were being marketed. In a few years, atomic power was being promoted as a new source of energy too cheap to meter. Only later in the 1950s, with recurrent testing of nuclear weapons, did fears of radioactive fallout become widespread. Public anxiety peaked during the Cuban missile crisis of 1962, but waned before emerging again on a wide scale in the 1980s. Although the reality of nuclear weapons was a constant, the perception of their danger clearly was not.

The ebb and flow of public concern has been noted by nearly all historians of the nuclear era. What is more interesting is how the public came to view nuclear weapons as a problem—not only in the negative sense, but often as a positive opportunity to be exploited—and how rolling up its collective sleeves to work on this problem became the accepted way of coexisting with the threat of nuclear annihilation.

Unlike the prospect of one's own death and the death of a loved one, and even unlike the occasional airplane crash or earthquake that takes dozens or hundreds of lives, the possibility of a nuclear conflagration—a holocaust from having unlocked the basic power of the universe and creating weaponry capable of putting the world in danger of sudden destruction—was anything but normal. Yet it became normal. After the initial emotional shock, when Americans inescapably experienced bewilderment, uncertainty, and some level of grief for those who had died, attention turned to more practical concerns. The nuclear era became one of problem solving. People decided that whatever it had taken to produce such powerful weapons could surely be harnessed for other commendable purposes. They looked to government officials to protect them and occasionally searched for better measures to protect themselves.

The incomprehensible possibility of nuclear annihilation was carved into more manageable tasks, such as guarding against fallout and keeping ahead of the Russians. As the decades passed, a large infrastructure became so thoroughly institutionalized that it governed the public's response even at times when nuclear war itself seemed unlikely. Few would have described the problem solving that took place as a way of making the prospect of peril meaningful. However, it was exactly this prospect that increasingly shaped how people thought of themselves and their responsibilities, how they imagined good and evil, and what costs they were willing to incur to survive.

THE INITIAL REACTION THAT AUGUST to the news about Hiroshima and Nagasaki, which has been chronicled in painstaking detail by historian Paul Boyer, was heavy with emotion.[3] There was the kind of apprehension people feel when any unexpected event promises to redirect their affairs. For a nation that had invested so much in fighting a war that had lasted so long, any such news was bound to stir the deepest emotions. There was pride, tempered with awe, certainly at the extent of destruction, but even more at the power that had caused it. The power now in America's possession, most commentators agreed, was testimony to the nation's native ingenuity and progressive leadership in science and technology. There was relief bordering on elation when Japan surrendered within days of Hiroshima and Nagasaki. There was also fear, voiced by a few in those early hours, that weapons of this kind could be unleashed against the United States, perhaps by Russia, whose scientists were suspected of working on a similar project, or by Japan, which circulated propaganda threatening to do exactly that.

The words in which these initial responses were preserved were almost always those of journalists. What may have been going through people's minds as they contemplated the news was never recorded. Polling, still in its infancy, did little to capture the public's mood. Nobody thought to conduct interviews with ordinary Americans. It was a time, though, when journalists were popularly regarded as the people's voice. Editors and writers put into words what people were thinking. Audiences read and listened to see and hear what they felt somehow they would have said themselves if they had known how. While the War Department released stories it had been preparing for months about how the bomb had been made, writers moved quickly to reflect on what it all might mean and what would need to be done now.

Word that a weapon of unimaginable power had been used was news indeed. Yet it is important to understand what exactly the news was. It was not that such a large number of people died, but that they had been killed by a single bomb. With vision obstructed by smoke and dust, the first reports described death and destruction only in general terms. The target was characterized as an army base in a location of 318,000 people, but civilian causalities received little attention in the initial stories. It was not until eyewitness reports from Japanese sources started to circulate a few days later that the grisly details began to emerge. Corpses were charred beyond recognition. People closest to the blast had simply vanished, presumably incinerated by the intense heat. The numbers were staggering. Yet the world was accustomed to such numbers. It was hard to forget that many thousands of soldiers and civilians had been killed in Europe and the Pacific. Thus, it was less the death toll than the power of the new bomb that writers struggled to find adequate words to describe.

It was like the dynamite or TNT with which everyone was familiar, only more like a ton of it, actually 20,000 tons. Had it been a conventional bomb, it would have taken 2,000 planes to deliver this much tonnage. Instead, one plane had done it. Compared to one of the largest explosions in living memory, that of a munitions ship that blew up in the harbor of Halifax, Nova Scotia, in 1917, killing 1,500 people and leveling more than a square mile, the atomic bomb was at least seven times more powerful. Indeed, the force packed into this one bomb was like the power of the sun itself. It was the basic power of the universe, a destructive weapon like no other before it, a harbinger of a revolutionary new era in warfare and technology.

An interest that developed among social scientists in the 1970s and has continued to the present emphasizes that social problems are socially constructed.[4] Drunk driving is an example. People had been driving automobiles while intoxicated and causing accidents since the beginning of the automobile era, but it was not until the late 1960s and 1970s that drunk driving became identified as a large-scale public problem.[5] Fetal alcohol syndrome (FAS) is another example. Although doctors had written about the possible effects of expectant mothers drinking for more than a century, FAS was not officially recognized until 1973, and even since, debate has continued about how seriously it should be taken and whether the public is worrying too much or too little.[6] Historically, witchcraft was often a commonly accepted practice, but on occasion, as in Salem, Massachusetts, in 1692, it became a matter of communitywide hysteria.[7] Other issues, such as pornography, prostitution, spousal abuse, and even national defense seem to wax and wane as matters of public concern. It is often difficult to know why they become defined as social problems when they do, and the reasons may have as much to do with community dynamics, demographic change, and shifts in power as with the gravity of the issue itself.

The nuclear era was not like that. Not only did it begin as far as the public was concerned at a specific moment on a particular day, it was also of such profound significance that it could not be ignored. Unlike the death toll from automobiles, which took the lives of some 20,000 Americans in 1945, but did so a life or two at a time in scattered locations throughout the year, the deaths at Hiroshima and Nagasaki were notably concentrated and simultaneous. Statistics did not have to be compiled or activists mobilized to get the public's attention. In the twelve months after August 6, 1945, the New York Times alone published more than 4,500 articles—an average of 12 a day—in which the atomic era was featured or mentioned. The Washington Post, Chicago Tribune, and Los Angeles Times each published more than 2,000 such articles in the same period. Television, still in its infancy, radio, news magazines, and local newspapers carried many of the same stories.

Having been developed in secrecy, the atomic bomb drew media interest in the way any surprise does, especially one that put Americans on the winning side and ended the bloodiest war in history. It was not that nothing at all like an atomic bomb was expected. There had in fact been much speculation about "splitting the atom" during the 1930s and early 1940s until government censorship quashed such discussion. Science fiction magazines had carried numerous stories during the war about atomic bombs, radiation, and mutant life forms resulting from radiation. Yet the details that could not be revealed until the bomb was used now came rushing forth: the fact that two entire cities of people had been working secretly on the bomb, for instance, and that a trial bomb had been exploded in New Mexico or that the wives of the leading scientists and military administrators had not known what their husbands were working on.

It was the sheer power of the atom that continued to attract attention long after the initial stories about making the bomb had been told. Newspaper articles dealing with the implications of the atomic era focused more often on this aspect than on any other. Of the more than 11,000 relevant articles that appeared in the *New York Times, Washington Post, Chicago Tribune,* and *Los Angeles Times* between August 6, 1945, and August 5, 1946, 54 percent mentioned "power" or "energy." The mushroom cloud became the first symbol of this power. Its towering size and the brilliance and roar of the explosion were hard to describe. News stories circulated about a blind girl hundreds of miles away from the test blast in New Mexico who claimed to have seen it. Aerial photographs were published of the utter destruction around ground zero in Hiroshima. Journalists followed Truman's lead in emphasizing social organization, money, and intellectual power that had been harnessed to create the bomb. "We have spent two billion dollars on the greatest scientific gamble in history," Truman said, "and won."[8] If Japan did not surrender, the War Department bluffed, U.S. forces were prepared to unleash a nonstop barrage of atomic terror. Scientists involved in making the bomb described in general terms how it resembled the power of the sun. They also described scenarios in which atomic energy would reduce conflicts between nations, stimulate economic growth, and make lives more comfortable for everyone.

The cultural significance of this emphasis on power was simply the fact that it had to be reckoned with. Atomic power was like nothing the world had ever known, more lethal by far than most natural disasters, and more destructive than anything else humans had devised. Its invention was thus a turning point in history, the mark of a new age, a test of character. As much as its potential for harm was evident, its possibilities for good were even more intriguing. The modern American, declared science writer William L. Laurence on the first anniversary of Hiroshima, "stands on Pisgah in the desert, gazing at a land of promise. He has within reach the philosopher's stone and the elixir of life combined in one."[9]

Speculation was rife that the nation's electricity would soon be generated from atomic energy and that miniature atomic reactors would be powering airplanes and automobiles within a few years. Before long, the public would be able to heat their homes at no cost, purchase cheap goods produced by factories run with atomic energy, and zip from place to place in newly invented vehicles. "Transportation anywhere on, over, or beyond the earth will be at your personal touch," a Cal Tech physicist predicted. "The face of the earth will be changed—with rails, houses, and roads gone. Everything—your clothes, food, health—will be touched by the wand."[10] The speculation about cheap heat and transportation was so rampant that press releases were put out to quash fears that the value of stock in oil and coal companies would plummet.

In these respects, the nuclear era posed a "problem" unlike any of the ones that students of social problems have emphasized. Nuclear energy differed not only in magnitude but in kind from drunk driving, prostitution, youth gangs, and juvenile delinquency. It was not a problem in the sense of posing a difficulty with which society needed to deal. It was rather a profound opportunity to choose between good and evil, to exercise moral responsibility in the face of great urgency and uncertainty. The challenge was not finding a way to eradicate atomic power, for the genie was truly out of the bottle, but in adjusting to it and learning to make the best use of this new reality. "Certainly with such godlike power under man's imperfect control," a writer for the New York Times editorialized, "we face a frightful responsibility. Atomic energy may well lead to a bright new world in which man shares a common brotherhood, or we shall become—beneath the bombs and rockets—a world of troglodytes."[11]

As the reality of the nuclear age sank in, though, it soon became clear that the choice was not as simple as that of a bright new world or a planet of troglodytes. Between a vast utopia and utter destruction lay innumerable possibilities. Some were clearly dangerous and frightening, but most fell into the gray zone of the imagination where it was impossible to know immediately how to think or respond.

The first order of business was thus to ponder the possibilities—to think about how to think. This in itself was a task of immense proportions. Nearly every prominent writer and public figure felt compelled to define the situation. Journalists who wrote about it included the Alsop brothers Joseph and Stewart, Herbert Block, Walter Lippmann, James Reston, Lowell Thomas, and many other opinion makers of lesser prominence. The era's most distinguished novelists and essayists, including James Agee, Saul Bellow, Erskine Caldwell, William Faulkner, Norman Mailer, John Steinbeck, and Kurt Vonnegut, all offered interpretations. The academic world saw contributions from historian Roland Bainton, anthropologist Ruth Benedict, psychologist Kenneth Clark, economist Ansley J. Coale, sociologist W. E. B. Du Bois, and philosopher Sidney Hook, among others, including many college administrators. Recognizing the deep moral implications of atomic weapons and warfare, the nation's leading religious figures—Harry Emerson Fosdick, Billy Graham, Mordecai Kaplan, Carl McIntyre, Reinhold Niebuhr, and Harold Ockenga, along with statements by denominations and clergy councils—also weighed in. Norman Cousins exaggerated only slightly when he predicted in a *Saturday Review* essay a few days after Hiroshima that the atomic era would touch "every aspect of man's activities, from machines to morals, from physics to philosophy, from politics to poetry."[12]

The cultural landslide following the first use of atomic weapons was an instance, only on a much larger scale, of the feverish talk, conjecture, commentary, speculation, scripts, frames, and repertoires that scholars have come to associate with unsettled times.[13] When previously established meanings can no longer be taken for granted, people scramble to offer new interpretations. "We have fought and won the freedom to work out our own future," James Reston editorialized. "But it must be worked out not in the old world, which is gone, but in a new world which will test our character equally as much as did the war itself."[14] The historian Arnold Toynbee asked, "Along what path are we to look for salvation in this parlous plight, in which we hold in our hands the choice of life or death not only for ourselves but for the whole human race?"[15] "Like the sorcerer's apprentice," George Bernard Shaw observed, "we may practice our magic without knowing how to stop it, thus fulfilling the prophecy of Prospero."[16] For Reinhold Niebuhr, the atomic bomb seemed mostly a continuation of the destructiveness evident during the war and indeed throughout human history; yet he, too, acknowledged that "the atomic bomb heralds the end of one age and the beginning of another."[17]

Others agreed that a new age had dawned, but interpreted it in a more favorable light. "It is the consensus among those present," concluded a gathering of scientists at Princeton University, "that the new era of atomic power can be subjected to a process of development that [can be] harnessed to the problems that face the post-war world for the benefit of mankind and its economy."[18] Atomic scientist and Washington University chancellor Arthur C. Compton saw the new era less in purely technological terms and more as a time for capitalizing on the spirit of cooperation the Manhattan Project had successfully illustrated. "Above all," he observed, "the atomic project is an example of the supreme value of a purpose." It demonstrated that "when people are working with a will to attain an objective, they will strive to learn how to do their part, and will willingly work with others as may be necessary for the desired result."[19] A few years later, William Faulkner, in accepting the Nobel Prize in Literature, expressed a different view. "Our tragedy today is a general and universal physical fear so long sustained by now that we can even bear it," he declared. "There are no longer problems of the spirit. There is only the question: When will I be blown up?"[20]

Other responses ran the gamut from extreme optimism to extreme pessimism. A poll of American adults conducted a month after the bombing of Hiroshima found that only 37 percent thought it a "real danger" that an atomic bomb would be used against the United States in the next twenty-five years. Yet 83 percent thought it a "real danger" that if there were another world war, "most city people on earth [would be] killed by atomic bombs."[21] One writer likened the moment to ancient times when people feared the worst and looked to prophets for guidance. "The destructive powers . . . are so great that civilization, already racked by so many torments, trembles in apprehension. [People] peer about seeking wisdom in their extremity, but no oracle can be found that can inspire faith in more than a few followers. They talk and pray and prophesy and speak in tongues, while time passes and the cloud grows larger."[22]

Yet it was not so much that people were simply torn with uncertainty, but that a range of thoughts and emotions needed to be entertained. A high school senior wrote, "Never before has the world been confronted by an instrument of such potentialities for wholesale destruction." But, on a more optimistic note, he added that the atomic age "vividly magnifies the need of people to learn to live together."[23] Another senior observed that great strides in medicine, industry, power, and agriculture were possible through atomic energy. "I want to walk through this doorway," she wrote, "and live when these things are a greater reality than they are at the present time." However, she noted, reading the newspaper did not make her hopeful, so it would be a matter of will to "be a part of that group that still has some optimism left regarding the human race and wants to see it preserved." Like other writers, she believed the appropriate response was neither despair nor utopian dreams, but "new obligations for us all."[24]

There was plenty in the varied responses to suggest that at some deep level people were terribly frightened. In its editorial the day after Hiroshima, the New York Times described the "horrible prospect of utter annihilation opened by the atomic bomb."[25] A few months later, delegates at an Ohio meeting of the Federal Council of Churches concluded that "a world of fear, hatred, cruelty, misery, and violent death" was replacing one of fellowship and love.[26] A journalism professor at New York University imagined a "blasted estate" in which "possible survivors" would use "flint and tinder to light flares on the road back from the Dark Ages."[27] In any future war, concluded an Advisory Commission on Universal Training headed by General Dwight D. Eisenhower, the "indescribable horror" of a single day's attack involving atomic weapons would level the nation's twelve largest cities and draw every factory and farm into the combat zone. Chaos, civil disorder, and sabotage, with millions of persons sick, wounded, and dying, would be the result.[28]

To imagine, though, that the fear of nuclear peril was so profound as to sink into the unconscious and there deter constructive thinking would be mistaken. Whenever the most fearful scenarios were mentioned, it was almost inevitable that writers also argued for plans to be conceived and work to be undertaken. "Tremendous tasks remain to be done without loss of time," wrote the New York Times editors.[29] Christians everywhere, declared the church leaders in Ohio, should engage in "practical applications" of their faith to help erect a new world order. The journalism professor at New York University suggested building underground repositories to preserve books and documents in case of attack. The Eisenhower commission focused on strategic military plans.

The point was not, as some argued at the time, that Americans were an innately optimistic people who took a can-do approach to even the greatest challenges. It was rather that an emphasis on the worst conceivable scenario went hand in hand with, and indeed served as justification for, arguments about specific actions that should be taken. It was as if the prospect of inconceivable peril required people to think about concrete ways of fighting back, of minimizing the danger, even though the specific problems to be tackled were already quite familiar and the solutions diverse. Faced with stupendous bewilderment, writers urged the public and its leaders to lower trade barriers, build faster airplanes, impose a universal draft, eliminate conscription, invest in science, support the humanities, organize civil defense units, work for peace, and hunt for saboteurs and enemy sympathizers.

What emerged from this initial period of wide-ranging commentary and opinion—this "great psychological surge of mixed fear and hope," as one *New York Times* writer put it—was a set of assumptions that gained broad consensus.[30] Together, these assumptions defined a problem that, in turn, identified how people in various capacities should respond, and thus was repaired the breach, as it were, in responsibilities that had once been taken for granted. A moral order was re-created that told people what they themselves should do and what they should expect others to do. The central assumption of this new order was the belief that nuclear weapons were indeed a sufficient threat to prompt urgent and continuing action. The nuclear era had come about for a reason. That much was clear.

But the nuclear era also marked a significant turning point in history and thus was a problem, challenge, and opportunity all in one. Less of the discussion focused on deep soul searching than on understanding the specific reasons why the bomb was necessary and the process by which it came about. Constructing the atomic bomb in the first place had been necessitated by the belief that German scientists were working to develop such a weapon. It was featured prominently in Truman's initial announcement about Hiroshima and widely repeated in subsequent months. It was in the nature of scientific progress itself that if the Americans and British had not discovered the secret of splitting the atom, their enemies would have. Once the bomb was developed, justification for actually using it was based on arguments that Japan had attacked first and would not surrender if only pictures were shown or a test bomb were dropped in international waters. Soon after, writers warned that other nations, the Soviet Union in particular, would have atomic weapons at their disposal within three to five years. It was therefore incumbent on the United States, in their view, to push ahead on all fronts to develop more advanced weapons, to demonstrate the peaceful uses of atomic energy, and to encourage moral leadership and international cooperation.

Observers held different views about how long it might be before other nations had atomic weapons and about what the most urgent tasks should be. For instance, some argued that the United States should retain its nuclear secrets, while others suggested sharing them through some international agency such as the United Nations. Other debates focused on how strong the United Nations should be and whether it was feasible to outlaw further development of atomic weapons. There was also disagreement about how quickly the positive uses of atomic energy could be developed. Always, though, the proposals were advanced with great moral urgency. Atomic power was not something that knowledgeable people could simply ignore. It required responsible engagement, perhaps to prevent human annihilation, but, if not that, then at least, in the words of the *New York Times* writer quoted above, "to prevent man's reversion to the Dark Ages and the spiritual, mental and political loss of all that our material progress has made possible."[31]

A second assumption was that the appropriate use of atomic power would require close and continuing supervision by government. Disagreement was present from the outset about how much of this supervision should be in the hands of the military and how it should be shared with industry, the public, and representatives of other nations, but the central supervisory role of government was never questioned. The Atomic Energy Commission (AEC), established in 1946, was the agency in charge of government oversight. Nominally led by "citizens," the six-member commission was composed of men with careers in public administration, the military, and science. Through this commission, the federal government exercised what one writer at the time described as "the most austere guardianship ever attempted in peacetime in a parliamentary country."[32] All fissionable materials were to be held under government monopoly. Under penalty of death, no private person could distribute any information about atomic weapons. International control through the United Nations was proposed but defeated in favor of exclusive U.S. supervision. Through an amendment to the initial legislation, contracting arrangements for industrial applications were initiated, but government alone held the right to produce plutonium and civilian organizations were permitted to possess only industrially insignificant quantities of uranium. So centralized was the control that even members of Congress felt excluded from the decision-making process.

It is difficult to imagine that the prospects and perils of nuclear energy could have been handled in any other way. The atomic bomb had been developed through a centrally organized program and under wartime conditions when public support of government action was high. All the initial publicity emphasized that the project had been of such financial magnitude and had required coordination of such extensive activities that only government could have been effective in managing it. Early projections indicated that hundreds of millions of dollars would have to be spent to develop further defense and peacetime uses. Yet it is important that the nuclear era firmly established a precedent for dealing with major catastrophic perils through centralized government action. "As a plain statement of fact," political scientist Robert A. Dahl wrote in 1953, "the political processes of democracy do *not* operate effectively with respect to atomic energy policy." The major decisions, Dahl observed, were being made largely in secret by an exceptionally small policy-making elite.[33]

Culturally, this arrangement was also significant, both in defining the nature of the problem and in discouraging the general public from taking an interest in it. Henceforth, peril would be understood less as a philosophical or moral problem and more as a technical and policy concern. If annihilation was to be prevented, it would not be through an act of public will, but through carefully conceived diplomatic initiatives and increasingly sophisticated scientific applications. By assuming such a large role, government also became responsible to a much greater extent than industry or the public for whatever hopes and fears were attached to nuclear power. The choice between good and evil that so many writers associated with atomic weapons in the days and weeks after the bombings of Japan was increasingly placed in the hands of high-level policy makers.

As problem solving became the accepted way of managing the nuclear era, the key problem solvers were of course scientists. Between 1940 and 1952 the number of professional scientists and engineers grew from 375,000 to 600,000. Physicists increased fourfold and chemists more than doubled. Nearly all of this growth was in applied research sponsored by government and private industry. Nonmilitary research expenditures increased by a factor of four, while military research expenditures grew by a factor of forty. Scientific conferences, wrote two young scientists in the early 1950s, had become "like anthills to which thousands of ants each bring a pine needle or a small straw to throw on the heap," and the typical pattern of daily scientific work was "that of a crowd of intelligent and competent young men assembled, not around a master, but around a giant atom-smashing machine."[34] The physical power of the atomic bomb conferred cultural power on those who understood how it worked. Whether they were credited with good or with evil, they were increasingly viewed as people with power. They held secrets that could make the world better, but they could also be dangerous spies, selling those secrets to foreigners. It was not that scientists themselves necessarily believed they were more influential than in the past; indeed, many expressed frustration at government policies and censorship. Yet, increasingly, it was to scientists that the public looked to handle the perils that the world faced. It was in their hands to invent better weapons, to predict the likelihood of enemies' developing more powerful weapons, and to realize dreams of cheaper fuel and more efficient transportation.

Besides government and science, there would also be a role in the new moral order for the educated elite and for specialists trained to guide that elite. At a conference of educators, University of Chicago chancellor Robert M. Hutchins argued

that the atomic age could bring about the "death of civilization" unless public support for higher education among adults dramatically increased. "If we want to save
adults in the atomic age from the suicidal tendencies which boredom eventually
induces," he said, "if we want to build a world community, we must regard the continuing education of our people throughout life as our principal responsibility."[35]

Others saw the atomic age as an opportunity to champion the merits of government funding for their particular professions. American Sociological Society president William Fielding Ogburn argued in the *American Journal of Sociology* that his
discipline was especially well suited to study the atomic bomb because of its
expected effects on social institutions. "Just as it takes time, money, and research
on the part of physicists, chemists, and engineers to produce an atomic bomb," he
argued, "so time, money, and research are necessary for sociologists to uncover the
social effects of this new source of power." Cautioning against the ill-informed
advice of columnists and preachers, Ogburn was optimistic that social scientists
could tell better what the consequences of atomic energy would be. "No doubt," he
contended, "if sociologists had the two-billion-dollar fund, which the physicists
and engineers had to finance constructing the bomb, then in several years' time
they could advise adequately on the social adjustments to this new source of
power."[36] Demographer Ansley J. Coale, writing in the *American Economic Review*,
considered the alternatives that might be required, not in response to atomic energy but to reduce vulnerability to an atomic attack. Besides "deep shelters of sufficient size to house a large proportion of urban populations," he suggested, the
density of urban centers should be greatly limited by "unprecedented government
intervention" involving slum clearance and subsidies to encourage people to live
in less populated areas.[37]

It was perhaps inevitable that representatives of different fields and institutions
would seek to exploit as many of the new opportunities as possible. The nuclear
era was a bit like a land rush in this respect. Fear focused less on possible annihilation than on being left behind. With billions of dollars at stake from government
contracts, and with potential earnings from new technology estimated to be astro-
nomical, the problem ceased to be one of survival and turned to proposing how
this industry or that profession could contribute and thus benefit. The National
Association of Manufacturers argued that controlling nuclear energy would wipe
out free enterprise and drastically impede social progress.[38] Not to be left out, the
leading journal of clinical psychology editorialized that research in that field should
be "imbued with the same intensity of purpose and given the financial support as
society now grants to atomic research."[39]

Yet there was also a sense that the atomic era would necessitate the various
roles involved working together to produce something greater than their separate
parts. Few expressed this view as clearly as Arthur C. Compton, the atomic scientist and Washington University chancellor mentioned above, who played an

important role not only in talking about scientific cooperation, but also in promoting it through the United Nations, the Atomic Energy Commission, and other organizations. The efforts of so many to create the atomic bomb, Compton wrote, "epitomizes certain major social trends, such as growing specialization with its implied coordinated cooperation, increasing emphasis on better training and education, and the growing awareness of the need for generally accepted social objectives as coordinating principles in setting a pattern for our social and political development."[40] Harnessing such cooperation in the future, Compton believed, would require setting aside "emotional or unconsidered living" in favor of commonly accepted objectives. It would also necessitate a greater emphasis on performing specialized roles for the common good. "Management and labor, the various trades and professions, government with its many branches, business and agriculture, school and church, each is developing toward doing a better job in a narrower field."[41]

On the whole, the average citizen was left with few responsibilities—and this lack of well-defined obligations would continue through later phases of the response to nuclear weapons. However, there were efforts from the start to draw ordinary people into the response. The idea was that atomic power posed too great a challenge to be left entirely in the hands of scientists and government officials. If the tide was to be turned from evil to good, the average, common citizen would need to be active.

One of the most vocal advocates of citizen involvement was Atomic Energy Commission chair David E. Lilienthal. At a speech to the American Society of Newspaper Editors in Washington in 1947, Lilienthal described the power of nuclear energy, its destructive as well as its humanitarian potentialities, and the need for an informed public. "How well the people understand," he argued, "depends largely upon our institutions of education and communication, the schools and universities, the churches and religious organizations, the radio and most of all, the press." By enlisting all of these cultural institutions, the nation would learn more clearly "what is at stake for themselves and their children." The issues needing to be understood, supported, and acted on by the public included both peaceful and military uses of atomic energy and better knowledge of the science on which it was based. Decisions about the control of nuclear weapons should not be made in secret by the government, Lilienthal contended, but through a democratic process. "What I am proposing, therefore, is nothing less than a broad and sustained program of education at the grass roots of every community in the land."[42]

At the time of this speech, Lilienthal was involved in high-stakes political maneuvering to win support for the Atomic Energy Commission and to define and gain funding for its continuing mission in the postwar era. His proposal was in no way to turn over the AEC's authority to the public. Yet at least two aspects of his argument were notably inclusive. The first is the role he saw for cultural institutions.

Whereas the initial response after Hiroshima had largely been the voice of scattered journalists, writers, and scientists, Lilienthal recognized that a more sustained public engagement would require "our schools and universities, the churches and lay religious organizations, the radio and the press." It would be the job of these organizations, he said, "not only to disseminate the facts, within the limits of security, but to interpret and give meaning to those facts." The second aspect was that the proper response was to *do something.* The role of these cultural institutions was not to vent the public's fears or to play on other emotions, but to enlist citizens in such concrete tasks as learning about the atom and discussing how best to guide its uses. Like others, he emphasized the peril in which humanity found itself ("destructiveness beyond our imagination"), not because fear was the only response, but to dramatize the urgency of his call to action.

Over the next few years, the response to nuclear energy did enlist the public in a variety of concrete activities. In Marengo, Iowa, a town of about two thousand people, a quarter of the residents attended lectures and viewed films about atomic energy at the local school auditorium. In Charlottesville, Virginia, and Portland, Oregon, women's clubs and churches sponsored public lectures and discussions about the implications of atomic power. The Atomic Energy Commission sent scientists to visit community groups in Idaho, Texas, Washington, New York, and other states. Brookhaven National Laboratory in New York created a traveling exhibit for museums and schools. The Great Books Foundation organized book discussion groups in seventeen cities in hopes of helping the public "reach the right answer to living with the atomic bomb."[43] More than a million copies of a comic book General Electric produced to explain atomic power were distributed to schools. Through the League of Women Voters in St. Louis and through the Citizens' Committee in Stamford, Connecticut, guest speakers and exhibits engaged the public in thinking about the atom. Stamford's "Atomic Energy Week" drew national attention.[44] High school and college students were especially affected as educators focused on expanding the younger generation's knowledge of science. At Yale, the entering class of 1947 was asked to take two full-year courses in science, doubling the previous requirement. Many other colleges followed suit. At a large high school in Kalamazoo, Michigan, a model program, jointly initiated by students and faculty, emerged in which students read John Hersey's *Hiroshima*, viewed a film about hydrogen bomb tests, discussed ways of improving human relations, and considered the advancement and control of nuclear technology. A follow-up study showed that more than half concluded they "would like to help" do things to make the world better, while only a quarter came away fearing the future.[45]

To be sure, these activities engaged the public quite selectively. Formal responsibility for meeting the challenge of the nuclear era was assigned largely to people with specific institutional roles to fulfill, especially scientists, experts working in industry, and government officials. There was less for the ordinary person to do, other than be respectful and supportive of these elites. Urgent warnings about the peril of nuclear destruction—warnings that were aimed at motivating moral action—were harder for the average citizen to heed. A person might hear that the world was in danger and that moral responsibility should be exercised, and yet be frustrated in finding reasonable and practical ways in which to fulfill those expectations. For instance, attending a town meeting about atomic energy could hardly be regarded by any truly conscientious citizen as a way to save the nation from terrible destruction.

Thus, it might be argued that fear, pure and simple, was the dominant response to coexisting with the possibility of nuclear annihilation. This, in fact, is the conclusion drawn by historian Paul Boyer, who writes that the "dreamscape of the nuclear future" that emerged between 1945 and 1950 had as its central motif "palpable fear"—fear that humanity would be annihilated, that progress was now a lost hope, and that even death could no longer be anticipated as the rational ending to a life well lived.[46]

However, the most systematic research conducted at the time suggests otherwise. Studies of public opinion by researchers at Cornell University in 1947 and at the University of Michigan between 1951 and 1953 concluded that the public was keenly aware of living in a nuclear age (there was almost universal awareness of the existence of atomic weapons, for instance, compared with far less awareness of any other issue or event pollsters asked about), but that the public's response could not be understood simply as one of fear or fear suppression. People did indicate that they were afraid of the atomic bomb, but more often said they were unconcerned or had complicated opinions. Had there been a great deal of suppressed fears, the researchers argued, "we might expect wild rumors and bizarre ideas to spread easily," but hardly any such behavior was evident. Far more common was the sense that government officials and scientists were making the important decisions. As a respondent in one of the studies explained, "I let the people who are qualified in those things do the worrying." Or, in the words of another, "Why should I worry about the bomb. There's not a thing I can do about it except make myself sick. If there's a war or not, bombs or not, the people in Washington decide—not me." The researchers also found that even by 1953 opinions had not crystallized into any single, stable pattern. People believed atomic power could result in some horrible outcome or could lead to peace and prosperity. With such a huge range of possibilities, people naturally entertained mixed views.[47]

Although observers in later years would look back on the first decade after Hiroshima and view it as a time of rising apathy and thus as a missed opportunity for the antinuclear movement, it is more accurate to describe the period as one of intense cultural preoccupation with the implications of atomic power. The public response clearly acknowledged that atomic power could be a blessing or a curse. It was indeed an important development that certainly demanded a moral response and was regarded as a major turning point in human history.

The response was not to sit back and let emotions rule, but to identify tasks that needed to be done. Most of these tasks were ones that policy makers, public administrators, and scientists would perform on behalf of the wider population. The elites in government, research, and industry accepted these responsibilities and the public willingly acceded. The technical and administrative nature of these tasks, and the necessity for secrecy, made it seem reasonable to do so. Nobody would have found it plausible for individual citizens to shoulder the responsibility of finding a solution to nuclear peril on their own. Not having much of a role to play, other than as taxpayers and consumers, the average citizen undertook the problem solving tasks that were within reach. Despite the possibility of atomic destruction, people went to work, raised children, and generally got on with the daily business of their lives.

THE COLD WAR BETWEEN THE UNITED STATES and the Soviet Union increasingly shaped the cultural response to nuclear weapons during the 1950s and 1960s. Especially during the Cuban missile crisis in October 1962, the standoff between the two superpowers provided the American public with one of the most vivid re-alizations of the catastrophic peril it faced. The prospect of major U.S. cities being destroyed by a rain of nuclear warheads was now something that could be imag-ined happening at any moment, not a theoretical possibility that might occur in ten or twenty years. For about two weeks—thirteen days, in the title of Robert F. Kennedy's memoir of the crisis—the nation stood on the brink of war as the United States mounted a naval blockade to prevent further Soviet shipments of nuclear ballistic missiles to Cuba and to force the removal of those already brought in.[48] Tapes released years later showed President Kennedy and his top advisors considering how Soviet premier Nikita Khrushchev might respond if the Ameri-cans tried to prevent missiles from being located in Cuba and how the public would react if they did not. In these private discussions, the topics that were seri-ously in play included invading Cuba, establishing a blockade, complying with the Russians' request to remove U.S. missiles from Turkey, and considering whether an overreaction might result in a Soviet takeover of Western-controlled sections of Berlin.[49] Public rhetoric and the speculation it encouraged were apocalyptic. "Let no one doubt that this is a difficult and dangerous effort on which we have set out," Kennedy said in an eighteen-minute radio and television address to the nation. "No one can foresee precisely what course it will take or what costs or casualties will be incurred. The path we have chosen for the present is full of hazards."[50] A viewer in Philadelphia called the broadcast "the most dangerous thing we've heard since Pearl Harbor." A woman in New Jersey lamented, "There's no civil defense here. We just have to sit." Merchants in Atlanta reported brisk sales of groceries, flashlights, transistor radios, water purification pills, first aid supplies, and camp stoves. As people left work the next day, farewells included, "See you later—if at all."[51] A woman who was in high school in Florida at the time remembers seeing squadrons of bombers heading south and thinking that at any minute missiles might be coming back. A journalist who would later write a book about the crisis observed, "I remember the look on my fifth-grade teacher's face when she told us that nuclear war might begin at any minute. . . . I wonder what could be worse than telling a child that both he and his country might be obliterated within minutes."[52] In a Gallup poll that fall, fully 85 percent of the public mentioned something about the crisis—the Cuban situation, war with Russia, atomic war—as the nation's most serious problem.[53]

To understand ideas about public responsibility during the Cuban missile crisis, it is necessary to recall the concerns that had gradually escalated over the previous fifteen years about nuclear fallout. The danger of being exposed to radiation, as much as the threat of nuclear annihilation, was the problem with which the public increasingly became concerned. Unlike negotiating arms agreements or developing the technology for nuclear-powered submarines, protecting oneself and one's family against radiation was something an ordinary person could think about and take steps to (try to) prevent.

Concern about long-term radioactivity was first expressed the day following the bombing of Hiroshima by Harold Jacobson, a scientist who had played a minor role in the Manhattan Project. In response, FBI agents threatened Jacobson with espionage charges, interrogated him at length until he suffered a physical collapse. The agents coerced a public retraction from Jacobson and solicited a counterstatement from physicist J. Robert Oppenheimer denying that radioactivity could possibly be a problem.[54] Within a year, reports of radiation sickness and death among the victims at Hiroshima and Nagasaki began to appear in the American press.

For a time, it appeared that science had come to the rescue, as reports of medical research suggested that heparin, an anticoagulant, and blue dye could dramatically reduce the effects of radiation poisoning. Initial reports from bomb tests at the Bikini atoll in the Pacific indicated that concrete walls would also provide sufficient protection against radiation. However, physician David Bradley, a member of the monitoring team, wrote in *No Place to Hide* that radioactivity would linger after a blast for centuries.[55]

Concerns deepened in the early 1950s. The first victim of postwar nuclear testing was a crew member of the Japanese fishing vessel *Lucky Dragon* who, along with his shipmates, was exposed to radiation from the Castle Bravo test of a hydrogen bomb at the Bikini atoll in 1954, even though the boat was outside the danger zone that U.S. authorities had defined. Over the next few years, scientists became increasingly interested in the spread and effects of radiation as testing of hydrogen bombs continued. By the end of the decade, the public had come to realize that they were in danger from radiation even if their community did not experience a direct nuclear attack. In 1959, the *Saturday Evening Post* carried an extensive two-part article titled "Fallout: The Silent Killer."[56] Harmful radioactive particles, the public learned, would not stay high in the stratosphere until they ceased to be dangerous, as the Atomic Energy Commission had predicted, but would fall much more quickly and thus be more deadly. One of the most troubling aspects of the new information was that as many as 40 million U.S. children under the age of ten had been exposed for four or five years to higher than normal doses of radiation from drinking milk. Nobody knew how many might contract thyroid cancer as a result.

Fearful as it was to imagine that the nation's children were already hopelessly exposed, fallout brought home the new nuclear age and turned it into the kind of problem that the average person could consider doing something about. The activities people engaged in were not necessarily the most appropriate or likely to be effective, and thus engaged fewer people in practice than in thought, but these activities shifted the responsibility for preventative action slightly more toward the public than before. As estimates of risk from fallout rose, officials increasingly called on citizens to take their own precautions, rather than rely on the government for protection.

One such activity focused on the milk supply. Between 1955 and 1959 newspapers and magazines carried numerous replies to readers who wanted to know if it was safe to drink milk. The experts advised that it was, although the same newspapers carried stories about levels of radioactivity rising as a result of Russian nuclear tests. Pocket-size "Geiger scopes," radiation detectors simple enough for a child to use, became increasingly popular. Government pamphlets encouraged the nation's farmers to do their part to protect the food supply, for instance, by keeping grain and hay fed to cows covered with tarpaulins or stored in stout weatherproof buildings, by deep-plowing fields, and by wearing rubber boots and gloves after an attack.[57] By 1961, warnings about food contamination and other ill effects of fallout had become part of the government's effort to mobilize public opinion against the Soviet Union in the arms race. A report early in 1962 showed that Americans' milk consumption during the previous year had fallen by approximately 375,000 gallons. Worried dairy farmers persuaded President Kennedy to encourage the public to drink more milk. That summer farmers shifted dairy cows from pasture to stored hay and grain to reduce levels of radioactive iodine 131.[58]

Another activity that ordinary people could do was to instruct children in ways to protect themselves. The most famous of these efforts were the "duck and cover" drills that began in schools in 1951 in conjunction with a Civil Defense Administration film by the same name. In the film, a black and white animation followed by real-life footage, Bert the Turtle counseled children to find shelter as soon as they were warned or heard an extremely loud blast overhead.[59] Schools developed air raid drills that variously called for children to evacuate to a shelter or duck under their desks. In most schools these drills occurred at random intervals every two weeks.

Adults who experienced these drills as children remember them vividly. "The dread of the atomic bomb was the equivalent of Anthrax and chemical weapons or dirty bombs now," wrote one. "Then as now, there was a need to feel a sense of control and understanding to make life tolerable." "As a child," recalled another, "one of my big fears was that this horrible thing called the 'Bomb' would happen when I was not at school! To my 6-year-old mind, the only safe place in the world was under my desk!" Memories of the drills sometimes include reflections about their ineffectiveness, but more often depict them as reasonable and reassuring. The film has a "scientific basis," one man explained, echoing the sentiments of another who mentioned the number of people at Hiroshima who were killed by flying debris. A history teacher emphasized that Soviet planes could have dropped bombs and the duck and cover advice "could have significantly improved your chance of survival."[60] At the time, these civil defense drills were also widely regarded as effective ways to quell fear. The more children practiced, educators argued, the better prepared they would be to withstand the emotional shock of a nuclear attack. "Action, and plans for action," advised one report, "make for the release of tension and a greater feeling of safety."[61]

Perhaps the most widely discussed response involved fallout shelters. The earliest of these were simply an extension of civil defense programs established during World War II and were generally located in basements of public buildings in major cities. As the possibility of radioactive particles from atom bomb tests or attacks became more familiar, a few people constructed their own shelters. A much publicized example was Kathleen MacDonald, a widow who hired an "X-ray expert" in 1950 to build her a steel-reinforced fallout shelter with thirty-two-inch walls of reinforced concrete.[62] The Eisenhower administration periodically encouraged people to have plans for fallout protection in case of nuclear attack. It was not until President John F. Kennedy took office (1961), though, that much attention was given to developing a systematic plan for fallout protection.

One of Kennedy's first acts was to direct Secretary of Defense Robert S. McNamara to determine what resources were available and what were needed. The administration soon decided that public shelters were more feasible, but in the meantime launched a major campaign to prompt action among individual homeowners. A few days after Christmas in 1961, the Defense Department's Office of Civil Defense published a booklet titled "Fallout Protection: What to Know and Do about Nuclear Attack" that could be obtained separately or as a cutout section in major newspapers and newsmagazines. The booklet showed a mushroom cloud distributing particles of fallout and told citizens how likely they were to die or be exposed to radiation at various distances from a nuclear attack. A section titled "Individual Action" told families how to construct fallout shelters in their basements and back-yards for as little as $150. One drawing showed a father and son building a base-ment shelter of sand-filled concrete blocks with Mom attentively engaging the two in conversation. The booklet provided a detailed list of food, medical items, and other supplies with which to stock home shelters and counseled those who had not built a shelter that in case of attack they should dive under or behind the nearest desk or sofa.[63] After President Kennedy's telecast about the emerging crisis in Cuba, New York's civil defense director, Lieutenant General Francis W. Farrell, said at a press conference, "Not everyone can come up with a concrete-and-masonry shelter in the next few days, but everyone should be able to improvise some kind of protection."[64]

Fallout left the public with a significant moral dilemma. On the one hand, individ-uals were being called upon to take more responsibility to protect themselves from nuclear peril than ever before. Their lives and the safety of their children, they were told, depended on having constructed a shelter and in other ways learning to take cover. "The country's survival depends on individuals," a civil defense official explained to a national women's conference in 1959; every homemaker should stock food and water, buy a first aid kit, and store emergency clothing and blankets.[65] Government and scientists were no longer the sole solution. Indeed, the greatest danger might be from one's neighbors attempting to break into one's shelter or steal one's food. "My mother tells me," one woman recalled, "that my father's whole response to the Cuban Missile Crisis was to purchase a handgun."[66] On the other hand, the actions that ordi-nary citizens could reasonably take were actually quite limited. They could instruct their children to duck and cover—knowing that this would probably not help much. They could imagine themselves being safe if only they had a bomb shelter.

However, hardly anyone had a shelter and, for that matter, there was consider-able skepticism about how effective a shelter might be. A national poll in July 1961 found that 21 percent of the public had stored food in case of a nuclear attack, and by November of that year 12 percent said they planned to make changes to their home to protect themselves in case of a nuclear attack. Yet only 3 percent said they had actually done so. A poll in Illinois found that only 4 percent had engaged in any safety or survival-related activities during the crisis. It was not that people were unmindful of the danger—quite to the contrary: 60 percent said they were "very" or "fairly" worried about the chance of a world war breaking out in which atom and hydrogen bombs would be used, and 53 percent believed that in the event of war their own locality would be one the Russians would strike. It was rather that con-structing home shelters was impractical for those who did not own their homes or have money to spare. Home shelters were unappealing to those who took seriously the news that Russia could launch more than 350 nuclear weapons—enough to destroy the entire United States.

Thus, it was unsurprising that people gravitated to solutions they could more easily manage. As the missile crisis unfolded, newspapers were flooded with advertisements for gadgets. Radiation detectors sold especially well. Some entrepreneurs sold potions to remove fallout from water. People also seized on routine activities to maintain a sense of order and security. They worried about war, but worried more about aspects of their lives over which they had greater control. A national poll of women in June 1962 showed that 20 percent worried a lot about the "possibility of war," but 34 percent worried a lot about their "children's behavior" and 33 percent listed debts and bills as their main concerns.[67]

Through novels and films it also became possible to imagine what people might do if an attack actually took place and they were unable to escape from radiation. *On the Beach,* by Australian novelist Nevil Shute, was published in 1957 and became a widely viewed motion picture starring Gregory Peck and Ava Gardner in 1959. The story, set in Australia and aboard a submarine after a massive nuclear war had exterminated human life in the northern hemisphere, offered a haunting look at ordinary people in the southern hemisphere as they waited to die from fallout. Throughout the story, naturally, the characters act out their fear; for instance, the submarine's crew is described as doing well at the start of the narrative "though various neuroses were beginning to appear, born of anxiety."[68] At one point, Commander Dwight Towers speculates about the possibility of anyone surviving in the northern hemisphere by living in a fallout shelter: "He'd have to be living in an hermetically sealed room with all air filtered as it comes in and all food and water stored in with him some way. I wouldn't think it practical."[69] As the radiation comes closer, the main characters occasionally raise philosophical questions. "All those cities, all those fields and farms, with nobody, and nothing left alive," Moira Davidson muses. "Just nothing there. I simply can't take it in." Towers responds: "It's too big for me too . . . I can't really believe in it, just can't get used to the idea. I suppose it's lack of imagination."[70]

However, the story is far less about fear or resignation than about the irrepressible drive to take action, however modest, and to keep busy in the face of overwhelming danger. Although it is too late, naval officer Peter Holmes (played by Anthony Perkins) reflects that more should have been done to educate people about the dangers of nuclear weapons. "We liked our newspapers with pictures of beach girls and headlines about cases of indecent assault, and no government was wise enough to stop us having them that way."[71] Others stay active by solving the practical problems of living as death approaches: finding blankets to stay warm, turning off the electricity to prevent fires, caring for children and pets, saying their good-byes. In the closing scene, Commander Towers is on the bridge of his ship, heading to sea on a final cruise.[72]

On the Beach and other works, such as Helen Clarkson's novel *The Last Day* and Walter M. Miller Jr.'s novel *A Canticle for Leibowitz* (both 1959), Roger Corman's film *The Last Woman on Earth* (1960), and Sidney Lumet's 1964 film version of

Fail-Safe (novel by Eugene Burdick, published 1962), supplemented the public's imagination about the threat of radiation beyond what could be learned from newspapers and magazines.[73] Unlike the news that Hiroshima had been bombed, the events culminating in the Cuban missile crisis were not announced to the world as a fait accompli. There was time to prepare and to think about moral responsibility in advance rather than after the fact. Although most Americans did not build fallout shelters, they did follow the news, register their views about what should be done in opinion polls, and huddle close to their families.

Their responses showed clearly that people were willing to delegate most of the responsibility for solving the missile crisis to those with the power to do so, just as they had in the opening years of the nuclear era. It was as if the public recognized that its own responsibility was quite limited compared to the tasks it had entrusted to its leaders. Kennedy's decision to impose a naval blockade received overwhelming approval. Indeed, an analysis of polls conducted at the time shows that the public largely believed that officials were doing the right thing. Citizens "absorbed the shock, backed their leaders, and carried on with their lives."[74]

Segments of the public, though, were more willing to criticize the president's actions than had been evident in 1945. They had lived with the Cold War and nuclear weapons long enough to have formed a clearer opinion about what should be done. They had also elected a president by the narrowest margin in U.S. history and were initially unsure if he was the right man for the job. A vocal minority thought the president should have acted sooner and more decisively against the Russians. "What did they think the Russians were doing down there," asked a woman in Los Angeles, "playing tiddlywinks?" She added: "It seems awfully late in the game—maybe too late."[75] A resident of Central City, Nebraska, complained, "We're a little sick and tired of that crowd up there in Washington. We was crazy that we didn't stop [the Soviet buildup in Cuba] right at the start."[76] At a Conservative party rally in New York City, eight thousand people booed Kennedy for doing "too little, too late" about Cuba.[77] A poll in Michigan showed that 32 percent favored invading Cuba. A survey in Kentucky found 27 percent did so. Nationally, 17 percent wanted an invasion.[78]

In the weeks leading up to the crisis, Republican leaders had been especially critical of Kennedy, arguing that he was downplaying the Russian threat rather than paying sufficient attention to the impending crisis in Cuba. Other leaders were equally critical of what they perceived as an overly belligerent response. Harvard's H. Stuart Hughes (then campaigning against Edward M. Kennedy to represent Massachusetts in the Senate) distributed a statement calling for a peaceful resolution involving the United Nations.[79] A student group at the University of California at Berkeley held a rally urging "no invasion, no blockade."[80] The head of a pacifist religious coalition in New York issued a statement of "grave concern and regret."[81] A women's organization dedicated to the elimination of nuclear testing staged a peace rally at the United Nations.[82]

In all of this, the primary response to the Cuban missile crisis was of course the decision by Kennedy and his closest advisors to be tough, but also to move cautiously, to keep options open, and to provide both themselves and the Russians with room to maneuver. Firsthand accounts of the meetings of EXCOMM (the Executive Committee of the National Security Council) provide a rare glimpse of the process by which decisions are made in the face of peril. The worst-case scenario was hardly denied or neglected, as some scholars have argued from considering other such instances. For example, at one point in the discussion Kennedy said, "It isn't the first step that concerns me, but both sides escalating to the fourth and fifth step—and we don't go to the sixth because there is no one around to do so."[83]

Robert McNamara recalled later, "What the missile crisis impressed upon me was that, yes, we *could* stumble into a nuclear war."[84] The worst-case was not so much something to be planned *for*, as others have emphasized, but to be guarded *against*. It served as a rhetorical reminder of the need to seek practical solutions. Kennedy's caution against escalation to the point of annihilation came at a moment when some of his advisors were urging an attack on the missile sites in Cuba and led to the conclusion that an invasion was unwise. (Despite assurances by the CIA, shortly after taking office Kennedy had been burned by a botched, abortive invasion at the Bay of Pigs in Cuba in April 1961.) McNamara said the thought of stumbling into a nuclear war persuaded him that this option was totally unacceptable and must be avoided.

HAVING AVERTED PERIL, the key players and subsequent policy analysts were quick to draw lessons from it. Robert Kennedy's account in *Thirteen Days* encouraged future leaders to plan, consider varying opinions, and trust experts. He also encouraged paying attention to world opinion, not humiliating one's opponent or backing him into a corner, and anticipating the unanticipated. There was something basically affirming about our humanity in these lessons. The nation had faced near destruction and survived. Humans were rational after all. We could invest in expertise and count on it to protect us.

Over the next quarter century, the crisis was examined again and again. It played a central role in theories about deterrence and in arguments about the value of game theory. The explicit lesson was that informed and cool-headed professionals at the highest levels of government were in the best position to deal with any crisis that might arise in the future. They not only had a responsibility to make the right decisions, but also required depth of character and courage. The implicit lesson was that the world would continue to exist in peril, even with those in power doing their best. "Risks of accident, miscalculation, misperception and inadvertence" would always be present, McNamara observed. A statement of these risks, he said, "ought to be inscribed above all the doorways in the White House and the Pentagon."[85]

THREE

WHAT TO MOBILIZE AGAINST

OPPOSITION TO NUCLEAR WEAPONS EMERGED soon after the bombing of Hiroshima and grew into a significant popular movement by the 1980s. It was through this movement, more than anything else, that efforts to redefine the public's moral responsibilities in the face of nuclear peril took place. The Federation of Atomic Scientists, founded in 1945 (later renamed the Federation of American Scientists), became an early foe of nuclear weapons and included many critical essays in its *Bulletin of the Atomic Scientists.* In 1949, a group calling itself the Committee for Peaceful Alternatives to the Atlantic Pact petitioned the U.S. delegation to the United Nations to prohibit the use of atomic energy for warfare. The petition was signed by more than 1,100 clergy, educators, scientists, and writers. In 1950, seven hundred members of an organization called American Women for Peace, an outgrowth of a tenants' council in New York City, held a demonstration in Washington. Other organizations pressing for a nuclear ban included the Federal Council of Churches, the Synagogue Council of America, the American Friends Service Committee, the Women's International League for Peace and Freedom, and the American Red Cross. Throughout the 1950s, these groups continued, but organized opposition to nuclear weapons remained sparse. Protests were more common in Europe and for the most part received negative press in the United States.[1] That changed, at first slowly and almost imperceptibly, in the months prior to the Cuban missile crisis. Scattered groups of activists formed to protest the Soviets' tests of nuclear weapons and to oppose the United States' retaliatory termination of the test ban treaty. By the end of the 1960s, much of this antinuclear energy was subsumed within the larger protest movement against the Vietnam war, but specific concerns about nuclear weapons remained. In the 1970s and 1980s, concerns about the safety of nuclear power plants helped the movement mobilize further. During the final years of the Cold War, opposition to nuclear weapons gained an even wider hearing. Although the antinuclear movement never attracted a large majority of Americans, it did represent a marked change in thinking from the prevailing mood of the late 1940s and 1950s.

The growth of the antinuclear movement raises interesting questions about the cultural response to peril, such as how does one's understanding of individual moral responsibility shift from being largely concerned about oneself to promoting action on behalf of the public good? What do these changing understandings imply about the formal roles delegated to public officials, scientists, and other specialists? With so much of the discussion about nuclear weapons having been dominated by experts, one of the most significant challenges of the antinuclear movement was to present itself in a way that could attract and indeed enfranchise ordinary people. The challenge was magnified by the fact that the public had been trained to think of nuclear weapons—and atomic energy more broadly—as a topic that only scientists and well-informed government leaders could understand, and thus to imagine that their own responsibility was quite limited. In the rising discussion of fallout, individual responsibility included moral connotations only in the sense of protecting oneself. For instance, in the civil defense film "Duck and Cover" starring Bert the Turtle, children were warned repeatedly to dive for cover, but never to help someone else find shelter. For an antinuclear movement to arise in which the public took collective responsibility for itself, this self-interested logic had to be extended to the point that a small share of the public could imagine itself acting on behalf of a common good beyond themselves. Doing so was further confounded by the Cold War penumbra of suspicion toward activists who might be categorized as communists, deviants, or beatniks. If citizens were to take responsibility for their own safety, the message also had to be different from the ones government had used to encourage construction of fallout shelters. Responsibility needed to be linked with a clearer sense that action could be efficacious.

THE ANTINUCLEAR MOVEMENT DEFINED ITSELF as a representative of the wider public and, at the same time, resisted being pegged as deviants by asserting repeatedly that its members were ordinary citizens. An interesting illustration of this emphasis on the ordinariness of its activists was Dagmar Wilson, a mother of three who became one of the prime movers of Women Strike for Peace (WSP), one of the most successful antinuclear movements of the early 1960s. Addressing a crowd of five hundred activists at the Washington Monument in 1962, Wilson asserted that she was not really an activist or a leader at all, but that nuclear weapons had been "bugging" her to the point that she "decided that there are some things the individual citizen can do." She observed, "I'm not a professional peace worker and I am not an organizer. . . . I've never done anything like this before. . . . I suppose I'm the ordinary housewife. I symbolize something."[2]

The "concerned, average mommy" image was a self-conscious persona that did not exactly square with the facts. A survey of more than two hundred Women Strike for Peace activists conducted by sociologist Elise Boulding showed that two-thirds held college degrees, 70 percent were married to professionals, and 41 percent were involved in other civic, race relations, civil liberties, or political groups. Wilson herself had been educated in Germany and England, was married to an employee of the British embassy in Washington, and pursued a successful career as an illustrator of children's books from her home in Georgetown. WSP's appeal to the "lady next door" was nevertheless considerable. By mid-1962, nearly four dozen local WSP chapters had enlisted more than 14,000 participants. The movement eschewed formal organization, styling itself as an informal network of housewives and working women.[3]

Another significant aspect of redefining moral responsibility involved pushing back the space, as it were, occupied by those in specialized roles to permit more of the terrain to be claimed by ordinary people. It was necessary to challenge expert authority, but on grounds that did not cast the challengers as amateurs or naïve idealists. From Dagmar Wilson, for instance, one finds statements that defy authority but that also express misgivings about doing so. "It was a hard thing for us to do," she told a reporter. "We were brought up to believe in a civilized world where our leaders were wise men, acting on principles we were taught to believe in in school. You are reluctant to buck that." Going against those leaders was enough, she said, to make you think "maybe you are the one who is crazy." Only through the affirmation of finding that other people felt the same way did she feel empowered to continue.[4]

Against the authority of scientific expertise and the formal administrative power of policy makers, WSP activists developed a rhetoric of "maternal outrage."[5] They were indignant mothers seeking at first to protect their children from the radioactive iodine 131 and strontium 90 that was thought to be contaminating milk and other food products. Their maternal outrage appealed to the universalism of motherhood and the fact that mothers could presumably speak on behalf of other mothers' children as well as their own. Moral responsibility extended beyond the United States in claims that mothers in Japan, Russia, Cuba, Vietnam, and elsewhere were similarly concerned about their children's safety and future. As mothers and homemakers, WSP leaders argued that they knew what was best for families and children and that they had insights no man could understand, no matter how technically knowledgeable he might be. The disagreements among nations that fueled the arms race, they contended, were like disagreements in families that could be settled amicably as members sat around the table and discussed their differences. The problem was that men in leadership positions had betrayed their wives and children. Reluctantly, the women were now having to sacrifice their domestic obligations to do what their husbands had failed to

accomplish. Mothers and housewives could hardly be accused of being communist sympathizers. The movement's moral appeal rested on arguments about
nurturance, the enduring instinct to sacrifice for one's children, and the claim
that children were now being victimized by nuclear weapons, just as they had
been by slavery, child labor, and oppression.

During the late 1960s, much of the antinuclear movement's energy was directed toward protesting the escalating war in Vietnam. Women Strike for Peace
protested U.S. involvement in Vietnam as early as 1964, and by 1969 was sending
delegations to meet with women in Hanoi. After 1964, the National Committee for
a Sane Nuclear Policy (SANE), cochaired by socialist leader Norman Thomas and
baby care specialist Benjamin Spock, focused less on nuclear disarmament and
more on condemning the Vietnam conflict as an immoral war. Students for a
Democratic Society (SDS) increasingly became a leader of campus protests against
the war, after having included in its Port Huron Statement (1962) an extended
discussion of nuclear energy being used to "unleash destruction greater than that
incurred in all wars of human history" and detailed recommendations about
achieving nuclear disarmament to avoid an "illimitable holocaust."[6]

Although protests against the Vietnam war overshadowed discussions of
nuclear weapons, the protest movement succeeded not only in mobilizing larger
numbers but also in broadening the public's sense of moral authority and responsibility. Claims could be made by ordinary citizens who knew nothing about the
technicalities of nuclear science or deterrence strategy, but who could argue that
atrocities were being committed in Southeast Asia, that the United States was
engaged in a war that was really a civil conflict in a distant country, and that young
Americans were dying needlessly. This progression in moral reasoning was evident in the rhetoric of activist organizations. The Port Huron Statement, for example, acknowledged the need for language that "can be understood and felt close-up
by every human being" and yet emphasized the relatively elite significance of intellectual skills, the central role of universities, and technical analysis of nuclear arms
policy. Its arguments included a detailed analysis of the Kennedy administration's
nuclear policies, a discussion of Western Europe's role in U.S.-Soviet relations, a
critique of military arguments about deterrence, and a set of alternative policy
recommendations. By 1965, as antiwar protests drew thousands of participants
and attracted national media attention, the language had become considerably
less technical. SDS spokesman Paul Booth argued that student protesters were
behaving morally in exercising their civic responsibilities as concerned citizens,
were advancing civil liberties and freedom just as the civil rights movement was,
were opposing administrative policies that had become morally bankrupt, and were
against the bombing of innocent women and children in another country.[7]

The broader mobilization of antiwar sentiment naturally faded as U.S. involvement in Vietnam diminished in the early 1970s. Apart from the fact that antiwar

protests had been controversial, they also deflected attention from specific concerns about nuclear weapons and other possible dangers from nuclear energy. Periodic protests in the late 1970s, such as those staged in 1976 and 1977 by the Clamshell Alliance to block construction of a nuclear reactor at Seabrook, New Hampshire, drew up to 2,000 demonstrators, but similar protests in Western Europe attracted upwards of 30,000. Pacifist religious organizations, such as Catholic Worker and the American Friends Service Committee, and the remnants of antiwar groups, provided most of the impetus for these protests. Indeed, the continuities in personnel and tactics were sufficient that critics readily branded activists as radicals and spoke of a regrettable "Vietnamization" of the nuclear question.

Public interest in the possible dangers of nuclear energy increased significantly after the March 1979 disaster at the Three Mile Island installation near Harrisburg, Pennsylvania, in which one of the reactors experienced a partial meltdown. Although a full investigation was ordered by federal and state authorities, the initial response from experts was largely to downplay the event's significance, comparing it to risks associated with electricity, immunology, automobiles, and hydroelectric dams. "Everything has finite hazards," an MIT scientist who had worked on the atom bomb at Los Alamos explained, "and if society won't accept that, then it has to stop moving ahead."[8] Public reaction was at first restrained as well. Person-on-the-street interviews in New York City after the incident suggested "blithe unconcern" about a threat that remained two hundred miles away. The longstanding assumption that government was in charge of such technical matters was still evident. "I expected government control to be watching out for me, as a private citizen," one man proclaimed. "Obviously somebody's not doing their job, somewhere."[9] Within weeks, though, the public mood began to change. Some 15,000 demonstrators joined a rally at a proposed nuclear reactor site on Long Island a few months later, and 20,000 did so at the contested Diablo Canyon site in California. In September 1979 an estimated 200,000 people participated in an antinuclear rally in New York. Besides the fears of radioactive contamination that had been heightened by Three Mile Island, the rising public turnout stemmed from a greater sense that collective action could make a difference. Unlike action aimed at nuclear war or fallout, which seemed to have little effect on national policy, demonstrators at reactor sites were confident they could persuade utility companies to forestall construction. In short, public responsibility was reinforced by a perception of efficacy.

Efficacy grew not only from evidence that power companies were canceling contracts for reactors; it stemmed as well from scaling down the problem of nuclear peril to manageable problem-solving size. Earlier discussions of a nuclear attack led citizens to believe that a massive explosion could happen at any moment, killing everything in sight. A person might hide, but there was little else to be done, and if the threat was from a standoff between superpowers, it was un-likely that the average person could do much to change that. In contrast, nuclear power plants were visible, planned, local, and controlled by state and regional au-thorities. Further, they were to be paid for (or not) by local customers. In addition, the appeal at mass rallies was not the grandiose hope of ending the threat of total annihilation, but the more modest objectives of being patriotic, stabilizing the arms race, or merely registering opposition to the Reagan administration.[10] Leaders told citizens that participating was something practical they could do. It was a way to fight cancer, for instance, just as giving to the American Cancer Society was, and it was even a way to fight inflation by discouraging utility companies from raising rates to pay for nuclear plants. The peace movement gave people *simple* tasks that they could accomplish with little risk or sacrifice—signing petitions, collecting signatures, writing letters, attending meetings, watching videos.

Psychological studies conducted at the time showed that feelings of efficacy and personal empowerment were stronger among antinuclear activists than in the general public. Activists felt that they, personally, were in control of their lives, rather than being controlled by external forces, and they believed that citizens working together could influence government policies in ways that would reduce the risk of nuclear war. Research also demonstrated that anxiety about nuclear peril was lower among people who imagined themselves doing something to reduce the likelihood of nuclear accidents and war. "Hope through action," as one psychologist termed it, was accomplished in modest, nonheroic ways, such as writing to congressional representatives and donating money to an antinuclear group. Researchers had few techniques to examine the underlying cognitive pro-cesses involved, but the results suggested that problem solving was an effective way of dealing with what otherwise would have been an immobilizing outlook on the future.[11]

The sense that a person *can* do something in the face of peril rings false, though, unless there are persuasive moral arguments that one *should* do something beyond simply looking out for one's own survival. These arguments were seldom spelled out among the signs protesters carried or in the pencil and paper tests psycholo-gists used, but were amply discussed in the antinuclear literature. The most detailed explication of the moral case against nuclear weapons was presented in a series of *New Yorker* articles in 1981 that subsequently appeared as the widely reviewed 1982 book by Jonathan Schell, *The Fate of the Earth*. The book ranked elev-enth in sales that year among nonfiction books, slightly ahead of Richard Simmons's *Never-Say-Diet Cookbook* and far behind the top-selling *Jane Fonda's Workout Book*, yet another indication that Americans were more preoccupied with daily life than with the threat of annihilation. *The Fate of the Earth* nevertheless served as a kind of bible for the antinuclear movement, drawing together in persuasive prose what scientists were saying about the consequences of nuclear war and presenting readers with a bleak scenario of the future if activism did not succeed. It won the *Los Angeles Times* book prize and was nominated for a Pulitzer Prize, the National Book Award, and the National Book Critics Circle Award. A quarter of a century later, New York University's journalism department selected it as one of the 100 best nonfiction works of the twentieth century. From the start, reviewers loved it or hated it. Sociologist Michael Useem called it a "defining document, a preamble for action" that was "deservedly acclaimed as one of the most compelling documents of the antinuclear movement."[12] Writer John Leonard described it as "a saving sneeze of Zeitgeist" offering no useful clues about what should be done.[13]

Schell argued that the American public was living in denial, incapable of an appropriate emotional or intellectual response to the unthinkable, and thus content to ignore the grave peril threatening the world. He recounted in graphic detail the hideous death, mutilation, and despair at Hiroshima and Nagasaki, and described how much worse the capacity for destruction had become. An all-out nuclear war between the United States and the Soviet Union, he contended, would leave the world a "republic of insects and grass." The complexity of the ecosphere would be reduced to the simplicity of nothingness. "We—the human race—shall cease to be."[14] The end of human existence, moreover, was so profoundly different from the ordinary deaths of individuals and loved ones that it could only be described as a second death involving the loss of all memory that humanity had ever existed.

Reviewers who favored the book's grisly depiction of nuclear war and those who accused it of being impractical missed its significance as a contribution to the *moral* debate about nuclear weapons. Drawing on Hannah Arendt's reflections about death and transcendence, Schell emphasized the "common world" into which each individual is born and to which all individuals owe responsibility. The common world exists before and after any particular person and is thus imperceptibly affected by the death of an individual. However, the common world depends completely on the survival of humanity as a species and is thus jeopardized by nuclear weapons. Extinction of the species would be more than death. It would be the death of death, the loss of future generations and the loss of ethical judgment itself. A threat to the common world, therefore, demands that individuals do more than struggle to save themselves or their families. A person's moral responsibility is to humanity itself, to the preservation of society and all that it stands for and has accomplished. "Each person alive is called on to assume his share of the responsibility for guaranteeing the existence of all future generations."[15]

The impact of Schell's argument, limited as it was to a relatively small part of the population, was nevertheless to broaden the response to nuclear peril beyond the question of how an individual might escape radioactive fallout or how a policy maker might negotiate an arms agreement. In demonstrating that in the event of human extinction nothing would matter, the argument showed how much it *should* matter to prevent extinction. Though it was framed in philosophical terms, the argument circled back to include the claims about nurturance articulated by Women Strike for Peace and an ethic of love from Catholic Worker activists and clergy. Working for the survival of humanity was a higher form of love than seeking to save oneself. The biblical admonition against killing was to be extended, Schell argued, to letting future generations be born. "Universal parenthood, which would seek to bring life into existence out of nothing, would embody the creativity and abundant generosity of love, and its highest commandment, therefore, would be, 'Be fruitful and multiply.'" To confront the nuclear peril was to be "the parents of all future generations."[16]

The Fate of the Earth appeared in bookstores just as the antinuclear movement was gaining its widest appeal. Activists and religious leaders increasingly challenged the moral validity of the arms race.[17] Polls showed a majority of Americans in favor of reducing or freezing the number of nuclear weapons.[18] A survey in May 1982 found that 53 percent of the public claimed to be paying attention to the issue of a nuclear freeze.[19] A demonstration in Central Park that June drew an estimated 700,000 people. News reports described the participants as a broad spectrum of humanity, including young and old, rich and poor, and representatives of different occupations, ethnic groups, regions, and national backgrounds. "We got rid of Lyndon Johnson—we stopped the war," one of the leaders explained. "This movement is much bigger. It combines the issues of bread and bombs."[20] That fall nuclear freeze referendums appeared on the ballots in 39 states, and passed in 36 of those states.

NEITHER ACTIVISM NOR MORAL APPEALS brought the Cold War to a close, although both played a role. A juxtaposition of special circumstances and strategies—including military threats, rhetoric, diplomacy, economic pressures, and personality factors (which historians are still sorting out)—was involved. By 1984, the National Committee for a Sane Nuclear Policy (SANE), responding to concerns about proposals for funding of MX missiles (dubbed "Peacekeeper" by President Ronald Reagan), had enlisted 80,000 members, a sixfold increase in four years. In 1987 President Reagan and Russian leader Mikhail Gorbachev signed the Intermediate-Range Nuclear Forces Treaty (INF Treaty) that removed 2,600 nuclear missiles from Europe. In 1989, Gorbachev refused to respond militarily as Hungary and Poland allowed free elections. In November of that year crowds tore down the Berlin Wall. Unrest in Eastern Europe continued, with Soviet military leaders placing Gorbachev under house arrest in 1991 and Boris Yeltsin successfully surviving an attempted coup. In December 1991 the Soviet Union officially dissolved.[21]

The end of the Cold War did not mean that the threat of nuclear warfare was over. Although the United States and Russia reduced nuclear weapons stockpiles, the potential for danger from the remaining weapons and from accidents at nu-clear reactors continued. In 1992 and 1993, policy analysts registered continuing concern about who would emerge to lead the former Soviet Union. By 1995, despite reductions of up to 70 percent in parts of the U.S. arsenal, an estimated 9,000 nuclear warheads remained, stored at 33 locations in 17 states and at 13 airbases in seven foreign countries.[22] A large study conducted in 1997 showed that 64 percent of scientists believed the Soviet breakup had decreased the likelihood of U.S. in-volvement in nuclear war, but only 42 percent of the public felt this way. Among the latter, a slight majority (51 percent) felt the breakup had actually increased the likelihood of nuclear war happening somewhere in the world. China loomed as the most likely threat. By a margin of two to one, the public worried that nuclear weapons were more, rather than less, likely to spread to other countries.[23] Continu-ing concern was also evident in popular entertainment. From 1989 to 2002 approximately five hundred motion pictures dealt with nuclear issues.[24]

The Soviet Union's dissolution nevertheless marked a turning point in discus-sions about the threat of nuclear war and in policy analyses of how to prevent one in the future. Hailed as the most important historical development in half a cen-tury, the conclusion of the Cold War was an event requiring a cultural response, just as the bombing of Hiroshima and the Cuban missile crisis were. "At stake," wrote political scientists Daniel H. Deudney and G. John Ikenberry, was "the vin-dication and legitimation of an entire world view and foreign policy orientation."[25] Leaders, activists, and ordinary citizens drew lessons about what had gone right and what had been learned from the long years of living in extreme peril. How the world was understood to have saved itself would be an important part of how it would hope to respond whenever the next crisis arose. The question of how much to trust leaders and how to think about moral responsibility remained central in these interpretations.

The view that nuclear annihilation was a problem best addressed by scientists and policy experts gained new credibility in interpretations of how the Cold War had ended. In this view, the high-stakes strategy of protecting the public from nuclear attack by threatening the Soviets with ever more destructive potential was vindi-cated. John F. Kennedy had been right to stare down Khrushchev during the missile crisis in 1962. Although Johnson and Nixon had perhaps overextended U.S. mili-tary forces in Vietnam, they were arguably correct in taking a realpolitik approach to foreign policy by dealing with Russia and China. Carter's administration could be said to have held the nuclear threat at bay by initiating the neutron bomb and MX missile programs and by strengthening missile defenses in Europe. Reagan's tough talk and his proposed Strategic Defense Initiative (the so-called Star Wars missile defense program) dealt the Soviets a final hand they could not match.

In what came to be known as the "Reagan victory" interpretation, the way to confront danger was to stand tall, look evil squarely in the face, and simply outmuscle it. America had been saved by a brave leader—a role fittingly played by a former actor who posed as a cowboy. Reagan received far more of the credit than his successor, George H. W. Bush, even though the latter was in office when the Soviet Union actually unraveled. A leader like Reagan could be trusted. The moral strength of the person would ensure that good policies resulted. Defenders of this interpretation emphasized that it vindicated faith in science and technology. The bold Star Wars initiative (proposed by Reagan in 1983 but never completed) was their best example. Proponents of soft power also found support for their views in Reagan as the great communicator. Threats of the most serious kind could be successfully confronted if leaders were sufficiently skilled in the use of incisive rhetoric. At the end of Reagan's term, 68 percent of the public said they approved of his handling of the presidency, the highest approval rating any outgoing president had received since polling began, and 88 percent approved of his handling of U.S. relations with the Soviet Union.[26]

An alternative interpretation credited scientists with having provided the technical information required to persuade U.S. and Soviet leaders to end the Cold War. In this interpretation, policies are determined by rational consideration of the facts—which scientists are in a better position to understand than either the unknowledgeable public or bureaucratically entrenched public officials. Critics of the arms race argued that scientists had played an especially important role in discrediting nuclear weapons from about 1980 to 1982 by demonstrating that the danger they posed to the planet made them unusable. "Within these two years," writer John Tirman observed, "the conventional thinking about nukes went from a shadowy concern about the Russians being 'ahead' to abhorrence at the thought of the weapons ever being used. Even Reagan, in this most hyperbolic phase of his belligerency, was forced to state that the weapons could not be used."[27] In this interpretation, science trumped ideology, providing hard evidence that even a militarist like Reagan was forced to accept. The lesson for the future was that peril can be averted if only the public and its leaders will listen to scientists.

The idea that individual citizens could somehow face down nuclear peril by themselves—by purchasing Geiger counters, building bomb shelters, and avoiding contaminated milk—seemed less persuasive than ever. The fact that these individual measures had never been tested by an actual attack meant that they had not been fully discredited. But belief that such measures would ensure survival had been shaken by the antinuclear movement in the early 1980s. The American and Soviet nuclear arsenals had grown to such magnitude, activists claimed, that spending a few days in a shelter was no longer a credible option. Fallout would be too pervasive and social services would be completely disrupted. By the early 1990s, vivid memories of duck and cover drills remained for people who had lived through them, but could hardly be fathomed by the generation just coming of age. "Like, you know," an eighteen-year-old asked a visiting lecturer, "what was that Cold War thing, anyway?" (to which the baffled lecturer replied, "[It] was the ever-present prospect of the Northern Hemisphere's incineration").[28]

The most ambiguous aspect of the debate about how the Cold War ended was its meaning for organized civic activism. On the one hand, writers argued that grassroots mobilization played a significant role in reducing the danger of nuclear annihilation. They pointed to Reagan's apparent softening on nuclear weapons in support of this claim. As activism mounted in the early 1980s, Reagan's poll numbers fell to the point that he responded in November 1983 by declaring, "I know I speak for people everywhere when I say our dream is to see the day when nuclear weapons will be banished from the face of the earth."[29] British historian and activist Mary Kaldor remembered "having a drink with a senior Reagan Administration official the night the zero [nuclear arms] option was announced" who told her "we got the idea from your banners."[30] Other Reagan officials were said to have confirmed the impression that White House policies and congressional perspectives shifted as the antinuclear movement grew. If the antinuclear movement had indeed made a difference, the implication for future threats was obvious. They should be dealt with by encouraging ordinary citizens to take greater responsibility for policies affecting their collective survival. On the other hand, protest rallies were easily forgotten or remembered as the work of hippies and agitators. Writer George Weigel observed that "domestic turmoil" involving the "nuclear-freeze and Central American agitations" merely distracted the public from seeing Reagan's personal role in ending the Cold War.[31] More significantly, the collapse of the Soviet Union drained energy from the antinuclear movement. A national study of local peace movement organizations found that more than a third (35 percent) of those active in 1988 had ceased operations by 1992.[32] The National Committee for a Sane Nuclear Policy (known as SANE/Freeze after 1986) shifted its attention from nuclear weapons to broader peace efforts and held its last large-scale rally in 1991 in protest of the Gulf War. In 1993 it changed its name to Peace Action. For those who had been at the forefront of struggles against the Vietnam War and nuclear proliferation, the causes of the 1990s seemed almost trivial by comparison. "Across the country, self-described aging hippies," wrote a bemused journalist, "are fighting to keep their communities free of Wal-Mart."[33]

The logical resolution of the two interpretations of organized activism was to argue that civic involvement had indeed been vibrant in the early 1980s, just as it had been in the 1960s, but was experiencing a worrisome decline. The Cold War had barely ended when writers across the political spectrum began to express concern that America was now endangered by a collapse of community. The new threat was not as scary as the possibility of being annihilated by nuclear weapons, but those who wrote about it viewed it in nearly the same terms. The civil society debate, as it came to be called, emerged first in discussions about what might replace Soviet totalitarianism in Eastern Europe. The question was whether

Hungary, Poland, the Ukraine, and other new democracies could mobilize enough grassroots civic involvement to establish stable regimes or whether they would succumb to new totalitarian leaders. If civil society could not be strengthened, the Soviet Union might reappear and with it the threat of nuclear war.[34] The civil society debate increasingly focused on concerns about civic involvement in the United States as well. In a widely circulated 1995 essay, political scientist Robert D. Putnam presented evidence that Americans were less likely to vote, sign political petitions, engage in demonstrations, or join civic associations than in the past, and even less likely to spend evenings with their neighbors or participate in bowling leagues.[35] In his subsequent best seller, *Bowling Alone: The Collapse and Revival of American Community*, Putnam assembled additional evidence in support of these conclusions and called on Americans to rekindle their civic passion.[36]

Despite the commentary it evoked, the Cold War was notable for generating no more attention at its demise than it did. Although social scientists examined how and why the threat of nuclear war had subsided, there was less discussion in the popular press than would have been expected in view of the long years in which the world had stood on the brink of annihilation. The reason was partly that the Cold War did not end in a single moment, but stumbled through a succession of agreements, relapses, and failures that lasted for most of a decade. Just as the Soviet Union was disbanding the world's attention was captured by Saddam Hussein's invasion of Kuwait (August 1990). From the discussions that did emerge, though, it was clear that the lessons to be drawn after the fact were not greatly different from those learned during the Cold War. When the world faced grave danger, the average citizen could do only a little. From day to day, life had to go on, filled with earning a living and caring for one's family. A person might be worried, but in most instances there was little reason to alter the pattern of daily life. Instances did arise when collective action made a difference, and in those instances a person might join a peace march or write to an elected official. Otherwise, the problems were of such magnitude that it took high-level leaders to deal with them. It was imperative that these leaders perform their duties as responsibly as they could. Even in so doing, the risks of failure were always present.

THREATS FROM NUCLEAR WEAPONS AND RADIATION since the end of the Cold War have continued from two sources. One is the danger from regional conflicts, such as between India and Pakistan and between Israel and its neighbors. The other is from exposure to radiation from nuclear waste, through accidents at nuclear power plants, and from industrial and military uses of nuclear materials. The likelihood of nuclear weapons being used in regional conflicts has been reduced by nonproliferation treaties and deterrence measures. However, large quantities of nuclear weapons remain in existence. In 2006, Russia's nuclear arsenal included approximately 16,000 warheads, of which a third were estimated to be active and operational; China had approximately 200 nuclear warheads; Britain and France each had between 200 and 300; India was assumed to have at least 40 to 50; and Pakistan was estimated to have nearly as many as India. Israel was thought to have about 60 nuclear warheads, and Western leaders worried that Iran and North Korea were aggressively pursuing such capability. The U.S. arsenal included 10,000 stockpiled nuclear warheads, of which about 5,700 were active and operational.[37] Besides the continuing presence of nuclear weapons, exposure to radiation has been an ongoing concern. Studies of Gulf War veterans suggested that illnesses may have been caused by exposure to depleted uranium used for penetrating tanks because of its exceptional hardness. Waste from nuclear plants and deactivated nuclear weapons has accumulated for lack of appropriate storage and disposal sites. After 9/11, people living in the vicinity of nuclear reactors worried that terrorist attacks would unleash radiation from those plants. Not surprisingly, a 2006 survey showed that 81 percent of the public would object to having "a nuclear power plant reactor constructed next to or otherwise close to" their home.[38]

The nature of these continuing threats is quite different from the peril facing the world during the Cold War. It is unlikely that, intentionally or accidentally, there would be unleashed a barrage of missiles of such magnitude that the entire ecosphere would be destroyed. American schoolchildren are not instructed that a nuclear attack could come at any moment. Scenarios of what would happen if nuclear war erupted anywhere in the world nevertheless depict serious global consequences. Chief among these are the economic costs from physical destruction, panic, and long-term dislocation and reconstruction. A nuclear conflict between India and Pakistan, for instance, is predicted to affect not only the billion or so people directly involved, but also to send the global economy into a serious nosedive and strain the resources of governments around the world. In these scenarios, radioactive fallout is assumed to be a significant danger to much of the world's population.

Public concern about nuclear peril has understandably been lower in recent years than during the Cold War. People nevertheless acknowledge that they worry about the possibility of nuclear warfare. "It scares me that Iran or some country of that type might get two or three of these nuclear weapons and turn them loose," says a resident in Maryland. "I think it will cause another major war. It could be a catastrophe that could wipe out much of the world." A man in Arkansas says more countries with nuclear weapons is a threat to the entire world. "You get a guy who believes he has the power to release havoc upon his perceived enemy [and] he may do just that." With any use of nuclear weapons, a woman in Indiana says, "we'd end up with a world war that would destroy everything. I just think that would be the beginning of the end." A woman in Ohio echoes this view: "I think if some country actually used nuclear weapons, the ones being attacked would send something back, so you have two countries blown off the map. That would be the beginning of the end of the world as we know it."[39]

In these comments, the logic of the Cold War remains very much in evidence. People believe that a nuclear attack by one country would result in a devastating response by another country. Although the countries potentially involved are no longer limited to Russia and the United States, the principle is the same. Once it began, a nuclear war would escalate out of control. Among the consequences, death and illness from radioactive fallout continue to be salient concerns, as does destruction of the environment. Perhaps even more worrisome is the likelihood of economic and political chaos. Being somewhat removed from possibilities of a direct attack, Americans imagine their lives being disrupted by worsening social turmoil until humanity literally destroys itself. People would stop spending and thus force businesses to close. Others would stockpile necessities and shoot their neighbors if it meant protecting their own families. Political factions would rise and regimes would fall. As one woman explained, "The whole world is gonna be in an uproar. I think it would just turn into sheer chaos."

Concerns about nuclear weapons are clearly evident in national surveys. Ninety-four percent of the public surveyed in 2005 regarded "the global spread of nuclear weapons" as an important threat to the United States in the next ten years," and 67 percent thought they would be "personally affected" by the global spread of nuclear weapons.[40] Fifty-two percent thought it likely that "one country will attack another country with nuclear weapons in the next five years."[41] Eighty-two percent regarded "North Korea's nuclear weapons program" as a threat to the security of the United States.[42] In 2006, seventy-four percent said they would be concerned about an attack on the United States "if Iran obtains nuclear weapons."[43] Seventy-four percent thought "countries that now do not have nuclear weapons [should] be stopped from developing them."[44] Only 14 percent gave the United States a grade of "A" in "stopping countries or groups from getting nuclear weapons."[45]

The worries people express about nuclear war are not without qualifications, though. People register trust in the continuing effectiveness of deterrence. "I have faith in the U.N.," says a man in California. "I feel it is very unlikely that countries are going to try to nuke America." Yet this man thinks it possible that India and Pakistan could start a third world war. That, he says, would be a "terrifying prospect." A man who feels it would be better if nuclear weapons had never been developed thinks they are nevertheless necessary because "you can't sit by and be defenseless." Another qualification concerns the timing of the danger posed by nuclear weapons. To some, the geopolitical situation is so unstable that nuclear warfare could happen at any moment, while for others the danger is less imminent. "I don't worry for myself," says an older man, "but I do for my children and grandchildren." A woman who grew up with civil defense drills and people talking about fallout shelters during the Cold War says she does not think as much now about a nuclear attack. "We were so afraid of the Russians and you never knew if this might be the day" for an attack. "I don't feel like that threat hangs over us like it did for a number of years. Plus, there's a lot more people saying, hey, let's stop this."

As they imagine worst-case scenarios, people hedge their remarks by emphasizing as their counterparts did in the past that these are issues about which they have too little knowledge. It is possible, they say, that a war with catastrophic consequences could happen, but it is also imaginable that the effects could be local or not as severe as the media suggest. They are willing to let experts be the authorities in such matters. As one man said when asked what he thought the economic consequences of a nuclear war might be, "I don't know. I am no economist." Believing that expert knowledge is required continues to persuade people that the average individual is powerless to do much about nuclear weapons. Nuclear war is "definitely a possibility," one woman mused, but "I feel like it is something beyond my control. I don't know what I could do as an individual that would make much difference."

Citizens' groups nevertheless continued to express hope that ordinary people could be effective in reducing the risks of nuclear weapons and energy. For instance, a group calling itself the Citizens Awareness Network petitioned officials in December 2001 to convert the Indian Point nuclear power plant in New York state to natural gas. Although the effort failed, eleven municipalities and one school board adopted resolutions calling for the plant's closing.[46] In 2005, some 40,000 activists participated in a march at the United Nations urging diplomats to endorse a nuclear nonproliferation treaty.[47] As in previous decades, instances could also be found of individuals taking the initiative to protect themselves and their families. In communities near the Indian Point power plant, for example, families were reported purchasing potassium iodide, a substance thought to have been effective in blocking thyroid cancer among people exposed to radiation at the Chernobyl nuclear plant explosion in 1986. Catering to the demand, the Nuclear Regulatory Commission budgeted $800,000 to distribute the drug free in thirty-one states with nuclear plants.[48]

Although the mass rallies of the 1980s became less frequent after the Cold War ended, mobilization in response to concerns about nuclear power plants and weapons continued. The larger national organizations that survived until 1992 remained active more than a decade and a half later. The Federation of American Scientists, with annual revenue of more than $3 million and assets of almost $7.5 million, continued to enlist the expertise of scientists in advocating for control of the development and testing of nuclear weapons. On an even larger scale, the Union of Concerned Scientists took in more than $10 million annually in its efforts to focus public attention on nuclear power plant safety and reductions in nuclear weapons. Smaller organizations emphasizing similar issues included the

Nuclear Policy Research Institute, with yearly revenue of approximately $600,000; Peace Action, whose annual budget exceeded $1 million; and the Wisconsin Project on Nuclear Arms Control, with annual revenue of approximately $750,000. Smaller organizations, such as Albuquerque's Peace and Justice Education Project, Seattle's Alliance for Nuclear Accountability, San Francisco's Bay Area Nuclear Waste Coalition, Denver's Colorado Coalition, and Santa Fe's Concerned Citizens for Nuclear Safety, also remained active.[49]

Many of the antinuclear groups broadened their base by including environmental concerns, campaign finance reform, corporate responsibility, and numerous other issues among their agendas. Ohio Citizen Action, for instance, monitored Nuclear Regulatory Commission activities through petition drives and participation at NRC meetings. Founded in 1975, the organization had an annual budget in 2004 of nearly $2 million and approximately 100,000 members, making it the state's largest nonprofit consumer and environmental advocacy group. More than its numbers, the organization's technical expertise enabled it to challenge the NRC on such detailed questions as whether a reactor should be placed in a "multiple/repetitive degraded cornerstone" category or had experienced an interruption in a "control rod drive source device."[50] Other advocacy groups with broad-based constituencies and agendas included the Union of Concerned Scientists, with interests in global warming, renewable energy, and sustainable agriculture, as well as nuclear safety; Pax Christi, with programs on nuclear disarmament, nonviolence, interracial justice, and human rights; and Public Citizen, with interests in nuclear waste, automobile safety, and economic justice. From 1987 through 2006, these and more than two hundred other regional, state, and local advocacy groups waged an ultimately unsuccessful campaign to halt the deposit of nuclear waste at Yucca Mountain in Nevada.[51]

DEATH, DESTRUCTION, AND ANNIHILATION are recurring themes of the nuclear era. Fear has been a significant part of the response, but is by no means the dominant one or the key to interpreting others. Had fear been the prevailing reaction, it would have been particularly evident during the Cuban missile crisis, when the overwhelming majority of the public was aware of the danger and when leaders themselves warned of impending doom. Far more research was being conducted on the public's mood by that time and more sophisticated measures of anxiety and depression were being used than was true earlier in the nuclear era. The research demonstrated convincingly that the Cuban missile crisis "was on most people's minds," as one review of the evidence says, but that the public "was not overwhelmed by worries" about death and survival. "Nor were there notable declines in psychological well-being." The various measures of psychological reactions produced mixed and muted results. "Positive affect was down, general happiness was up, and negative affect changed little. Likewise, measures of stress and anxiety showed little alteration and clearly presented no evidence that people were traumatized or debilitated by worries over the crisis."[52] Two decades later, following Three Mile Island and the inauguration of Reagan, when public concern about the arms race and about accidents at nuclear reactors was at an unprecedented level, researchers came to the same conclusion. People were aware of the dangers, but were by no means obsessed with them. Observers considered this lack of attention disturbing, but found little evidence that it stemmed from suppressed fear.[53]

These conclusions cast doubt on some of the most popular interpretations of how nuclear peril affected American life during the Cold War. One interpretation is that Americans were so driven by fear that they devoted themselves to their families, where they felt more secure than when they thought about the insecure world in which they lived. This argument is at best shaky, for if Americans were so afraid, they would just as likely have refused to bring children into the world as have lots of them. It has no empirical basis in surveys or psychological studies and it is incongruent with the fact that so few people actually built fallout shelters to protect their families. The simplest explanation for Americans' emphasis on family life is that large numbers of families had small children, and the reason for that was marriage and childrearing having been postponed until the end of World War II. Another popular view is that the 1950s witnessed a religious revival because people were afraid of dying in a nuclear blast. An uptick in religious participation, though, can be explained in the same way as the emphasis on home and family. More people raising children meant more of them going with their children to church and synagogue. Yet another interpretation of how the nuclear threat affected postwar life is that Americans engaged in wild, unpredictable behavior because their suppressed fears drove them to be irrational. Certainly the nuclear era evoked erratic responses, but if this "wild behavior" interpretation were correct, it is odd that the 1950s was also considered a time of exceptional conformity. A related view is that fear led to widespread panics and hysteria (such as the bank panics of the early 1930s and the hysteria prompted by the 1938 broadcast of Orson Welles's radio play "War of the Worlds" about a Martian invasion). However, there were remarkably few instances of such behavior during the 1950s and 1960s. Given the number of false alarms, close calls, and near accidents, it is indeed surprising that mass hysteria was so rare.[54]

Culture is always more than the sum of individuals' emotions and attitudes. It is produced by journalists, actors, academics, teachers, public officials, scientists, administrators, clergy, and other writers and speakers through news stories, films, books, reports, lessons, and sermons, and less formally through discussions among neighbors, phone calls, and conversations in living rooms. The scripts people read, hear, and invent provide cues about how much or little is appropriate to say, what to think, and whether something is worth attending to or is better left for others to worry about. The mental processing involved focuses a considerable share of the public's attention at least periodically on the threat of nuclear weapons, but has also encouraged optimism about the wonders of atomic power and concentrated considerable effort on practical measures, such as disarmament, arms control, and nuclear power plant safety. Leaders and the media routinely conferred the authority to make major decisions about the uses of these discoveries to scientists and officials, suggested a few concrete activities for ordinary citizens to become involved in if they chose, and largely encouraged people to get on with the daily chores of life. From this broader vantage point, writers who concluded that the public response to the existence of nuclear weapons was fearful are simply wrong. There is too little evidence to support the claim that Americans had succumbed to psychic numbing or that most people were, as one recent book concludes, "silently paralyzed by fear or cloaked in denial."[55] Conclusions of that nature locate the American public too squarely on the psychiatrist's couch.

It is understandable that psychological interpretations of the public's response to nuclear peril would have been emphasized at the start of the nuclear era. Psychology had blossomed as an academic discipline in the 1930s and become common fare in college curriculums by the start of World War II. It was part of the training teachers received and increasingly was included in seminaries, business schools, and even in a growing number of high schools. Popular books depicted psychology as the key to success in sales careers and in marriage and parenting. Over the same period, psychiatry grew rapidly in medical schools, especially through large infusions of funding from the Rockefeller Foundation. During World War II, psychology and psychiatry contributed sufficiently to the war effort that the federal government established the National Institute of Mental Health (NIMH) in 1949 to continue research and training in these fields. Arguments for expanding the mental health movement frequently associated its benefits with the Cold War. Good mental health was part of a strong national defense, while poor mental health weakened it. The schools became an ideal venue for promoting mental health. In 1951 the National Parent Teachers Association (PTA) launched a "positive mental health program" to help teachers and parents face the anxieties of the atomic era. The campaign warned that anxious children would become neurotic adults. If an attack occurred, teachers and parents were to "maintain calmness and transmit a feeling of assuredness." They were to practice these attitudes during civil defense drills.[56] By the 1960s, the mental health movement had expanded to the point that insurance companies were beginning to provide coverage for psychological counseling and the military was experimenting with sensitivity training groups.[57]

Although its practitioners included Rogerian, Jungian, humanistic, and other schools of thought, the mental health movement emphasized assumptions originating in Freudian theory throughout the Cold War. Denial and repression of fear as psychological defense mechanisms received frequent attention. Anna Freud's research among children exposed to trauma during World War II had popularized these ideas. In her formulation, denial was troublesome because it sometimes resulted in asocial behavior among children themselves and in other instances led to neuroses that lasted into adulthood.[58] Psychiatrist Robert Jay Lifton attached similar importance to denial in his research among survivors of the bombing of Hiroshima. By the late 1960s, when Lifton was completing his research, denial had come to mean more than simply a defense mechanism with psychological consequences. It had taken on political overtones through assertions that denial was the reason for the public's lack of opposition to nuclear weapons. Lifton, for instance, asserting that "we are all survivors of Hiroshima and, in our imaginations, of future nuclear holocaust," argued that "psychic numbing" or a "cessation of feeling" was the natural response to the resulting anxiety and called for the public to move past this numbing in order to avoid "massive extermination."[59]

What appears to have been a purely psychological reaction to fear—denial—is better understood as part of the culturally constructed response to nuclear peril. This response included arguments about the ways in which individuals could exercise moral responsibility. Being calm in the face of anxiety and helping children avoid becoming neurotics was something the public could do. It was a way of taking responsibility in small and relatively easy steps amid the threat of a nuclear holocaust. If the public seemed calm, it was not only because they may have been avoiding fear, but also because they were instructed to be calm. Again and again, officials counseled the public that "civil defense begins with you."[60] Since nothing much could be done by the average citizen to prevent a nuclear attack, the appropriate response was to take things in stride and thus reduce the likelihood of panic and hysteria. Later, as the nuclear freeze movement emerged, the discussion of denial took on a broader meaning. Whether individuals were somehow repressing their fears could seldom be determined, but accusations of denial became an argument for greater public involvement in the antinuclear effort.

Once culture is understood in terms other than individual psychology, the importance of distinguishing among the various players involved in producing it comes more clearly into view. The reason why people respond to nuclear peril as they do is that they are not just isolated individuals, but members of the social order. Society assigns people different roles in responding to perceived threats and catastrophes, just as the economy does through occupational specialization. The most important players in defining the response to nuclear capabilities were elite decision makers. Individual citizens who either trusted these decision makers or felt there was little the average person could do were hardly acting irrationally, and they were not "doing nothing" because their fears had immobilized them. From the start, atomic energy was associated with the most brilliant minds of the twentieth century. Only the experts, the public learned, could fully assess the dangers and opportunities involved. When it appeared that those in charge might not be able to protect the public, such as during the Cuban missile crisis, officials called on individuals to look out for themselves. As the nuclear industry grew, scientific expertise became embedded in an ever-widening governing apparatus. The Atomic Energy Commission evolved into the Nuclear Regulatory Commission (NRC) and the Energy Research and Development Administration (ERDA) in 1975, with the latter becoming the Department of Energy in 1977. Besides oversight of nuclear weapons, these agencies supervised the growing nuclear power industry. The public entrusted its safety to these agencies, thereby limiting the need for individuals to exercise moral responsibility on their own behalf. The agencies, in turn, became a major source in the cultural response to nuclear energy. Besides the vast volume of scientific and technical reports produced by scientists, engineers, and military planners, this response included thousands of detailed transcripts and assessments. For instance, the NRC alone produced between 200 and 300 documents every day.

The highly institutionalized response to nuclear peril minimized what ordinary people could reasonably expect to do but also shaped the grassroots response that did occur. Although public involvement waxed and waned, there was a noticeable increase over the years in the technical sophistication of advocacy groups. With the exception of the Federation of American Scientists, the earliest organizations were composed largely of writers, clergy, philosophers, and other members of the lay public, whereas the later ones drew more heavily on the expertise of professional activists, full-time organizers, bureaucrats, and scientists. Students, homemakers, and others swelled the ranks during mass protests, but the professionals who campaigned against nuclear weapons and power plants were highly educated activists who relied increasingly on legal, scientific, and technical arguments.[61] It was necessary to do so, not to sway public opinion, but because such arguments were the lingua franca of the agencies through which decisions were made. As the level of required expertise increased, the problems to which various groups directed their attention also became more specialized. In the weeks and months after Hiroshima, activists looked to the United Nations or wrote about nuclear peril as if it were a single topic. By the 1980s, even though the very survival of humanity remained at issue, most discussions dealt with arms treaties, the merits of particular weapons, a freeze that would keep the nuclear arsenal from growing (but not eliminate it), and questions about the safety of proposed and existing nuclear reactors.

With so much of the nuclear debate decided by policy makers and advocacy groups, the residual sphere of moral responsibility assigned to the average person was quite small and for the most part scripted by officials and other leaders. The response to concerns about radioactive fallout in the late 1950s and early 1960s, for instance, was by no means random, but was encouraged by policy makers who believed individuals could protect themselves in the ways experts envisioned. It made sense to participate in civil defense drills when officials said it was necessary, but not to be overly concerned about matters beyond one's control. Later, movement organizers told followers it was now effective to sign petitions to regulate power plants and reduce nuclear weapons. During much of the nuclear era, experts told the public there was little else to be done. One woman expressed the idea well when she remarked that nuclear war would "certainly be a horrible thing to contemplate" because it would "obliterate a lot of humanity and the environment," yet she seldom worries about this possibility because her "energies are better spent on things I can do something about." To say merely that this woman is in denial does not capture her way of thinking. Her point is rather that a person has control over what one chooses to worry about. Worrying is energy well spent if it is connected with the possibility of action. If there is a chance of eliminating nuclear weapons, then action directed toward that end is worthwhile. If nuclear weapons are being dealt with as best they can by decision makers in high office and by scientists, then the better use of one's time is on more practical things.

Focusing on the routine problems of daily life shielded the public from having to accept the more ambitious challenges they may have been expected to undertake—and avoided the disruption that may have occurred. When Seattle newspapers warned citizens in April 1954 that nuclear fallout was pitting automobile windshields, the public largely believed the reports (which proved false after a few days) but responded by keeping their automobiles garaged at night.[62] When the American Institute of Decorators encouraged consumers a few years later to construct the "Family Room of Tomorrow" (equipped with sleeping equipment, a forty-gallon water tank, two weeks' worth of food, and an exercise machine to circulate air during a nuclear attack), people quietly ignored the suggestion.[63] While a few people were moved by reading *The Fate of the Earth* to quit their jobs to become full-time antinuclear activists, most Americans responded, if at all, by showing up at a meeting or rally.

Doing something, either to reduce the risk of nuclear annihilation or simply to keep life on an even keel in the midst of peril, is a way to focus mental attention on practical problems, as opposed to responding emotionally or empathically. Some of what the public did in response to the dangers of nuclear annihilation involved behavior that was scripted for the particular problem at hand, such as learning to duck and cover. Other activities carried on the daily tasks of life, which had to be done no matter how perilous the circumstances may have been. In either case, the response to danger so extreme that life itself could have been terminated was to find some act to be taken, some problem however large or small to be tackled, and thus to believe that life was both manageable and worthwhile. One man, likening basement fallout shelters and other precautions against nuclear war to the activities that take place among the dying in hospices, put it this way: "[They are] a way to keep going with pride and dignity even when hope cannot rationally be measured."[64]

FOUR

WAGING WAR ON TERROR

THE THREAT OF PERIL DRIVEN HOME TO AMERICANS by the September 11, 2001, attacks on New York and Washington was quite different from the dangers the world faced during the Cold War. The response to weapons of mass destruction, as they became known, and to terrorism was nevertheless shaped by those earlier dangers. Moral responsibility in 2001 reflected how it had come to be understood during the preceding half century. Government officials, scientists, and policy makers continued to be the professional experts who set the agenda for how the public would think about and respond to the attacks. People feared for their safety, thought it likely that terrorists would strike again, and registered doubt that they could do much to protect themselves. The initial sense of loss led quickly to calls for retaliation, as if a stricken nation needed to demonstrate its strength. Interpretations of 9/11 came at first from all quarters—artists, journalists, academics, clergy, writers—who focused on the broader implications of living in a fragile world. But within days public officials turned the response from questions about why the attacks had occurred to plans for retaliation. The Cold War was thus replaced by a new war, a controversial war that dominated public debate and again divided the world into defenders of freedom and purveyors of evil. Whereas nuclear weapons had connoted strength as well as danger, the possibility of bombs on planes, anthrax, sarin nerve gas, and buildings destroyed with loads of fertilizer left the public feeling weak, anxious, and vulnerable. Nuclear arms were generally described by public leaders as defensive weapons, but the idea of a preemptive war to decimate extremists before they could act required a new framework of understanding. Weapons of mass destruction symbolized a continuing peril that people would have to live with for a long time. The sporadic and largely ineffective civil defense measures advocated during the Cold War gave the public scant hope that they could do anything on their own behalf, either to defend their families or to ameliorate the grievances motivating terrorist attacks. It was unnecessary to deny fear because waging a "war on terror" became the accepted way of expressing it.

THE NEWS THAT PLANES HAD SMASHED into the World Trade Center and Pentagon was as startling to the world as the bombing of Hiroshima was in 1945. The quiet of a breezy, sun-filled Tuesday morning was abruptly shattered when American Airlines Flight 11 flew into the north tower at 8:46 A.M. Word spread immediately that something unprecedented was taking place. Millions watched as a second plane struck the south tower, and one by one the twin towers collapsed. In stark contrast to 1945, the target was not an enemy on the far side of the world but ordinary Americans. Horror bordered on panic as people tried in vain to telephone relatives and friends in the affected cities. Journalists picked up rumors of additional planes being seized. The crash of United Flight 93 in a Pennsylvania field confirmed that the devastation could have been much worse.[1]

Over the next few days, personal engagement with the tragedy spread from coast to coast. People heard that a neighbor's son or daughter had been on one of the planes or working at the Pentagon. Newspapers and television stations found links between their own locales and the events in New York and Washington. Reports featured a local resident killed in the attacks or a relative who narrowly escaped. Other stories suggested that danger was closer than people had realized or that threats of this kind would likely continue. In Boston authorities questioned cab companies about a driver suspected of ties with Osama bin Laden (a name most Americans had never heard before). Residents in New Jersey and Florida learned that the attackers had been their neighbors. Lawmakers in Buffalo created a task force to prepare for a bioterrorist attack. Citizens in Chattanooga, Tennessee, speculated about an attack on the nearby Sequoyah Nuclear Plant. Justice Department officials cautioned that supporters of the 9/11 attackers might still be at large. In less than a week, investigators received more than fifty thousand tips from vigilant citizens. Editors printed letters calling for quick and effective retaliation. "An eye for an eye," wrote one citizen. "If Muslims around the world do not want to be bombed out of existence, they had better step up to the plate."[2] "They should take all of the Muslims that live in New York and send them back to where they came from," a teacher heard someone in the line behind her at McDonald's say. A second person replied, "That's too good for them. We should just execute them all."[3] Not surprisingly, violence flared. In Bangor, Maine, a customer at a Pakistani restaurant threatened to kill the owners unless they went back to their country. In Queens, New York, a South Asian man was assaulted with a baseball bat. In Mesa, Arizona, a gunman shot and killed a Sikh service station owner. The FBI opened forty investigations involving attacks on Muslims and mosques. Watchdog groups said there were probably ten times that many.[4]

Just as the dawn of the atomic era had done a half century earlier, the 9/11 attacks obliged every cultural producer to weigh in with information and interpretations. Newscasters filled the first hours with commentary about what they knew and what they knew they did not yet know. As the weeks unfolded, the nation's major newspapers carried stories not only in the front section but also in business, local, sports, entertainment, and food sections as well. In the twelve months after 9/11, the *New York Times* alone published more than 14,000 articles mentioning the attacks. Within the first *week*, it published more than 500. Interest ran high in newspapers around the nation. The *Seattle Post-Intelligencer* published 300 articles mentioning these topics during the first week, the *Denver Post* and *San Francisco Chronicle* each published more than 400, the *Pittsburgh Post-Gazette* published nearly 500, the *Boston Globe* published approximately 600, and the *Atlanta Journal-Constitution* printed more than 700.[5] Every major newsmagazine published cover stories about the attacks and most did so again the following week.[6] Between September 11 and September 15, the four major television networks devoted a total of 262 hours of special programming to the events.[7] Nationally, 83 percent of the public said they had watched at least four hours of the coverage, and 74 percent said they had been following the news about the terrorist attacks that first week "very closely."[8] Google searches for news-related content that week shot up sixtyfold.[9]

Almost immediately, the gifted and articulate offered words of consolation and hope at prayer vigils and memorial services and through editorials and essays. Evangelist Billy Graham exhorted mourners at the National Cathedral in Washington to become stronger through trusting in God. Tom Hanks hosted a telethon in New York that included performances by Bruce Springsteen, Mariah Carey, Bono, Robert De Niro, Kelsey Grammer, and numerous other musicians and actors. The producers of *Sesame Street* put together a web site about helping children cope with the crisis. Nearly every well-known writer—Toni Morrison, John Updike, Galway Kinnell, Robert Pinsky, Wendell Berry, Joyce Carol Oates, Susan Sontag, Erica Jong, Richard Bernstein, William Safire—wrote something. In the following months, academic papers, journal articles, and edited volumes poured forth. By the fifth anniversary, more than two hundred books bearing "September 11" in their titles or subtitles had been published, and many more dealt with such related topics as terrorism, al Qaeda, and radical Islam. The commentaries ranged from straightforward accounts of the day's events and firsthand memoirs to analyses of why the attacks were successful or how they had changed America, and from novels and collections of poetry to discussions of the tragedy's implications for business, religion, journalism, civil liberties, law, education, ethics, and international relations.

Although the bombing of Hiroshima and Nagasaki had prompted a great flood of commentary and interpretation, the attacks on New York and Washington differed in that they were broadcast live and were witnessed firsthand by so many Americans. The news in 1945 had been carefully scripted by the War Department. Hardly anyone had seen the test explosion in Nevada. Black-and-white photos in *Life* provided the public with only a glimpse of the physical devastation in Japan. After a year, John Hersey's book *Hiroshima*—which first appeared in *The New Yorker* on the first anniversary (there was no other content in that issue)—remained one of the few accounts written from the perspective of the survivors. Robert Jay Lifton's extensive research among survivors was not published until 1968. In contrast, the 9/11 attacks occurred at the centers of the nation's news industry. Network and cable television crews were on the scene within minutes. In New York, professional photographers ran down the street to take pictures. Hundreds of essayists, poets, playwrights, scriptwriters, journalists, and academics viewed the World Trade Center collapse from their own windows, balconies, and rooftops. If the aim of terrorism is to gain attention, observers remarked, better targets could not have been chosen.

Television played such an important role in framing perceptions of the attacks that nearly everyone who wrote about their experiences commented on this role. Eyewitnesses likened what they saw to images of violence on television or in movies—and then struggled for words with which to express the differences. "I see imagery that until now did not exist in reality, only in the fiction of film," writer A. M. Homes observed. "Seeing it with your own eye, in real time, not on a screen, not protected by the frame of the television set, not set up and narrated by an anchor man, not in the communal darkness of a movie theater, seeing it like this is irreconcilable, like a hallucination, a psychotic break."[10] Another eyewitness in New York e-mailed her friends, "It looked like a movie. It was a cheesy Hollywood blockbuster movie. But the screen was really fucking big, and about the best resolution I've seen."[11] Fittingly, some who took live photographs also shot pictures through windows or captured images on their television screens because they realized that these would be how most of America would remember the event.[12] Other eyewitnesses described how they turned on their televisions even while they watched the towers burn and fall firsthand. The newscasters' running commentary informed them of what was happening, but also shaped how they experienced what was happening. "By late in the day I have the sense that my own imagery, my memory, is all too quickly being replaced by the fresh footage, the other angle, the unrelenting loop," Homes added. She felt herself surrendering to the "collective narrative" the newscasters were imposing.[13] People living farther away necessarily relied on television. They watched the same clips being shown again and again. It was as if their mental hardwiring needed the repetition to get used to the enormity of what had happened. "This has become our modern therapy in catastrophes," essayist Phillip Lopate suggested, "the hope that by immersing ourselves in the media, by the numbing effect of repetition we will work through our grief."[14]

Inevitably, the networks began framing the story for viewers beyond New York and Washington. At first, eyewitnesses who were only a few blocks away told themselves that the World Trade Center or Pentagon had been attacked. Over the next several days, as they learned of casualties, witnessed the changed skyline, and breathed the lingering smoke, New Yorkers talked and wrote about their *city* having been attacked. Increasingly, though, the definition of what exactly was under siege widened. CBS News labeled its special coverage "Attack on America." CNN headlined its programming "America Under Attack." "Freedom itself was attacked," President Bush said in a nationally televised statement before the day was over. "We will do whatever is necessary to protect America and Americans," he promised.[15]

It was a new era, the commentators concluded, just as they had after Hiroshima. Americans were living in "a different world," columnist Anthony Lewis wrote on September 12.[16] "I don't think our lifestyles will be the same for a long time," said Arizona senator John McCain. New York senator Charles E. Schumer said it was as if America had wakened in a "new world."[17] Florida congressman Cliff Stearns told his colleagues in the House, "Life in America as we know it will change."[18] The *Economist*'s editors titled their September 15 cover story "The Day the World Changed."[19] The response to the event would shape American civilization for the "next 100 years," historian Kevin Starr predicted.[20] Comparing the terrorist attacks to Pearl Harbor, historian David M. Kennedy wrote that the "new threat of catastrophic terrorism," so spectacularly real on September 11, was "more insidiously consequential" because the "very character of our society is at risk."[21] In an address from Atlanta on November 8, 2001, President Bush told the nation that the world "seems very different" than it was on September 10 and that "we are a different country," engaged in a "different war from any our nation has ever faced." "We've added a new era," he said, "and this new era requires new responsibilities."[22] "The world would never quite be the same," CNN declared on the first anniversary of the attacks.[23] Holt, Rinehart and Winston offered every public high school a free video titled "September 11, 2001: A Turning Point in History." Foreign commentators largely agreed that the world was entering a new epoch. September 11 might one day be viewed as only the beginning of a new terror composed of powerful, invisible, and uncontrollable microbes and bacteria, mused the French writer Jacques Derrida.[24] German sociologist Jürgen Habermas called it a "caesura in world history," a turning point in geopolitics like the French Revolution and the outbreak of World War I had been for Europe.[25]

The sense that everything had changed proved to be wrong of course. Clergy facing packed houses of worship on September 16 found audiences gone back to their usual numbers by a week or two later. Volunteering and such civic-minded activities as working on community projects or attending political meetings rose temporarily but soon diminished.[26] Movie and television critics saw little evidence that tastes in popular entertainment had changed.[27] A rupture in time had nevertheless occurred, providing an opportunity for Americans to return again and again in brief moments to questions about what it had all meant and how, if at all, they should think or behave differently. Studies showed that people remembered exactly where they were and what they were doing when they heard the news, just as an earlier generation had recalled about President Kennedy's assassination. In a poll five years later, 98 percent of the public still claimed to recall exactly where they were when they heard the news about the 9/11 attacks.[28] In focus groups, even those who lived a considerable distance from New York and Washington felt as if their own lives had been altered—that their thoughts and feelings *should* take account of this momentous occasion and in some way learn from it. Some imagined what it was like to have been in the towers; others, how it would have felt to lose a loved one. People not only felt upset, but heard others on television say they were traumatized and talked with friends and family about each new revelation. In so doing, the drama came at once to be personal—embedded in individual narratives about how one felt—and a collective story about what the nation had experienced and how it would respond.[29] "It was an invasion—the violation of sovereign American soil, the erasure of a visible monument to American success and energy and civilization," essayist Andrew Sullivan wrote in *Time*. "The whole dream of this continent—that it was a place where you could safely leave the old world and its resentments behind—was ended that day. A whole generation will grow up with this as its most formative experience."[30]

As though trying to imagine the explosive power of an atomic bomb, commentators searched for comparisons to establish the scale of 9/11. For those who believed the world *had* changed, the historical parallel that came to mind was not Hiroshima but Pearl Harbor. Recalling that history "changed forever" on December 7, 1941, Vice Admiral Conrad C. Lautenbacher Jr. said the 9/11 attacks would now be the "solemn day of infamy" embedded in memory for horror "unequaled in our nation's history."[31] Retired war correspondent James M. Cannon remarked, "There has been nothing like this since Pearl Harbor."[32] "A Day of Infamy" in large bold letters covered the front page of the *Tulsa World*. It was the twenty-first century's "day of infamy," CNN.com headlined. "New day of infamy," declared the *Boston Globe*. Two days after the attacks the Congressional Research Service provided legislators a summary of the "federal budget response to the 1941 attack on Pearl Harbor."[33] The loss of life and the surprise of the attacks on Pearl Harbor and 9/11 bore obvious similarities. Interpreters quickly speculated about other parallels: poor intelligence, missed warnings, lack of military preparedness. Others saw differences, yet agreed that Pearl Harbor was the obvious comparison. The new enemy was harder to identify or to respond to militarily than the one that brought the nation into World War II.[34] "It's really worse than Pearl Harbor," declared historian David McCullough, "because it was an attack on innocent civilians, not a military target." Another difference, observed presidential historian Wayne Fields, was that Franklin Delano Roosevelt was a seasoned leader with nearly nine years in the Oval Office at the time of the attack on Pearl Harbor, whereas on 9/11 George W. Bush had held office only eight months.[35]

Hardly anyone wrote specifically about the similarities between September 11 and the dangers the nation had faced from nuclear weapons during the Cold War—most of the comparisons focused on Pearl Harbor. Yet the connections with August 1945 were evident. Without quite realizing what he was saying, an eyewitness of the Pentagon attack remarked, "I saw the mushroom cloud."[36] "It was like the onset of a nuclear winter," an eyewitness in New York wrote.[37] A woman in Georgia wrote to an online site that her husband recalled a dream about a nuclear attack when he saw the twin towers crumble.[38] Playwright Wendy Wasserstein wrote that the World Trade Center attack reminded her of "hiding under our desks" during atomic bomb drills in grade school. She was "riddled with fear" as she had been as a child during the Cuban missile crisis.[39] Striking a very different note, Boston Globe columnist James Carroll observed, "The nation had lived for two generations with the subliminal but powerfully felt dread of a coming nuclear war. Unconsciously ashamed of our own action in using the bomb, we were waiting for payback, and on that beautiful morning it seemed to come. The smoke rising up from the twin towers hit us like a mushroom cloud, and we instantly dubbed the ruined site as Ground Zero."[40] "I thought of the firebombing of Dresden, of Hiroshima, and Nagasaki," Erica Jong wrote. "Here too, people had been vaporized and would never be found. Their relatives would wander from hospital to hospital, from morgue to morgue and finally, go home not quite knowing how to grieve."[41]

News of the first atomic bomb had excited interpreters as a boon, a plus, a powerful new source of energy with positive potential at least as promising as its destructive capabilities. Further, it was ending a war, whereas 9/11 inaugurated something dreadful. The dominant imagery was one of loss, a minus, a lack of good information, of insecurity, a paucity of readiness and communication.[42] Hastily composed flyers showed photos of the missing. "You needed to imagine a legion of the missing," poet Robert Polito wrote, "wandering New York, lost, amnesiac, waiting for someone to recognize them from their photo and life story, and send them home."[43] A large section of New York City once brimming with vibrant business activity was now a vacant, smoldering space. Sightseers came that fall to view the void, even as the wreckage was being cleared, and went away shaken by its emptiness. Ground zero, Richard Rodriguez wrote, was so obviously reminiscent of the point at which a nuclear explosion occurs and now designated a "vast, gaping wound in lower Manhattan and in our heart."[44] Themes of lack, loss, and vacancy played out in myriad ways. "Earth wasted bare and rotten," the poet Alicia Ostriker wrote, "and all this while I have been shopping."[45] "It was a week of what was not—of not seeing a familiar skyline, of not knowing how to answer a child's questions, of not being able to sleep, of not understanding why," journalist Dean E. Murphy observed.[46] The burning and falling of the towers prompted the poet Galway Kinnell to recall that the nuclear era had also been a time of vast loss: "atomic blasts wiping cities off the earth, firebombings the same, death marches, starvations, assassinations, disappearances, entire countries turned into rubble, minefields, mass graves."[47] Toni Morrison in a short essay addressed to the dead of September 11 declared the need even to set aside words and to purge language itself. "I have nothing to say," she wrote, "no words stronger than the steel that pressed you into itself; no scripture older or more elegant than the ancient atoms you have become."[48]

A GREAT LOSS, like news of a powerful new weapon, shocks the collective psyche in a way that inevitably generates excitement, along with other emotions. Nearly two decades before 9/11, the novelist Walker Percy had invited readers to imagine talking with a neighbor in Englewood, New Jersey, when "an earthquake levels Manhattan." Of course it would be putatively bad news, Percy argued, but there would also be a sense of excitement at having witnessed such a spectacular event—the same sort of excitement, he wrote, that had dramatically dampened the suicide rate after Pearl Harbor.[49] At 9:20 A.M. on 9/11, an eyewitness to the unfolding tragedy wrote in her diary that she was experiencing a "rush of adrenaline." She felt "mesmerized by the awesome beauty of destruction." Two hours later, having rushed to the grocery store for emergency supplies, she wrote, "I ponder the meaning of this, feeling a bit crazy. An adrenaline high, the thrill of fear."[50] "You won't believe your eyes . . . the Trade Center is burning," a computer specialist e-mailed a friend that morning. "No friggin way!" the friend replied.[51] Others wrote of feeling restless, eager to run out and find someone to talk to, or glued to their television sets, waiting to see if anything more was happening. Walking the streets of Lower Manhattan a few days later, a resident wrote, "The stunned walkers who crowded the avenue were wary and fatigued. Even the bland September weather seemed suspicious. But there was also a kind of shared electricity among the people on the street, an almost festive unease."[52]

Fear was as palpably evident in the days following 9/11 as it had ever been during the Cold War. People feared that loved ones had been killed, that rumors of other bombs and fires were true, and that more attacks were imminent. Muslims feared that they would be victimized on the street or that their mosques would be burned. Many Americans worried that it was no longer safe to fly. In a poll on September 15, 65 percent of the public expressed worry about "traveling by commercial airplane because of the risk of terrorism."[53] More than three-quarters of the public said it was "frightening" to watch the terrorist attacks on television.[54] A national poll in late September found 53 percent of the public "very" or "somewhat" worried that they or their families "might become a victim of a terrorist attack." By mid-October, that figure remained unchanged. In that survey, 69 percent said they were very or somewhat worried that "there will soon be another terrorist attack in the United States."[55] In another poll, nearly half (46 percent) of the parents surveyed said their children had expressed "fears about the terrorist attacks."[56] In yet another study, 34 percent of the public said they "personally worry about terrorism" when they are in public places.[57] Being afraid in those first days after 9/11 seemed utterly reasonable. It seeped into the bloodstream until it poisoned life itself, *NewsHour* essayist Roger Rosenblatt wrote that fall. "Even in those moments when nothing is going wrong, a sweet time with family, a walk in the park, one feels that life is on the verge of a mad explosion."[58] A Unitarian pastor who watched the towers collapse from his window in Brooklyn told his congregation the next Sunday, "I know something I did not before, namely the experience of being assaulted by fear. One of the products of terrorism is to rip away a person's sense of understanding, to pulverize one's most basic assumptions, namely: that I and my home will be here at the end of the day."[59]

Surveys inadequately captured the fact that there were actually two kinds of fear. One was the fear of immediate, specific danger. Concern that other planes would be hijacked forced the grounding of all commercial aircraft. When flights resumed three days later, they ran at 16 percent capacity. People were indeed afraid to fly. It was unclear for weeks just how many workers and firefighters had been killed. A plot so successful suggested that others may have already been set in motion. Anthrax-laced letters, which began appearing a week after the attacks, posed new risks. Beyond the fears aroused by these specific threats, there was also the longer-term, diffuse fear of terror itself. This second fear was very much like the generalized anxiety that had been present during the Cold War. The danger was lethal but hidden and could strike at any moment. Nobody knew the extent of the threat or how powerful it might be. Just as there had been fears of secretive communist cells operating within the United States, now there was concern about sleeper cells of terrorists. "The enemy," Secretary of State Colin Powell warned, "is very often right here within our own country."[60] The terrorists' mindset was so alien that their actions could not be predicted. The enemy was a shadowy threat that functioned through clandestine networks and in many scattered locations throughout the world. This enemy could not be defeated easily or with conventional warfare. It would be around for a long time. The fear evoked by this threat required an adjustment of how one thought about life and safety and happiness, just as the fear of nuclear annihilation had done.[61]

Yet pollsters and commentators focused far more attention on other emotions than they did on fear. In a national poll conducted by NBC News on September 12, thirty-seven percent of the public said "anger" best described their emotions, followed by "sadness" (24 percent) and "disbelief" (21 percent).[62] In another poll,

87 percent of the public said they "felt angry" about the terrorist attacks, and in yet another study 64 percent said anger described their "very deepest feeling" about the event.[63] Besides anger, grief was especially evident. "Our feelings are carried, bleeding and raw on gurneys through the streets of Manhattan," poet Emily Borenstein wrote.[64] In a poll taken on September 14 and 15, seventy percent of the public reported having cried in response to the attacks.[65] A few days later, 49 percent said they were having difficulty concentrating on their usual activities.[66] Thinking about the tragedy, observers suggested, was causing stress and contributing to heightened levels of generalized anxiety. "People are terrified, stressed out, disgusted," one Manhattan resident wrote. "And the anger, anxiety, and sadness is only starting to hit."[67] Reporters used words like broken, bent, impotent, agonized, disoriented, and shaken. Clinicians focused on distressing dreams, hyperarousal, insomnia, lack of concentration, and depression. A national poll conducted ten days after the attacks discovered that 71 percent of the public "felt depressed" because of their concerns about terrorist attacks or the war against terrorism and 33 percent said they had "trouble sleeping" because of these concerns.[68] Psychiatrists suggested that a quarter of those with symptoms in the days after the attacks might suffer long-term effects.[69]

Sorrow, rage, anxiety, and fear were impossible to suppress when there were so many public displays of emotion. Newscasters wept openly and essayists described their feelings in intimate detail. "Never have I seen so many men expressing their anguish in public—fireman, journalist, comedian, mayor, and cop—all wounded into expressing an anguish that cut to the soul," wrote Alison Hawthorne Deming. "Everyone knew the hard truth: It could have been me."[70] Unlike during the Cold War, hardly anyone argued that the public was in denial. Even some months later, when the initial flurry of public venting had quieted, it was uncommon to find experts arguing that Americans were stifling their fears. The very idea of people being in denial seemed to have gone out of vogue. A reporter visited psychiatrists and talked with people on the streets in New York the following summer to hear what they might say about denial. The story took a satirical turn. "Sociologists and psychiatrists have long considered denial to be an essential component of the human survival instinct," the reporter ventured. Yet among those interviewed, the most common response was to poke fun at the idea. "If I'm in denial," an art consultant told him, "how would I know?" A psychologist suggested that denial could just as well be termed "overlooking"—a healthy way to quit obsessing and move on. Another said it was impossible to decide if someone was in denial or "just confused," especially when expert advice was so often contradictory. They agreed that total denial was probably unhealthy, but doubted that many people could be oblivious to terrorism and similar dangers.[71] Another journalist reported similar views. In the few instances in which experts talked about denial, the advice was far different from earlier arguments in which it was viewed as pathological. "There is a certain level of denial that is necessary," one psychiatrist summarized. "You can't function thinking that at any moment you're going to be struck by lightning or receive an anthrax letter."[72]

In clinical research, a new language largely replaced the earlier emphasis on suppressed fear and denial. This was the language of post-traumatic stress disorder (PTSD), or syndrome. Using scales developed in previous studies, government-funded research sought to measure how traumatized the public might be. A study of New York residents a month after the attacks suggested that about 8 percent were suffering from stress-related trauma and nearly 10 percent from severe depression. Among those living closest to the World Trade Center, the prevalence of symptoms was closer to 20 percent.[73] A random-sample survey in spring 2002 concluded that 15 percent of New Yorkers and 8 percent nationally were suffering from trauma-related stress.[74] A third of New Yorkers said they had been extremely bothered or bothered quite a bit since the attacks by disturbing memories. Twenty-eight percent said they had been bothered this much by feeling upset, as had 23 percent by being on guard. At least one New Yorker in ten had been bothered quite a bit by reliving the event, having disturbing dreams, being unable to sleep, finding it difficult to concentrate, and being easily startled. The percentage for each of these symptoms was approximately twice as high in New York as in the national sample.[75]

In popular treatments, the word that came increasingly into prominence was *vulnerable.* A body, structure, or nation that experiences a loss is weakened as long as that loss remains. The collapse of the twin towers, a writer observed, was like a "sudden amputation."[76] A person who has lost a limb or loved one or home feels less capable of responding because he or she is no longer whole. "This is the end: the end of an era, the era of our invulnerability," international relations specialist Ronald Steel wrote in the *New York Times.*[77] America had been violated and the psychological impact of that breach would continue, Steel argued, long after Lower Manhattan was rebuilt and even if further attacks were not imminent. From the start, with only the British invasion in 1812 as an exception, the nation's identity had been shaped by its insulation from foreign intruders. The two world wars had left the homeland unscathed. Continental America was a safe haven, a retreat, a protected zone—by divine intention, some said. It was now evident that the corporeal body could be wounded. The scar would likely be permanent. Vulnerability, in this sense, was profoundly symbolic. It meant that geography was no longer as secure as had long been presumed. It also implied questions about America's defensive strategies and even the ideals to which it was committed. Vulnerability was now "mutual," anthropologist James W. Fernandez contended. As long as poor countries were economically vulnerable, rich countries would be vulnerable both to attacks on their security and doubts about their principles.[78]

Vulnerability was deeply personal as well as national, especially for those living close to the attacks. "From serene confidence, even at times arrogance, New Yorkers became vulnerable and very exposed," Robert Jay Lifton and Charles B. Strozier wrote a few days after the attack. "We were exposed and raw, suddenly weakened, even somewhat helpless."[79] "To be in New York last week," a reporter explained, was to know "the hole in your stomach, the aching at the center of your being." It was a time, he said, to be "afraid of things known and unknown, to miss both loved ones and people you had never met."[80]

A nation that for half a century had felt endangered from nuclear weapons now found itself confronted with a new peril that had hitherto been associated only with embassies and military installations and with bombings in Northern Ireland, Israel, and other places of turmoil. Life in the United States was markedly less certain when it was possible for ordinary men and women, as they had on September 11, to go to work and be killed by suicide bombers. If that could happen, it was also more conceivable that other dangers could be realized. "I am scared of what is still to come because I am sure this is only the beginning," a woman said when asked her response to the tragedy.[81] Within a month, the nation became preoccupied with a mysterious attack of anthrax-tainted letters that killed five people, infected seventeen others, and resulted in hundreds of millions of dollars being spent cleaning contaminated office buildings and postal facilities. Other threats came increasingly under scrutiny as well. In communities across the nation leaders worried if the local water supply was safe. A bottle of botulism could wipe out an entire city. Public health officials warned that terrorists could easily spread smallpox. The breakdown in communications on 9/11 suggested strongly that telephone systems were vulnerable. Electrical grids, nuclear reactors, and chemical plants probably were too. Security checks at airports reminded passengers that weapons could still be smuggled aboard aircraft. Little was being done, it seemed, to guard trains, buses, bridges, and tunnels. For older people, reared on nuclear fears, the new threats seemed continuous with the old. "E. B. White saw it coming," a journalist wrote, recalling the famous writer's 1949 essay "Here Is New York." The city was vulnerable from easily delivered nuclear weapons, White had written. "A single flight of planes no bigger than a wedge of geese can quickly end this island fantasy, burn the towers, crumble the bridges, turn the underground passages into lethal chambers, cremate the millions." White's prediction seemed to have come true.[82] For younger people, 9/11 was like an initiation into a dangerous new reality. "We grew up with nothing bad ever happening to us," a college sophomore told a reporter. "Not the Bay of Pigs, not the cold war, not the threat of nuclear terror."[83] In her mind, 9/11 was a pivotal historical moment. The world would never be as safe or the outlook of her generation as innocent as it had been before the attacks. Seventeen-year-olds worried that they would be drafted and sent off to be slaughtered. They wanted to be heroic and wondered if they would have the courage. They looked forward to enjoying life and worried that they might not have a chance.[84]

The prevailing response to this new peril, like the reaction of people faced with the possibility of nuclear annihilation, was to take action that in some small way persuaded them they were doing something and that life would go on. The reality that attacks had actually happened, as opposed to the more diffuse worries of the nuclear era, provided a focal point for individual and collective activity. "The natural response is to do something," a twenty-year-old told a reporter shortly after the attacks. "I'd like to be lifting something or doing something."[85] In New York and Washington and in neighboring communities people phoned and e-mailed friends to find out whether buses and subways were running and if bridges were open. They asked if the air was safe to breathe and if buildings were being evacuated. Bystanders rushed to donate blood. People draped American flags from backpacks, hats, and windows. A United Way volunteer said its web site was receiving donations at the rate of four or five per minute compared to an average of four or five per week prior to the tragedy.[86] Taking action in these ways was not in any literal sense meant to solve the tragedy of the attacks, for that could not be fixed. It was rather that action, however modest, helped people to feel they were doing what they could and thus was a way of addressing their own needs and feelings. "How could we fix this thing?" a writer asked herself as she sat down to craft an essay. "What lesson, what warning could we write or speak?"[87] Writing, speaking, phoning a friend, or merely fixing dinner was a way of demonstrating that one had not been rendered helpless. "Tomorrow, I'm going to make blueberry pancakes," a blogger wrote at the end of a long essay about his visits to the World Trade Center.[88] "What we want to do as survivors," explained anthropologist Anthony Oliver-Smith, "is to reassert our control."[89] For some, reasserting control involved showing their concern by attending vigils or memorial services on campuses or in their communities. For many, gaining control meant mastering the details of the event by religiously following television coverage. Storytelling was another part of the adaptive process. People regained control of their own story—the story of their self-identity—by telling again and again where they were when they heard the news and how they had responded. Repeating the same narrative to different friends and relatives was a way to cement that new part of one's identity into a familiar relationship.

Storytelling, watching newscasts, donating blood, hugging one's children, attending memorial services, and contributing to charities were ways Americans could respond as *individuals* and thus feel they were doing something in the face of fear and tragedy. Yet the attacks were a wound to the nation and to its national identity, not just to individuals. There was talk from the first moments about how the *nation* should respond. In the initial confusion, it was clear that something should be done but a lack of clarity about what that should be. "America must do what it can to ease the suffering of those who have been injured, comfort the families of those who were killed and quickly repair or clear away the physical damage," the *Washington Post* editorialized at the end of the first day.[90] These ameliorative activities would need to be shouldered by government as well as by private citizens. Besides helping those directly affected, the government's use of armed force was clearly warranted, many argued. The nation was at war, leaders declared, but with whom? And for what purpose? "The enemy is faceless and placeless," Native American writer Diane Glancy remarked. "Who should we attack? The air?"[91] It was harder to know in a world that had become globalized and deterritorialized. "Having prevailed in the great 'hot' and 'cold' wars, the bloody muse of history now gives us the Gray War," columnist David Von Drehle wrote, "a war without fronts, without armies, without rules, in which the weapon can be any commercial jet and the target any building anywhere."[92] A study involving in-depth interviews with more than a hundred residents of Lower Manhattan concluded that "in the first days and weeks after the events there was confusion about the origin and meaning of the attacks, which promoted a deep disquiet over the definition of the enemy."[93]

Being at war, even being engaged in a Cold War, had always involved fighting a clearly defined enemy. The effort to identify America's new enemy began immediately, not only in secret intelligence briefings with the president, but also in the press. By nightfall of September 11 it was widely reported that the most likely suspect was Osama bin Laden, the forty-four-year-old Islamic militant from a wealthy Saudi Arabian family who had been living under protection of the Taliban regime in Afghanistan since 1996.[94] U.S. officials with access to intelligence reports said there was credible evidence pointing to this elusive leader. Manifests from the hijacked flights included at least two names linked with al Qaeda (Arabic for "the base"), an Islamic terrorist organization founded by bin Laden in 1988 originally to expel Soviet forces from Afghanistan. Foreign journalists claimed to have heard bin Laden's followers boasting that an attack on the United States was imminent. If bin Laden the *person* provided an identifiable enemy, the exact nature of this person as *enemy* nevertheless needed to be defined. Journalists described him as a highly talented master impresario with wealth and expertise in business, on the one hand, and as a cowardly thug at the head of a thoroughly premodern network of extremists, on the other hand. His followers were "people who would like to return the world to the 8th or at most the 9th century," wrote Joel Achenback in the *Washington Post*.[95] Among government experts the debate was less about bin Laden's personal characteristics and more about U.S. policy toward terrorism. Clinton administration policy had favored targeting individual terrorists and groups rather than governments. The new thinking, articulated most clearly by Defense Policy Board Advisory Committee chair Richard N. Perle, was "to hold responsible governments that support terrorism."[96] That perspective was evident in the official definition of America's enemy given by President Bush in a speech to a joint session of Congress nine days after the attacks. The enemy was "a collection of loosely affiliated terrorist organizations known as al Qaeda." They were "to terror what the mafia is to crime." Al Qaeda was responsible for murdering Americans in Tanzania and Kenya and for imposing radical beliefs wherever it went. The reference to the mafia suggested that al Qaeda might be a shadowy target, but additional words implied precision. It was headed by one man, Osama bin Laden, operated in sixty countries, and was being sheltered by the Taliban regime in Afghanistan. The true enemy thus was the Taliban in Afghanistan, to whom the president directed specific and nonnegotiable demands. Al Qaeda, the president argued, was the successor to enemies that the United States had fought during World War II and the Cold War. "We have seen their kind before. They are the heirs of all the murderous ideologies of the twentieth century. By sacrificing human life to serve their radical visions—by abandoning every value except the will to power—they follow in the path of fascism, and Nazism, and totalitarianism."[97] The U.S. war on Afghanistan began two and a half weeks later.

THE MOST INTERESTING ASPECT of the cultural debate that took place between September 11 and the October 7, 2001, invasion of Afghanistan was the shifting meaning of retaliation. The initial meaning—best expressed as *revenge*—was closely aligned with anger. It was the primordial urge to strike out when stricken, to hit back when hit, to return blow for blow, to inflict pain on those who had caused pain, to show strength more powerful than one's foe, to do something physical with emotions ready to burst. "We'll smoke the asses of whoever did this," a blogger wrote on 9/11, adding, "I'm not usually like this but I really want revenge."[98] These terrorists, wrote a man in Ohio, "are less than animals and are deserving of nothing more than extermination."[99] "Somebody's got to pay for this," a young man told an army recruiter in Colorado as he rushed to enlist. "I know just what to do with these Arab people," a retired truck driver told a reporter in Wyoming. "We have to find them, kill them, wrap them in a pigskin and bury them. That way they will never go to heaven."[100] Otherwise staid New Yorkers were overheard telling their neighbors that Osama bin Laden's head should be carried through the streets on a pike. "I want to strike back, pulverize, kill, obliterate anyone who has caused this harm to my city," a New York resident from Australia wrote. "I have become like the dangerous American the world has most reason to fear."[101]

The raw passion expressed in these calls for revenge gave them a kind of unbridled legitimacy. They came from the heart, or from somewhere lower, the gut perhaps, driven by a visceral urge that could not be suppressed. They were authentic words that instantly drew assent from the large number of Americans who felt outraged by the attacks. Striking back was simply the obvious way to respond. Kick back and kick hard. The impulse to retaliate was ratified by the frequent use of "we." *We'll* smoke them. *We* have to find them. "We should retaliate with the strongest force," wrote a citizen in Dayton.[102] "We will bring the full power of this great nation against the criminals responsible for this evil," echoed an official in North Dakota.[103] The response was a "communal fury," columnist John Tierney wrote.[104] *We* implied that America, the people, the nation, the amassed force of a great power would mobilize. There was strength in the unity implied in this response. The victims' families were not alone. The whole nation had been attacked. It was united in its determination for revenge.

The rage brimming in the media and in these calls for revenge evoked an immediate counter-discourse urging a more temperate view of retaliation. "Retribution fails to resurrect our dead," counseled writer Dan Giancola. "I have a 15-year-old daughter and a 9-year-old son; I want more for them than a future charged with danger and fear, a future of ash."[105] The phrase "rush to judgment" that had been heard so often during the O. J. Simpson trial in 1995 now attached itself to the discussion of 9/11. "The lesson is not to rush to judgments," George F. Will cautioned," or "to rush to actions" that would "embolden America's enemies."[106] He did not mean that America should turn the other cheek but that whatever revenge was inflicted should be carefully planned. It would need to be effective, he said, not merely a catharsis for riled emotions. An alternative perspective emphasized the importance of not overreacting. "We are all angry and want revenge," a Manhattan resident acknowledged, "but I fear errors of judgment." "We must remain objective," she wrote, "especially at a time as emotionally trying and confusing as this."[107] Seeking vengeance, critics argued, was unwarranted even on practical grounds. "A violent response will not bring back loved ones, bring justice or increase our safety, and may increase the likelihood of more terrorist acts," said an American Friends Service Committee spokesperson.[108] Yet another view held that the United States should respond but do so more creatively than brandishing swords. "As if might and retribution were a sensible response in a world where anyone with a flight simulator and enough hate can change the New York skyline," one woman e-mailed.[109]

If the urge for massive forceful retaliation commanded attention through its passion and by claiming to speak for the American people, the voice of moderation gained credence by insisting that reason should trump emotion. The proponents of caution further distinguished themselves by arguing that they were also Americans and that they spoke for many others besides themselves. They were the *loyal* opposition at this critical moment in history when disloyalty was out of the question but expressions of honest disagreement were sorely needed. They were *not* the majority, or the intemperate masses, or the hotheads in Washington seeking to exploit the tragedy for political gain. They were the thoughtful minority who could keep their emotions under control and understand the need for a reasoned response. "We all need to keep our heads," said one. "We have to do this right," said another.[110] The proper reaction, they said, was not to overrespond but to inflict punishment proportionate to the tragedy. That meant going after specific persons identified with planning the attack—presumably bin Laden. An appropriate reaction was one that did not result in escalation. The Cold War served as a negative example. "Stop this stupidity now," one man e-mailed, "Pearl Harbor. 2 atomic bombs. Need I say more."[111]

Fear was a common theme both among those who sought aggressive revenge and among those who argued for caution. The first group argued that revenge was a way of overcoming fear, not by whistling in the dark, but by standing tall in the face of adversity, spitting in the devil's eye. Striking back at the terrorists would bring them to their knees. Wiping out bin Laden would end the threat, send a defiant message to other would-be attackers, and thus conquer the collective fear. For those who wanted moderation, fear served in two ways. It connoted the kind of emotion that needed to be surpassed with reason. Seeking revenge to conquer one's fears was not an appropriate way to proceed. "Fear may get the better of people's nature," one writer cautioned. If it did, Americans might voluntarily give up their freedom or succumb to political appeals exploiting the nation's sense of vulnerability. Fear figured importantly, too, as a reason not to overreact. People said they were less afraid of another terrorist strike than of their own government escalating the violence and thus creating more danger. "I am scared, my friends," an office worker in Lower Manhattan wrote three days after the attacks. "Scared of the repercussions that will occur because of this disaster. Already, our president has used the word 'war.'" People should draw on their "collective morality," he urged, to make certain that we do not go too far.[112]

It was true that the president had focused on war from the start. "When chief of staff Andrew H. Card Jr. whispered in the president's ear that morning in a Sarasota schoolroom that "America is under attack," Bush later told journalist Bob Woodward, "I made up my mind at that moment that we were going to war." One plane slamming into the World Trade Center might have been interpreted differently, but two planes persuaded the president that "they had declared war on us." That evening he dictated into his diary, "The Pearl Harbor of the 21st century took place today." Pearl Harbor was not only a national tragedy but symbolic of a nation that had been weak, unprepared, caught off guard, and thus badly damaged. The same national weakness that had now been revealed on 9/11, Woodward believed, corresponded with Bush's personal insecurity of being widely viewed as a "lightweight." It was thus essential to appear manly. Whatever America did, it could not be an "impotent" nation, Bush said, not a "flaccid, you know, kind of technologically competent but not very tough" country.[113] Chief counterterrorism advisor Richard A. Clarke remembered Bush and Defense Secretary Donald Rumsfeld that evening discussing whether using force for revenge was consistent with international law. "I don't care what the international lawyers say," Bush exclaimed, "we are going to kick some ass."[114]

The debate about revenge evolved from an expression of outrage into a discussion of how best to compensate for the damage the nation had sustained. It was this shift from instinctive revenge to retaliation as public policy that proved most interesting. Behind the scenes, military planners discussed alternative scenarios for retaliating against Osama bin Laden and al Qaeda. The White House crafted words with which to frame the meaning of 9/11 and to suggest what an appropriate response would be. "This enemy attacked not just our people," Bush told reporters on September 12, "but all freedom-loving people everywhere in the world."[115] Reasonable retaliation is a prescriptive action grounded in a diagnosis of the harm that has been inflicted on the aggrieved party. The definition of what exactly had been harmed was thus central to how retaliation would be discussed. Was it the kind of terrorism, only on a larger scale, that the FBI routinely tracked in order to bring domestic perpetrators to justice? Was it an attack on a specific building as the 1993 and 1995 bombings in New York and Oklahoma City had been described? Was the target specifically the World Trade Center and the Pentagon—something about the financial and military apparatus of global markets, as some said—or was it something larger? Few doubted that America itself had been attacked, but the official rhetoric suggested that something even larger was at stake. "This is the world's fight," the president's speechwriters wrote in a draft of the speech he was to give to Congress and the nation on September 20. It had something to do with freedom and fear. The final version read: "This is not, however, just America's fight. And what is at stake is not just America's freedom. This is the world's fight. This is civilization's fight. This is the fight of all who believe in progress and pluralism, tolerance and freedom."[116]

To say that "freedom itself is under attack" was to use language reminiscent of the Cold War when the free world was deemed to be in a death struggle with totalitarianism. Civilization was again threatened. Damage had been done to other countries on 9/11, not just to America. The entire free world, the civilized world was in danger. The rhetoric signaled the need for an international coalition and in this way served a strategic purpose as leaders sought to enlist allies for the coming war. It also significantly broadened the definition of what damage had been done and what potential harm could be inflicted. The attack was an act of war carried out, not by the enemies of America, but by the enemies of freedom. Like other totalitarian leaders, these enemies were seeking to impose their will on free peoples and were known for their brutal repression. If this grave evil was not stopped, governments would be destabilized, prosperity would end, and cherished principles would be lost.[117]

America was thus engaged once again in a struggle to preserve civilization itself. There was no time to be hamstrung by fear or simply to pursue such private activities as grieving, working, and tending to one's family. A massive response was necessary. The gaping vacancy in Lower Manhattan had to be filled. The hole in America's soul needed to be repaired. The apparent vulnerability, the evident weakness of America revealed on 9/11 needed to be countered by a show of strength. "No one anywhere should doubt our national strength and resolve," Minnesota senator Mark Dayton declared in calling for retaliation.[118] "We must be strong," a reader wrote to the *Washington Post*. "We cannot give one inch. We must . . . exact retribution."[119] The deep threat to freedom had to be balanced by a great mobilization of collective energy. It would not be enough to track down bin Laden or to identify others who may have assisted the attackers. What that larger struggle would be became the subject of intense debate among the president's top advisers. Bin Laden was an attractive target because he was a specific villain who could plausibly be connected with the attacks. His picture alone provided an enemy against which the public could vent its wrath. However, bin Laden also presented problems. If he were captured too easily, the public would not be satisfied, advisers reckoned, especially if other terrorist threats remained. This outcome, Rumsfeld argued, could also reduce the public's willingness to engage in a larger war. Worse, bin Laden might elude capture, leaving the public disgruntled with the administration's response. Attacking the Taliban regime in Afghanistan was a better way to retaliate. Like bin Laden, it could be vilified. It held an entire country in subjection and was especially notorious for abusing the rights of women. It occupied a territory that could be invaded. It was not a shadowy figure that could only be chased. Again, there were worries that it might be difficult to conquer Afghanistan, just as there were that it might be hard to locate bin Laden. Afghanistan was a landlocked country the size of Texas thousands of miles away and it had held the British and the Soviets at bay in the past, and for this reason was known as "the graveyard of empires." Attacking it might destabilize Pakistan or let al Qaeda slip into other countries. In some ways, though, these very concerns made the invasion of Afghanistan more attractive. The point was less to kill terrorists than to show that America was strong. "Do something and do it well," Bush concluded.[120] Even the rhetoric anticipating the invasion had to show strength. This is "the moment for America the Determined," wrote columnist Jim Hoagland, "an America that takes its time" and that "matches its bountiful resources and abilities to the challenge."[121] "We have suffered great loss," Bush told the nation. "And in our grief and anger we have found our mission and our moment." Repeating the theme of loss being replaced by resolve in more personal terms, he added, "I will not forget this wound to our country or those who inflicted it. I will not yield; I will not rest; I will not relent in waging this struggle."[122]

As the United States embarked on a new campaign with stakes as vast as those of the Cold War, the idea of massive retaliation took on a different meaning than it had acquired when the issue was nuclear weapons. Its earlier meaning was *threat* for the sake of deterrence. The United States and the Soviet Union each threatened the other with retaliation so severe that any first use of nuclear weapons, analysts hoped, was out of the question. Massive force on one side was meant to match massive force on the other side. It was a dangerous game, should force ever be used, but the expectation was that it would not be used. Retaliation implied the capacity to even the score, not that one side actually had evened the score. The principle of commensurate strength necessitated being able to demonstrate that each of the players had the weapons to destroy the other but not to have actually used those weapons.[123] The new meaning of retaliation was that threat now had to translate into *action*. The 9/11 strike, having already occurred, could not be deterred. The resulting loss of national dignity could only be restored by doing something. Aggressive retaliation could be undertaken in the name of deterrence—scaring terrorists from trying again. Yet there was little hope that terrorists would behave like a nation-state. That was what made them terrorists. They played by different rules, judging from the experience of other countries, and were seldom deterred by reprisals.[124] Massive retaliation was thus a way to heal the nation's own wounds. It was action for the sake of action—big action to compensate for a big loss.

This new kind of retaliation, the use of force as "payback," had to be on a sufficient scale not only to prevent terrorists from striking again but also to make up for everything that America had lost symbolically. During the Cold War the nation's leaders had often imagined that retaliation would be so severe that civilization itself might not survive. The stakes were that high. Leaders now found themselves in their own defining moment, in a new era, defending civilization all over again. This time it would take the courage required not only to build weapons but also to use them. The struggle would be long and hard. It would demonstrate the nation's strength and its leaders' resolve. Those were the cultural stakes as the nation launched its attack on Afghanistan. Pushing the Taliban out would be not only a reprisal for the lives lost in New York and Washington but also the first major battle in the new struggle for civilization.

If taking action is an effective means of confronting fear, the invasion of Afghanistan served that purpose admirably.[125] In reality, the threat of another terrorist strike could have come from anywhere and was perceived that way by top officials. The CIA estimated that al Qaeda was operating in and from as many as eighty different countries. The FBI figured there might be as many as three hundred terrorists with al Qaeda connections inside the United States. There was plausible "chatter" from terrorist networks in Europe and Africa. Nobody knew who was sending the anthrax letters delivered to the offices of major news networks and Senate Majority Leader Tom Daschle, among other recipients. Yet the war on Afghanistan became the principal means through which the nation perceived itself to be fighting terrorism. Instead of terrorism being an ill-defined, shadowy enemy with decentralized leadership and semiautonomous embedded sleeper cells, it became popularly understood as a highly centralized organization located somewhere in Afghanistan and controlled by one man. Both the administration and the media needed a specific enemy against which to direct their rhetoric and take action. In the four weeks between 9/11 and the announcement that military action in Afghanistan had begun, major news coverage referring to Afghanistan doubled.[126] At the White House, daily National Security Council meetings focused almost exclusively on planning the invasion.[127] By driving the Taliban from power, or better, by capturing or killing bin Laden, terrorism could be decapitated, officials argued, thus rendering it symbolically powerless.

As the war in Afghanistan began, the public overwhelmingly supported the administration's actions. One poll showed that 92 percent approved "the way Bush is handling the U.S. campaign against terrorism." Inside the White House, there was considerable urgency to, as the president insisted, "do something and do it well." Political adviser Karl Rove analyzed polls following previous crises and concluded that the administration had at most eight months to show results before public support would fade. However, progress was painfully slow. Diplomacy with Russia, Uzbekistan, and Pakistan involved tedious negotiations. The military said bombing could not begin until teams were in place to rescue downed pilots. Reconnaissance showed that Taliban training camps were empty and few other attractive targets could be identified. It was uncertain which of the tribal leaders could be counted on to provide ground combat units against the Taliban. After a month of planning, the CIA had been able to plant only one paramilitary team in Afghanistan. Three weeks later, there were only three. By early November, columnists were beginning to ask if Afghanistan was becoming a quagmire, like Vietnam had been. "Massive military force," wrote political scientist John J. Mearsheimer in the *New York Times*, "makes the problem worse." The struggle against terrorism would only be won, he counseled, through diplomacy and better intelligence-gathering.[128] Yet in mid-November, a notable shift became evident as the Northern Alliance forces—anti-Taliban Afghans allied with the United States—began pushing back the Taliban and opposition forces in the south became more effective. On December 7, the fall of Kandahar effectively left the country in the hands of the Taliban's opponents. It was a striking victory for the Bush administration. Polls in early December showed that nine Americans in ten approved his handling of the campaign against terrorism. Expelling the Taliban had been accomplished with only 110 CIA officers, 316 special forces personnel, and massive airpower. The new regime in Afghanistan, sworn in on December 22, became official only 102 days after 9/11.[129]

Inevitably, the war in Afghanistan fell seriously short of fulfilling the high symbolic expectations with which it had begun. Al Qaeda was dislocated but not decapitated. Of the twenty-two al Qaeda leaders the CIA had been able to identify, the whereabouts of sixteen remained unknown. Bin Laden had not been killed or captured. The press was still more eager to know what the president thought about him than about the new regime in Afghanistan. Was bin Laden running? Was he still capable of masterminding another terrorist attack? A poll taken at the conclusion of the military campaign found that only 48 percent of the public felt it had been successful.[130] From the start, officials had cautioned that success in Afghanistan would be only the beginning. "We need to be patient," President Bush told reporters. "The world will learn that when the United States is harmed, we will follow through."[131] The war on terror would last a long time. Striking the Taliban had satisfied some of the public's appetite for revenge, but the victory had come almost too easily. Before it started, nearly two-thirds of the public had expected military action in Afghanistan to last a long time and result in many casualties or defeat.[132] After it was over, nine Americans in ten said the "most difficult part" in the war on terrorism was "yet to come."[133] The war to save civilization certainly had not been won. Something else needed to follow. A month after the fighting in Afghanistan ended, public approval of the president's campaign against terrorism began to slip, and over the next nine months approval fell 22 percentage points.[134] The nation was set on engaging in a larger struggle that would last a long time and demonstrate its hardened convictions. Yet it was not immediately clear what that struggle would be or how it would be justified. That response would require stepping back from the tragedy of 9/11 and taking a longer perspective—one that looked further into the future but also more explicitly to the legacy of the Cold War.

FIVE

WEAPONS OF MASS DESTRUCTION

THE BROADER UNDERSTANDING OF PERIL that evolved from the 9/11 attacks focused on weapons of mass destruction, or WMDs as they soon came to be called. The peril of WMDs subsumed the earlier threat of nuclear weapons and significantly enlarged the danger Americans felt from watching planes hitting the twin towers. The public now increasingly perceived itself to be at risk of waking up to find their city's air contaminated with radiation or poisonous gas, their water fouled with toxic chemicals, or their food laced with biological agents. As one man observed, "It's just a matter of time. Things are becoming so sophisticated that somebody could come in with a test tube full of destruction—hide it in their garments and walk the waterways and reservoirs and maybe walk into buildings and drop a little here and a little there. Who knows what would happen!"[1]

By the first anniversary of 9/11, public officials and commentators were focusing less attention on how or why the World Trade Center and Pentagon had been attacked than on the far more lethal and presumably prevalent danger posed by weapons of mass destruction. The truly terrifying danger that now faced the world, officials argued, was the likelihood that terrorists would use WMDs to inflict casualties on a larger scale than ever imagined. Over the next few years, concern about WMDs grew dramatically. "Weapons of mass destruction," an international policy analyst wrote in 2006, "have become the bête noir of the 21st century." Policy makers justified spending billions of dollars in the name of combating this perceived threat. Grants for bioweapons research were fifteen times higher in the five years after 9/11 than in the preceding five years. Federal spending on biodefense rose almost twentyfold between 2001 and 2005.[2] In 2003, the *New York Times* carried fourteen times as many stories about weapons of mass destruction than it had in 2000.[3] Television coverage rose even more dramatically.[4] Yet this emphasis on WMDs did not appear immediately after 9/11. It emerged gradually as a topic of public discussion, grew into its own during the half year leading up to the war on

Iraq, and then eventually came to be viewed by critics of the Bush administration as having been cynically manipulated to justify the war. In reality, weapons of mass destruction had already been a topic of considerable discussion in policy circles well before 9/11, and then took on new meaning as public officials debated them and linked them with new policies. WMDs acquired the same kind of cultural prominence as an abiding source of unease that nuclear weapons had gained during the Cold War. How the 2001 attacks merged with and animated the discussion of WMDs is thus one of the more important chapters in the changing response to peril in the post–Cold War era.

A CONNECTION BETWEEN THE ATTACKS ON 9/11 and weapons of mass destruction was implicit in concerns about the possibility of terrorists using lethal chemicals, anthrax, and other biological agents. However, hardly anyone mentioned weapons of mass destruction explicitly in the first hours after 9/11. The focus was more on the specific attacks, the casualties, and the response. One who did raise the larger question was columnist George F. Will, who wrote on September 12 that "weapons of mass destruction are proliferating" and might include nuclear weapons in shipping containers or suitcases and an anthrax attack. Significantly, Will was one of the few writers who also drew a connection between 9/11 and "a half-century of war and Cold War." In his view, the 1990s had been an abnormal period of calm. The nation would now return to the same sort of steely resolve and readiness it had shown for so long since the end of World War II.[5] Inside the government, Vice President Dick Cheney, who had served as secretary of defense under President George H. W. Bush from March 1989 to January 1993, became one of the most persistent advocates of concern about weapons of mass destruction. Beginning in May 2001, one of Cheney's principal assignments had been to study the nation's vulnerability to chemical and biological threats. The 9/11 attacks convinced him that these threats necessitated urgent vigilance.[6]

Policy makers understood that the potential devastation from weapons of mass destruction could be horrific. A thorough 127-page report produced by the Office of Technology Assessment in 1993 concluded that "biological weapons efficiently delivered under the right conditions against unprotected populations would, pound for pound of weapon, exceed the killing power of nuclear weapons." A single aircraft carrying 100 kilograms of anthrax on a windless night over Washington, D.C., could result in as many as three million deaths. In less favorable weather, as few as 130,000 and as many as 460,000 deaths could result. An attack of sarin nerve gas would be far less lethal, but could lead to as many as 8,000 dead.[7] Many more would experience debilitating respiratory, vascular, and neurological effects. The potential danger of WMDs, including so-called dirty bombs spreading low-level radiological contamination, was estimated to have increased by the relative ease of gaining access to relevant materials, possibilities for clandestine production, and their compatibility with various delivery systems. As early as 1992, the CIA reported that as many as fourteen nations—including Iran, Iraq, North Korea, Libya, Syria, Myanmar, Vietnam, and China—either had or were on the verge of acquiring nuclear, chemical, or biological weapons capabilities.[8] The broader question that remained unaddressed in such assessments, though, was how WMDs might come to be perceived by the American public as a significant danger and what the response to that danger would be.

Although concern in the general public about WMDs was present prior to 2001, there is little evidence that rank-and-file citizens thought much about them, other than as nuclear weapons, until the 1990s. The first known usage of the phrase itself was in a 1937 Christmas broadcast, reprinted in the *Times* of London, in which the archbishop of Canterbury referred to the "appalling slaughter" in Spain and China from "new weapons of mass destruction."[9] A well-known instance of what would later be included among weapons of mass destruction was the use of chlorine gas in World War I.[10] German agents' unsuccessful attempt to infect horses shipped out of the country with glanders and anthrax bacteria was less widely known.[11] There had been evidence, too, of chemicals and disease being used as weapons in earlier wars.[12] After World War I, Germany, France, Britain, Canada, Japan, and the United States all experimented with pathogens designed to kill crops and livestock. In 1947 the United Nations Security Council formally listed "radioactive material weapons" and "lethal chemical and biological weapons," in the same category as "atomic explosive weapons."

During the Cold War, far less was said about chemical and biological weapons than about the nuclear arms race, but after the superpowers signed a chemical arms treaty in 1990 the U.S. Army disclosed that it had retained 60 million to 70 million pounds of deadly mustard gas and nerve agents.[13] Such disclosures accounted for some of the renewed interest in WMDs in the 1990s. The sarin nerve gas attack in which twelve people died and fifty-four were seriously injured in the Tokyo subway system in 1995 prompted U.S. officials to look more closely at the possibility of terrorist groups using similar methods. Sporadic civil defense drills drew additional attention. For instance, emergency personnel simulated a nerve gas attack in New York City on November 9, 1997, in which six hundred people took part. However, wider public interest in weapons of mass destruction remained limited. Polls in the 1990s seldom asked questions about WMDs and those that did ask yielded inconclusive results. For instance, a Times Mirror poll in 1993 found that 69 percent of the public regarded "preventing the spread of weapons of mass destruction" as a "top priority" among possible long-range foreign policy goals for the United States, and polls conducted in 1995 and 1997 found similar results.[14] Yet, in another poll in which people were asked which of six issues should receive "greatest attention from the federal government at the present time," only 4 percent of the public selected "weapons of mass destruction," putting it in a last-place tie with "unfair trade practices" and far below "street crime and violence," "public education," and "economy."[15] In a 1997 survey, "proliferation of weapons of mass destruction" came in first among "dangers in the world," but was selected by only 22 percent of Americans, placing it only slightly ahead of "international drug and crime cartels" and "nationalism and ethnic hatreds."[16]

In the decade preceding 9/11, media discussions of WMDs focused more on Iraq than on any other nation or group. Sixty percent of *New York Times* stories that mentioned weapons of mass destruction during the 1990s also mentioned Iraq. The largest number of such stories occurred in 1991, when planning for the Gulf War sparked speculation that Iraqi leader Saddam Hussein might use chemical or biological weapons against U.S. troops, and again in 1998, when Hussein's efforts to keep United Nations inspectors away from alleged biological and chemical weapons programs eventuated in a four-day air campaign by U.S. forces in late December. The inspectors' lack of access to suspected weapons production sites encouraged speculation about the dangers involved. Columnists who thought Hussein's programs presented little danger beyond the immediate region worried that any use of biological or chemical weapons might result in nuclear retaliation by the United States or Israel. Armageddon, some writers suggested, could follow. Others doubted that Hussein yet had a nuclear arsenal, but worried that he was hiring unemployed technicians from the former Soviet Union. These writers effectively saw the Cold War continuing, only with Iraq as the United States' main antagonist. Still others imagined Hussein as Dr. No (as in Ian Fleming's James Bond novel of that title) with scientists huddled over poisonous concoctions in underground laboratories. The speculation was reinforced by evidence that Hussein had used chemical weapons against Iraqi Kurds in Halabja in northern Iraq in 1988, killing some 5,000. There was fear that a leader irrational enough to have launched a hopeless venture into Kuwait might be planning WMD attacks on other countries in the Middle East. Reports circulated that Baghdad had medium-range missiles loaded with botulinum toxin, anthrax, aflatoxin, and other deadly agents. Perhaps he was just crazy or reckless enough to be planning total annihilation, a few argued. As one journalistic team observed, Iraq has "enough deadly microbes to kill all the people on earth several times over."[17]

It was thus not surprising that the 9/11 attacks immediately drew speculation about Iraq. A poll conducted only two days after the attacks showed that 78 percent of the public thought it likely that Saddam Hussein was personally involved in the terrorist attacks (34 percent said "very likely").[18] In another poll four days after the attacks, 63 percent of the public blamed Iraq.[19] Behind the scenes, policy makers shared the public's suspicion that Iraq was involved. In National Security Council meetings on September 12, Secretary of Defense Rumsfeld and Vice President Cheney speculated that Iraq was behind the attacks. Discussions of this possibility continued at NSC meetings over the next three days. The Pentagon had been working on plans for a possible campaign against Iraq prior to September 11, and key White House advisors urged that these plans now be given high priority.[20] Stories about whether Iraq was or was not involved implicitly drew it into the discussion. In the *New York Times* only fifteen articles had mentioned both "Iraq" and "terrorism" in 2000; that number jumped to 73 in 2001, to 302 in 2002, and to 990 in 2003. Iraq served as the critical symbolic link between the specific loss the nation had experienced on 9/11 and the new peril the American public perceived in weapons of mass destruction.

The Bush administration's decision to go to war with Iraq was connected with concerns about weapons of mass destruction, but less closely so than critics of the war were to argue when no WMDs were found. Secretary of State Colin Powell's speech to the United Nations on February 5, 2003, arguing that Hussein's regime had WMDs, merely added to the momentum that had been building over the preceding year. Key advisors such as Paul Wolfowitz and I. Lewis "Scooter" Libby Jr. argued that the post-9/11 mood presented a ripe opportunity for ousting Hussein. Rumsfeld was keen on identifying other targets beyond Afghanistan. Cheney believed the no-fly zone and embargo strategy of containment used by the Clinton administration was impractical as a long-range solution. At huge expense and risk to planes and pilots, since the end of the Gulf War in 1991 the United States had flown more than 150,000 flights over southern Iraq in this containment effort.[21] In October 2002, shortly before the midterm elections, the U.S. Congress passed a joint resolution authorizing the use of armed forces against Iraq. The vote was a comfortable 296 to 133 in the House and 77 to 23 in the Senate. At no time, judging from the various behind-the-scenes accounts published later, did the president's political advisors worry that negative sentiment might be aroused by going to war. Although the president's job approval ratings had slipped since the high-water mark reached soon after 9/11, they were still above 60 percent in late 2002. At least 70 percent of the public approved of the president's handling of the campaign against terrorism.[22] The sense of loss, fear, and desire for retaliation that emerged after 9/11 was still prevalent. A year after the attacks, nearly three-quarters of the public was at least somewhat worried that "there will be another major terrorist attack in the United States" and a third thought they might be among the victims.[23] Arguments that removing the threat posed by Iraq was part of the continuing war on terror played well in the media and with most of the public. In late January 2003, only weeks before the war began, 81 percent of the public in one poll said they believed Saddam Hussein had ties to al Qaeda.[24] A few weeks after the war began, a poll showed that 77 percent considered it "part of the war against terrorism."[25] Organized protests by antiwar and pacifist groups were present but relatively weak. Those who argued against war with Iraq on the basis of just war theory found it difficult to make the case that Saddam was not a menace to his neighbors or that war would incur unwarranted costs in lives and materiel.[26] The successes in Afghanistan sparked optimism that the military had discovered a low-risk way of winning battles with special operations units and laser-guided air strikes.

What the buildup for war in Iraq accomplished *culturally* was to popularize and legitimate the idea that WMDs were the greatest peril the world faced—indeed, a danger as perilous for its time as the atomic and hydrogen bombs had been in theirs. Mass destruction is itself an ominous phrase, suggesting that many people may be killed and property destroyed. And yet the scope and significance of peril is never defined solely by estimates of physical damage. The nuclear era had shown that beyond doubt. Nuclear fears were communicated through the symbolism of the mushroom cloud, in duck and cover drills, and in stories about radiation-contaminated milk and leaky power plants. Weapons of mass destruction required similar connections with concrete images and rituals to be more than an abstract concept easily bracketed from mind. Saddam Hussein, as crazed dictator of Hitler-like deceptive ruthlessness, was one such tangible symbol. Weapons of mass destruction could be visualized in yellowcake uranium and Scud missiles loaded with botulism. The distance between Baghdad and American neighborhoods shrank. One U.S. household in ten made emergency plans and other special preparations—as many as during the Cuban missile crisis—as the nation prepared for war.[27] Nearly three-quarters of the public feared there would be "all-out war in the Middle East." Ninety percent were worried that Iraq might use biological or chemical weapons against U.S. troops.[28] It became easy to imagine that bottles of anthrax filled in secret facilities in Iraq could wind up in Los Angeles or New York.

No single speech or statement did as much to focus public consciousness on the threat of weapons of mass destruction as President Bush's State of the Union address on January 29, 2002. In an interview with Bob Woodward, speechwriter Michael Gerson explained that establishing a connection between terrorism and weapons of mass destruction had been a key aim of the speech. An initial draft written by fellow speechwriter David Frum characterized this connection as an "axis of hatred," a phrase inspired by Frum's reflections about Pearl Harbor and World War II.[29] Gerson changed it to "axis of evil." The result, in Woodward's view, was to render the connection "more sinister, even wicked. It was almost as if Saddam was an agent of the devil." Gerson knew that plans for war with Iraq had begun. It was important to communicate the president's concern without literally announcing these plans. National Security Advisor Condoleezza Rice suggested mentioning North Korea and Iran as well as Iraq. The three became the axis of evil.[30] "States like these, and their terrorist allies," Bush said, "constitute an axis of evil, arming to threaten the peace of the world. By seeking weapons of mass destruction, these regimes pose a grave and growing danger." The president's comments about Iraq provided the most graphic evidence of evil. Iraq had "plotted to develop anthrax, and nerve gas, and nuclear weapons for over a decade." It had already "used poison gas to murder thousands of its own citizens—leaving the bodies of mothers huddled over their dead children."[31]

A survey conducted a few weeks after the president's speech showed that the axis of evil rhetoric resonated with a wide swath of the American public. Nearly eight in ten (79 percent) said the statement that "rogue nations like Iraq, Iran, and North Korea constitute an axis of evil and threaten the safety of all peaceful nations" was true.[32] Eighty-two percent in another poll agreed that the government of Iraq was evil.[33] An axis of evil was reminiscent of Ronald Reagan's characterization of the Soviet Union as an evil empire, as much as it connoted Nazism and the Axis Powers in World War II (headed by Germany, Italy, and Japan). What made WMDs truly frightening was the possibility of their being used by terrorists harbored by evil regimes. "Our greatest threat comes not from the specter of nuclear war between two superpowers, as it did during the Cold War," explained Under Secretary of State John R. Bolton, "but from transnational terrorist cells that will strike without warning using weapons of mass destruction."[34] Critics seized on the fact that Iraq, Iran, and North Korea were not militarily aligned and thus were not a Soviet-style bloc or an axis like Germany and Japan were. Condoleezza Rice defended the wording arguing that the three regimes were oppressive and opaque. The fact of "aggressively seeking weapons of mass destruction," she said, was what truly mattered.[35] The technical debate about what constituted an axis only contributed to the phrase's popularity. The message was less about alliances than about evil. Weapons of mass destruction and the terrorists who used them were evil. The term significantly upped the stakes in the war on terror. America was no longer a nation striking back or defending itself but engaged in a cosmic struggle such as the Cold War had been. Evil was "radioactive," a foreign relations specialist noted in an interesting choice of words. "You can't make a deal with evil. You can only kill it."[36]

Invading Iraq was thus a way of combating evil. As explained by Henry Kissinger, former secretary of state and a frequent visitor to the Bush White House, "Afghanistan wasn't enough." There was a "need to humiliate" the enemy.[37] Launching another war demonstrated that America could look fear in the eye and do something about it. The vulnerability the nation had felt after 9/11 was gradually being replaced by a plan of action. Weapons of mass destruction were a far greater peril than al Qaeda. It was incumbent on people of good will to eradicate this evil. American forces, President Bush told the nation as bombing began on March 19, 2003, were engaged in operations "to defend the world from grave danger."[38] The most vocal proponents of war viewed it as a way to side with the forces of good. "All that is necessary for evil to prevail is for good men to do nothing," a letter to the editor observed, quoting Edmund Burke.[39] The struggle was not for the faint of heart or for those who wished for an international consensus. There could be no negotiation when good and evil were at stake. "We will pass through this time of peril and carry on the work of peace," the president said. "We will bring freedom to others and we will prevail." For their part, opponents of the war generally agreed that America was pitted against evil and disagreed only with the methods being taken. Speaking against the war was a way of taking action.

BETWEEN SEPTEMBER 11, 2001, and the start of the Iraq war commentators argued increasingly that the nation had not been well prepared to identify terrorist threats before they became reality. The FBI in particular seemed to have missed information that would have alerted it to the attackers' plans. Months after the tragedy, officials labored to identify and implement new procedures. A survey of state-level security chiefs in mid-2002 showed general frustration with the information and support they were receiving from Washington.[40] Amid these concerns, rumors spread of new threats and impending danger. There were vague warnings about the Brooklyn Bridge and the Statue of Liberty, about the Sears Tower in Chicago, the Space Needle in Seattle, and Los Angeles International Airport. Other targets about which public speculation surfaced ranged from nuclear power plants to shopping malls. No additional attacks occurred, but tests of security arrangements at airports and in transit systems and chemical plants showed major gaps that could easily be exploited by terrorist groups.

Public officials spoke often of the dangers facing Americans and of the need to be watchful. On the first anniversary of 9/11, as the color-coded terror threat level rose to orange or "high," Attorney General John Ashcroft urged citizens to be alert and defiant. Terrorists "are coming after us," CIA director George J. Tenet told a congressional panel the following month.[41] "It would take one vial, one canister, one crate slipped into this country to bring a day of horror like none we have ever known," President Bush declared in his 2003 State of the Union address.[42] The question of which party was more capable of defending the nation against terrorism emerged as a prominent campaign theme over the next year and a half. "The biggest threat we face now as a nation," Vice President Cheney said in a speech in Ohio, "is the possibility of terrorists ending up in the middle of one of our cities with deadlier weapons than have ever before been used against us—biological agents or a nuclear weapon or a chemical weapon of some kind—to be able to threaten the lives of hundreds of thousands of Americans."[43]

Critics speculated that the administration was stoking public fears for political purposes and perhaps dampening these same fears for opportunistic reasons at other times. The criticisms began soon after 9/11 and became particularly evident during the 2004 presidential election campaign. Writing in the *National Journal* on October 6, 2001, Alexis Simendinger observed: "There can be no question about it: The Bush Administration is in the fear business." The more the president and other top officials talked about fear, Simendinger argued, the more the public supported them.[44] In a *New York Times* essay the following June, Bill Keller complained of "silly color-coded gimmicks," "hype and spin and bluster and political opportunism," and "willingness to make terrorism a lobbying prop for every cause on the Republican agenda."[45] In 2003, as campaigning began for the 2004 presidential election, one of the first television ads in Iowa included a clip of the president's statement about a vial, canister, or crate producing horror. "Well, that's a comforting message from our commander in chief," columnist Maureen Dowd quipped. "Do we really need his cold, clammy hand on our spine at a time when we're already rattled by fresh terror threats at home and abroad?"[46] As campaign rhetoric reached a climax the following fall, an expert on risk analysis argued that fearmongering had grown to such proportions that public health was at stake. "People are being harmed as politicians frighten us to curry our votes," he wrote. "It is fair to demand that they stop, and we should hold them accountable at the polls if they don't."[47] Another writer drew parallels between the 2004 campaign and the McCarthy era of the early 1950s, when Wisconsin senator Joseph R. McCarthy played on public fears with unfounded charges of communist infiltration in the (mainly Democratic) State Department, and encouraged Americans to make the fight against communism their highest priority.[48] Former vice president Al Gore wrote shortly after the election, "President George W. Bush and his administration have been (wittingly or unwittingly) distorting America's political reality by force-feeding the American people a grossly exaggerated fear of Iraq that was hugely disproportionate to the actual danger posed by Iraq."[49]

Allegations of fearmongering facilitated the rise of an alternative perspective on fear. In much of the writing about the nuclear era, commentators interpreted fear as a natural psychological response to danger. The threat of nuclear annihilation was, in this view, real, and thus it was inevitable that people would be afraid. Fear arose unbidden within the individual psyche and was then in most instances denied because it was too painful to face squarely. These repressed emotions were sometimes articulated for the public by fiction writers, motion picture producers, and psychiatrists. After 9/11, the view that fear was a natural response continued, of course, but was edged aside by a different perspective. Tragic as the attacks had been, they had been catastrophic only in limited parts of Manhattan and Washington, but in a broader sense they had achieved the attackers' goal of evoking terror nationwide. The response was to some observers out of proportion. Fear was being produced, even manipulated, by political candidates, the media, and other special interests. At a conference in 2004 on the politics of fear, scholars drew on this perspective to reexamine not only the response to 9/11 but also the role of fear in other contexts. Conference organizer Kenneth Prewitt wrote that the central challenge was sorting out "the fear that is grounded in real threats from that which is manipulated by those in power for reasons less connected with objective conditions than private goals, such as holding on to power."[50] There was an underlying propensity for fear, an endemic anxiety that was probably hardwired, the scholars concluded, but conscious fear capable of inducing action was usually the result of specific circumstances, some of which were organized for the explicit purpose of evoking fear. One had only to think about *Jaws* or *The Omen* to understand that fear was easily manipulated. Prophets of old stirred followers to action by instilling fear of divine wrath. Newscasters now encouraged people to stay tuned around the clock for fear of missing a breaking story about terrorism. Demagogues in Congress and other elective offices, who have often shown a talent for stirring racist fears, red-baiting, and doomsaying about threats to the economy, were playing the war on terror for political gain.

If fear was being manipulated by politicians, the question of how the public should respond nevertheless remained. Was it entirely irrational to be afraid? Or was it prudent to be prepared? The long decades of the Cold War had inadvertently taught the American public two important lessons about taking responsibility for its own protection. One was that investing much time and personal resources into safeguarding one's family was probably futile. If destruction came, it would be so massive and sudden that preparations would do little good. What may have appeared to some critics as a head-in-the-sand fatalism was actually a quite realistic appraisal on the public's part about how best to invest scarce time and energy. The other lesson was that the most important sources of preparedness would come from government in the form of missile defenses, military technology, and civil defense. Cold War preparedness essentially came to be a *national* response to a perceived international threat. It was a matter of national security and thus was centrally coordinated by the National Security Council, which came into existence in 1947. National security was quite different in vision and orientation from preparedness for natural disasters, the response to which was largely in the hands of state and local officials. The public's role in national security differed from its role in preparing for natural disasters. Tornadoes, fires, and floods necessitated purchasing whatever insurance might be available, having a household emergency plan in mind, and supporting local fire and rescue workers. National security meant delegating responsibility to federal officials, paying taxes, and patriotically supporting political decisions involving the military. It seldom meant taking action as private citizens to protect oneself and one's family.

The public's response to 9/11 followed suit. Few Americans altered their lifestyles or undertook special precautions in preparation for subsequent attacks. A 2003 survey of New York residents found that 76 percent had no family emergency preparedness plan at all, while only 14 percent had food and water, a flashlight and portable radio, and a place for family members to meet in case of evacuation.[51] Nearly five years after 9/11, a summary of national surveys and other research concluded that "the failure of the U.S. public to be prepared for terrorism . . . bears little difference to the state of public preparedness during other periods in which national calls were issued." The authors argued that the public remained "confused about what 'prepared' means," was increasingly disengaged from leaders' rhetoric about preparedness, and had little understanding of who was responsible for what in cases of terrorist attacks and natural disasters.[52] Another survey of available evidence came to the same conclusion. "America does not have a culture of preparedness," it said. While many Americans believed the *nation* would be attacked by terrorists, few believed they or their property would be targeted and thus failed to take precautions.[53]

The lack of preparedness by individual citizens reflects the reality that responses to peril are as much social as they are psychological. The social response occurs through organizations, usually ones that are appointed by government officials for the purpose of protecting the public through the mobilization of specialized expertise. The public reaction—trusting, favorable, attentive, cynical, critical, fearful, indifferent—is thus directed as much toward these agencies as toward the crisis itself. In the early years of the atomic era, the Atomic Energy Commission governed the national response through a highly centralized decision-making process. After 9/11, the administrative response was far more complex because government bureaucracy itself had grown immensely and because the threat was deemed to require vigilance at many levels. The World Trade Center and Pentagon were places of employment and the attacks occurred during business hours. Postwar civil defense had been modeled largely on anticipation of nighttime air raids like those on London in the Battle of Britain and the Blitz (1940–41); the 9/11 attacks gave notice that an entirely different response would be required. Basement bomb shelters would be of little value if people were not at home. Preparedness implied greater attention to corporate evacuation plans, building design, and emergency communication networks, all of which were deemed particularly deficient in New York by the 9/11 Commission (formally, the National Commission on Terrorist Attacks Upon the United States), whose report was released in July 2004. Among its conclusions, the commission emphasized that "private-sector challenges," including a lack of protocol for rooftop rescues, improper evacuation orders, locked exits, and poor coordination among first responders, had contributed to the casualties. Observing that "the private sector controls 85 percent of the critical infrastructure in the nation," the commission recommended significantly increased attention to private sector preparedness, including the adoption of national standards for emergency management and business continuity. "Private sector preparedness is not a luxury," the commission stated, "it is a cost of doing business in the post-9/11 world. It is ignored at a tremendous potential cost in lives, money, and national security."[54]

This was by no means the first time private sector preparedness had been emphasized, but two aspects of the 9/11 Commission's recommendations are especially worthy of note. The first is that the recommendations focused on adopting national standards. The second is that these standards were concerned with minimizing casualties *after* a terrorist strike, rather than avoiding one in the first place. Both underscored the fact that the nation's response to 9/11 was shaped by long-established institutional arrangements. The national standards recommended by the commission were ones developed by the National Fire Protection Association (NFPA). This organization had been founded in 1896 by a coalition of municipal and regional insurance companies. Patterned after the Underwriters Electrical Bureau of 1894, which promoted national uniformity in implementing electricity technology, the NFPA established uniform standards for sprinkler systems and thus standardized the procedures insurance companies used to assess risks. Within a few years, other insurance companies joined the NFPA and railroad executives, fire chiefs, sprinkler manufacturers, and government officials became active among its leaders.[55] As the NFPA expanded, it took pride in keeping in step with "progress in science, invention, and the industrial arts."[56] The national standards recommended by the 9/11 Commission originated in a Technical Committee on Disaster Management established in January 1991 by the NFPA Standards Council. The committee produced a document, *Recommended Practice for Disaster Management*, which was adopted by the NFPA in 1995 and became known as NFPA 1600. The 2000 edition incorporated a "total program approach" for disaster and emergency management and business continuity programs. This program specified a wide range of disaster management activities and considerations, including hazard identification, risk assessment, legal restrictions, warning systems, coordination of medical and rescue personnel, equipment, training, and communication.[57] Other than emergency management workers, few of the wider public would likely have been aware that such national standards existed. Yet it was a well-established cultural assumption that in times of crisis more than the impromptu actions of individual citizens would be needed. Professional expertise was required to know how much steel reinforcement a building should have to avert a collapse or how to reroute 911 calls if telephone computers became overloaded. The public response to 9/11 was, in this respect, much like its reaction to the earlier threat of nuclear weapons. In both instances the public knew implicitly that safety was less in its own hands than in those of scientists, engineers, technicians, and other professionals. This did not mean that the public's confidence in these specialists was always high. In fact, polls suggested that confidence was often low.[58] However, there was little reason to believe that any other solution would be better.

The administrative response to the need for public preparedness was the formation of a new governmental unit. On September 20, 2001, President Bush announced the creation of a cabinet-level position to be filled by former Pennsylvania governor Tom Ridge. The new Office of Homeland Security was charged with preparing a comprehensive national strategy for protecting the nation against future attacks. The task of coordinating communication among dozens of agencies further suggested the need for a larger-scale reorganization of intelligence and security activities. In a televised speech to the nation on June 6, 2002, the president proposed to Congress that a "single, permanent department with an overriding and urgent mission [of] securing the homeland of America, and protecting the American people" be formed. The new Department of Homeland Security, Bush said, would shoulder responsibility for preventing terrorists and explosives from entering the country, help state and local officials respond to emergencies, develop new technologies, and review intelligence and law enforcement information.[59] With passage of the Homeland Security Act on November 25, 2002, the department became official and commenced operations on January 24, 2003. Subsuming 22 federal agencies with more than 170,000 employees, it became one of the largest departments, exceeded only by the Department of Defense and Department of Veterans Affairs.[60]

From its inception, the idea of *homeland* security was a matter of symbolism as much as it was of administrative policy. In its editorial on September 12, 2001, the *New York Times* described the attack as a "frightening assault on the American homeland."[61] The very soil of America, where its values were rooted, was under siege. Jewish Theological Seminary chancellor Ismar Schorsch recalled the high priest's special prayer for the inhabitants of ancient Israel that "their homes might not become their graves." Modern terrorism, he observed, "can turn our homeland without warning into a graveyard."[62] Homes should be the cradles of life, not of death. This had been their meaning from earliest times. Those who likened the tragedy to Pearl Harbor emphasized that the two were singular events in which the very bosom of America had been violated. Some recalled that a panel chaired by former senators Gary Hart and Warren Rudman only months before 9/11, the U.S. Commission on National Security/21st Century, had cautioned about homeland vulnerability. "A direct attack against American citizens *on American soil* is likely," they wrote.[63] Terrorism could no longer be considered a danger only in distant locations. A homeland is defined by "we-ness," belonging, affinity. It is where we live and work, the space in which we enjoy our loved ones and treasured possessions, the ambience that becomes part of our personal identity. Homes are places of safety, sanctuaries of warmth, havens against the dangers of life among strangers and in the street. Both familial and familiar, homes are the repositories of local knowledge. They hold uncertainty at bay. To speak of homeland security is thus to imply that one's home is *not* in fact secure, at least not in a way that can be taken for granted. "Homeland security" should be a redundant term, but juxtaposing the words achieves exactly the opposite of what either word separately connotes. A homeland requiring security is in reality not a safe haven by virtue of its very existence but one that must be defended. The homeland becomes a territory that must be protected from dangerous enemies outside of it so that the inhabitants within can feel secure.[64]

The symbolism was thoroughly evident but unlikely the result of any conscious decision to promote it for political purposes. In August 2002 an effort by journalist Elizabeth Becker to trace the origins of "homeland security" as the name for the new department turned up empty. "Etymology unknown, don't have a clue," her sources told her, "no one can remember," although it was evident that the phrase bore connotations of World War II, both with German references to *heimat* or homeland and with the British Department of Home Security.[65] Bob Woodward's account of high-level meetings has the president saying on the evening of 9/11, "We need to stress homeland defense" and assigning the task to Cheney.[66] If Woodward's information is correct, it would have been likely that the president's choice of words was influenced by briefings based on the Hart-Rudman Commission report, in which the phrase "homeland defense" was first used in an official document and which urged that Congress establish a special body to deal with "homeland security." Indeed, the new Office of Homeland Security was patterned almost exactly on the commission's recommendation to establish an agency "to consolidate and refine the missions of the nearly two dozen disparate departments and agencies that have a role in U.S. homeland security today."[67] The commission also devoted extensive consideration to the evolving role of the National Security Council since its creation in 1947. The NSC had become increasingly preoccupied with foreign policy, thus creating a vacancy needing to be occupied by an agency similarly concerned with domestic security. The frequency with which policy makers interchanged discussions of national defense and homeland security suggests that the new office might have been named differently, had an NSC not already existed. Yet *homeland* served the useful purpose of distinguishing those aspects of national defense that concerned the actual physical territory of the United States, as opposed to the much broader, even global, connotations of defending the *nation's* interests, whether on the high seas, in space, or in the Middle East.[68]

The Department of Homeland Security's cultural imprint was most visible in color-coded terror alerts featured on television news programs and through airport security screening. However, a less public but equally important aspect of the department's work was its emphasis on science and technology. The war against terror was never as clearly associated in the public's mind with science as the discovery of atomic weapons was. Yet the same faith in scientific and technological prowess that prevailed during the Cold War remained evident in the response to 9/11. The Hart-Rudman report mentioned science more than 250 times. "We have concluded," the authors wrote in the report's opening paragraphs, that "despite the end of the Cold War threat, America faces distinctly new dangers, particularly to the homeland and to our scientific and educational base." The report's recommendations included "recapitalizing America's strengths in science and education."[69]

In his June 6, 2002, address to the nation, President Bush echoed this recommendation, emphasizing that the new department would "bring together our best scientists to develop technologies that detect biological, chemical, and nuclear weapons, and to discover the drugs and treatments to best protect our citizens." The Homeland Security Act of 2002 created a Directorate of Science and Technology to conduct basic and applied research and to develop counterterrorism technology according to "research-based definable goals" and in other ways to support "United States leadership in science and technology."[70] On October 1, 2003, President Bush signed the Homeland Security Appropriations Act in which $5.6 billion over the next decade was allocated to Project BioShield for the development and procurement of vaccines against biological, chemical, and radiological threats, and an additional $918 million was to be devoted to other science and technology projects, such as building a facility to study biological pathogens, promoting the rapid adaptation of commercial counterterrorism technologies, creating an urban Bio-Watch monitoring program, and developing sensors for monitoring the transportation of nuclear materials.[71] By 2006, these outlays for additional science and technology projects had risen to nearly $1.2 billion.[72] "As long as there are groups and individuals willing to use terror against us," a 2005 Office of Science and Technology Policy report declared, "we must continue to maintain a posture of high alert and focus on protecting our citizens. Science and technology is a key foundation in this national effort and one that will continue to make the homeland stronger, safer, and better equipped to respond to national emergencies."[73]

Individuals and organizations scrambled to participate in the new opportunities presented by the homeland security effort. In 2003, the department advertised one hundred scholarships for students interested in the study of counterterrorism. Nearly 1,000 undergraduates and more than 1,500 graduate students applied.[74] The Association of American Universities sent its president to Washington to ask Congress for $40 million to set up new university-based research programs for homeland security. MIT began hosting an annual symposium on the role of science and technology in homeland security. Texas A&M established an Integrative Center for Homeland Security. The Maryland-based Association of Analytical Communities set up a committee to evaluate handheld tester kits for biological hazards.[75] A team of information technology specialists outlined a broad program of IT applications, from Arabic character recognition to biometric signature analysis.[76] Publishers got into the act, bringing out not only best sellers by authors involved in national defense but also textbooks, such as McGraw-Hill's annually updated *Homeland Security*.[77] Others, more remotely connected to the science and technology effort, also sought to forge connections, if in name only. A book review entitled "homeland security" described two books about the World War II era; another by the same title reviewed a pair of monographs about the Civil War.[78] As they had done in the atomic era, social scientists proposed new ways to apply their expertise. "Basic units of social organization—families, work groups, neighbor-hood associations, community-based organizations, schools, church groups, and other civil-society institutions—are the building blocks of meaningful homeland security," a sociologist advised.[79] A journalism professor argued that better courses should be offered about democracy, the First Amendment, and freedom from religious orthodoxy.[80]

If homeland security was principally in the hands of scientists, educators, policy makers, and other professionals, average citizens were nevertheless expected to share in the responsibility for their own safety. The Federal Emergency Management Agency (FEMA) put out a 200-plus-page comprehensive guide to individual and family preparedness titled *Are You Ready? An In-depth Guide to Citizen Preparedness*.[81] Resembling the civil defense manuals of the nuclear era, the guide pictured a mother, father, and two children happily collecting canned food, toilet paper, and a flashlight. A section on terrorism advised people to be aware of their surroundings, leave if they feel comfortable doing so, take precautions when traveling, and learn where emergency exits are located. More detailed instructions described how to whistle or shout to signal rescuers if trapped in a fallen building, to wash with soap and water if exposed to a biological attack, and to seal a room with duct tape in the event of a chemical attack. "Terrorism, by nature, is unpredictable," the guide warned, but good preparation would reduce fear and anxiety.[82] *Preparing Makes Sense: Get Ready Now* distilled the essential points of the longer guide into a sixteen-page pamphlet that families could download from the Internet or order by mail. The pamphlet warned, "Terrorists are working to obtain biological, chemical, nuclear and radiological weapons and the threat of an attack is very real."[83] Just as it had done during the Cold War, the government sponsored a major advertising campaign to inform the public about the preparedness advice it was offering. This time the ads were carried on television and the Internet instead of as foldout sections in newspapers and magazines. The cost was upwards of $40 million, supplied mainly as in-kind contributions and monetary donations from television networks and foundations. The spots featured firefighters and their families encouraging fellow citizens to read "Preparing Makes Sense" and to stock up on food and water, radios, batteries, and other emergency items.[84] Normally critical of administration policies, the *Bulletin of the Atomic Scientists* reviewed its advice over the past half century about civil defense and concluded that following the pamphlet's advice was probably a good idea. "Preparing one's residence is something akin to wearing seatbelts," the author observed.[85] "Both are inexpensive and imperfect safety measures that nevertheless improve the odds." Temporarily at least, the public responded. Our stores are "really crankin,'" a Home Depot spokesperson reported amid the campaign. It is "not unlike the spikes we see when people prepare for hurricanes."[86]

Radios and other household items were a small part of the commercial activity generated by the new interest in homeland security. A hardware store owner in the Midwest marketed home preparedness kits for $15 plus shipping and handling on eBay. A military surplus store in Alabama reported a fivefold increase in business.[87] Some of the new products, such as the "Terrorist Hunting Permit (No. 91101)" marketed by an online military supplier were as gimmicky as "atomic" sandwiches had been in the 1940s. Other marketing efforts were no-nonsense ventures. RAE Systems, Inc., a manufacturer of chemical-detection monitors advertised its new ToxiRAE II, a "single-gas personal monitor that provides continuous readouts of toxic gas concentrations."[88] The Intelligent Automation Corporation (IAC) offered a "portable, web-enabled, real-time early-warning biomonitoring system" of electrodes attached to bluegill fish. The system's "monitoring applet" displayed alarms when biotoxins altered the fishes' ventilatory behavior.[89] Artificial intelligence scientists at the University of Maryland developed a "semantic web" program to monitor Internet traffic among networks of supposed terrorists.[90] At a small business expo organized by the Public Forum Institute in 2002, approximately fifty companies exhibited products ranging from voice intelligence monitoring equipment to a lotion aimed at preventing exposure to anthrax.[91] Vermont's Commerce and Community Development agency organized a similar meeting for small business entrepreneurs interested in pursuing the new contracting and research opportunities sparked by homeland security concerns.[92]

The sense that none of these solutions—governmental or commercial—offered much protection was captured in what became known as homeland security humor. Cartoons and satire about ineffective security measures frequented newspapers, web sites, and comedy shows. Duct tape was a favorite target, especially after a Homeland Security official in February 2003 encouraged the public to prepare for a terrorist attack by purchasing duct tape and plastic sheeting. One cartoon showed large bags of "intelligence" being loaded into the Department of Homeland Security and the building emitting duct tape to a waiting family. In another, showing a television set well wrapped in duct tape, a man says to his wife, "Wow! I do feel more secure!" Talkshow host Phil Hendrie quipped that a man was filing suit against Homeland Security officials, alleging he suffered emotional distress after duct-taping his genitals. Other cartoons and satire focused on the department's color-coded alerts, the frustrations of airport screening, gaps in border security, Big Brother, and paranoia. There were homeland security astrological calendars counseling people to purchase pepper spray and avoid people with beady eyes. A fake news headline announced that al Qaeda might attack the United States with a giant man-eating pterodactyl. Another declared that homeland security officials had raised the Reptile Terror Alert to red after picking up chatter about a plot involving snakes. An online news service advised readers that it was un-American not to be terrified. Another web site offered a Homeland Security Self-Exam to sort out good citizens from evildoers.[93]

Polls showed that Americans generally favored the idea of having a Homeland Security Department, but were less sure that having one would make them any safer. In a CBS News poll in June 2002, seventy percent of those responding said they approved of the "recent proposal to create the Department of Homeland Security, a cabinet department, which would unite a number of government agencies into one department," while only 15 percent disapproved and 15 percent neither approved nor disapproved. In the same survey, 66 percent said the new department would "help in the fight against terrorism," while only 4 percent thought it would hurt, and 30 percent thought it would have no effect or were unsure.[94] A poll conducted for *Time* magazine the same month showed that 58 percent of the public thought the department would make them "feel more secure personally," but 37 percent said it would not (5 percent were unsure).[95] Two months later, in August 2002, a *Los Angeles Times* poll found that only 13 percent had "a lot" of confidence that the "newly-created Department of Homeland Security will be able to protect the country from terrorist attacks," while 55 percent had "some" confidence, and 30 percent had "not too much" or "none at all."[96] In November 2002, a Gallup poll showed that 13 percent of the public felt "a lot safer," "now that the government has created a new cabinet Department of Homeland Security," but 47 percent felt only "a little safer," and 39 percent felt "not any safer."[97] A more sharply worded question a few weeks later in a Fox News poll registered only 30 percent saying that the recently created department "will make the United States safer from terrorism," while 39 percent said it will "mostly increase Washington bureaucracy."[98]

There were ample reasons for the doubts expressed in these polls. The department's proposals about public safety were widely criticized. International Association of Fire Fighters president Harold Schaitberger observed in 2003 that "most of the suggestions, I don't believe, are effective at all in really helping to protect anyone from many of these biological and chemical threats." Former senator Gary Hart, who with Warren Rudman had cochaired the Clinton-era panel on terrorism, was equally critical. "It's almost back to the duck-and-cover days of the nuclear exchange in the '50s," he said. Partisan disagreement about the run-up to the war in Iraq spilled into debates about homeland preparedness as well. Senate Minority Leader Tom Daschle complained that the Republican majority was dragging its feet on important appropriations legislation. "We had an amendment that would have allowed $5 billion to go to more FBI agents, more Customs agents, more infrastructure investment, more protection—and again we were told it was unaffordable."[99] A citizen in Chattanooga wrote, "If something happens in any of our cities . . . whose responsibility is it to prepare our communities and administer emergency procedures, how will the plans become known and how will these activities be financed?"[100]

Doubts about the government's role in public preparedness became more pronounced in 2005 when FEMA was widely perceived as having failed to help victims of Hurricane Katrina in coastal Louisiana and Mississippi after the hurricane struck on August 29. The scope of the disaster temporarily removed the war in Iraq from headlines and put the spotlight more clearly on domestic needs than at any time since fall 2001. If insufficient resources and inadequate coordination hampered emergency and rescue operations when disaster was known to be approaching, it seemed unlikely, critics charged, that homeland security would be any more effective in the event of an unanticipated terrorist attack. Investigations further suggested that FEMA's difficulties were present well before Katrina. Trouble in coordinating efforts among states became apparent in 1979 when Hurricane Frederic hit the Gulf Coast. FEMA ran into conflict with the FBI and Department of Justice during the Los Angeles Olympics in 1984, and came up short in relief efforts associated with Hurricane Andrew in 1992. As policy experts debated possible solutions, the images that registered in the public's mind were of people huddled in the Superdome and outside the Convention Center and of homes submerged from broken levees.[101] A poll for *Time* magazine that September showed only 5 percent of the public convinced that "federal government agencies, such as the Department of Homeland Security and FEMA," had done an excellent job in responding to the hurricane. Only 23 percent thought the government's response had been good, while 70 percent thought it was only fair or poor.[102] On a broader question, only a minority now felt that the Department of Homeland Security had made Americans safer.[103] Another survey showed that 42 percent of the public was confident or very confident that the government could "protect the area where you live from a terrorist attack," down from 62 percent in 2003.[104] The danger, one commentator remarked, was that people would adopt a fatalistic attitude, feeling that if even their government was unprepared, they themselves could do little, either.[105]

DISCUSSIONS OF PREPAREDNESS do not exhaust the questions of moral responsibility that arise in times of peril. Any serious shock to a society necessitates reflection about the strength of its values, what it means to defend those values, and why they are under attack. The Cold War generated its share of such questions. On the one hand, Americans generally perceived communist totalitarianism as a threat that demanded a moral response. It was obligatory for good Americans to stand up for freedom. Communism was a danger that ordinary men and women were morally obliged to resist, whether that meant being on the lookout for infiltrators or supporting the nation's nuclear arms policies. On the other hand, there were moral principles of other kinds to be upheld. These included principles of free speech and freedom of association. To the small but growing number of peace activists, the massive stockpiling of nuclear weapons was also morally wrong. Competing ideas about what principles must be upheld and what dangers must be resisted result in uncertainties and differences of opinion about moral responsibility. What we might call *moral ambiguity* was even more apparent in the war on terror. Whereas totalitarianism was widely viewed by the American public as a top-down system of repression, Islamic radicalism was harder to sort out. It was in some respects like the totalitarianism against which the U.S. had mobilized in World War II. For instance, the opening lines of a 50-page report entitled *The National Security Strategy of the United States of America*, released by the White House in March 2006, reminded readers that the twentieth century had been a struggle against fascism and communism, and suggested that "a new totalitarian ideology now threatens." The new totalitarianism was like the old in promoting "intolerance, murder, terror, enslavement, and repression."[106] Osama bin Laden, al Qaeda, and Saddam Hussein represented this kind of totalitarianism, the report argued. It other respects, though, radical Islam presented greater ambiguity than totalitarianism had. It was a religion that people presumably espoused freely, rather than a repressive regime imposed on otherwise innocent citizens. Islam was, along with Judaism and Christianity, one of the world's three great, centuries-old monotheistic religions.

The war on terror thus involved American leaders and the broader public in an interesting process of religious interpretation. It became necessary to determine what kind of Islam was implicated in 9/11, how to distinguish among friends and foes, and how to think about America's relationship with them. The task was only partly about foreign policies toward such countries as Kuwait, Syria, Saudi Arabia, and Iran. It was much more about making sense of the peril now confronting America. Was it the kind that could be understood with reference to dictators, fanatical leaders, and other enemies of freedom, as some officials called them? Or was the American way of life being challenged by a religious system that espoused alternative values? If the former interpretation was correct, an appropriate response was to be resolute in waging war on the enemies of freedom. If the latter made sense, the responsibilities implied might range from thinking harder about excesses within America's own system of values to encouraging greater understanding of other traditions, especially Islam.

Efforts to distinguish among kinds of Islam were part of the public rhetoric about 9/11 almost from the start. The president's address to the nation on the evening of the tragedy characterized the attacks as evil, but mentioned nothing further about the attackers. The president's first public comment about Islam came on September 17 during a visit to the Islamic Center of Washington, D.C., aimed at quelling anti-Muslim sentiments. Distinguishing "the true faith of Islam" from the "face of terror," the president described Islam as a religion of peace that provides comfort to millions of American citizens and to many others around the world, whereas terrorists represent evil and war.[107] In his September 20 address to Congress, the president asserted that the teachings of Islam are "good and peaceful" while "those who commit evil in the name of Allah blaspheme the name of Allah." The terrorists, he said, were "traitors to their own faith" and were trying to "hijack Islam."[108] Meanwhile, commentators had been quick to give their own interpretations of how to think about Islam. On September 12, religion writer Laurie Goodstein gave it a human face, describing Muslims as innocent women and children who disapproved of the attacks and were themselves in danger of reprisals. Columnist Thomas L. Friedman, on assignment in Jerusalem, painted a rather different picture of America, on the one hand, as the "quintessential symbol of liberal, free-market, Western values" and, on the other hand, "super-empowered angry people" from "failing states" in the Muslim world who "resent America's influence over their lives." *Los Angeles Times* reporter Richard Boudreaux also wrote of a fundamental conflict between America and a popular movement of "radical Islam" in which the "capitalist West" is regarded as an "infection of immoral values," including the spreading of "alcohol, drugs and pornography." "There is no shortage of reasons in much of the world to dislike the United States," he observed, adding that "the nation can appear arrogant and selfishly fixated on its own politics and interests."[109]

Surveys suggested that the public was divided in how to think about Islam. In one national study, 40 percent said the term "peace loving" applies to the Muslim religion, just as President Bush had argued, but 47 percent thought Islam was fanatical, 40 percent said it was violent, and 56 percent said it was close-minded. Concern about Islam's growing influence in the United States was evident in the fact that 60 percent thought the U.S. government should collect information about Muslim religious groups in the United States, 38 percent thought the U.S. government should make it harder for Muslims to settle in the United States, and 23 percent said it should be "illegal for Muslim groups to meet in the U.S." The study found that negative views of Muslims were somewhat more common among Americans who feared another terrorist attack than among those who were less fearful. However, there was also a broader sense that Islam simply represented different values than those of the predominantly Judeo-Christian heritage in America. For instance, 64 percent said the beliefs of Muslims and Christians are "fairly different," while only 24 percent felt "Muslims and Christians pretty much believe in the same things." That being the case, people interviewed in the study said, Muslims might well have different views about democracy, gender, and child rearing, and they might be critical of the permissiveness and materialism of American culture.[110]

Most of the discussion about Islam that ensued in the mainstream media, however, drew a distinction similar to President Bush's. Islam, the Islamic world, or large segments of the world's Muslim population were not engaged in a fundamental critique of American values, commentators argued. Were that true, it might have been necessary, as Richard Boudreaux did, to acknowledge that all was not well with America. Instead, the attacks were said to have come from a small group of evildoers who could be set apart from the Islamic mainstream. Michael Kilian in the Washington bureau of the *Chicago Tribune* described the attackers as a "handful of fanatics." Israeli writer Amos Oz wrote of a "lethal fanatic tide" driven by "Muslim fundamentalism." Americans, he counseled, should avoid drawing a line between themselves and Muslims, and focus instead on the "evil" of "hatred and fanaticism." Other observers separated the attacks from broader characterizations of Islam by arguing that the attackers were not true Muslims. For instance, profiles hastily pieced together from intelligence information suggested that the hijackers drank alcohol and played video games. Other reports noted that Osama bin Laden frequented nightclubs, drank heavily, and engaged in drunken brawls.[111]

However the line was drawn, it described a contest between a virtuous, progressive, civilized America and a dark network of benighted evildoers that had little in common with the rest of the Muslim world. "This is good versus evil," President Bush said at a meeting on September 25, 2001. "These are evildoers. They have no justification for their actions. There's no religious justification, there's no political justification. The only motivation is evil." Writer E. L. Doctorow said in a radio interview that the attack had been against the "democratic heart of the post-Enlightenment world" by "ancient storytellers" and their "fundamentalistic fanatic interpreters." A reporter for the *New York Times* wrote that "Islamic terror groups have their own ideology, rooted in a deeply conservative reading—and Islamic moderates say, a distortion—of the Koran, Islam's holy book." Not only was this militant interpretation a distortion, it was also at odds with what this reporter regarded as a broader fascination with things American throughout the Muslim world. From "visa seekers, desperate for their chance at the American dream," to "an unquenchable appetite for Marlboro cigarettes and Levi's jeans," the dominant view among Muslims was of an America "as a place where everyman can pursue his dreams." Thomas L. Friedman drew a similar distinction, arguing that the terrorists held a "medieval" view of the world and "pray to a God of Hate," whereas the civilized world is characterized by "Muslims, Christians, Hindus, Buddhists and Jews with a modern and progressive outlook."[112]

This way of dividing the world into good and evil was clearly reminiscent of thinking during the Cold War, observers suggested. "Today we are the product or children of the Cold War," wrote defense analysts Nadine Gurr and Benjamin Cole shortly before 9/11. "We made ourselves absolutely self-righteous . . . the repository of all things good, of all civilized values, whilst the Soviet Union became the place of absolute evil." The temptation now was to conceive of radical Islamists in the same way. "The cold war is back," *Newsweek* essayist Fareed Zakaria wrote more approvingly after 9/11. It would be a "long twilight struggle," like that against communism. And, just as the first task of the earlier war was to "discredit communism," the "task now is to make sure that radical Islam is not seen as an attractive option." In a more critical vein, *Washington Post* columnist Donna Britt wrote that 9/11 had given Americans, long accustomed to "simmering anxieties and muted dreads," an "enemy worth wrapping our terror around." But, she warned, "those who would label others as monsters risk becoming monsters themselves." There was also a twist that had served as a minor theme in Cold War rhetoric. This was the view that reining in fanatics lay primarily with America's more moderate enemies, not with America itself. In similar fashion to arguments about Moscow restraining Castro, Tito, or Ho Chi Minh, the new rhetoric held moderate Muslims responsible for dampening the fanaticism of their radical brethren. "Mainstream Muslim clergy need to step up in their mosques and in public," columnist William Safire argued, "to give the lie to the fanatics' perversion of their faith." Somehow, he urged, local communications networks among clergy and their followers could stem the tide.[113]

Of course the rhetoric about Islam did not appear ex nihilo. There was the long historic legacy of what comparative literature scholar Edward W. Said had termed orientalism in the West, which ranged from viewing Muhammad as a false teacher to being fascinated with tales of exotic sheiks and harems.[114] For more than two decades since the revolution in Iran, the overused phrase Islamic fundamentalism had been used by journalists and academics to suggest that fanaticism and zealotry were rife within the Muslim world. In a 1993 *New York Times* essay, Said observed that "phrases like 'Mohammed's armies' or the 'Islamic threat' suggest an emanation from out of the desert into otherwise faceless societies," adding that "it is as if a tribe of aliens had suddenly appeared over the horizon and invaded a placid village."[115] In a 1993 *Foreign Affairs* article and subsequent book, political scientist Samuel P. Huntington argued that Islam and the West would increasingly be engaged in a "clash of civilizations." This clash, rooted in language, religion, and ethnic customs, would dominate international relations, Huntington predicted, as pervasively as the Cold War had during the preceding half century. It would not negate the continuing importance of Indic and Asian civilizations, but it would be of special significance to the United States because of Christianity's long history of conflict with Islam and because of increasing economic and military tensions. Huntington acknowledged the significance of ethnic and political differences within Islam, but emphasized its linguistic and religious unity, its demographic and economic resources, and its capacity to mobilize against Western exploitation.[116]

After 9/11, Huntington's image of competing value systems was mentioned frequently, but usually to argue that his diagnosis was wrong. Writers did so, it appears, for the well-intentioned purpose of preventing the vilification of Muslim terrorists from broadening into negative characterizations of Islam. The enemy was a more specific variant or even a perversion of Islam, rather than an entire culture. "This is not a clash of civilizations," New York mayor Rudolph Giuliani told the United Nations General Assembly a few weeks after 9/11. "It's a conflict between murderers and humanity."[117] *Los Angeles Times* columnist Ronald Brownstein wrote that it was tempting to think of America now engaged in a clash of civilizations, but that the struggle was really against "fanatical terrorism" more "like the Cold War—an amorphous, ambiguous, often frustrating conflict."[118] Historian Arthur Schlesinger Jr. emerged from retirement to warn that America should make every effort to avoid engaging in a civilizational war with Islam, thus proving Huntington wrong.[119]

Yet it was difficult to maintain the view that America was somehow waging war on evil without implying that America was necessarily on the side of good. To speak of a clash of civilizations in a less tension-fraught climate might have suggested that two different but equally valid systems of moral obligation were at odds with one another. Had that been the case, Americans might have asked themselves what they could learn from Islam or in what ways they were failing to live up to their own values. The difficulty increased, moreover, as the definition of evil expanded. Seeking the evildoers who had murdered innocent civilians on 9/11 was one thing. That could be done by a people who were otherwise flawed and yet committed to fundamental human principles of justice. As the rhetoric enlarged into a war, not on terrorists but on terror, and no longer against hijackers but on the enemies of freedom, it became much harder for officials to state that America was anything but good and decent, strong, right, and filled with resolve. The struggle was not between an America that might have its differences of opinion with some other system of moral obligation. The great divide was between evil and good, and thus between the purveyors of darkness and a people of light.

Whether the tragedy had been caused by a few extremists or represented some larger evil in the world, there was nevertheless a sense at least initially that it held some deeper meaning that would require time and effort to comprehend. On a national scale, 9/11 was like the accidental death of a loved one that causes family members to ask if there is some lesson to be learned, some insight to be gained, or some new responsibility to shoulder. The very possibility of living a better life makes the grief more endurable. It is at this more personal level and in their more private moments that people contemplate anew what it means to live responsibly. When Americans told themselves in the first hours after 9/11 that the world had changed, they meant partly that they intended it to change. The tragedy would harden their resolve. They would learn from it, rise phoenixlike from the ashes of their collective despair as better persons with clearer insight and a stronger commitment to high values. Their concerns prior to the attacks, they confessed, had been trivial and trite or selfish and materialistic. They would henceforth be more patriotic, more civic-minded, and would encourage their friends, their coworkers, and their children to be the same. A man who had stood on the Key Bridge in

Washington watching smoke rise from the Pentagon said, "I thought about our civic responsibility to teach all our children that bravery, courage and strength . . . has made our way of life in the United States possible." On the Sunday after 9/11, a Baptist pastor encouraged his flock to "become better people, more loving people, caring people, not only for the victims and the victims' families but also those who are impoverished in our nations, caught in the prisons of injustice and inequity." At a Zen monastery in New York a woman prayed, "In the dark night, silence speaks, 'I will die only when love dies.'" A woman in Great Falls, Virginia, wrote, "I know we will all come out of this as changed people. Hopefully, we will be better from this and learn that all of our petty differences between races, nationalities, religion, etc. do not outweigh the importance of life."[120]

The harder question was whether ordinary Americans should live in some other way that would ease the tensions from which terrorism had been birthed. Fundamentalist Jerry Falwell said the blame should be laid at the feet of secular humanists and homosexuals, but his pious finger-pointing evoked well-deserved ridicule from public officials and fellow clergy alike.[121] The question of how Americans might resolve to do better was posed more compellingly in quieter ways. It was the distraught citizen, writing a letter to the editor as a private person, or the occasional artist, rather than the mainstream media or public officials, who could suggest the need to reflect about these larger meanings. The attacks, poet Wayne Visser wrote, required Americans to "venture beyond the fortress / of our comfortable self-indulgence" and to "dig deeper than the shallow well / of our cultural arrogance."[122] A letter to the Washington Post expressed a similar view. "Our policies of political and military intervention from the Balkans to the Middle East to Africa and beyond have exposed civilians in these societies to destruction that bears unfortunate similarity to what we ourselves now witness," the woman wrote. "Blame ourselves for the horrifying and evil acts of September 11? Absolutely not. Seek to understand what may have prompted them? Yes, absolutely. To question ourselves, bravely, in the most trying of circumstances, is our surest road to security."[123]

MORE CIVILIANS DIED ON AMERICAN SOIL ON 9/11 than from nuclear weapons during the entire Cold War. That fact was significant. It meant that the cultural patterns that had become so familiar during the Cold War needed to change. Most notably, the fear that had supposedly been so long repressed could now be released. The unthinkable had happened, not in the way that it had been anticipated, but indeed in a way that had not been conceived of. In less than a morning, nearly three thousand people had perished. Fear could finally be expressed in grief. The nation learned, as Anne Taylor Fleming put it, "that it is fragile in ways we had never imagined, and we with it."[124] In that realization, Americans also resolved that they would need to be strong—perhaps to foolish extremes, not as a denial of fear but as a way of overcoming it.

Naturally, there was more to it than that. The earlier obsession with fear and denial was not repeated because the clinical frameworks for interpreting emotions had changed. Fear had been replaced by anxiety and extreme phobias by post-traumatic stress disorder (or syndrome). Anxiety could be treated with new medications, such as Zoloft, Paxil, and Prozac. PTSD was a more plausible concept after 9/11 than it would have been during the Cold War, since an actual trauma, a tragedy, had occurred. However, PTSD was also an example of cultural institutions providing a framework in which to think about 9/11. Although stressful reactions to traumatic events had certainly been present much earlier, PTSD as such was first studied among Vietnam veterans and appeared as a diagnosis in the American Psychiatric Association's *Diagnostic and Statistical Manual of Mental Disorders (DSM-III)* only in 1980. Through the Department of Veterans Affairs, a National Center for PTSD was created in 1989 to improve the well-being of veterans by engaging in research and education about post-traumatic stress. Subsequent efforts focused largely on clinical studies of veterans and on assessment and pharmacological treatment techniques.[125] In this respect, the history of PTSD was much like that of fear-repression and denial in that both dealt initially with victims, survivors, and combatants of war. As in the earlier era, the diagnosis was then extended to the general population. By the mid 1990s, researchers using survey techniques claimed that as many as 5 percent of American men and 10 percent of American women were suffering from PTSD.[126] In addition, hundreds of scientists and social scientists were conducting PTSD studies through government and foundation grants using such diverse techniques as questionnaires, clinical evaluations, and brain imaging, and reporting results for doctors, nurses, psychiatrists, emergency management personnel, and social workers. In all, the government had spent approximately $153 million sponsoring more than 400 peer-reviewed research projects, trained more than 5,300 mental health practitioners, and produced nearly 30,000 publications.[127] Not surprisingly, the response to 9/11 focused on PTSD.

Unlike the 1950s, when fear and denial dominated discussions of the public's response to peril, the emotional response to 9/11 was thus described in terms of trauma and stress. Reports varied but generally showed that people living closer to the attacks experienced stress more often than those who lived farther away, and sometimes claimed to estimate the incidence of trauma with startling accuracy. For instance, in one report about New York City, exactly 11.2 percent of the population were determined to be afflicted with PTSD (although another report fixed the number at 8.8 percent), while in Washington, D.C., the rate was 2.7 percent. In other metropolitan areas, 3.6 percent of the public was diagnosed with PTSD, as was 4.0 percent in the rest of the country.[128] Despite their proximity to the Pentagon attack, Washington residents were thus apparently relatively less distressed than people in other cities. And, compared to the rates of PTSD suggested in research a few years earlier, the nation at large seemed to have experienced a decline in PTSD. The researchers speculated that as many as 80 percent of those with acute PTSD from having witnessed the World Trade Center attack firsthand would likely continue to experience emotional distress, but argued that people having become upset from watching the event on television would not experience any long-term consequences. Hardly any of the research focused on fear. However, it was evident from the results that many Americans were troubled with such symptoms as feeling irritable or angry, insomnia, hypervigilance, and lack of concentration. One report, for instance, characterized 44 percent of the adult population as experiencing "one or more substantial symptoms" of emotional distress.[129] It was also apparent from the numerous polls conducted by media organizations that worries about terrorism and concerns about personal safety typified many Americans.

Indeed, evidence collected long after 9/11 showed clearly that a large proportion of the public remained concerned. In late August 2006, as the nation prepared for the fifth anniversary of the attacks, CBS News and the *New York Times* conducted polls and interviews in New York City and nationally. A majority of those polled—57 percent in New York and 59 percent in the national survey—thought it "very" or "somewhat" likely that "there will be another terrorist attack on the United States within the next few months." Only 22 percent nationally said they were "very concerned about a terrorist attack" in the area where they lived, but in New York this proportion rose to 69 percent. Nationally, 46 percent said they personally felt uneasy or in danger; in New York 63 percent felt this way. "Any day, our life could be turned upside down or destroyed by a terrorist attack," said a woman in Houston. "Every time I step onto a subway car or airplane, I'm thinking of terrorists," a Manhattan resident confessed. "This is virtually every day." Most of the public had not become obsessed with thinking about terrorism all the time, but to say that people were "in denial" would have been seriously inaccurate. Forty-four percent nationally said they still thought about September 11 every week; in New York, 46 percent did.[130] The result of thinking about 9/11, people said, was neither to be consumed with anxiety nor to lapse wearily into resignation. One man articulated the prevailing sentiment especially well: "I am not paralyzed by fear or sadness," he said, "just aware of what was lost 5 years ago and the feelings forever embedded in me."[131]

The most common response was to think or behave deliberately, as if to make a statement in the face of an ever-present but invisible threat. A quarter of the public said they had made decisions that dramatically altered their pattern of living.[132] "I do everything differently," one woman remarked, noting that she avoids crowds and elevators, does not travel in bridges or tunnels, and works mostly from home. Another woman said she "walked away" from her job in Manhattan shortly after 9/11 and took a part-time job in the suburbs where she could give priority to keeping her children safe. One man said his interest in daily news had become much sharper. Another said he had quit smoking. Many reacted against the view that the world had changed or that they should live differently. "Why do anything differently?" a combat veteran asked. "Let's just get on with life." Several said they resisted doing things differently because that would make it seem that the terrorists had won or because they disagreed with government policies. For many others, the effect of living in a post-9/11 world was less a change or lack of change in lifestyle than a renewed appreciation of basic principles and a commitment to upholding these values. Recognizing that civil liberties are fragile, one man said he had a stronger resolve to protect those liberties, especially in view of prejudice toward Muslims and immigrants. "I'm more respectful of human life," a woman said, adding that "9/11 lives in all of us, perhaps not so literally, but everyone has a tragic moment." Having courage and being able to "move on," she said, was key. A teacher at a Quaker school said his personal values, especially peace, simplicity, and integrity, had deepened. A nurse who cared for people burned on 9/11 said he had redoubled his efforts to be compassionate. "I saw for a time the pure selflessness and humanity that the terror evoked," he said. "I know it exists and I still seek it out."[133]

Whether they felt changed, strengthened, or merely vulnerable, Americans were largely agreed on one thing: the world was less safe than they would like it to be. September 11 had wakened them to the fact that terrorism could strike at home as well as abroad and could happen on any sunny day or rainy night when they were least expecting it. Although the threat of a nuclear holocaust now seemed to have receded into the background, it was replaced by a new awareness that life was fragile for reasons equally difficult to comprehend or control. There was no easy escape or remedy. The war on terrorism would be a long one—probably a war that would never be won. Individual Americans vowed that they would make an effort to do better or at least to live on unperturbed. It was far less certain that America as a nation could find the will to exercise such resolve.

The difficulty of sustaining resolve was not so much a matter of collective will as of the agenda-setting power of government. The attacks on 9/11 caught government officials off guard. Even though an attack had been predicted and various contingency plans were in place, the timing and location made it impossible to shape the news as had been the case on August 6, 1945. There was no way to filter interpretations though the stories of journalists hand picked by the War Department. People wrote and reflected about what they had witnessed firsthand. Yet the power of Washington to shape how the public responded was remarkable. From the first hours, officials told the public that America was at war. Meetings at the White House with national security advisors focused on what was known about al Qaeda in Afghanistan, how quickly an attack on Afghanistan could be mounted, and whether Iraq should also be punished. There was almost complete silence about why the attacks on New York and Washington had not been prevented. Robert

S. Mueller III, the newly appointed director of the FBI, to which blame for lack of domestic intelligence could most easily be laid, had little to say.[134] The president, who had done nothing to focus on homeland security, had no reason to pursue the topic, either. War served not only as retaliation but as a way of filling the silence.

The resolve that might have emerged from sustained reflection about the meaning of 9/11 was soon diverted. People wondered privately what it must be like to know that one's spouse or sibling had gone off for a routine day at the office and died in a raging inferno. The unspoken fear was partly that another terrorist strike might happen—as polls showed—but also that a person might die unexpectedly from some other accident or tragedy. It was a concern, too, that the nation had not effectively grieved or commemorated its loss or learned enough from it. The failure to keep talking about these important issues could hardly be understood as some form of individual psychological denial. It was much more straightforwardly the fact that all the public discussion about terrorism now focused on something else. The way to think about terrorism was to talk about war, for a short while in Afghanistan and then increasingly in Iraq. The *New York Times* carried three times as many stories about Iraq in 2002 as it had in 2001, and that number tripled again in 2003. Meanwhile, stories about the World Trade Center fell by 25 percent in 2002 and by 50 percent in 2003.[135] Had it not been for the heated debates within the city itself about how to build an appropriate memorial and replacement structure, stories about the twin towers would have been even fewer. After a few highly publicized meetings in Washington, the families of 9/11 victims faded from view, and only their quiet persistence succeeded in persuading the administration to authorize the investigation by the National Commission on Terrorist Attacks Upon the United States that released its *9/11 Commission Report* in 2004. Ironically, the very fact that the Iraq war became as controversial and extended as it did helped to divert public attention from other aspects of the 9/11 tragedy.

If denial is better understood as a social or even political act than as a psychological reaction, the role of fiction in exposing denial also needs to be rethought. It is not that writers and artists somehow overcome their own repression, although that may be true, but that they find a venue in which to construct alternative interpretations. Comedy is one such venue. It occupies a demarcated space in the cultural landscape, set apart by such identifiers as the cartoon or humor section of newspapers, the opening monologue on late night television programs, programs on a comedy channel, and performances in clubs and concert halls by stand-up comedians. Comedy with a political edge typically uses satire to suggest the irony, absurdity, or banality of official statements by exaggerating them, altering the context in which they occur, or substituting words with double meanings. It thus becomes possible to make pointed critical observations, while bracketing these observations with remarks, such as "I'm only kidding" or with laughter. Comedic criticism of administration policies became an important part of the cultural response to 9/11 and the war on terror. Comedy Central's *Daily Show with Jon Stewart* and HBO's *Real Time with Bill Maher* were among the most popular of these venues for comedic criticism. Jay Leno's *Tonight Show* and Conan O'Brien's *Late Night* monologues typically included political satire, as did special comedy performances by Whoopi Goldberg and George Carlin and "Connie Rice" appearances on National Public Radio's *Tavis Smiley Show*.

The arts were the other main venue for expressing nonofficial interpretations of 9/11 and the war on terror. Box office film hits provided entertainment renditions of terrorist plots, just as they did of nuclear conflagration during the Cold War. Two of the most successful were *Sum of All Fears* (2002), which grossed more than $118 million, and *Collateral Damage* (2002), with gross revenue of $40 million. Neither film dealt directly with 9/11 or offered veiled criticisms of the response. Two releases in 2006—*United 93* and *World Trade Center*, respectively earning $31 million and $70 million—emphasized heroism during and after the tragedy.[136] A widely publicized television miniseries, "The Path to 9/11," which aired on ABC in September 2006, blamed the Clinton administration for inaction leading to the attacks on New York and Washington, but was in turn criticized by reviewers and officials associated with that administration.[137] Director Michael Moore's 2004 film *Fahrenheit 9/11* was critical of the Bush administration's promotion of war in Afghanistan and Iraq, and was similarly criticized by defenders of the administration. On a smaller scale, documentary filmmakers, writers, and other artists sought to provide factual information and critical interpretations they felt were being ignored or misrepresented by the mainstream media. One example was a group of artists and political activists on the West Coast calling themselves Weapons of Mass DistrACTION that performed on campuses and in churches on such topics as fearmongering and the relationship between oil and the war in Iraq. Another example was a network calling itself Loose Change that produced downloadable films about what it regarded as a government cover-up of events leading to the 9/11 attacks.

Yet it is testimony to the power of government to set the agenda for interpreting major crises that even artistic and humorous responses focused so often on criticisms of particular decisions, public statements, and news coverage, rather than pointing to the silences about why the nation moved so quickly to war or how preparedness and responsibility could have been improved. Criticism of stories already told is quite different from changing the story altogether. The war on terror picked up the story of a nation under siege, a narrative that had been learned so well over the decades of nuclear arms race and confrontation that it seemed only natural to engage once again in a struggle of good and evil. There was reason to fear, enough reason to keep slightly on edge, worrying, looking to the nation's leaders for guidance and strength. It was a war that would last a long time, as President Bush said in a 2006 speech on national security. It would be "a long struggle, similar to what our country faced in the early years of the Cold War."[138]

SIX

PANICS AND PANDEMICS

PANIC, WROTE FREUD, IS A COLLECTIVE FEAR so gigantic that it bears almost no relation to an actual threat. Ordinary bonds of civility that maintain social order break down. Contagion and hysteria predominate. Individuals take flight and otherwise seek to protect themselves from the imminent danger they perceive. Someone yells "fire!" and theatergoers trample each other in a stampede to the exit. An army hears that its leader has been killed and soldiers scatter in disarray. Examples can be found throughout history. On a cold December afternoon in 1903, the Iroquois Theater in Chicago caught fire and within eight minutes more than five hundred people died trying to flee. An eyewitness wrote, "The heel prints on the dead faces mutely testified to the cruel fact that human animals stricken by terror are as mad and ruthless as stampeding cattle."[1]

Panics of a different sort are common to the banking industry. The bank crisis of 1857 was typical. On August 24, the Ohio Life and Trust Company, a large bank with substantial holdings in western land and railroad securities, collapsed over uncertainties about whether Kansas and Nebraska would become slave states. The stock market declined and Eastern banks tightened credit. Over the next month, deposits in New York City banks fell by 12 percent. On September 26, banks in Philadelphia and Chicago suspended payments. Heavy runs on New York banks ensued. Newspapers reported long lines on October 13 as people waited the whole day to withdraw funds. On October 14, banks throughout the city suspended payments and did not resume until the middle of December. Later studies showed that women were more likely than men to close accounts and that married people with children were somewhat more likely than other individuals to do so. Those most vulnerable to loss—domestics, servants, washerwomen, drivers, porters, factory workers, seamstresses—were the most likely to close their accounts, even if it meant losing some of their meager savings. Panics on this scale or larger occurred again in 1861, 1873, 1884, 1890, 1893, 1896, 1907, and 1914. Between 1929 and 1932, thousands of banks failed again.[2]

One of the most celebrated panics occurred in October 1938 in conjunction with the radio dramatization of H. G. Wells's science fiction novel *War of the Worlds*. It was the night before Halloween, and as at least a million Americans listened, many in New York and New Jersey (although not as many as initial reports suggested) became convinced that Martians actually were landing in their communities. People phoned police, fled their homes, ran into the streets, and covered their faces with towels as protection against gas the invaders were expected to release. Residents of Grovers Mill, New Jersey, where the broadcast said the invasion was located, mistook a wooden water tower for the landing craft and riddled it with bullets. An investigation of the incident concluded that most people took the event in stride but that panic-stricken individuals were particularly susceptible to suggestion and had simply lost their critical faculties.[3]

After World War II, fears of widespread panic among a public frightened by imagined or real nuclear attacks were a recurring concern among civil defense planners. New York City's civil defense director, Herbert R. O'Brien, said in a widely publicized statement that moving people out of the city, "even with several hours' warning of approaching attack, is one that staggers the imagination of anyone who has tried to get out to the country even on an ordinary holiday weekend." The result, he said, would be "uncontrollable panic, with hundreds of thousands trapped on exposed bridges and in the under-river tunnels." A Civil Defense bulletin in 1955 echoed this sentiment, observing that it was widely assumed, correctly or incorrectly, that the use of atomic and thermonuclear bombs by an enemy nation would "strike terror into the hearts of Americans" and lead to "panic or mass hysteria" that would result in "devastating disorganization and paralysis."[4]

Yet the most notable aspect of large-scale panics during the six decades after World War II was their absence. True, people phoned police stations to see if pitted windshields were from radioactive fallout, scrambled to find their children when air raid sirens blew, and purchased duct tape in larger amounts than they would ever use. But when schools taught children to duck and cover and presidents encouraged people to build basement bomb shelters, this behavior was hardly surprising. The orderly lines at checkout counters of people stockpiling flashlight batteries and water could scarcely be called mass hysteria. Recurrent threats of nuclear meltdown led concerned citizens more often to sign petitions than to flee into the streets. Even the 9/11 tragedy evoked little evidence of outright panic. Occupants of the World Trade Center described a methodical evacuation down darkened flights of stairs. Those who ran for their lives through ash-covered streets fled real danger. As the day wore on, New Yorkers walked home, watched television, and expressed their fears by phoning friends.

Rare in reality, panic is nevertheless a recurrent theme in the popular mind. Ironically, the *New York Times* titled its editorial the morning of September 11, 2001, "The Politics of Panic," noting a "whiff of panic in the air" as the Bush administration discussed reviving a faltering economy. On other days, television viewers learn that villagers in some remote corner of the world panicked during an earthquake, or that smart investors were not panicking about a dip in stock prices. The word "panic" is used in all kinds of contexts, sometimes carefully and other times not: listeners might hear that everyone experiences panic on a daily basis as a result of lost keys, a missing wallet, turning onto a wrong street, forgetting a name, wearing an inappropriate party dress, or breaking a heel. Panic, it seems, hovers on the edges of sanity, waiting to push people into bizarre activity or just reminding them to slow down.

Academics who write about panic have acknowledged this ambiguity. "The term is vague, ill-defined, and commonly used to designate a wide variety of behaviors ranging from wild flight to paralysis, from the actions of a solitary individual to those of an entire nation," Ralph H. Turner and Lewis M. Killian observed in a classic text on collective behavior. Others have noted that almost any socially disorganizing or personally disrupting activity might qualify. The sell-off of stocks and bonds is often referred to as an investor panic. Increasingly, social scientists wrote about "moral panics," meaning only that groups periodically became concerned about child abductions, drunk driving, or pornography, while psychologists spoke of "panic attacks" to designate bouts of acute anxiety.[5]

Terminological ambiguity provides one of the best keys to understanding the place of panic in current thinking about peril. The panic that interested Freud and that broke out at the Iroquois Theater is spontaneous. It arises unbidden and unplanned from stark fear as people flee for their very lives or imagine that they must. That sort of panic is rare, but does occur as a collective phenomenon when people have reason to think that immediate action is necessary, as in the case of a run on banks, and happens to individuals when circumstances bring them to the brink of desperation. The more common kind of panic is the one that is largely produced by organizations or the media, as in the case of *War of the Worlds*, and by civil defense and risk assessment specialists. These panics are usually grounded in real concerns about possible dangers, and they sometimes are in fact accompanied by people taking extreme actions to protect themselves. But we miss their importance by focusing only on such behavior. It is rather the warnings themselves and the way they keep the public on edge that are the defining elements. Warnings about panic are modern morality tales. They tell us what rational people should do when faced with a possible crisis—how the responsible heads of institutions are making appropriate plans and why we can trust them to protect us from harm. The possibility of panic and what must be done to avoid it are core themes in contemporary discussions of peril. Freud's point was that panic can be judged objectively irrational because the response is out of proportion to the danger. But Freud was not entirely correct in that respect. Rationality is also a matter of cultural construction. Through stories of people who do panic, we learn by negative example what it means to be an extremist and how the behavior of extremists leads to chaos. Tales of panic distinguish paranoia from prudence. They express fear and at the same time channel it. When the crisis has passed, the process of interpretation continues, offering post hoc explanations of how it was averted or could have been worse.

Although the actual occurrence of panics is rare, discussions about the possibility of panics are thus rich with cultural significance. Hardly a year passes without some major threat arising that could potentially be the source of mass death, widespread panic, and ensuing chaos. One year it is the threat of a massive collapse of computers and electrical systems. Another year brings fear that millions will die from an unstoppable illness carried by pigs or birds or insects. Or fears of an economic meltdown followed by a contagion of joblessness and widespread poverty. As concern mounts, public officials caution against undue alarm but at the same time promote it by publicizing worst-case scenarios and recalling times of devastation in the past. It is difficult for reasonable people to ignore their warnings. The officials, after all, are trained experts—professionals paid to anticipate danger and guard against it. There is in fact danger, they say. "Better safe than sorry," the adage goes. At some level, it becomes impossible not to think about the impending peril.

THE YEAR 2000 PROBLEM, OR Y2K BUG as it came to be called, was a perfect occasion for discussions of panic, its possible consequences, preparations to avoid it, definitions of what action was and was not appropriate, and after-the-fact considerations of lessons learned. Nobody knows who exactly first thought of the problem, but sometime in the early 1990s computer programmers realized that two-digit dates would cause problems when the year 2000 rolled around and programs assumed the date was 1900. By 1995, a few scattered observers were imagining bizarre scenarios. A person who started a phone call before midnight on December 31, 1999, and finished it after midnight might receive a bill for a 100-year call. Someone 104 years old might receive a notice to attend kindergarten. Many of the examples were lighthearted. Others offered heavier predictions. Electrical grids might power down temporarily. Airplanes might not fly on schedule. If nothing else, the problem was ugly and expensive, as one programmer remarked. "There are time bombs out there in every facet of society," he said.[6]

At first, computer specialists worked quietly to check and rewrite programs, largely unnoticed by the mass media and general public. A brief article in an insurance journal in 1997, for instance, noted that Data Dimensions, a computer systems firm in Bellevue, Washington, had corrected the "millennium bug" for 400 to 500 companies in fifty-three countries over the past six years. The company was insuring itself against "errors and omissions." People with programming expertise agreed that the problems were serious, but cautioned against alarmist responses. Technology never worked perfectly, they counseled, and the public might experience some inconvenience, but corporations and the government were on track to have millennium-compliant systems ready in time and nobody should rush out to purchase new personal computers or invest in expensive software.[7]

A few months later, the story turned dark. "Some experts are warning of world-wide chaos and economic ruin just 18 months from now," declared a front-page *Wall Street Journal* article entitled "'Y2K' Is Scarier Than the Alarmists Think." What was scariest? Not that an estimated $50 billion would be spent by the time programmers finished. The worrisome part was that people fixing the problem were from "populations with a disproportionate number of disgruntled workers," meaning that the potential for vandalism was great. Besides that, hostile governments could use the occasion to infiltrate agents into the nation's infrastructure. Mayhem could ensue, as technicians planted "viruses, logic bombs or trapdoors" in delicate systems. Moreover, the problem would not end in 2000. Y2K was merely a hint of things to come. "Criminals, terrorists and hostile governments will find opportunities in the confusion." Dangerous people were "probably at work even as we speak."[8]

The *Wall Street Journal* was not alone. An anonymous Barclays Bank official told the *Times* of London that people should sell their homes, stockpile cash, and purchase gold in anticipation of a global economic collapse. A *Business Week* editorial predicted "panic in the year 2000." For companies and government agencies, the situation "could be a disaster," the essay said. This mind-boggling problem was symptomatic of government's typical slowness to respond. More should have been done earlier. Corporate executives whose lives were already dealing with overwhelming technological complexity were now having to face the prospect of "financial chaos" that would at a minimum reduce productivity growth and perhaps even tip the economy into a recession. The *Chicago Tribune* echoed the same grim prediction. Experts, it said, believed the economic outlook was pessimistic because of this "information-age gotcha."[9]

Not everyone agreed, but plenty of people had reason to heed warnings or to utter them. Bruce D. Berkowitz was one. Writer and consultant to the Center for Strategic and International Studies, a think tank specializing in reports about threats to national security, Berkowitz was the source of the *Wall Street Journal* article. Another was freelance writer Edward Yourdon. His book *Time Bomb 2000* sold 250,000 copies. Computer programmers, insurance companies, and lawyers also had a special stake in Y2K. One attorney was reported to have earned two million dollars defending software companies against class-action lawsuits. Journalists and news commentators vied with one another to get their stories placed on the front page or the evening news. The writing was both restrained and alarmist, focusing on technical details about bytes and digits and attributing the most extreme language to others—"insiders call it a computer holocaust"—but grabbing audiences' attention with colorful phrases like "gnashing of teeth," "fear and trembling," and "major league bad news."

Early warnings of impending doom also came from religious fundamentalists. One of the first was Gary North, a conservative Christian economist whose numerous books included such titles as *The Threat of Nuclear War*, *Twelve Deadly Negatrends*, and *Is the World Running Down?* In the 1980s, North argued that the world economy should return to the gold standard and predicted that AIDS would bring about the apocalypse. By 1997, North was predicting on radio talk shows that Y2K would be the end of the world. People who wanted to learn more could subscribe to his newsletter, "The Remnant Review," for $129. Those who did found scenarios that were highly specific and in many ways more frightening than just a prediction that the world would end. One described standing in a bank line because all of one's checks had bounced, despite a balance of a few thousand dollars on last month's statement. The computer has closed your account and the teller is powerless to reopen it. Because this has happened to everyone, "Western civilization will shut down." As if that were not enough, it would be impossible to dial 911 for emergency help, your retirement money would be gone, all gasoline station pumps would malfunction, and all railroad deliveries of grain and coal would stop. The bottom line: "A billion lives lost, if things go fairly well."[10]

For those who found North's predictions untenable, there were arguments almost as scary about the possible consequences of panic. The glitch inside computers would set off a chain reaction. Those concerns, coupled with fears aroused by biblical prophecies and widespread anxieties about technology and social change, would greatly increase the likelihood of mass hysteria. "If even a small proportion of the population starts to panic," a newsletter for homesteaders counseled, "the social and economic results could be catastrophic." The true difficulty was that people were no longer self-sufficient. Everyone was dependent on large organizations. If anything went wrong, nobody would be able to control the outcome. People would react as best they could, but their reactions would initiate a downward spiral. A few smart investors would sell their stocks, causing markets to fall until the economy collapsed. Nobody would get paid. Emergency shelters would shut down for lack of heat and water. The military would be unable to function. The specter of collapse showed that social organization was fragile and yet in many ways extraordinarily powerful. Its scope was almost inescapable. Only the hardiest could free themselves from its grasp. To do so required complete withdrawal from society: living "off the grid," away from any city, having one's own water and fuel supply, growing one's own food, and being skilled at making one's own tools.[11]

Although it became easy to criticize alarmists' warnings when the Y2K crisis turned out not to be the catastrophe foretold, the question at the time was determining what a reasonable response should be. Reason in such situations is always a matter of implicit mental negotiation. It depends on listening to authorities, but it also involves stories about Chicken Littles who are worrying too much, ostriches who are not worrying enough, and prudent people who are planning properly. For the leaders of major organizations, it made sense to err on the side of caution. In January 1998, President Clinton signed an executive order to create a Council on Year 2000 Conversion and asked for nearly $5 billion to pay for the task. In London, Prime Minister Tony Blair announced that his government would be hiring 20,000 additional programmers to work on the problem. The Federal Reserve banking system printed an extra $50 billion in case money became scarce. In the private sector similar precautions took shape. Intel purchased backup generators and worked out contracts with alternative suppliers of critical materials and services. Mutual funds giant Vanguard had more than a hundred workers assigned to the problem as early as mid-1998. IBM, Microsoft, and most of the major banking chains announced they would open round-the-clock call centers to handle problems that might arise. Humana, the Louisville-based healthcare insurance provider, tripled the number of pages in its disaster preparedness manual. A survey of the top one hundred businesses in Chicago showed that half were planning to spend more than $5 million apiece on Y2K preparation.[12] Oil companies collectively spent an estimated $2 billion upgrading pumps and credit card readers.

The more leaders talked about what they were doing to prevent Y2K problems, the more ordinary people began to worry. By August 1998, forty-five percent of the public told pollsters they had heard a lot about the "Year 2000 problem, the millennium glitch, the millennium bug, or the Y2K problem." Only a quarter said they had heard very little or nothing. Among those who had heard about the problem, 36 percent thought it was a serious problem. Eighteen percent thought there would be "widespread dislocation and possibly chaos, even a collapse of law and order at all levels of government." The poll itself went on to encourage respondents to accept the view that Y2K was a grave problem, telling them that experts said it would indeed be serious. With this additional information, 59 percent said they agreed that the problem was serious.[13] In December 1998, a Gallup poll disclosed that 79 percent of the public thought the Y2K problems would last for at least several weeks after January 1, 2000. Half thought it would last for several months or more. The extent of the public's concern was evident in responses to other questions. Sixteen percent planned to withdraw all their money from the bank, 17 percent said they were planning to purchase a generator or wood stove, 26 percent were going to stockpile food and water, and 65 percent were going to document their bank accounts in case records were lost.[14]

Everywhere, judging for news accounts, prudent people seemed to be planning for the worst. A welder in Iowa purchased a gas-powered generator, stocked up on food, and took extra cash out of his bank account. A family in Atlanta stored enough food to feed a dozen people for six months. A couple in Pittsburgh stored up enough firewood to last the winter and purchased a solar cooker in case there was no electricity. A woman in Berks County, Pennsylvania, bought fifteen gallons of kerosene and formed the Daniel Boone Y2K Preparedness Group to advise her neighbors how to plan. Others attended emergency preparedness meetings, stocked up on medical supplies, and set up crisis centers in church basements. Behavior that in other situations would have been considered unusual increasingly came to be described as normal, prudent, rational. These were not extremists, reporters declared. They were people who decided they would rather "be safe than sorry." They were simply following the Boy Scout motto: Be prepared. They were levelheaded citizens who knew things could get ugly. They realized full well that experts running the government and big companies made mistakes. "Better to prepare and have nothing come of the millennium bug than go unprepared and have disaster strike."[15]

In view of these rising concerns, it fell to public officials and corporate leaders not only to ensure that computers worked but also to manage public opinion. The message shifted from urging cautious preparation to warning against panic. "Calming nervous citizens," was how John Koskinen, chair of the President's Commission on Year 2000 Conversion, put it. The danger was that the public would overreact. People would hoard food and gasoline and cash out their bank accounts. Worse, houses would burn down as residents experimented with wood burning stoves and bystanders would be killed by unseasoned owners of handguns.[16] Buzz Weiss, the spokesperson for Georgia's Emergency Management Agency, assured residents that "the lights are going to be on, the heat is going to be on, and communications will be up."[17] When NBC planned a television thriller featuring scary Y2K scenarios, utility company executives asked that it be toned down or not shown at all.

As the new millennium approached, the number of Americans who took precautions was considerably smaller than the number who thought they would a year earlier. Fewer than 1 percent purchased a generator, 2 percent took money out of the bank, and 4 percent bought a flashlight. The most common response— among 24 percent of the public—was to stock water or food. Sixty-one percent did nothing.[18] It would be easy to go to "one of those big wholesale chains" and buy "a couple of shopping carts full of canned chili," a woman in New York explained. But what if it was not enough? Or what if no one wanted to eat $75 worth of canned chili?[19]

If few ordinary people did anything unusual to hedge against disaster, organizations did. MIT was as well prepared as any university in the country. Its computer scientists knew the problems that could arise and some of its programmers had been consulting with companies for the past several years about the technicalities involved. Administrators learned in September that the university had a Y2K team in place to help anyone who still needed help updating their computers. Easy-to-follow instructions were downloadable on the university's web site. Critical supplies even as minor as toner cartridges and paper should be ordered well in advance in case of delays. More than five hundred of the university's vendors were required to provide information assuring that their materials were Y2K-compliant and more than 6,300 items on campus with embedded processors—from elevator controls to lab equipment—were checked. As the New Year's weekend approached, faculty and students were advised to avoid engaging in any research that might involve hazardous experiments. Backup copies of computer files should be made. Batteries should be purchased. If anyone was planning to travel, they should check with airports and the State Department. In case the worst happened, the university had purchased emergency power generators, spare bedding, and stockpiles of food and water.[20]

MIT's actions were not unusual. Officials at Princeton University announced in late November that the university would be closed from 1:00 P.M. on December 31 to 1:00 P.M. on January 2. Only essential personnel were allowed on campus during this 48-hour period. All nonessential devices, including desktop computers, departmental servers, fax machines, and copiers, were to be shut down to avoid power consumption and possibilities of damage from power surges. In New York City, 114 emergency work stations that formed the mayor's Office of Emergency Management on the twenty-third floor of the World Trade Center were fully staffed through the weekend. More than $750,000 worth of spare parts were on hand at the city's computer center in Brooklyn. The corporate world was more secretive about what exactly it had done, but one survey of large corporations concluded that at least a quarter of the two million information technology workers they employed had devoted at least some of their time to Y2K planning and repairs. California Edison reported spending $70 million retooling its computers. Merrill Lynch spent $520 million. Overall, the tab was approximately $250 billion in the United States—as much as $600 billion worldwide.[21]

Y2K was by far more about organizations than about individuals. This was in no small measure because organizations depended so heavily on computers and stood to lose if the technology failed. Nevertheless, the episode revealed perhaps even more clearly than the Atomic Energy Commission after World War II or the invasion of Afghanistan after 9/11 that the response to peril is only in minor degree about the thoughts and feelings of individuals. Peril is defined by organizations that have the public's blessing to "do something." And they respond in ways that reflect what their leaders feel must be done in order to maintain the public's confidence, as well as serve their own interests.

Because so much was spent and so little happened, a great deal of cultural work occurred after the turn of the millennium as interpreters competed to say what it had all meant.[22] On the lighter side, the stock of groups that poked fun at the whole episode went up. Few at Princeton talked of having been worried, while many recalled the football halftime spoof suggesting that students purchase a thousand-year supply of clean water, a wall calendar for 1900, and some Y2K-Y Jelly. Others who claimed to have been skeptical from the start enjoyed tracking down Y2K stories and labeling them as urban legends. One was a story of a supermarket chain in the Midwest that had shut down because a credit card reader malfunctioned—impossible, a cashier declared, looking back. Another was an urban legend of large quantities of meat having to be destroyed because a computerized inventory system said the meat had expired. The story turned out to be about cans of corned beef that were not in fact destroyed.

More serious discussion focused on whether the huge expenditures had been unnecessary or whether they were the reason why catastrophe had been averted. The answer hinged partly on demonstrating that at least a few problems—ones that apparently could have been worse—actually did happen. Americans "would have felt better," tech reporter Steven Levy wrote in *Newsweek*, "if at least one crummy power facility had gone down."[23] It was especially embarrassing that in places like Italy, Austria, and Venezuela—countries that spent hardly anything on Y2K compliance—no major problems had occurred. So writers searched and came up with evidence that things had indeed gone wrong. Texaco reported heading off a problem with computers being unable to monitor its output from offshore drilling rigs.[24] A man in upstate New York reported receiving a $91,000 bill for a video the computer deemed a hundred years overdue. A frozen security system left doors unlocked at a building in Omaha. "Common sense suggests that inaction was not an option for government and business leaders," the *New York Times* editorialized, "once the experts determined the existence of a threat to power grids, defense systems, air transport, financial communications and other vital linkages."[25] And skeptics remained unconvinced. "Glitches, patches, crashes—these are as inherent to the process of creating an intelligent electronic system as is the beauty of an elegant algorithm," one programmer wrote.[26] The fact that problems occurred in connection with Y2K, she felt, did not mean that anything particularly extraordinary had taken place. As if to prove the point, the National Security Agency reported on January 30 that its computers that handled highly sensitive intelligence information had malfunctioned for the past 72 hours. There was "no evidence of a Y2K problem," the report stated.[27]

The broader question was whether businesses and government had acted rationally. "There hasn't been so much disaster preparedness since the bomb shelter era," *New York Times* columnist Gail Collins wrote. "Now a lot of people are sitting around with two years' supply of peanut butter on hand."[28] It was one thing to observe that survivalists were left with extra supplies on hand, quite another to wonder if $600 billion had been wasted. Perhaps this was a new kind of panic, one in which private individuals largely behaved themselves while corporate and government leaders acted foolishly. Two lines of defense emerged. The first, advanced mostly by experts directly involved in Y2K compliance work, argued that it was too soon to tell. Like prophets of doom who acknowledge the world did not end as predicted, these experts claimed that many technical problems were just waiting to appear. "There is a good chance the world's going to have a digital hangover for three to six months," a computer magazine publisher said. Gartner Group officials, whose business had been almost completely concerned with Y2K, told *Business Week* that "some 90 percent of Y2K glitches won't show up for months." Problems might not appear because programs had not yet been used. Others might emerge at the end of January, on leap year, or not until 2001. Apparently the idea was that if some did appear, their presence would demonstrate that money had in fact been needed to prevent others from occurring. The second and more common argument was that the money had not only fixed Y2K problems but had also resulted in significant technological improvements. In the absence of concrete information about any specific expenditures, anecdotes served this purpose. For instance, Marriott reported that Y2K fixes had made it possible to put more Internet connections in hotel rooms. DaimlerChrysler plants were now linked into a single network. Washington Gas & Light could schedule customer service calls more precisely.[29] "The world in general," an insurance industry newsletter declared, "is a more sophisticated, efficient and productive place as a result of Y2K remediation."[30]

In the end, the public remained divided about Y2K. A Fox News poll taken in mid-January 2000 showed that 37 percent thought the Y2K bug had been a "major threat that was avoided by spending millions of dollars in preparation," while 54 percent regarded it as a "minor threat that was exaggerated causing millions of dollars to be wasted."[31] By March, media interest in the topic all but disappeared, but surfaced again briefly as the year closed and people recalled what had happened the year before. One lesson seemed to evoke general agreement: there were nutty ways to deal with impending crises and there were reasonable ways. The nutty response was characterized by fundamentalists and survivalists who went to extremes to protect themselves. The reasonable response involved conforming to social norms—being cautious but not going overboard. Explicitly, the message was, yes, problems occur and if people stay calm and avoid panicking, these problems can be fixed. It pays to worry some; it does not pay to become caught up in fear. There was also an implicit message: how the problem is defined and what the appropriate level of fear should be is largely beyond any ordinary person's control. Power resides in large organizations. It will be their response, their ability to mobilize the right measures of technical expertise, that matter.

IT WAS PROBABLY NOT SURPRISING that the two most frequently used designations for the Year 2000 Problem were "millennium bug" and "Y2K bug" and that malicious computer programs came to be known as viruses. Bugs and viruses were among the oldest and deadliest killers of humankind. In 430 BC a plague that recent epidemiologists believe may have been a hemorrhagic fever similar to the Ebola virus originated in Ethiopia and spread to Egypt and then to Athens where it killed tens of thousands over the next four years. Thucydides, who suffered from the plague, described it vividly in the *History of the Peloponnesian War*. In early stages of the disease, people suffered headaches, rash, and fever; in later stages, stomach cramps, diarrhea, severe vomiting, and coughing blood. Chaos resulted, he observed, as people became indifferent to the laws and turned to self-indulgence. Lucretius later based his arguments about human vulnerability and the futility of religion on Thucydides' account.[32]

In 550 AD the Byzantine historian Procopius described what came to be known as the Justinianic plague. Starting in 541, a disease that historians now regard as bubonic plague spread throughout northern Africa and Central Asia along trade routes and among soldiers, reaching Constantinople within a year and extending into Italy and Western Europe. Drawing parallels between his own account and Thucydides' experience, Procopius suggested that as many as 10,000 people died each day over a four-month period. Though the number was undoubtedly exaggerated, historians agree that Procopius' description and those of several contemporaries provided images capable of instilling dread among later writers whenever plague was rumored. Victims' bodies were covered with black blisters. Many sufferers developed gangrene, became mad, experienced hallucinations, and died vomiting blood. Those who survived often had withered thighs and tongues. In Constantinople, grave sites quickly filled beyond capacity, huge burial pits were dug, and piles of corpses rotted in the streets, causing a stench that pervaded the entire city.[33]

Less is known about subsequent outbreaks of plague, but it is assumed that they occurred intermittently during the seventh and eighth centuries. Bede, the famous monk and chronicler of the British Isles (widely known as the Venerable Bede), wrote of an onset of pestilence in 664. A second outbreak occurred from 684 to 687, and sporadic attacks continued until the 760s.[34] The famous Black Death that infected England in 1348 killed one-third of its population, with many dying from what would now be called pneumonia as well as from bubonic plague itself. In some parts of Europe, the death toll was as high as 60 percent.[35] An eyewitness in Messina, Italy, wrote of terrified citizens with burn blisters on the groin, arms, and neck. "Soon the boils grew to the size of a walnut, then to that of a hen's egg or a goose's egg, and they were exceedingly painful, and irritated the body, causing the sufferer to vomit blood."[36] After three days, the sufferer usually succumbed. During the following century, plagues were recorded in approximately one of every three years. Although many were confined to local areas and none took as many lives as in 1348, at least a dozen affected all parts of Europe.[37] Besides the sheer magnitude of suffering itself, the Black Death was widely viewed by contemporaries as having dramatically affected the lives of those who survived. The frequency with which suffering and death were associated with religion necessarily influenced interpretations of the divine. One writer observed at the time that "no one was secure, whether rich, in moderate circumstances or poor, but everyone from day to day waited on the will of the Lord."[38] Images of Sebastian, the suffering saint, became increasingly popular—his bleeding body martyred by arrows that represented the plague, and his countenance communicating both acceptance of divine will and the promise of salvation.[39] Interpreters inevitably stressed the shortness of life and grief for the missing. However, there were also complaints that the social order had given way to the rising demands of workers whose diminished numbers gave them new and unanticipated bargaining power.[40]

Although subsequent studies discounted many of its presumed effects, the Black Death came to occupy a singular place in continuing discussions of the devastation that humanity has experienced and could experience again if appropriate measures are not taken. It served often as a comparison point for assessing recent threats; for example, to show that death rates from AIDS in sub-Saharan Africa reached similar levels and lasted over a longer period of time.[41] It provided a standard against which to judge the progress of modern medical science. "Medieval man," the eminent historian Phillip Ziegler wrote in 1969, "was equipped with no form of defence—social, medical or psychological—against a violent epidemic of this magnitude."[42] In contrast, modern man enjoys these defenses and thus has no need to feel baffled or terrified. For others, the Black Death was a starting point for considering the public health challenges of recent pandemics, such as the need for careful monitoring of tourist-borne disease. For still others, it served as a reminder of the importance of good methods of sanitation and the dangers of corrupt officials.[43]

The fact that large numbers died from influenza in 1918 and that smaller outbreaks occurred again in 1957 and 1968 gave continuing currency to fears of pandemic disease. The outbreak in 1918 was the largest instance in North America but by no means the first. John Winthrop wrote in 1647 of an "epidemical sickness" in Massachusetts and Connecticut. A "general catarrh" swept North America in 1675. Cotton Mather chronicled a period of "distress" from 1697 to 1699 when many died "in a strange and unusual manner."[44] The medical historian John Mote traced severe epidemics in 1757 to 1762, 1767, from 1780 to 1782, between 1798 and 1803, in 1857 and 1858, from 1873 to 1875, and in 1889.[45] More limited outbreaks occurred in nine of the years between 1901 and 1917. The first reported illnesses in 1918 were at Fort Riley, Kansas, when more than a hundred soldiers reported to the infirmary on March 11 with severe coldlike symptoms. Within three weeks, more than eleven hundred were sick.[46] Similar outbreaks occurred at other training camps. By the end of the month more than four hundred servicemen had died nationwide. With the onset of warmer weather, the problem seemed to have disappeared, only to surface again during the summer as reports of deaths in Europe emerged. In mid-August scattered reports appeared in East Coast newspapers of ships arriving with passengers and crew members suffering from "Spanish grippe." After several deaths were confirmed, health officials reassured the public that there was little danger of the disease spreading. A month later, nearly 7,000 soldiers at Camp Devens in Massachusetts were suffering from influenza. Within a week, the number of cases at the camp climbed to 23,000.[47] Older adults and children in New Jersey, New York, North Carolina, California, and Washington became ill following visits from family members in uniform. In all, officials reported outbreaks in twenty-six states. Over the next twelve months, the epidemic spread. A report compiled by the Bureau of Vital Statistics of the Department of Commerce estimated that 500,000 had died by the end of 1918 and another 45,000 in 1919.[48] Later calculations based on statistical models of mortality data placed the toll closer to 675,000.[49]

The Asian flu pandemic of 1957 was first observed in February, peaked in October, diminished by December, then surged again in January and February of 1958. It resulted in 69,800 deaths in the United States. Health officials termed the 1968 outbreak Hong Kong flu. It was detected in September of that year and became severe during December 1968 and January 1969. It was responsible for 33,800 U.S. deaths.[50] The diminishing death rates compared with 1918 demonstrated that medical knowledge could greatly reduce the likelihood of people dying from influenza. Researchers identified a virus they named influenza A in 1933 and a B strain in 1940. The World Health Organization established a network of laboratories in 1947 and began conducting epidemiological studies of influenza outbreaks in 1949. In 1957, through a special appropriation from Congress, a widespread vaccination program was initiated. In 1968, some residual immunity from the earlier vaccinations remained in effect and antibiotics were more readily available to combat secondary bacterial infections. Yet the possibility of widespread illness and death was a continuing concern.

On March 15, 1976, Health, Education, and Welfare (HEW) secretary David Mathews sent a memo to Office of Management and Budget Director James T. Lynn stating, "There is evidence there will be a major flu epidemic this coming fall. The indication is that we will see a return of the 1918 flu virus that is the most virulent form of flu." He went on, "In 1918 a half million people died. The projections are that this virus will kill one million Americans in 1976."[51] The events leading to this memo began in mid-January with cases of respiratory illness at Fort Dix in New Jersey. On February 4, one of the stricken soldiers, Private David Lewis, died. A week later tests at the Center for Disease Control revealed that some of the throat swabs from Fort Dix contained a swine flu virus. After further testing and emergency meetings at which the need to develop a vaccine was discussed, CDC Assistant Director for Programs Bruce Dull held a press conference on February 19. Media coverage the next day avoided alarmist predictions, but reminded readers that the greatest pandemic the world had ever seen had taken place in 1918 and suggested that the virus causing it may have returned. On March 24 President Gerald Ford announced that he would ask Congress for $135 million to launch a national vaccination program. On April 9 the Senate passed an appropriations bill. The House approved an amended bill three days later, and on April 15 President Ford signed the bill into law. Pharmaceutical companies worked over the summer to manufacture a vaccine in sufficient quantities. As the program began that fall, the U.S. Public Health Service provided the public with an information sheet. Acknowledging that "no one can say for sure" that an outbreak would occur, the statement cautioned that "if an epidemic were to break out, millions of people could get sick." The statement added that "swine flu caused an outbreak of several hundred cases at Ft. Dix" and that nothing like this had occurred since the 1920s (it did not mention that only one death had occurred).[52] Polls at the time showed that 93 percent of the public were aware of the inoculation program and 54 percent planned to participate. A survey three months later showed that 31 percent had actually participated.[53] Those who did participate, a study in Michigan showed, were strongly influenced by how severe they believed the problem to be and whether they personally felt susceptible.[54] On December 16, the program was suspended after reports that at least fifty persons receiving the inoculation had died and several hundred were suffering from paralysis of the face and limbs. When asked in February to rate the government's handling of the swine flu vaccine program, 66 percent of those polled in a Harris survey said only fair or poor. Fewer than a third said excellent or pretty good.[55]

Like the Y2K crisis a quarter century later, there was considerable discussion during and after the swine flu scare about how serious it was and what measures should be taken. The debate occurred largely among experts at HEW, the CDC, among public health officials, and in legislative hearings. In the general public, few had the ability to judge whether claims about genetic similarities between the virus at Fort Dix and the scourge of 1918 were true or untrue. Public anxiety about the possibility of a pandemic was entirely a function of what officials said and how the media interpreted their statements. Internal memos released later showed that officials were deeply influenced by what they had read or heard about the 1918 pandemic. If death and illness on that scale were likely, it was clearly the job of any responsible official to sound the alarm. Nobody could say for sure what would happen, but the prudent course was to take action. It was a situation of "go or no go." The tab was small compared to the estimated billions of dollars that would be lost if large numbers died.[56] Officials stopped short of predicting massive death, but as critics questioned whether an inoculation program was necessary, the warnings were sometimes pointed. As assistant secretary for health at HEW, Theodore Cooper, observed in a lengthy *Washington Post* essay, "We are not dealing with a trivial 'bug,' but with the last major scourge of mankind."[57] Three years later, CBS's Mike Wallace asked Cooper's former boss at HEW, David Sencer, how many cases of swine flu had been reported by the time the inoculation program started. "There had been several reported," Sencer replied, "but none confirmed."[58] Nevertheless, Sencer wrote later, "When lives are at stake, it is better to err on the side of overreaction than underreaction."[59]

Second-guessing what went wrong with the swine flu inoculation program largely deterred similar efforts in the future, but worries about pandemic death and illness continued. In 1983 a poultry virus mutated in Pennsylvania and over the next six months killed 17 million chickens. Experts saw parallels with what could happen to humans. As one virologist remarked, "There are millions of us 'chickens' just waiting to be infected."[60] In 1989 the Ebola virus, which kills 50 to 90 percent of those it infects, was found in imported laboratory monkeys in Reston, Virginia, the first time the virus was observed in the United States. As symptoms spread among employees, the CDC went into action to dampen panic and contain a potential epidemic. The incident was popularized a few years later in Richard Preston's best-selling thriller *The Hot Zone*, which one reviewer described as a wake-up call about the "very real global threat of emerging infections."[61]

Neither scenario materialized. Instead, the AIDS crisis did. Acquired immunodeficiency syndrome (AIDS) caused 234 deaths in 1981. Two years later the number climbed to 2,304. By 1989, it grew to 14,544, and in 1995 peaked at 48,371. Figures compiled in 1997 revealed that approximately 6.4 million worldwide had died of AIDS and that 22 million were HIV-positive. Cumulative U.S. deaths reached nearly 525,000 by the end of 2003.[62] AIDS was, as one writer put it, "the first plague in the history of mankind whose regulation is entirely dependent upon our knowing behavior."[63] It nevertheless was a source of widespread anxiety, both reasoned and unreasoned, as people searched for ways of understanding it, avoiding it, living with HIV (human immunodeficiency virus), and grieving for lost loved ones and friends. In September 1985 *Time* magazine conducted a national poll in which registered voters were told that "you can't worry about everything all the time," and then asked what worried them personally "right now." A striking 57 percent said they worried at least a little about the possibility of "catching AIDS." Twenty-eight percent said they worried a lot.[64] "AIDS anxiety has reached phobic proportions," a reporter in San Diego wrote at the end of 1986, noting examples of people refusing to eat at restaurants and avoiding all physical contact for fear of contracting the disease.[65]

Over the next decade and a half, public anxiety about AIDS diminished as better understanding of the disease and new treatments emerged. The rate of new infections also declined. In 1999, about 40,000 Americans contracted HIV, down from approximately 100,000 in the mid-1980s. Experts nevertheless worried that the public was becoming complacent. A widely publicized report suggested that as many as 5 million Americans were at high risk of contracting AIDS as a result of unsafe sexual practices. "I'm scared by the trends we are starting to see," AIDS director at the Centers for Disease Control and Prevention, Helene Gayle, told a conference sponsored by the American Medical Association.[66]

After 9/11, the threat of terrorist attacks overshadowed concerns about viral pandemics, but left many Americans feeling more vulnerable than ever. On March 15, 2003, as U.S. military leaders made final preparations for the invasion of Iraq that was to begin in five days, the World Health Organization issued a global alert about a mysterious respiratory illness that it termed a "worldwide health threat." Little was known other than the fact that it had killed at least four people (possibly six) and left hundreds of others with severe breathing difficulties. Most of the cases were in Vietnam, Hong Kong, Singapore, and China, but the illness had apparently spread to Canada, where at least one death had been reported. A health care worker suspected of being ill had also traveled from Singapore to New York and from there to Frankfurt. Besides its virulence, the disease, which health officials named Severe Acute Respiratory Syndrome or SARS, was especially troubling because laboratory tests had thus far been unable to identify its origins. In Atlanta, CDC director Julie Gerberding told reporters, "[Asia] is a part of the world where we have a great concern for viruses." Daniel Yee of the Associated Press reminded readers that in 1918–19 as many as 40 million people worldwide died of influenza. The last major outbreak, he wrote, occurred in 1968–69. Thus, "health officials long have feared the world is overdue for a major flu attack."[67]

SARS quickly became a matter of widespread concern. Initial WHO advisories were directed at organizations whose employees were considered especially vulnerable. Hospital workers were advised to take special precautions in treating patients who might be carrying the virus. Airlines were instructed to refer passengers and crew with high fevers and respiratory symptoms to airport health authorities for assessment and management. Hospitals and airlines were the principal means through which the spread of the disease could be monitored and controlled. Through the CDC and counterpart organizations in other countries, significant resources were being devoted to the disease. The extent of mobilization was meant to be reassuring, but also communicated that health officials were worried. Daily updates showed how rapidly the disease was spreading. In the first week, known cases increased to 456 and the death rate climbed to 17. Travelers and anyone exposed to tourists, immigrants, and employees of international corporations were particularly vulnerable. Within days, tour group bookings to Hong Kong dropped by 80 to 90 percent.

By the first of April, just two weeks after the public first became aware of SARS, there was growing concern that the pandemic could trigger a worldwide recession.

Morgan Stanley economist Andrew Xie predicted that Hong Kong, Singapore, and Taiwan would be in recession if the disease was not brought under control in two months. Economists at Merrill Lynch, Deutsche Bank, JP Morgan, and HSBC agreed that the illness would significantly lower growth projections for the region, raise joblessness, dampen international trade, and spark concerns among investors. A few days later, observers noted that Americans were purchasing vitamins and respiratory masks in record quantities. Doctors and public health officials were inundated with inquiries about risks to families, in schools, and at businesses. Chinese restaurants reported that business was down by as much as 70 percent. At a hastily convened briefing at Harvard University, an expert in infectious diseases estimated that 90 percent of Americans would contract the disease within five months and that four percent of the public would die. "Rumors and angst about SARS, fueled by the Internet and a public primed for biological apocalypse," a journalist wrote, "appear to be accelerating faster than in previous disease outbreaks and spreading more widely than the disease itself." One rumor held that a genetic engineering experiment had gone wrong; another, that the CIA was somehow involved. "What I'm trying to understand," asked a doctor in California (who insisted he was not on the "lunatic fringe"), "is the government for whatever reasons, political or economic, going to allow this deadly virus, and that's not an exaggeration, to spread throughout this country?"[68]

The idea that government agencies were responsible for disease prevention and perhaps for allowing the spread of disease was not that far-fetched. By 2003, the CDC, which had been formed in 1946 with a staff of fewer than 400 to monitor infectious diseases, had grown to more than 7,000 employees at ten locations, not counting at least that many working as independent contractors.[69] In each instance when a major public health crisis was feared—the influenza outbreaks of 1957 and 1968, the swine flu panic of 1976, and the Ebola scare of 1989—CDC officials shouldered responsibility to warn the public and organize methods of studying and combating the disease. Early CDC successes, especially its role in identifying poliomyelitis and developing the Salk vaccine, raised public confidence in its work and encouraged the agency's expansion. In 1957 and 1968, far more of the public heard about the possibility of influenza than were actually exposed. In 1976 and 1989, public awareness of possible danger was largely the result of CDC warnings. The AIDS epidemic demonstrated that it was important to take these warnings seriously. SARS was another case in point.

Through aggressive CDC and WHO action, health officials monitored the spread of SARS with astonishing precision. Although its origins in Guangdong Province, China, remained murky, the first case treated there occurred on November 16, 2002, after which international transmission was attributed to a Chinese physician who exposed guests at the Metropole Hotel in Hong Kong on February 21, 2003, and they in turn spread the virus to Vietnam, Singapore, and Canada.[70]

The Canadian case illustrated the level of detail health officials were able to attain. After her stay at the Hong Kong hotel, Mrs. K (whose name was withheld), a seventy-eight-year-old matriarch of a large family, returned on February 23 to her home in Scarborough, British Columbia. She died from apparent heart failure on March 5. Two days later, her son, Mr. T, came to the Scarborough Grace Hospital suffering from a respiratory illness and waited for sixteen hours in the crowded emergency room. A total of eighty-four cases were traced directly to the emergency room and to members of Mr. T's immediate family.[71] Monitoring of this kind permitted health officials to isolate and contain the virus. A report in April 2004 showed there had been 8,098 probable cases of SARS worldwide, resulting in 774 deaths—a far cry from the millions some experts had feared. Only twenty-seven cases had been identified in the United States; the death rate was zero.[72]

The same governmental action that curbed the spread of SARS heightened fears and sometimes frustrated the public's expectations. Experts offered alarming predictions that were later refuted. One report concluded that cases were multiplying exponentially and would total more than 70,000 in sixty days. Later analysis, showing the rate to be linear, demonstrated that only 2,400 cases would emerge over the same period.[73] A survey conducted one month after the initial WHO travel advisory found that 47 percent of U.S. adults were very worried that they or someone in their immediate family would contract SARS. In the same study, 46 percent were convinced that SARS spreads "very easily." Another poll revealed that almost as many Americans were worried about SARS as were about another terrorist attack.[74] Cautious administrators at the University of California at Berkeley refused to admit students returning from the Far East. Fears of traveling dampened airlines' earnings from trips to China by 24 percent, to Hong Kong by 41 percent, and to Singapore by 43 percent. In all, Asian economies lost between $11 billion and $18 billion, or as much as 2 percent of gross domestic product.[75] In Ontario, an investigation concluded that public health preparedness "through three successive governments of different political stripes" had failed miserably.[76]

Twelve months after the first WHO health alert, new reports of SARS cases fell to a trickle, leaving health officials and academics to consider what had been learned. Almost immediately, finger-pointing focused on the media for having hyped the story. Discussions mentioned the media's penchant for "killer virus" rhetoric and the relatively new role that web sites were playing in publicizing unfounded rumors. There was also increasing awareness, though, that health officials themselves were a decisive factor in shaping public anxiety. "Containing fear" was recognized as an integral feature of public health crisis management. CDC infectious disease experts, for instance, established a community outreach team to deal with issues of fear, stigmatization, and discrimination. Health officials not only contained fear, but also perpetuated it as they warned of new viral killers and anticipated that SARS could reappear after lying dormant or mutate into novel strains. As CDC director Julie Gerberding observed in September 2003, "We have to expect that sometime, somewhere, this virus is going to rear its ugly head again."[77]

The fears experienced by those closest to the virus itself were quite different from those who heard about it from press conferences and web sites. "Mommy, are you going to die?" asked a nine-year-old in Canada. Her mother was a nurse caring for SARS patients at a local hospital.[78] In the coastal province of Zhejiang, China, angry villagers stormed government offices to protest the conditions under which eight residents had been quarantined—the only panic anywhere that resulted in collective violence.[79] The vast majority of people in America and elsewhere who panicked did so in quieter ways, usually by telling pollsters they were worried and sometimes by purchasing masks and canceling trips. Their exposure to SARS was mediated. They worried because of what they thought health officials were saying *could* happen.

RENEWED FEAR OF PANDEMIC INFLUENZA only months after the SARS scare subsided revealed more clearly than ever how perceptions of peril were mediated and shaped by institutions. On July 5, 2003, WHO officials declared that SARS outbreaks had been contained worldwide. Six months later, on January 13, 2004, the deadly avian flu (H5N1) virus was identified in laboratory samples from patients hospitalized with a severe respiratory illness in Hanoi. Three of the patients died. This was not the first time the virus had been observed. In 1997 it infected eighteen people in Hong Kong, resulting in six deaths. A million and a half chickens were slaughtered to curb the outbreak. In 2003 the virus appeared again in Hong Kong, causing one death. Other strains of avian virus had been observed in Hong Kong and the Netherlands in 1999 and 2003, and in South Korea and Japan as far back as 1925. Although none of these outbreaks had caused large numbers of deaths, health officials registered particular alarm at the new outbreak in 2004.

The reason for concern was that poultry in several locations, including Vietnam, Korea, and Japan, were reportedly infected and dying at a high rate. In addition, advances in microbiology and genomics since the late 1990s gave scientists quicker and more accurate information about genes and genetic mutations. Although none of the initial deaths had been transmitted from human to human, scientists worried that the avian flu virus would mutate to include human flu virus genes and thus increase the rate of human transmission. Earlier discussions of influenza had largely focused on death rates and inoculation. The viruses themselves varied in lethality and were recognized as living entities but were relatively stable. In the newer understandings, they were more powerful, complex, unstable, and unpredictable—"inexorably evolving and changing," as one scientist put it. Viruses were increasingly regarded as highly adaptable compositions of DNA sequences capable of intertwining and exchanging with the DNA sequences of human hosts. The H5N1 virus was especially dangerous because it appeared to mix with human flu viruses without an intermediate host, such as pigs.[80]

In more imaginative depictions, H5N1 was likened to an incredibly clever antagonist in a deadly game of chess. It had supervillain flexibility that allowed it to jump from human to human, but could disguise itself as a simple avian predator. It was stealthy, waiting, watching, learning, and quietly becoming more deadly, attacking only a few at first, getting better, and then moving on before the health police could catch up with it. Not only was it physically strong and amazingly intelligent. It was also an astute user of the new global communications network. "It takes advantage of flights that connect Asia's major cities to the rest of the world, popping up simultaneously in Sydney, Los Angeles, and London," science writer Martin Enserink observed. Besides getting around easily, it would soon reveal the vulnerability of society itself. "Panic and riots erupt while schools, businesses, and transportation systems are shutting down." Hospitals become overcrowded, desperate patients are turned away. Coffin makers and grave diggers are in high demand. When the dust settles, "2 billion people have become ill, and more than 40 million are dead."[81]

By the end of 2004, avian influenza, or bird flu, as it was dubbed, remained confined to East and Southeast Asia. Only twelve deaths had been attributed to the disease in Vietnam and the same number were recorded in Thailand. Assessments of the risks involved nevertheless increased as infections occurred in ducks and pigs as well as in chickens. A year later, highly pathogenic avian influenza had been observed among poultry, migratory birds, and other fowl in fifteen countries. The virus killed twenty-two people in Vietnam, fourteen in Thailand, eleven in Indonesia, five in China, four in Cambodia, and two in Turkey.[82] Though the number of fatalities was small, the possibility of a major pandemic had become front-page news.

Health officials were the principal source through which the public heard about bird flu, in no small measure because of an international network the World Health Organization had established in 2000. The Global Outbreak Alert and Response Network (GOARN) was a partnership of more than 240 local and regional organizations in forty countries. Its purpose was to investigate epidemic disease threats, provide technical support to domestic officials, and share information about emerging health problems. Between January 2004 and December 2005, WHO officials posted an average of approximately one situation update a week about avian flu from information collected through this network. Most updates concerned a particular country, and many referred to a single patient being hospitalized, although some offered more general overviews and predictions. These updates, with related press releases and alerts, were covered closely by the media, thus ensuring wide exposure to the general public. CNN, for instance, mentioned bird flu more than nine hundred times during the same two-year period. Typically, a brief WHO update about a new confirmed or suspected occurrence or death in a particular country was followed the same day by an on-the-scene or in-country report or interview with a local official.

An example of the close connection between formal health reports and media coverage occurred on February 2, 2004, when health authorities in Thailand announced laboratory confirmation of H5N1 influenza in a fifty-eight-year-old woman who had fallen ill on January 19 and died eight days later. The WHO update added that this latest fatality brought the number of human cases in Thailand to four, of whom three had died. CNN's coverage included the same information. Following anchor Carol Costello's report that 30 million fowl had been destroyed and eighty-one people had been treated, Bangkok bureau chief Tom Mintier noted the fifty-eight-year-old woman's death and provided a video clip from a regional health official who said the "situation remains serious." Mintier further reported learning of the death of a six-year-old boy, whose illness may have been avian influenza. Two days later, a WHO update announced that the boy's death was indeed from H5N1 infection. On CNN, Mintier elaborated. Fifty million chickens in Thailand and Vietnam had been slaughtered. There was a "great deal of concern about the mutation of the virus" and "officials at WHO are saying that this is a long way from over."[83]

On both days, CNN's coverage was relatively brief and on point, differing from WHO's in being available to a far larger audience and including language conveying the emotional tenor of the story, such as "dreaded bird flu," "disturbing revelation," and "great deal of concern." Whereas the WHO information was authoritative because it came from an official health organization, the conversational style used by CNN reporters permitted one to speak for the public, expressing its presumed questions and concerns, as when Costello said to Mintier that "a lot of people are worried." Both WHO and CNN focused on individuals, thus personalizing the tragedy. Besides the death in Thailand, the February 2 WHO update described an investigation of respiratory illness among members of a family in Thai Binh province, Vietnam, involving a 31-year-old man, his two sisters, aged 23 and 30, and his 28-year-old wife, and noted that the man and his two sisters died and the wife had recovered. CNN's Mintier repeated the information, saying that two women in Vietnam had died, as had a brother.[84]

In subsequent months, as the human death toll remained low but incidents in poultry spread to new countries, WHO updates and media coverage expressed deepening concerns. On May 14, WHO observed that the latest outbreaks were "historically unprecedented" and that no vaccine or treatment was available. The update pointedly referred to the unpredictable periodicity of pandemics with high mortality rates, "great social and economic disruption," and the likelihood of new human virus subtypes occurring. It further warned against complacency, despite few deaths to date, and called for continuing vigilance and cooperation. A WHO update on July 8 reinforced the growing concern, stating that the virus was becoming "increasingly pathogenic," had the ability to "spread easily" from human to human, and could trigger a "global influenza pandemic." CNN gave only minimal coverage to the report, noting that new cases were being reported in Asia and thousands of birds were being slaughtered, but the New York Times carried a lengthy report indicating that WHO officials were preparing for the worst by conducting laboratory tests on the virus in hopes of learning how it worked and what kind of vaccine and antiviral treatment would be most effective.[85] The topic surfaced again in late November when Dr. Shigeru Omi, WHO's regional director for Asia and the Pacific, stated that in the event of a pandemic outbreak—which he termed "very, very likely"—local officials would need to close schools and office buildings and set in motion emergency plans to provide basic services. A week later, Paula Zahn's evening program on CNN led with the statement that "according to some medical researchers, one billion people could die from a worldwide outbreak of avian or bird flu." Acknowledging that only thirty-two people had died thus far, Zahn said World Health Officials believed there could be 100 million deaths. To dramatize what this could mean, the program reminded viewers of the 1918 pandemic and introduced a survivor who said "it was terrible" because "most houses were afflicted." The program further observed that global epidemics occur about four times a century and that the last one had occurred in 1968.[86]

Meanwhile, CDC officials in Atlanta were focusing increased attention on the nation's lack of preparedness for a global epidemic. On January 27, 2004, CDC director Julie Gerberding announced that an operation center was being established to cooperate with WHO investigations and that six scientists had been sent to Vietnam, noting that the situation in Asia was of serious concern but that danger to the United States was as yet minimal. Over the next six months, CDC infectious disease experts focused on overcoming an anticipated shortfall in vaccine supplies for the regular fall influenza season, while also developing plans for pandemic preparedness and response. In October, just as the vaccine program was to begin, the British government suspended the license of Chiron Corporation, one of two companies making vaccine, thus cutting the expected supply of 100 million doses in half. Inevitably, the problem prompted questions about what might happen if bird flu erupted. CDC officials announced that progress was being made toward producing an experimental vaccine from a seed virus of the H5N1 strain and stockpiling supplies of Tamiflu, the drug thought to provide the best protection against infection among those exposed. Efforts were also under way to educate the public about an impending pandemic and to determine how best to screen travelers, close schools, and quarantine those suspected of carrying the virus. Budget projections for the following year called for an almost ninefold budget increase on influenza-related work over five years earlier.[87]

In 2005, lawmakers became increasingly involved in efforts to get out in front of the rising concern about a possible pandemic. CDC was being criticized by watchdog organizations and disgruntled former employees over an administrative restructuring program initiated two years earlier. Concerns were also being voiced about political interference in scientific research and the departure of several dozen top scientists. A 2003 report by the Trust for America's Health, a nonpartisan organization, showed that only one-quarter of the states had pandemic flu plans. A 2004 General Accountability Office survey found that no state was prepared to hospitalize more than five hundred flu patients at a time. In February 2005, the Committee on House Government Reform held hearings about CDC's efforts to produce and distribute vaccine. At a subsequent hearing in April 2005, an executive of the Air Transport Association of America reported that airlines and CDC cooperation had increased since the SARS outbreak of 2003 and that a system was in place to track and notify passengers who may have been exposed to an infectious disease by another passenger. In May, CDC's Gerberding told a hearing of the Health Subcommittee of the House Energy and Commerce Committee, "we're sitting on a cauldron of flu virus incubation" that should be taken very seriously. Other witnesses provided updates on seed virus research, clinical trials, antiviral therapies, pilot vaccine programs, and public education. A month later, the House Government Reform Committee held additional hearings at which many of the same experts testified.[88]

News accounts of these hearings prompted polling organizations to assess the public's reactions. A survey for Fox News in October 2005 found that 30 percent of the public were very concerned about the spread of bird flu in the United States. Another 33 percent said they were somewhat concerned. In the same survey, almost as many respondents expressed concern about bird flu (29 percent) as about terrorism (32 percent). A Gallup poll that month showed that 62 percent of Americans considered it at least somewhat likely that the bird flu virus would strike the United States. In yet another survey, 71 percent said they were at least moderately concerned about avian flu. Underscoring the concern, 52 percent in an NBC poll said the United States was not very well prepared for an outbreak of avian flu.[89]

Feeling that America was unprepared undoubtedly stemmed from the fact that just a few months earlier, Hurricane Katrina had exposed just how poorly equipped to handle a major crisis government agencies were. By early October, the official death toll from the storm stood at 1,213, with 2,500 missing. More than 1.5 million had fled their homes; 75,000 were living in shelters. Much of the devastation and many of the deaths were blamed on the U.S. Army Corps of Engineers, whose levees and drainage canal walls failed to protect New Orleans (resulting in the flooding of 80 percent of the city), and on the Federal Emergency Management Administration, whose director, Michael D. Brown, was widely viewed as a political appointee lacking in relevant experience and administrative skills. A poll conducted by George Washington University showed that 58 percent of Americans thought the federal government had done a poor job of responding to the crisis; 53 percent said their opinion of President Bush had become less favorable as a result.[90]

On November 1, amid continuing coverage of Katrina and increasing bloodshed in Iraq, President Bush held a news conference at the William Natcher Center of the National Institutes of Health (NIH) to announce a plan to address the threat of pandemic influenza. The plan called for increased cooperation with WHO and other international organizations, expanded medical and veterinary research, and better communication among government agencies, the pharmaceutical industry, and the public. The proposed program, termed the White House's *National Strategy for Pandemic Influenza Implementation Plan*, included a major effort to develop and stockpile vaccine and antiviral treatments. In all, there would be $7.1 billion in emergency funding: $2.8 billion for cell culture technology, $1.5 billion to purchase vaccines, $1 billion for antivirals, and nearly $2 billion for other domestic and international programs. As if to limit public expectations about government responsibility, the report declared that "individual action is perhaps the most important element of pandemic preparedness and response." It counseled individuals and families to guard against spreading infection or becoming infected, stay away from public gatherings, forego travel if asked, and stockpile at least several days' worth of household necessities.[91]

The tone of the *National Strategy* report was evenhanded, and yet conveyed a message easily capable of arousing anxiety. It evoked the memory of previous outbreaks and predicted that another one was certain. Living in a "universe of microbes" that were "forever changing and adapting themselves to the human host" may have been scientifically accurate, but it was not very comforting. With vivid images of Katrina victims still in mind, it was hard to ignore the prediction that a pandemic would "threaten all critical infrastructure by removing essential personnel from the workplace for weeks or months." Covering the president's news conference, CNN anchor Daryn Kagan opened a discussion among a panel of fellow journalists by observing that bird flu was "causing a lot of fear." Jeanne Meserve, the network's homeland security correspondent, said the effort was problematic because it depended on the World Health Organization, which was "chronically underfunded and understaffed." Public health organizations in the United States, she observed, suffered from the same problem. Medical correspondent Elizabeth Cohen added that people are "very scared" because there is no vaccine, and observed that unspecified "experts" were calling the nation's vaccine production system "fragile and rickety." Later in the day, Wolf Blitzer repeated the story, calling the president's plan an effort to keep Americans safe from a "deadly threat that could strike terror around the world."[92]

Always in the background, the 1918 pandemic hung over the discussion of an impending outbreak as an ominous reminder of what could happen. That outbreak killed 20 million people, the president recalled, infected a third of the U.S. population, and reduced life expectancy by thirteen years. On Blitzer's program "The Situation Room," Elizabeth Cohen observed, "Experts say that H5N1 resembles the strain responsible for the 1918 flu pandemic [that] ultimately killed as many as 50 million around the world." One of those experts was Jeffery K. Taubenberger, whose team at the Armed Forces Institute of Pathology in Rockville, Maryland, in collaboration with researchers at the National Center for Infectious Diseases in Atlanta and Mount Sinai School of Medicine in New York, had succeeded in locating two samples of the 1918 virus and sequencing its genetic code. Taubenberger's evidence suggested that the H5N1 virus was evolving in ways that would make it as lethal and as easily transmitted from human to human as the earlier virus.[93]

Polls showed that people were increasingly worried. After the president's speech and CNN's news coverage, one survey showed that 21 percent of the public thought bird flu would either create a crisis or be a major outbreak, while 63 percent thought it would consist of a minor outbreak. Only 14 percent thought it would not strike the United States. A few weeks later, a Fox News poll found that 26 percent of the public were very concerned about the spread of bird flu. Another 31 percent were somewhat concerned. It was also evident that Americans were paying attention to the emerging news and discussions. The Fox News poll showed that 74 percent of the public claimed to be interested in news stories about bird flu. A survey sponsored by the Henry J. Kaiser Family Foundation found that 69 percent had been following news accounts of the president's plan to prepare for a possible outbreak of bird flu. [94]

Continuing news coverage reinforced the impression that the public was deeply worried. On December 10, 2005, CNN medical correspondent Sanjay Gupta presented an in-depth look at the potential "global catastrophe" from the "worldwide killer" known as bird flu. Laurie Garrett of the Council on Foreign Relations said the virus was "orders of magnitude more contagious than the dreaded Ebola virus." WHO consultant Ira Longini described the situation as a "disaster waiting to happen." The program introduced eight-year-old Firdaus Baskara, a Jakartan who had been diagnosed with bird flu and whose aunt had died of the illness. There were many unanswered questions about how the boy and others had contracted the virus, Gupta said, leaving people "just plain frightened." CDC scientist Tim Uyeki agreed. "We're very, very concerned," he said. The next day on a broadcast titled "Killer Flu: A Breath Away" Gupta continued the story, this time standing outside the home of a recent victim in Indonesia. It was the home of Agoos and Rinny Dinna, high school sweethearts, married fourteen years, and running a small business from their home. Rinny developed a cough and died a few days later. It was the killer flu known as H5N1.[95]

How Americans actually responded to news about a possible pandemic, though, was considerably more varied—and typically more cautious and pragmatic—than the coverage implied. Following the president's briefing at NIH headquarters, CNN had time to discuss some of the e-mails it was receiving. A viewer in California wondered if it would be safe to be inoculated both for regular flu and bird flu if a vaccine for the latter became available. An e-mail from Michigan asked if it was possible to catch bird flu by feeding birds in her backyard. The answer, a doctor on the program said, was no because birds in the U.S. did not have avian flu. A viewer in Hawaii e-mailed to ask if it was safe to eat poultry. Absolutely, the doctor replied.[96] Letters to the editor and postings on web site forums posed other practical concerns. Writers suggested that the Bush administration was spending too much or too little on the problem. Some drew parallels with FEMA's failures in New Orleans. Farmers wrote to say that eating poultry was safe. There were concerns about pharmaceutical companies' "massive profits," as one writer put it, and whether laws should be passed requiring these companies to spend more on developing vaccines. There were informational questions about how the virus worked and about how much Tamiflu was available, with responses referring questioners to CDC and Tamiflu web sites. Others wrote to offer advice about the proper temperature to cook chicken, how to protect pets, and where to find additional information. Notable, too, was the evidence in polls that most Americans were not alarmed. Despite reminders on television that a global pandemic could be as destructive as a thermonuclear war, only a quarter or fewer in polls expressed significant levels of concern.

In personal interviews, people talked more candidly and at greater length than in e-mails and letters to the editor. They said they would be scared, devastated, depressed—"freaked out," as one woman remarked—if people they knew started dying from a pandemic. Many described information they had seen on television and stories about the Spanish flu of 1918. A few acknowledged that the prospect of mass death was too "mind-boggling" to picture realistically. Most admitted they had done nothing special to protect themselves or their families. The reasons were revealing. Since the threat is "out there," a woman in Iowa said, there's not a "specific task" I can undertake at this point. A man in Illinois echoed her sentiment, noting that there is no "imminent threat," but if there were, he would cooperate with any quarantine program recommended. A man in Ohio said he hadn't prepared yet because the government's advice to purchase duct tape to guard against terrorism had turned him off. A man in Maryland said he trusted "the experts" to figure out a way to solve the problem. Although they considered a pandemic entirely possible, they also thought, with few exceptions, that the right steps were being taken. As a man in Georgia observed, "What we are seeing the world community do now seems like the right thing. We are attempting to monitor it and stave it off wherever it raises its ugly head." Or, as others noted, educating the public and working on a vaccine were sensible activities.

To be sure, alarmist views were evident. Bloggers frequently distilled the various government figures and news reports into frightening scenarios of what experiencing a pandemic would be like. If only 5 percent of the population were ill at any given time, a blogger calculated, many more would be preoccupied caring for the sick and dying, and people would be scared to go to work or travel. Supplies of food, water, and medicine would be disrupted.[97] Bird flu was, some fundamentalists said, a sign of living in the end times—a reminder of biblical warnings about the pale horse of the apocalypse and the coming of pestilence throughout the land.[98] Survivalists and "preppers" exchanged thoughts about protecting themselves from hapless neighbors. What would you do, wrote one, if you used your weapon to fend off a neighbor and he didn't die? "Well I'm not going to feed him or her," replied one. "Reload, then shoot him again," wrote another. "Keep shooting until he stops moving," advised another.

But even the views of alarmists were generally restrained. Apocalyptic writers more often encouraged people to repent and find hope in God than anticipate a catastrophic ending of history. On FluTrackers.com, which included posts by people who were clearly frightened, most of the information consisted of factual daily updates from WHO, the CDC, and other official sources, as well as maps, news summaries, and practical tips. On a home schooling site, a blogger responding to a message about the possibility of goods and services being disrupted, wrote, "I know what you mean. Limiting myself to grocery shopping only once a week is hard." Another popular web site, AvianFluTalk.com, included hundreds of posts on such topics as the comparative advantages of different brands of solar cookers, cooking beans, and living without bread (including numerous recipes). Others used the site to discuss their reactions to Stephen King's novel *The Stand*, in which much of the human population dies from a superflu virus, and to circulate information about their own little-known novels and books-in-progress.

IT WOULD BE EASY TO CONCLUDE that the media hyped the bird flu story, using sensationalist language about terror and mass death to scare viewers into staying glued to their televisions. In this interpretation, people who became distraught and filled their basements with bottled water and canned beans did so because the media engaged in fearmongering. And it could be argued that most of the public remained calm because they understood the media was doing this. People watched the news and read the reports, heard that tens of millions could die, and put about as much stock in the reports as they did a reality thriller. But this interpretation is too simple.

Public knowledge about bird flu, SARS, and even swine flu was greater than had ever been true of infectious diseases in the past. In 1918, it was nearly impossible for people outside of major cities to hear of outbreaks until they occurred in their own locale. By the time they were aware of its presence, it was often too late. With the discovery of viruses and knowledge about how they worked still well in the future, health authorities and army officials reported illnesses and deaths, but the reports often lacked specificity. Others were based entirely on rumor. A lengthy article in the *New York Times* on September 18, 1918—six months after the first outbreak, when more than a hundred soldiers and sailors had already died in various locations and more than 2,600 were hospitalized in Chicago alone—argued that the disease was being spread by German agents put ashore from a submarine.[99] In comparison, news of recent outbreaks spread almost instantly and in great detail. Anyone who might have been interested could learn the names of people who died, see what the hospital ward looked like, and hear their relatives talk, even if the occurrence was in a remote section of Thailand or Indonesia. This did not mean that large numbers of the American public understood the technical details of genetic differences among various strains of influenza virus or how it attaches to human receptors. It did mean that most of the public was at least minimally aware of the problem, whether or not it had claimed few lives and was in another part of the world.

The information networks from which this knowledge emanated had been set up specifically to monitor the spread of infectious disease. They were, in a sense, not only the institutional buffers that authorities had established to protect the public from disease, but also the source through which most of what the public knew about disease was filtered. Like the Atomic Energy Commission and the Intergovernmental Panel on Climate Change, the CDC was the organizer of expertise required to understand and develop solutions for a large-scale threat to public safety. Although its origins and expansion dated only to the 1950s, it was an outgrowth of the public-sponsored health services that had begun in 1798 under President John Adams with the establishment of the Marine Hospital Service and the Public Health Service in 1912. The World Health Organization had been established as part of the United Nations to coordinate international efforts. Had it not been for these organizations, the general public would have had far less knowledge of infectious disease outbreaks in other parts of the world. Although CNN and other news sources had reporters around the world, much of what the media reported derived from these official health networks.

Besides monitoring and conducting research on infectious diseases, the World Health Organization, CDC, and related agencies bore responsibility for identifying and anticipating worst-case scenarios. It was the job of employees at these organizations to think the unthinkable, to overcome whatever inherent tendencies toward optimism might be present in the culture at large, and to imagine possible catastrophes as well as less frightening scenarios. This meant that people working at these organizations had a stake in collecting information and considering its implications. Their jobs and the very legitimacy of what they were charged with doing depended on it. The public expected results, not failure. As one man observed, "I would be outraged at the World Health Organization if [a pandemic] happened." If they failed to predict the worst, and it happened, that was more blameworthy than if they exaggerated what could happen, and it did not come to pass. This meant that there was a built-in bias toward emphasizing the worst. Budgets were less likely to be cut if lawmakers thought serious danger lay ahead. Journalists were subject to the same biases. A headline about impending doom was more likely to make the front page than one saying there was nothing to fear.

However, health officials and medical correspondents often took care to provide balanced information and even to question reports that seemed exaggerated. In November 2004, when a WHO official in Asia announced that the death toll could reach 100 million, the *New York Times* made a point of stating that the official believed this was the worst-case possibility and that other estimates, including those by other WHO officials, were much lower. A WHO spokesperson said the Asian official's remarks had not been cleared by the agency. Another influenza expert called the estimate "unscientific, unjustified and an inaccurate extrapolation from the current situation."[100] A year later, as journalists expressed alarm at the lack of vaccine for the regular flu season, CDC's Julie Gerberding cautioned, "We all need to take a deep breath. This is not an emergency." Writing in the *Washington Post*, three specialists in infectious diseases charged that the public health community had long used fear as a strategy to promote flu vaccine, and counseled readers to be careful in interpreting statistics about possible illnesses and deaths.[101] As a follow-up to Taubenberger's research on the 1918 virus, *Nature* published a series of articles questioning the results and offering alternative interpretations.[102] PBS produced a full-scale lesson plan for high school students to learn the basics about viruses and to consider health preparation proposals, and WHO regularly publicized reports in virology journals about new discoveries.[103]

The public's worries in this context were shaped by the organizational apparatus through which information was produced and communicated. It was quite different from the fear that caused people at the Iroquois Theater to panic in 1903 and the raw emotion people experienced as they saw loved ones die in 1918. Fear mediated by health and news organizations was not an immediate threat, but a matter of calculation, of being aware that something catastrophic could happen, although the probability was low, just as a person knew death could come on the next business trip or during an outing to the grocery store. Such possibilities were insufficiently scary to require denial, and too remote to necessitate deviating from the normal business of daily life. The fact that larger numbers did not stockpile food and water was not an indication that they disbelieved catastrophe could come. It was rather the more complex expectation that other means, having to do with expertise and large-scale organization, were likely to be more effective, and that if these failed, stores of personal preparation probably would too.

With so much riding on expertise and organization, it would have been surprising if some of the public's anxiety did not focus on the capabilities of scientists and government officials. Besides the possibility of actually becoming ill and dying, there was the chance that those in charge might not be trustworthy or would fail in their appointed tasks. People who felt the danger was not great did not deny that it existed, but thought that officials and journalists were emphasizing the worst. Those who felt extreme action was necessary were responding partly from a sense of skepticism about administrators' ability to protect them.

There was also the recurring fear of social chaos, which itself was an indication of how much the concern about infectious disease had come to be understood through the lens of large-scale organizations. The reason to be informed about an impending pandemic was as much to preserve social order as it was to protect life. WHO and CDC updates went not only to the general public via CNN and other news media, but to state and municipal emergency planners, hospitals, medical associations, stockbrokers, and insurance companies. Some survivalists decided that the only way they could outlast a pandemic was to insulate themselves from all social relations—neighbors, utility companies, supermarkets, schools, doctors. Most people realized they were social creatures bound for better or worse to the social institutions on which they depended for almost everything. In for a penny, in for a pound.

SEVEN

ENVIRONMENTAL CATASTROPHE

IN THE MONTHS PRECEDING THE 9/11 TRAGEDY, public attention focused less on possible attacks than on new concerns about climate change and its effects on the natural environment. Just two days before the attacks, the *Washington Post* announced ominously, "The End Is Near." The accompanying story was not about impending terrorism but global warming. Quoting extensively from a recently released United Nations report, which it described as "unsettling," "authoritative," and "alarming," the story warned readers that glaciers were melting rapidly and could cause sea levels to rise by a projected three feet over the next century. People in low-lying areas would lose their homes, vital crop land would be flooded, and disease would become more likely.[1] A large share of the public agreed. In a Harris Poll that August, 88 percent said they had heard or read about global warming and 75 percent said they believed it was a reality. A CBS News poll showed that 72 percent thought it necessary to take steps to counter the effects of global warming "right away."[2] A citizen in Dayton likened global warming to a cancerous tumor. A professor in Pittsburgh noted that more people were dying from air pollution than from traffic accidents. A high school student in Vermont wrote, "Our reckless destruction of the environment through industrial pollution is creating a dangerous world." A writer in Wisconsin observed, "Hurricanes and tornadoes will multiply and become ever more fierce and unpredictable." "Unless we take drastic action—and soon," an environmental activist urged, "global warming threatens to plunge the world into a series of climatic crises."[3]

The U.N. report the *Washington Post* referred to was a 3,000-page "Third Assessment Report" from the Intergovernmental Panel on Climate Change. The IPCC report was a massive undertaking involving more than five hundred authors and some seven hundred reviewers. The study, which served as the key reference for delegates who met in Bonn, Germany, in July 2001 to consider policies for limiting greenhouse gas emissions, concluded that the 1990s had been the warmest decade in a century and a half and that there was a definite warming trend due to increased atmospheric concentrations of carbon dioxide, methane, and nitrous oxide. The study further argued, based on newly collected information, that global warming was the result of anthropogenic (human-caused) activities and not simply a reflection of long-term natural cycles. Many of the effects of global warming could already be observed. Ice coverage of rivers and lakes in the Northern Hemisphere had decreased by approximately two weeks during the twentieth century. Sea ice had thinned by as much as 40 percent. The growing season was lengthening. Plant and animal locations were shifting. "Overall," the report concluded, "climate change is projected to increase threats to human health, particularly in lower income populations, predominantly within tropical/subtropical countries." In addition, biodiversity would decrease, crop yields would be adversely affected, and water shortages would become more severe.[4]

The IPCC report attracted enormous interest. The long-awaited document was a cultural landmark representing the collective wisdom of the best minds from many countries—something like what the deliberations at the Council of Nicaea were for the early Christians. The report was all the more important because it seemed to ratify what the public had been hearing for the past decade about environmental destruction, even to the point of fueling apocalyptic predictions, and it was a political statement, a call for international action, rather than a mere academic exercise. It was also a significant moment for interpreters to read into it their favorite views about what was right or wrong with the world. Environmental reporter Andrew C. Revkin observed in the *New York Times* that the report pointed especially to a "widening gap between rich, industrialized countries and poor developing nations." *USA Today* published an essay by conservative Cato Institute fellow Patrick J. Michaels that critically examined the report, concluding that no policy action should be taken because "global warming has been a profound irrelevancy to the quality of our lives." A writer in *U.S. Catholic* likened the report to the prophecies of Cassandra—true but ignored—and called on readers to "wake up and smell the carbon." The left-leaning *Monthly Review* argued that the report demonstrated conclusively that capitalism was producing an ecological crisis that "will rapidly spin out of control, with irreversible and devastating consequences for human beings." The *Oil and Gas Journal*, an industry magazine, came to a rather different interpretation: "If consumers around the world want to mitigate climate change, they must be willing to pay higher prices for energy."[5]

The IPCC conclusions intensified broader discussions about the environment that had been at center stage throughout the spring and summer of 2001. Following a series of electricity shortages in California resulting in rolling blackouts and leading to projected rate increases in western states of 25 to 50 percent, the public and legislators were already concerned about energy policies. Unless better policies were implemented, Alaska Senator Frank H. Murkowski told his colleagues during a hearing in March, "we risk threatening our economic prosperity, our national security, and our very way of life." That same month, Environmental Protection Agency (EPA) administrator Christine Todd Whitman told a meeting of G8 ministers in Trieste, Italy, "Global warming is one of the greatest environmental issues we face, if not the greatest challenge." Whitman's remark led observers to believe Washington would support the Kyoto Protocol, a treaty under which industrialized countries agreed to reduce emissions of greenhouse gases by 2010. However, it soon became clear this was not the administration's position. "The Kyoto Protocol is an unfair and ineffective means of addressing global climate change concerns," President Bush explained on March 13. What some took to be a reversal of policy led to controversy throughout the summer and well beyond. A *New York Times* editorial on March 15 reminded readers that during the 2000 election campaign Bush had promised to "establish mandatory reduction targets" and thus was betraying his promise. The editorial continued, "One can conclude only that political considerations carried the day." That conclusion drew increasing interest from critics who noted that Vice President Cheney's Energy Task Force had held private meetings during the previous month at which top oil company executives had been present. Concern about the possible influence of these meetings on administration policy resulted in a lawsuit brought against Cheney and other members of the administration by the Sierra Club and a subsequent investigation by the General Accounting Office.[6]

Meanwhile, global warming drew increasing attention because of highly publicized policy debates and scientific reports. On May 7, Senator Robert C. Byrd of West Virginia addressed global warming in a speech to the Senate. On May 10, Department of Energy Secretary Spencer Abraham answered questions about climate change during a hearing before the Senate Committee on Energy and Natural Resources. At the River Centre Convention Center in St. Paul, Minnesota, on May 17, President Bush warned of a "darker future" being previewed in "rising prices at the gas pump and rolling blackouts" in California, but promised that a bright future of "efficient, clean, convenient and affordable" energy was achievable. The speech highlighted conclusions published in the administration's 170-page *National Energy Policy* that included approximately one hundred recommendations, ranging from opening the Arctic National Wildlife Refuge to oil and gas leasing to setting standards for air pollutants other than carbon dioxide.[7] In June the National Academy of Sciences published an analysis of current information about climate change that largely confirmed the IPCC's conclusions, but opened room for further debate by noting "considerable uncertainty" about models of the climate system and the need for "caveats" in assessments about the role of human activity. According to the report, global warming was in fact occurring, but at varied rates in different locations, and some mitigation of the greenhouse effect through the banning of aerosols had already taken place.[8] Commenting on the report at a meeting on June 13, President Bush acknowledged that "the surface temperature of the earth is warming" and "the increase is due in large part to human activity," but argued that so much remained unknown that policies should be flexible enough to "adjust to new information and take advantage of new technology."[9] At a Senate hearing on June 28, much of the discussion focused on finding practical solutions to the nation's growing energy needs. As Senator Murkowski observed, the way to manage the "risk of climate change" was to deploy "American technology and ingenuity and innovation, and America's can-do spirit."[10]

The various reports and policy statements elicited strong responses from advocacy groups and partisan spokespersons. One side emphasized the "increasingly united and alarming findings of mainstream science," as an essay in the Sierra Club's magazine described them, and argued that the time was short for taking major steps to curb greenhouse gases.[11] That view was contested by experts who felt the scientific evidence was far from settled and who opposed setting standards for carbon dioxide emissions. As one declared, "To insist on draconian measures designed to avert even a remote threat of harm from global warming is absurd."[12] Opponents of regulatory legislation also argued that nothing should be done that would adversely affect the economy. As a spokesman for the Global Climate Change Coalition, a group representing leading oil companies, observed, "To limit energy consumption is to restrict economic opportunity and increase consumer cost."[13] On the eve of 9/11, activists on both sides were fiercely engaged in the debate. As an article in politically conservative *Human Events* warned, a "liberal concept of global warming" that would increase government spending, create new layers of bureaucracy (such as a proposed National Office of Climate Change Response), and add "heavy-handed regulations" was making its way to the Senate floor.[14] And, on the other side, an article in the politically liberal *American Prospect* argued that "increasingly intense floods, droughts, heat waves, and storms" as well as "infectious diseases like West Nile virus and Lyme disease" were so inevitable that President Bush would experience a "prematurely crippled, one-term presidency" if he did not act.[15]

Amid these arguments, there was nevertheless little sense that the public was seriously engaged in the debate about global warming. Polls suggested that people were worried, but neither immobilized by fear nor motivated to become more personally active. A *Daedalus* essay that September by Pennsylvania environmental activist Donald A. Brown suggested that future generations would probably regard the period's inattention to global warming with the same puzzlement with which people looked back on Jim Crow segregation. The problem, he argued, was that no major crisis had galvanized Americans into action. It was too easy to ignore the consequences of burning fossil fuels for future generations when nobody at present was seriously affected or to understand how rich countries' overuse of energy supplies "hurt the poorest on the planet." Not only were the ecosystems of the poorest nations most at risk, but people living in those areas were most vulnerable to increased flooding from storms and rising sea levels, their health was at greatest risk, and their food supplies would be harmed.[16] These concerns were well established in discussions about the environment. Yet the question of how exactly to make compelling moral claims was one that remained unsolved. Global warming presented an unusual challenge in this regard. In other instances, people might take action against peril from considerations of self preservation, such as protecting themselves against nuclear radiation or a terrorist attack. But if global warming was not a serious immediate danger, what arguments might prevail? Was it enough to show that the poorest nations would suffer? Were calls for sacrifice realistic? Or would nothing be done until it was too late?

The debate about environmental devastation in the months preceding 9/11 were both the latest in a quarter century of discussions and a prelude to concerns that would ripen in the coming months. In the threat of global warming the fragility of life was evident in ways similar to that of nuclear annihilation and terrorism. Things were neither out of control nor fully under control, but perilously close to endangering all of humanity and thus a source of profound worry. The differences lay more in how immediate, unanticipated, or catastrophic the threat might be. Global warming would not obliterate the world in a sudden flash or wipe out large buildings in a vicious moment. If it was happening at all, as scientists largely agreed, it was a slow burn, like water in a kettle reaching the boiling point sooner than anyone realized. The cultural response to this sort of peril was thus in some ways unique and yet in other ways conditioned by the patterns of thought and relations of power that had become customary in the last third of the twentieth century. Fear served both as an underlying current and as a force that could be manipulated. With no single event as pivotal as the bombing of Hiroshima or the attacks on 9/11, interpretations were less frequent, more scattered, and less subject to the agenda-setting influence of government. Yet the same inclination to transcend fear with action, to engage in individual and collective problem solving, was evident, and with it, the same emphasis on seeking technological solutions and debating administrative policies. The cultural response was shaped by the creative use of the imagination and focused decisively on questions of moral responsibility.

AFTER 9/11, NATIONAL ATTENTION SHIFTED dramatically away from global warming. The *New York Times'* coverage fell by two-thirds in the half year after the attacks compared with the half year before. *Newsweek* mentioned global warming only ten times in these months compared with thirty-three times in the earlier period. Plans to introduce an alternative energy package in the Senate to one passed by the

House were put on indefinite hold. Efforts by the EPA to end the Air Force's use of Halon, a chemical known to deplete the ozone layer, were quietly set aside. As the nation rallied around the president, opponents of the administration's energy policies sidelined criticisms they feared would appear divisive and in any case gain little traction with the public. A spokesperson for a prominent environmental group, the Natural Resources Defense Council, told a reporter, "We've shifted from trying to win high-profile defensive battles to basically deferring most of those battles." When representatives from 150 countries met in Marrakesh in late October to discuss cuts in greenhouse gases, U.S. observers lacked an alternative plan they had hoped to have ready and participated only as observers. On February 15, 2002, when the administration finally released its energy plan, no new initiatives were included to reduce carbon dioxide and other greenhouse gas emissions. Meanwhile, a national poll in December showed that only 15 percent of the public thought global warming should be one of Washington's top priorities, compared with 78 percent who listed terrorism or chemical and biological weapons.[17]

Although it was less in the public eye, climate change drew increasing attention from scientists. Between 1997 and 1999, the annual budget for scientific research conducted under the U.S. Global Climate Research Program averaged approximately $750 million. Under the Bush administration, the global climate research budget averaged approximately $800 million annually, totaling more than $4 billion between 2002 and 2006. If arguments about scientific uncertainty inhibited stronger regulatory policy measures, they were nevertheless consistent with the view that additional research was needed. Eight principal agencies—the U.S. Department of Agriculture, National Oceanic and Atmospheric Administration, Department of Energy, Department of Interior, Environmental Protection Agency, National Aeronautics and Space Administration, and the National Science Foundation—administered the research. Major program areas included atmospheric composition, climate variability, the global carbon and water cycles, ecosystems, land uses, and human contributions to climate change. Questions posed by the National Academy of Sciences' 2001 evaluation of IPCC conclusions about the extent and sources of global warming were among the topics that received continuing emphasis, especially through the Climate Change Research Initiative that the Bush administration announced in June 2001. These questions were the focus of a conference attended by nearly 1,300 scientists in the nation's capitol in December 2002 and were addressed in annual reports assembled for the Global Climate Research Program. Private funding facilitated additional research. For instance, the Pew Center on Global Climate Change, founded in 1998, published almost fifty scientific reports between 2001 and 2006. From all foundations, grants for environmental research in these years totaled approximately $1 billion annually. Researchers accumulated basic data on climate change through an extensive system of earth satellites and stations monitoring surface temperatures, oceans, and storms. Through computer simulations, scientists also developed models of the effects of carbon dioxide, other greenhouse gases, and aerosols on the environment. Other activities included reconstructing long-term climate cycles through evidence from ice cores and tree rings and analyzing the role of vegetation in removing carbon dioxide from the atmosphere. Specific activities included establishing the Climate Modeling Center as part of the Geophysical Fluid Dynamics Lab in Princeton, New Jersey, and creating new Global Atmosphere Watch stations in 2003, producing an assessment of arctic climate changes and developing new techniques for aerosol measurements in 2004, and developing long-range models of the history of climate change in North America in 2005. Besides the sheer influx of funding, investigations were furthered by advances in technology. Larger supercomputers, for example, made it possible to run ten times as many simulations as had been run only a few years earlier and to incorporate more variables and estimate projections over longer periods. Whereas studies of climate change even as recently as the early 1990s had focused largely on land surface and atmospheric temperatures and observations of sea ice, research a decade later also took into account the effects of aerosols, carbon cycles, vegetation, and changes in atmospheric chemistry.[18]

The research from these studies left little doubt that global warming was a reality. An advisory committee to the U.S. Global Climate Research Program wrote that proxy data from ice cores and tree rings showed that there had been fluctuations in the past but little or no evidence of long-term average temperature increases for the thousand years prior to the mid 1800s. "Then, starting in the late 19th century, the temperature started to rise and has risen especially sharply during the latter part of the 20th century."[19] Temperatures in recent decades were noticeably higher even than during much of the previous century. "The trends in the temperature record, particularly in the last 20 years," climate scientist Kevin Trenberth observed in 2002, "are now outside the realm of natural variability."[20] Over the next few years, additional evidence accumulated in support of this conclusion. For instance, scientists succeeded in piecing together data about climate patterns in the western United States for approximately 7,000 years against which they could compare recent trends.[21] Through temperature profiles obtained from nearly 700 boreholes, researchers were able to chart relatively modest warming over most of the past 1,500 years.[22] Satellite-borne instruments confirmed that temperatures were rising in the lower atmosphere, as well as on the surface, in ways consistent with greenhouse climate models.[23] An evaluation of evidence from several long-term surface temperature studies found it "plausible that the Northern Hemisphere was warmer during the last few decades of the 20th century than during any comparable period over the preceding millennium."[24] A summary report by the National Academy of Sciences concluded that surface temperatures of the earth had risen about 1.4 degrees Fahrenheit since 1900, with

about two-thirds of that increase occurring since 1978. The report further concluded that changes in oceans, ecosystems, and ice cover were consistent with this
warming trend.[25] Scientists expressed the rate and intensity of global warming in
various ways. Atmospheric maps showed widening areas of red depicting temperature increases in the Arctic and Antarctic and in much of northern Africa, Central
Asia, and the western United States. Word pictures indicated the importance of the
recent trend by saying that the rise in temperature would exceed all increases over
the past 10,000 years. Others described the shift as a "planetary imbalance" of "no
known precedent," meaning that much more energy is absorbed from sunlight
than emitted to space as thermal radiation.[26] One of the most notable images likened the long-term temperature patterns to a hockey stick composed of a relatively
constant line extending from left to right with a sharp upward curve at the end.[27]

The research pointed clearly to the role of human factors in global warming, or
what scientists called anthropogenic forcing. The sharp rise in average temperature since the late nineteenth century coincided almost exactly with increases in
carbon emissions and carbon dioxide concentration, which in turn corresponded
roughly with industrial expansion and greatly increased burning of fossil fuels.
Data suggested that approximately two-thirds of greenhouse gas emissions were
from human sources, such as industry, power generation, and transportation.[28]
Research further demonstrated that alternative hypotheses, such as increased solar
activity or volcanic eruptions, could not explain the recent trend. In addition, studies showed that different factors resulted in distinctive atmospheric fingerprints
that were consistent with human activities. For instance, an observed rise in surface temperatures with a cooling influence in the stratosphere was consistent with
an increase of greenhouse gases. Patterns consistent with coal combustion and
aerosol concentrations were also evident. Moreover, the future rise in carbon dioxide as the world economy continued to industrialize would be significant. These
were important findings because they suggested that global warming was not simply the result of cycles in nature over which humans had no control. The present
era—the anthropocene period, as Dutch chemist Paul J. Crutzen termed it—was
thus unique in geological history. If humans were the cause of climate change,
then they also bore responsibility for doing something about it.[29]

Projections about short- and long-term impacts of climate change were more
speculative, but included new evidence and models incorporating more considerations. One of the most widely discussed impacts was rising sea levels resulting
from melting ice and thermal expansion of ocean water (that is, water expands as
it warms). A prediction in the 2001 IPCC report that sea levels would rise as much
as three feet by 2100 received much publicity. Subsequent studies projected smaller
increases ranging from a few inches to a foot and a half. However, other evidence
suggested that glaciers were disappearing at about twice the rate previously
thought. The apparent reason was that global warming caused glaciers not only to

melt but also to slide more quickly to the sea by lubricating them with meltwater. Other factors predicted to speed glacial melting included heavy rain, hurricanes, and soot. Scientists were unsure how these factors would converge and what their consequences might be, but some scenarios predicted that coastal areas would be flooded much sooner than initially expected.[30] A second prediction was that the frequency and intensity of hurricanes and El Niño–related storms was likely to be affected by climate change.[31] A third prediction based on proxy evidence from AD 900 to 1300 was that modest warming would likely result in epic drought across the western United States.[32] Abrupt changes in temperature and rainfall could also result from melting ice caps freshening the water of the North Atlantic, thus shutting down natural ocean circulation.[33] Other studies examined increasingly specific implications of climate change, such as the implications of global warming for electricity demand, risks associated with hydroelectric projects, the fishing industry, wheat production, medical disorders, and local flooding.[34]

Research also focused on what might be done to mitigate global warming or its effects and what the costs of various approaches might be. The controversial, highly publicized Stern report on the economics of climate change (2006) estimated the costs of doing nothing in the hundreds of billions of dollars. The principal costs, the report said, would include higher prices throughout the world for scarce food, the expense of treating widespread disease, the displacement of homes and businesses in flooded areas, and damage from more destructive hurricanes. These expenses could constitute between 5 and 20 percent of the world economy for the foreseeable future and thus be significantly higher than the costs of taking action to reduce global warming.[35] Other researchers concentrated on developing and estimating the effects of various alternative and sustainable energy techniques. The many possibilities ranged from more fuel-efficient cars and public transportation systems to wind and solar power generation and methods of capturing and storing carbon dioxide.[36] With heightened uncertainty about weather, researchers also paid closer attention to forecasting. For instance, studies examined how better to anticipate mosquito-borne viruses, droughts, and wildland fires.[37]

On the whole, the research provided a firm basis for concluding that significant climate change was taking place and would likely continue unless corrective measures were implemented to reduce carbon dioxide and other greenhouse gas emissions. In only a few years, the level of confidence in this conclusion had increased noticeably. In a 2001 report in response to the IPCC, the National Academy of Sciences agreed that global warming was taking place, but hedged its analysis with numerous expressions of uncertainty, such as the following: "Because of the large and still uncertain level of natural variability inherent in the climate record and the uncertainties in the time histories of the various forcing agents (and particularly aerosols), a causal linkage between the buildup of greenhouse gases in the atmosphere and the observed climate changes during the 20th century cannot be unequivocally established."[38] Four years later, however, the academy asserted confidently that "the scientific understanding of climate change is now sufficiently clear to justify taking steps to reduce the amount of greenhouse gases in the atmosphere" and observed that "failure to implement significant reductions in net greenhouse gas emissions will make the job much harder in the future."[39] In the short run, people might enjoy barbeques at Christmas, picnics in January, and lower heating bills in February, but in the longer term the effects of global warming would scarcely be welcome. The science had become more certain and yet the trends were a source of fear because of what remained unknown as well as what was known. The failure of scientific models to predict storms or to provide accurate estimates of glacial movement dramatized the possibility that things could be even worse than they seemed. For instance, scientists pointed to the fact that studies had anticipated the negative impact of chlorofluorocarbons on the ozone layer, but had failed to realize that the solid surfaces of ice cloud particles were making these effects happen even more rapidly. By analogy, some disturbances due to global warming could be leading to other disturbances not yet recognized.[40] Weather patterns remained ominously complex.

The larger implication was that humankind was living in an ecosystem that was fragile and susceptible to serious damage. No longer was it possible to assume that the planet was a naturally self-correcting system in which hot and cold spells would simply come and go like the ebb and flow of the tides. It might have been possible in the past to imagine the earth as a solid, stable place, a secure environment that had been home to humans for a long, long time and would continue to be well into the distant future. It was now easier to think the earth-home might become too despoiled to be habitable. The climate change that had taken place in recent decades distinguished the present from all that had happened before. The trend suggested a tipping point from which there might be no return. Perhaps that was long in the future. Yet it appeared that a relatively short span of human history had produced almost irreparable damage. In a few decades or centuries the planet could become as much of a wasteland as if it had experienced a nuclear war.

FIVE YEARS AFTER 9/11, global warming had acquired unprecedented standing within the lexicon of public concerns, even while the debates about the war on terror continued. In 2006, the *New York Times* carried over seven hundred stories about global warming, more than twice as many as it had in 2002. The *Washington Post* discussed it in over 550 stories, also more than twice as often as in 2002. In both newspapers the coverage in 2006 was higher than before 9/11 by almost 50 percent, and in both the coverage had increased steadily during each of the three preceding years. A national poll in August 2006 found that 67 percent of the public thought "global warming is an environmental problem that is causing a serious impact now," while only 28 percent thought it "isn't having a serious impact."[41] In another national survey, 77 percent agreed strongly that "global warming is becoming a major threat to our country and the world."[42] Yet another poll showed that 68 percent of the public thought "global warming is a problem that requires immediate government action."[43] Thus, it seemed plausible that the media and the public had finally been persuaded by the scientific evidence.

The consensus scientists reached by the early years of the twenty-first century was by no means complete or without gaps. However, it represented the culmination of research that had begun much earlier. For more than a century, scientists had been interested in collecting information about weather patterns and testing ways of understanding variations in climate. For anyone who may have been interested in this history—and scientists certainly were—it was thus possible to breathe a huge sigh of relief and argue that knowledge had been progressing fortuitously just in time to save humanity from destroying the planet. That story was in fact told by some of the best science writers of the early twenty-first century. It was a gripping story of courageous scientists pursuing esoteric interests in scattered corners of the world and of light gradually converging to illuminate the darkness. The lead characters were driven by curiosity and just enough fear to sense that they were on to something important. They were the prophets of their time whose warnings needed to be heard and whose research warranted further investment. This was the background narrative against which the response to global warming was inevitably situated. It was a story that contained a great deal of truth, and yet one that revealed as much about storytelling as it did about science. It showed that peril is an aspect not only of the human predicament but also of persuasion. Achieving consensus about global warming depended both on getting the facts straight and on convincing the public at strategic times that consensus had or had not been attained. The story was sometimes told by scientists themselves, but was more often crafted by journalists and policy makers. They were the mediators who instructed the public how to think about global warming and they were in this respect like the interpreters who shaped the cultural responses to Hiroshima and 9/11. The difference was that global warming did not emerge on the public stage in a single dramatic moment. It was rather the kind of fear that waxed and waned, surfacing in public consciousness, receding, and emerging in different forms.[44]

In two earlier periods public discourse about global warming had risen significantly, only to subside, and on at least one earlier occasion a credible warning from the scientific community had received only passing attention. Interest was high between 1989 and 1992, only to plummet between 1993 and 1996. It rose again in 1997 and 1998, but receded in 1999. Until 1987, it received hardly any attention in the wider public, despite growing concern among scientists. Thus, despite the fact that global warming was in reality becoming increasingly evident during the last quarter of the twentieth century, public interest in the problem ebbed and flowed.

The episodic nature of this response contradicted the view that the accumulation of scientific evidence alone was sufficient to motivate public concern. Had that been the case, public interest would have progressed in the same upward linear fashion that scientific research did. But global warming was the kind of peril that could easily slip from public awareness. There were no cataclysmic moments to rivet attention, no anniversaries to commemorate, and no organized enemy to wage war against. Global warming became a front-burner concern in tandem with other problems, such as rising fuel prices and international treaties, and then faded from view as interest in these issues declined.

Although scientists had long speculated about the possibility of global warming, the first report to grab significant—though short-lived—public attention was in 1977. *Energy and Climate*, a report submitted by the fifteen-member Geophysics Study Committee of the National Research Council after more than two years of study, concluded that significant global warming was likely during the twenty-first century as a result of carbon dioxide from burning fossil fuels.[45] The report likened carbon dioxide emissions to glass in a greenhouse that permits sunlight and absorbs infrared radiation. The prediction of future warming caused by this greenhouse effect, as it came to be called, was based on estimates that carbon dioxide concentrations had risen by about 12 or 13 percent since the beginning of the industrial revolution and would likely rise by at least 12 percent by the year 2000. A doubling of this kind, the report said, could raise temperatures by 2.5 degrees centigrade (2.5°C). Although the report emphasized the tentativeness of its conclusions and called for further research, it was a landmark study not only in the extent of material it summarized but also in contradicting recent speculation about global cooling and in suggesting that warming was more likely a function of human activity than of cyclical weather patterns.[46]

For anyone who may have been paying attention, there was plenty in news coverage of this 1977 report to stoke fears. An article in the *New York Times* suggested that temperatures could rise by 10 degrees Fahrenheit and by as much as 30 degrees in high altitudes. A rise of this magnitude, the article stated, "could radically disrupt food production, lead to a 20-foot rise in sea level and seriously lower productivity of the oceans."[47] An editorial in *Science* warned that "humanity is in the process of conducting a great global experiment" and cautioned that "unpleasant effects" could not be quickly reversed.[48] The *Washington Post* editorialized that the "adverse, perhaps even catastrophic" effects predicted in the report were "like a disaster-movie script." Iowa's corn belt, it suggested, "might wind up in Canada. The effects on world food supplies would be enormous, nearly irreversible and possibly disastrous."[49] The *Los Angeles Times* headlined, "Disaster seen if U.S. relies on fossil fuels."[50] The report itself warned against panic, but called for a "lively sense of urgency."

The timing of the report, though, linked it inevitably to larger concerns about U.S. energy supplies and thus destined the discussion of global warming to be sidelined as soon as these other concerns diminished. Since the 1973 OPEC oil embargo, the nation had been more concerned with finding enough oil than with the possibility of environmental damage from using too much of it. In 1970, Saudi light crude oil had sold for two dollars a barrel; by 1977, the price had risen to $15 and then increased to nearly $40 by 1981. The price of regular gasoline rose from only 40 cents a gallon in 1973 to 60 cents at the start of 1977, exceeded a dollar for the first time in October 1979 in conjunction with the Iranian revolution, and peaked at $1.40 in 1981 during the Iran-Iraq war. After that, prices fell steadily, reaching a low of $11 a barrel for oil and 82 cents a gallon for gasoline in 1986.[51] The Carter administration's energy policy was defined largely as a response to energy shortages. "Our energy problem is worse tonight than it was in 1973 or a few weeks ago in the dead of winter," Carter told the nation on April 18, 1977. "The oil and natural gas we rely on for 75 percent of our energy are running out." Conservation, coal, nuclear power, and renewable energy sources were needed, Carter explained, less to protect the environment from overheating than to reduce dependence on the Middle East and to promote economic growth.[52] News coverage of the National Research Council (NRC) global warming report three months later was framed by the administration's proposal to expand production of coal-derived synthetic fuel. Although the report indicated that carbon dioxide from all sources was a problem, commentators focused on whether or not coal was especially problematic. The most dire predictions were not that global warming would increase but that the world would simply run out of fossil fuel in the next thirty to fifty years. Not surprisingly, these discussions diminished a few years later when oil again became plentiful and gasoline prices dropped. In 1982, when the National Research Council again released a report about global warning, the *New York Times* mentioned it only in a brief column on page 14, and an editorial a few days later asserted "there is no clear sign yet that the predicted global warm-up has begun." The major television networks collectively devoted fewer than three minutes to the topic. For the next five years, global warming was seldom mentioned in any of the major newspapers or on television.[53]

The first significant surge of public interest in global warming began in 1988, reached a crescendo between 1989 and 1992, and then diminished sharply over the next four years. In June 1988, with global temperatures at record levels and 40 percent of U.S. counties experiencing drought, scientists and environmentalists from forty-eight countries met in Toronto to discuss climate change and form a panel to gather additional data. CBS News presented its first major story about environmental problems associated with global warming, including scenes of dying fir trees and interviews with scientists and policy makers.[54] That same month President Reagan and Soviet leader Mikhail Gorbachev announced a joint project to plan for global warming. In October, the Environmental Protection Agency produced a 700-page report estimating that climate change would necessitate spending billions to alter roads, bridges, and water supply systems. In November, representatives from thirty-five countries met in Geneva, Switzerland, under the auspices of the United Nations and the World Meteorological Organization to launch a program to assess scientific evidence about global warming and analyze its environmental, economic, and social impact. That meeting created the Intergovernmental Panel on Climate Change (IPCC). Efforts to ratify and implement an international agreement from the previous September to reduce the production and use of chlorofluorocarbons continued. The World Resources Institute, an environmental organization, reported that temperatures might rise by nine degrees over the next few decades and that the problem was being aggravated by rapid deforestation. The National Coal Association responded by arguing that it was impossible to know for sure whether a greenhouse effect was happening or if burning coal was a contributing factor. Over the next twelve months statements about climate change made frequent headlines as scientists and policy makers discussed ocean temperatures, natural gas, nuclear energy, rain forests, automobiles, and the latest EPA proposals. The *New York Times* and *Washington Post* carried a total of four hundred articles about global warming, more than three times as many as the year before.

Whether global warming was a reality and, if so, what to do about it continued to be topics of intense discussion in the early 1990s. The IPCC issued its first assessment of human-induced climate change in 1990. After much discussion about what the George H. W. Bush administration would or would not support, Congress passed an amended Clean Air Act that included provisions for a five-year phase-out of chlorofluorocarbons. That fall, Congress also established the U.S. Global Change Research Program to evaluate scientific evidence and analyze climate trends and their possible effects. In 1991 the National Academy of Sciences produced a report suggesting that adaptation to global warming could be relatively painless. Discussions continued about the United States' commitment to combat global warming in conjunction with an international Earth Summit in Rio de Janeiro in June 1992. In April 1993 the Clinton administration announced a Climate Change Action Plan that called for U.S. greenhouse gas emissions to be returned to 1990 levels by the year 2000. The following October the Office of Technology Assessment released a 700-page report entitled *Preparing for an Uncertain Climate.*[55] Besides policy statements and news articles, popular books and magazine essays spread information about global warming. David E. Fisher's *Fire & Ice* described the greenhouse effect and its likely consequences for ice caps, sea levels, weather, and crops in easy-to-read language. Articles in *Flower and Garden* and *Reader's Digest* described global warming in similarly simple terms.[56]

The debate about global warming in these years was more detailed than in 1977 and articulated themes that would continue along remarkably similar lines during the next two decades. Scientists were reasonably certain that temperatures were rising and that carbon dioxide emissions were a contributing factor. Experts, basing projections on computer models, were less sure about how much or how quickly temperatures would rise. It was certain that ice caps would melt and beaches would erode, but unclear when this would happen or how serious it would be. Questions remained about the ability of forests and oceans to counteract rising carbon dioxide levels. Some scientists predicted a coming ice age and some argued that current weather patterns were part of a natural cycle. Journalists typically associated stories about global warming with concerns about drought, floods, and other recent weather patterns while quoting scientists denying that any specific connection could be drawn. There was some speculation that crops would be more abundant in cold climates, but predictions more often focused on food shortages, rising costs, and long-term economic problems.

Amid the quieter give and take, leaders searched for metaphors to communicate the gravity of the issue. "Humanity is conducting an enormous, unintended, globally pervasive experiment whose ultimate consequences could be second only to global nuclear war," declared officials attending the 1988 Toronto conference. A month later, a Smithsonian Institution biologist predicted that "the great environmental struggles will be either won or lost in the 1990s. By the next century it will be too late." Not long afterward, the National Academy of Sciences released a statement that "global environmental change may well be the most pressing international issue of the next century." In what was to be the first of many statements about the environment, Tennessee senator Al Gore Jr. wrote in a 1989 *New York Times* op-ed piece, "Humankind has suddenly entered into a brand new relationship with our planet. Unless we quickly and profoundly change the course of our civilization, we face an immediate and grave danger of destroying the worldwide ecological system that sustains life as we know it." Gore likened the impending crisis to the Holocaust. In 1992, some 1,700 scientists issued a "warning to humanity" about "irreversible damage" to the environment that "may so alter the living world that it will be unable to sustain life in the manner that we know."[57] All of this made for riveting reading.

The first national survey to mention global warming specifically occurred in July 1988. A question in that survey explained that chlorofluorocarbons (CFCs) were depleting the ozone layer—which "partially screens ultraviolet rays and prevents skin cancer, cataracts, crop and fish damage, and global warming"—and asked whether or not the benefits of using CFCs outweighed the risks. Not surprisingly, only 15 percent said yes while 57 percent thought the risks outweighed the benefits and 27 percent were unsure. Three months later a national survey of registered voters described scientists' reports about a greenhouse effect that could lead to drought in farming areas, beach erosion, and deterioration of forests and asked if the reports were truthful warnings of real and important danger or exaggerated and alarmist. Seventy-two percent of the public agreed that there was real danger while only 19 percent thought the reports were alarmist. Forty-two percent, though, said they had never heard of a greenhouse effect prior to the survey.[58]

It was clear from these early polls that Americans were willing to believe something detrimental was happening but had little knowledge on which to base their opinions. A large share of the public did not know about global warming or were unsure how to think about it. Those who were informed associated it mostly with ozone depletion and CFCs. Subsequent polls showed further uncertainty. In October 1988, eighteen percent of the public said the greenhouse effect was already happening and 21 percent thought it would occur within a decade, but 18 percent said it was at least two decades in the future and 23 percent had no idea when it might occur. After being told that carbon dioxide and other gases were accumulating in the atmosphere and raising concerns about harmful changes in ocean levels and weather patterns, 77 percent of those surveyed agreed that the greenhouse effect was a serious problem (39 percent said it was very serious). Yet several months later only 29 percent of Americans said they had paid much attention to news about the greenhouse effect.[59]

Polls conducted between 1989 and 1992 suggested that news coverage about global warming was beginning to influence the wider public. During this period the proportion who claimed to have heard or read something about the greenhouse effect or global warming increased from 58 percent to 82 percent and one survey put the figure at 86 percent. By September 1992, sixty-eight percent of Americans said they were sure global warming really exists, while only 19 percent said it did not. The proportion who felt global warming was at least a somewhat serious problem climbed from 77 percent to 89 percent and those who viewed it as a very serious problem grew from 39 percent to 46 percent. The terms in which global warming was discussed also shifted. Increasingly, poll questions emphasized "global warming" as well as the "greenhouse effect." Whereas earlier polls focused on CFCs and ozone depletion, later polls showed increasing awareness of other factors. For instance, the poll conducted in September 1992 showed that only 6 percent of the public attributed global warming to CFCs and aerosol sprays while 37 percent mentioned automobile emissions, fossil fuels, industrial pollution, and carbon dioxide.[60]

This wave of interest in global warming coincided with a rise in oil and gasoline prices and a corresponding interest in conservation and alternative sources of energy, just as the short-lived attention in 1977 had. Imported crude oil jumped from $13 a barrel in 1988 to $33 a barrel in 1991 and then sank below $20 a barrel, where it remained for the next five years. Gasoline topped a dollar a gallon once again in April 1989 and reached $1.38 in October 1990. Prices declined temporarily and then peaked at $1.60 in June 1991, after which they returned to prewar levels almost immediately.[61] The rise in energy prices and the possibility of interruptions in Middle East oil supplies sparked broader interest in energy policies. Global warming attracted increasing attention because it was part of these larger discussions. Its inclusion in national polls reflected this fact. Between 1989 and 1992, 58 questions in national polls referred specifically to global warming. That compared with only one question during the previous four years. It was also more than twice as many as during the next four years. The organizations sponsoring these polls included national news organizations (such as Times Mirror, CNN, *USA Today*, and the Associated Press), the Alliance to Save Energy, the Union of Concerned Scientists, the National Association for Plastic Container Recovery, and various other marketing and industry firms. The polls located global warming in relation to wider concerns about energy supplies, the economy, and energy policy. A 1990 "national energy strategy" poll in which two-thirds of the public expressed concern that the nation was entering a period of energy crisis focused on Kuwait, domestic oil drilling, and renewable energy.[62] A 1991 Americans Talk Issues survey, paid for by Florida philanthropist Alan F. Kay, included one question about environmental pollution among more than fifty other questions about energy resources, automobile fuel economy, Japanese competition, taxes on oil, and the Middle East.[63] A 1992 survey included global warming in a battery of questions asking about government regulation, oil, and the economy.[64]

Interest in global warming waned between 1993 and 1996 only in part because of declining oil prices and decreasing concerns about energy supplies. A second reason was that the problem seemed rather easily solved, at least in the short run. Global warming proved to be an exemplary instance of people responding to fear by engaging in problem solving. Although much of the discussion during the late 1980s and early 1990s had been concerned with the science of how much climate change was occurring and how rapidly it was happening, even more focused on practical solutions. One idea was to curb global warming by seeding the oceans with iron to encourage more rapid growth of phytoplankton. Another was to plant billions of trees. Yet another was to give loans to developing countries that promised not to cut down forests or build coal burning plants. Proponents of these various solutions implicitly accepted that global warming was real. However, the driving assumption in their proposals was that solutions should take into account uncertainties about how serious the effects of global warming would be. Practical suggestions in effect reduced an otherwise vague and perhaps daunting threat to something that could be expressed in dollars and cents. If combating climate change would cost hundreds of billions of dollars and slow the economy, that was too much of a price to pay. If the cost could be reduced, then action could be taken. Reducing chlorofluorocarbons in a phased process was a simple and relatively easy step. Another step that most Americans could support without having to bear any real costs was protecting tropical forests that absorbed carbon dioxide. Yet another was to use more natural gas in place of oil or coal. The matter was in a sense temporarily settled, not because environmentalists had overstated their case, as some commentators argued, but because interim solutions had been found. The nation would not be required to make significant sacrifices, as Jimmy Carter had suggested it might a decade earlier. There would be no major shortages of oil and gasoline or exorbitant taxes on those cherished commodities. Opinion leaders could take a breather, having to worry less that some new proposal might escape their attention and feeling more confident that whatever happened would be incremental.[65]

The other explanation for the diminishing public interest in global warming was that Congress devoted less attention to environmental topics in the mid 1990s than it had earlier, which in turn gave commentators less reason to write about it. Under the Democratic-controlled 101st and 102nd Congresses, committees considered global warming or climate change 45 and 33 times, respectively, and during the first two years of the Clinton administration, Congressional committees still considered these topics on 30 occasions. Following the Republican victory in the 1994 midterm elections, committees addressed these issues only 19 times during the 104th Congress and on only two occasions focused specifically on global warming. The first occurred in November 1995 as a continuation of hearings by the House Committee on Science. EPA administrator David Gardner testified that "there is a growing consensus that human-induced climate change is a reality." However, the hearing also considered arguments that global warming could be economically beneficial and that climate models were uncertain.[66] The second hearing, convened by the Senate Committee on Energy and Natural Resources in September 1996, discussed the U.S. position on climate change in response to a United Nations meeting and concluded that clear evidence about global warming caused by human activities was lacking. Committee chair Frank Murkowski urged the administration to "not enter into any agreements that would compromise the competitiveness of the American steel industry" and not ratify or implement any United Nations agreements.[67]

Although global warming was less in the news between 1993 and 1996 than it had been during the previous four or five years, the organizations that had been created in the earlier period continued to accumulate evidence and produce reports. These efforts to institutionalize research, to ensure continuity of funding, and to bring scientists together for conferences and to write reports played a significant role in deepening the expert knowledge about climate change and preventing policy makers from ignoring the topic entirely. The Intergovernmental Panel on Climate Change produced its second assessment report about climate change in 1995. In conjunction with this report, the U.S. Global Change Research Program (USGCRP, formerly the U.S. Climate Change Science Program) issued its own report and program summaries. In 1995, the Environmental Protection Agency published projections about the extent and implications of rising sea levels for American coasts. In 1996, the USGCRP produced another report calling for increases in public funding for climate change research and the IPCC issued a report warning about the public health risks of climate change. Scientists conducted research through the National Science Foundation, the National Oceanic and Atmospheric Administration, and the Department of Energy. Private agencies, such as the Center for Environmental Information, continued to host conferences and produce reports as well.[68]

The wave of interest in global warming that occurred in 1997 and 1998 was unlike the previous one in that gasoline prices had been relatively stable at approximately $1.25 a gallon from 1992 through 1997 and then *declined* in 1998 and fell to below a dollar a gallon for the first time since December 1989.[69] The price of imported crude oil rose steadily from $13 a barrel in 1993 to $23 a barrel in 1997, before dropping to $10 a barrel in 1999. The temporary spike in oil prices gave journalists reason to be interested in energy supplies and made it more conceivable that cleaner alternative energy sources might become cost-effective.[70] In Washington, though, much of the attention devoted to global warming was driven by the United Nations convention on climate change, held in Kyoto, Japan, in December 1997, at which an agreement was formulated under which industrialized countries would reduce their emissions of greenhouse gases. In preparation for that meeting, the U.S. Senate Committee on Foreign Relations produced a report on climate change, and hearings were held by the Senate Committee on the Environment and Public Works and by the House Committee on Science. A Senate resolution, which passed on July 25, 1997, called on the administration to refrain from becoming a signatory to the anticipated agreement. After the Kyoto meeting, the House Committee on Science continued to hold hearings. Other hearings were sponsored by the House Committee on Commerce; the Senate Committee on Agriculture, Nutrition, and Forestry; and the House Committee on Government Reform. Amid statements by scientists about rising sea levels and predictions of future warming patterns, much of the discussion focused on fears that the Kyoto protocol would ruin the U.S. economy. What appeared only a few years earlier to be a resolvable environmental problem now loomed as a serious political threat to the American way of life. The scientific evidence thus came increasingly under fire. As Congressman Jim Talent, who chaired one of the hearings, declared, there was a "pretense of a consensus" within the scientific community, blatant use of "selective and misleading" data, and "utter failure" to acknowledge "that the Earth's warming trend is natural and beneficial."[71] The Clinton administration signed the protocol on November 12, 1998, but, in view of overwhelming opposition among legislators, did not submit a bill to the Senate for ratification.

The Kyoto Protocol ceased to be a front-burner issue in 1999 and 2000, and media interest in global warming weakened as a result. Continuing attention to the topic nevertheless reflected policy makers' efforts to prevent arguments for ratifying the treaty from reemerging and to suggest alternative ways of thinking about climate change. Most of the alternatives focused on technological initiatives, market-based strategies, and tax credits. Novel ideas ranged from using farmers' fields to sop up carbon dioxide to purchasing credits from countries with low emissions (the so-called cap and trade approach). State and local officials proceeded with studies of how to prevent shore erosion, construct cleaner sewage treatment plants, and encourage businesses to work on energy-saving technology. The particulars, which dealt with modest deeds rather than sweeping proposals, were less amenable to public controversy than the Kyoto agreement had been and were relatively more technical than could be easily addressed in the media and other popular forums. During the 106th Congress (1999–2001), the Congressional Research Service produced nearly four dozen technical reports and Congressional committees sponsored almost that number of hearings. Questions continued to be raised about the reliability of scientific predictions, but most of the discussions centered on specific policy issues, such as whether the EPA was empowered to regulate carbon dioxide emissions, which greenhouse gases could be curbed most economically, what state and local officials could do, how corporations could be rewarded for implementing voluntary emissions reduction plans, and which agencies should provide funding for scientific research.[72]

The consensus that emerged by the beginning of the twenty-first century was at best fragile, as subsequent debates would show, and it was less an explicit conclusion about the science of climate change than an implicit agreement about the place of global warming in American public life. It included tacit assent to the idea that the planet probably had been warming and would continue to do so, but largely endorsed the notion that there was too much uncertainty about scientific predictions to warrant significant government regulation. What was most worth preserving was economic well-being, jobs, familiar lifestyles, and the freedom for market forces to continue functioning with minimal government interference. This did not mean that global warming should be or was ignored, but that it should be taken in stride, using the best in American ingenuity to combat it. In the process, public discussion waxed and waned, less because of what scientists were finding, and more because of adjustments to the emerging consensus that climate change could be addressed without extreme measures. Climate change itself increasingly became the rubric used in these discussions, rather than global warming. Apart from the technical arguments involved, climate change signaled uncertainty, complexity, and multidirectionality more than global warming did, and its connotations were less negative. Climate change required adaptation and flexibility. It was not a concern around which a specific policy agenda could easily be set. As Senator John McCain declared at a committee hearing in September 2000, "I am interested in hearing about what else the government can do to improve the current situation or, again, if anything at all actually should be done."[73]

HOW COMBATING GLOBAL WARMING might become an explicit national priority, as the war on terror did, was a question asked repeatedly by environmental advocates and social scientists. The mounting evidence and frequent warnings from scientists over the last quarter of the twentieth century did not go unheeded, but neither did they result in widespread public anxiety or mobilization around a centrally coordinated effort. In one sense, the reason was perhaps obvious: there was no single event, no mass loss of life, and thus no sudden outpouring of sentiment for something to be done. Yet it was puzzling that the concern expressed by leading scientists and in public opinion polls did not crystallize into a more specific plan of action. At some deep level, Americans seemed willing to take a wait-and-see attitude and preferred to let modest proposals result, rather than engage in concerted activities to reduce the possibility of grave environmental damage. The puzzlement about this response came especially from writers who noted that environmental concern had on one previous occasion been mobilized with surprising effectiveness. That occasion had been the campaign against pesticides that began in the late 1950s and extended into the 1970s. This effort achieved remarkable success in little more than a decade and thus loomed as a milestone in subsequent discussions about environmental agenda-setting. The war against pesticides, though, was more a lesson in why establishing global warming as a national priority could *not* follow the same path than a story about why it would.

By all accounts, the decisive event in the war against pesticides was the publication of Rachel Carson's *Silent Spring*. Although scientists had questioned the safety of pesticide use, Carson's book drew public attention to the issue and significantly broadened the debate. The book appeared in September 1962 following publication of three lengthy excerpts in the *New Yorker* in June of that year. At a news conference in Washington on August 29, occasioned by the announcement of Felix Frankfurter's retirement from the Supreme Court, President Kennedy referred to Carson's forthcoming book in answer to a reporter asking whether the Department of Agriculture and Public Health Service were looking into concerns about DDT and other pesticides. The next day CBS announced that the book and reactions to it would be the focus of a telecast later that fall. The program eventually aired on April 3, 1963, receiving mixed reviews from commentators who found it informative and balanced but dry. Meanwhile, the book had sold 500,000 copies plus 150,000 copies in advance sales to the Book-of-the-Month Club. It stayed on the *New York Times* best-seller list for 31 weeks and sold another 600,000 copies in the first two printings of a paperback edition. By 1987, it had sold more than two million copies.[74]

Silent Spring warned that pesticides were endangering the environment by killing off many more insect species than was necessary to protect crops or guard human health. With no insects to provide food and with poisons transmitted directly to birds, it was possible to imagine a future when no birds would sing.

"The most alarming of all man's assaults upon the environment," Carson wrote, "is the contamination of air, earth, rivers, and sea with dangerous and even lethal materials."[75] DDT, Carson argued, posed one of the most serious threats. The insecticide had been developed during World War II and was said to have saved hundreds of thousands of soldiers and civilians from malaria and typhus, allowing the war to be the first in modern history in which more casualties were sustained from battle itself than from disease. Yet evidence increasingly showed that DDT was a health hazard when used indiscriminately and was resulting in pesticide-resistant adaptations among insects. DDT was shown to be especially harmful to bird populations by hindering effective reproduction through the thinning of egg-shells. The larger problem, Carson said, was that outmoded science and technology were being used by chemical companies and by the U.S. Agriculture Department instead of developing better scientific methods for insect control based on an understanding of natural predators.

Reviewers praised the book for its compelling scientific detail and its inspiring prose. Brooks Atkinson, who likened *Silent Spring* to Thomas Paine's *The Rights of Man*, described it as a "meticulously documented book." Harry Hansen observed that Carson "writes with deliberation, stating a startling fact unsensationally." *Science*, calling the book "superbly written and beautifully illustrated," predicted that it would "undoubtedly result in wider recognition of the fact that [there] are serious hazards involved in the use of pesticides." A spokesperson for the Ecological Society of America declared that the "importance of this book and its effect on public opinion, national scientific policy, and the status of professional societies with respect to public affairs can hardly be overstated." Another reviewer wrote, "Seldom has a case been more competently prepared or so carefully documented." A team of scientists commissioned to provide an independent assessment of Carson's evidence concluded that "her facts are unimpeachable" and urged that the book become a clarion call the way Upton Sinclair's *Jungle* and John Steinbeck's *Grapes of Wrath* had. A biologist, who cautioned that the book was "overenthusiastic," nevertheless credited Carson's convincing evidence that pesticides resulted in resistant insect populations and judged that the study's warnings "will ultimately result in good."[76]

The book figured prominently in policy discussions as well as in literary and academic circles. When President Kennedy mentioned it at the August 1962 news conference, a review panel including representatives from the Departments of Defense, Commerce, Agriculture, Interior, and Health, Education and Welfare was already evaluating the role of pesticides in government programs. The following June, Carson appeared as an expert witness before a Senate Commerce Committee hearing on pesticide research and controls. In a fifteen-page prepared statement she provided examples of chemicals harming the environment and called for legislation to restrict the sale of pesticides and better government funding for research on new methods of pest control. Senator Abraham Ribicoff, who chaired the hearing before a standing-room-only audience, described Carson as the "one person most responsible for the current public concern over pesticides."[77] Carson herself was suffering from cancer and died the following spring. Interest in pesticide regulation continued at a modest level for several years, with news stories occasionally recalling Carson's warnings, and then gained traction in 1969 and 1970, when it became a topic of more than forty congressional hearings. As one of its first actions, the newly formed Environmental Protection Agency initiated a review of DDT in January 1971 and announced plans to curtail its use. On June 14, 1972, all federal registrations of DDT products were canceled and at the end of that year domestic sales and use of DDT became illegal. In announcing the ban, Walter Cronkite told *CBS Evening News* viewers that it represented the culmination of a ten-year struggle initiated by Rachel Carson.[78]

In the years following the ban on DDT, writers gave much of the credit to *Silent Spring* and thus looked for equally compelling books that could raise concern about other problems. On the tenth anniversary of its publication, wildlife biologist John George told a *Washington Post* reporter that Carson was "the greatest biologist since Darwin" and credited her with having "spearheaded the revolution" in ecological awareness. Five years later, amid continuing discussions of whether the EPA was moving too aggressively or too cautiously, Barbara Walters reminded television viewers that the war on pesticides had been effectively launched by Rachel Carson. In 1982, CBS reporter Bill Moyers commemorated *Silent Spring's* twentieth anniversary with a story about concerns involving a new pesticide called Temik, and in 1987 Peter Jennings provided a retrospective on the book's twenty-five-year legacy. Another indication of the book's stature was that animal rights activists argued that ethicist Peter Singer's 1975 *Animal Liberation* was the *Silent Spring* of their movement, just as reviewers said Fred A. Wilcox's *Waiting for an Army to Die* could be the *Silent Spring* of Agent Orange. In the 1990s, books about global warming joined the list, either by authors mimicking Carson's style or by publishers and reviewers drawing the connections. Al Gore's *Earth in the Balance* and Bill McKibben's *The End of Nature* both drew on Carson's legacy and were likened to *Silent Spring*. A decade later, proponents of efforts to combat global warming continued to cite *Silent Spring* as a kind of talisman or cure-all. "What's urgently needed is a *Silent Spring* for climate change," a writer in *Nature* observed, "a book that will do for the fight against global warming what Rachel Carson's 1962 book did to protect the environment from chemical pollution."[79]

Books aimed at raising public consciousness occasionally enjoyed considerable success. John Hersey's *Hiroshima* and Jonathan Schell's *The Fate of the Earth*, both serialized in *The New Yorker*, were two prominent examples. Ralph Nader's *Unsafe at Any Speed* and Eric Schlosser's *Fast Food Nation* played significant roles in setting policy agendas. But none had quite the impact that *Silent Spring* did, and numerous examples could be found of attempts to write agenda-setting books that failed completely. Indeed, as historians of the environmental movement observed, three books were published about the same time as *Silent Spring* and dealt with essentially the same issues—Murry Bookchin's *Our Synthetic Environment*, Theron G. Randolph's *Human Ecology and Susceptibility to the Chemical Environment*, and Robert Rudd's *Pesticides and the Living Landscape*—and yet they received only modest attention.[80]

Silent Spring's success must be understood less as a model of how other books might achieve agenda-setting influence than as a unique publishing event. It derived in no small measure from the fact that Carson was already a well-known author. Although her first book, *Under the Sea Wind*, which was published six weeks before the bombing of Pearl Harbor, drew few readers, her second book, *The Sea Around Us*, was serialized in *The New Yorker* in 1951 and stayed on the *New York Times* best-seller list for 86 weeks. A second factor was that the book itself was exceptionally well crafted and thoroughly researched. As scholars of literature have noted from examining carefully preserved early drafts and correspondence, Carson went to great pains to revise the smallest details of her text. The "Fable for Tomorrow" that provides the compelling first chapter of the book was recast in more universalistic and thus mythically inflected language. Carson adeptly used quotes to objectify and distance herself from certain arguments and authors, while personalizing the work of others. Although it was written in nontechnical language, the book included approximately fifty pages of references to scientific studies. At the time, some reviewers registered surprise that a *woman* could be taken seriously as an authority in science. Yet the fact that Carson had worked as a scientist and written about scientific topics before helped to establish her credentials. Being referred to in the press as "Miss Carson" may have drawn attention to her as well, and as feminism strengthened during the 1960s, interest in Carson as a role model grew. The book evoked more than its share of controversy, especially from pesticide companies that funneled an estimated $250,000 into attacking it, and thus inadvertently contributed immensely to publicizing it.[81]

The book's popularity may have also been furthered by larger public concerns. Literature scholar Rob Nixon has argued that *Silent Spring* played off the "national anxiety" generated by the Cuban missile crisis, which came only a month after the book appeared. Carson, he writes, exhorted an America "awash in paranoia to take charge of its fears by changing the way it lived." Combating pesticides was more manageable than fighting the Russians and was thus a means of turning overwhelming fear into a solvable problem. The "landscape of fear" shifted from the Red Peril to the "doom perched on the kitchen shelf." Whether that was the case or whether the missile crisis might just as easily have overshadowed the book, *Silent Spring* did play on existing fears of radioactivity. The first substance mentioned by name is strontium 90 and, as Ralph H. Lutts has shown in a perceptive analysis, the book includes explicit and implicit references to the effects of atomic radiation. There is some evidence that Carson's editor, Paul Brooks, suggested that she emphasize these connections, and in her Senate hearing testimony in June 1963 she referred specifically to chemical particles as a "new kind of fallout." The most immediate danger that millions of Americans could imagine, either from radioactive fallout or from pesticides, was cancer. Suffering as she was from this disease, it is not surprising that Carson devoted an entire chapter of *Silent Spring* to the relationship between chemicals and cancer. Her death, though unrelated to pesticides, forged a lasting symbolic link between the two. Legislative interest in cancer, cancer research, and regulation of carcinogenic substances grew in the late 1960s, just as concerns about pesticides did, and then rose even further in the 1970s.[82]

The other lesson from the war on pesticides is that the success of this effort was not linked as exclusively to *Silent Spring* as has often been imagined. Senate hearings about the lingering effects of DDT in milk and butter had been held as early as 1949. Later the same year, DDT and other new insecticides were the subject of a ten-day conference sponsored by the United Nations. Two years later, the American Medical Association issued a warning about the adverse health effects of careless use of DDT. By the late 1950s, researchers and physicians were reporting that DDT might be a cause of leukemia, Hodgkin's disease, and other maladies in much the same way that atomic radiation was. There were public concerns about insecticides before the publication of *Silent Spring*, and although the book made a powerful impact, many more developments had yet to unfold during the subsequent decade before DDT was banned. With increased funding for cancer research, scientists conducted large-scale studies of the effects of pesticides in the mid-1960s. In 1967 a local lawsuit resulted in a ban on DDT in Suffolk County, New York, and in the same year the newly founded Environmental Defense Fund initiated a wider campaign. Although the eventual ban on DDT constituted a victory, it was by no means the end of the story. By the close of the twentieth century, an estimated 2.5 million tons of industrial pesticides per year were still in use.[83]

On balance, then, the fight against pesticides offered relatively few lessons that could be generalized to questions about agenda-setting for global warming. Best-selling books describing the effects of climate change, such as Al Gore's *An Inconvenient Truth*, Elizabeth Kolbert's *Field Notes from a Catastrophe*, and Tim Flannery's *The Weather Makers*, came to be compared with *Silent Spring* and played a role in publicizing the issue, though their influence thus far has not been as profound.[84] *Silent Spring* was a distinctive publishing feat that furthered but by no means singlehandedly set the agenda for public concern about pesticides. If it was gracefully written, it was also strategic in its approach to the problem at hand. Within Carson's larger appeal for a fundamental revision of humanity's relation to the environment was a much more manageable task. DDT was one product that could be banned while the chemical industry continued to produce alternative pesticides. Though the outcry from chemical companies was great, the end of DDT did not spell their doom, nor did the shift from one kind of pesticide to others necessitate vast international agreements such as those involved in the debate about global warming. Carson's perspective on science was also well suited to the times. Her harshest criticisms were not against science itself, but against what she termed primitive science. Rather than needing to reject the advances of modern science and technology, the public could thus move ahead toward a better relation with the environment by embracing science. None of this, though, occurred in a cultural vacuum. What the struggle to ban DDT did more than anything else was to contribute to the formation of an organized environmental movement. That movement was destined to play a significant role in the later debate about global warming, and—as with the movement's connection to *Silent Spring*—this role was by no means straightforward.

IN 1962, WRITERS GENERALLY REFERRED TO RACHEL CARSON as a conservationist and characterized *Silent Spring* as a contribution to the conservation movement. By the early 1970s, the language had changed to environmentalism. Reviewers of Frank Graham Jr.'s widely read *Since Silent Spring*, published in 1970, described Carson as an environmentalist. In his 1970 State of the Union address, President Richard Nixon spoke in detail of the need to reduce damage to the environment. A few months later, Earth Day organizers further publicized the idea of environmental activism. The following January, the editors of *Time* magazine declared the environment the "issue of the year" and observed that "the 'decade of the environment' got off to a good start last year and the pace seems unlikely to slacken." In 1971, the *Washington Post* mentioned environmentalists 147 times, up from only seven times two years earlier. Over the same period, mentions in the *New York Times* grew to 272, an elevenfold increase. The Environmental Defense Fund, Student Environmental Confederation, National Resources Defense Council, Greenpeace, and Friends of the Earth gained increasing attention as leaders of the new environmental movement. Newscasters said the struggle to ban pesticides was being waged largely by environmentalists. The label soon came to be associated with other causes as well. Environmentalists were assailing power companies, leading the fight against automobile emissions, encouraging citizens to recycle old phone books and aluminum cans, opposing the construction of nuclear power plants, urging legislation to protect wildlife, and raising questions about pipelines and oil drilling. In the ensuing years, these and other issues—ranging from clean water to the protection of endangered species—gave the environmental movement a firm organizational base and a highly visible public identity. By the time climate change became of interest to policy makers and the wider public, well-established environmental organizations were there to press the cause. Yet the very presence of these organizations influenced how global warming was perceived and shaped the public's response. In significant measure, the battle lines were already drawn.[85]

The conservation movement with which *Silent Spring* was popularly associated originated during the first decade of the twentieth century with the creation of wildlife refuges and an expansion of the national park system during the administration of Theodore Roosevelt. These efforts in turn grew from private initiatives such as the Sierra Club in 1892, Wildlife Conservation Society in 1895, and the National Audubon Society in 1905. "Conservation" meant the preservation of wilderness areas and wildlife, long of interest to naturalists, and increasingly included concerns about deforestation, topsoil depletion, and pollution from mining operations. The devastation caused by drought, dust storms, and soil erosion during the 1930s further broadened the idea of conservation to include such practices as planting shelter belts, terracing hilly farmland, building dams, and creating detention ponds. In the 1950s, with some 2,600 soil conservation districts in existence, the U.S. Department of Agriculture had become an active promoter of conservation in this familiar sense, but at the same time increasingly came to be viewed by opponents of pesticides as conservation's enemy. "Environmentalism" not only resolved some of the terminological confusion but also provided a new banner under which a broader and more youthful constituency could be organized. The term fit well with the fact that the Environmental Defense Fund became one of the most active organizations in the fight against pesticides. Environmentalism also signaled a different and growing constituency within the wider public. Whereas conservationists could include farmers and policy makers who wanted monies spent on agricultural subsidies and did not mind using pesticides, environmentalists were more likely to live in cities and suburbs and express concern about spraying in their neighborhoods or visit national parks where rare species were being lost. The grassroots organizing and sometimes confrontational tactics of environmentalists further set them apart from conservationists. As historian of the environmental movement, Robert Gottlieb, observed, "The characterization of a 'new environmentalism' especially grated on the conservationists, who insisted on the importance of 'the old values in their own right.'" Although conservationists continued to make news throughout the 1970s, the coverage increasingly consisted of obituaries and stories about wildlife preserves in other countries, whereas environmentalism became the accepted term for activists concerned with clean air and water, health and safety, endangered species, and a host of related issues.[86]

The Environmental Protection Agency, formed in 1970, reflected and further defined the emerging meaning of environmentalism. What was to be protected were those aspects of the environment in which humans lived that might cause health problems or in other ways compromise the safety and aesthetic pleasure of humans. Protection largely meant keeping the air people breathed clean and the water they drank pure. These objectives corresponded with the larger concerns that Rachel Carson had articulated, permitting proponents of the EPA to embrace Carson as its symbolic progenitor. "*Silent Spring*," a writer in the *EPA Journal* later mused, "played in the history of environmentalism roughly the same role that *Uncle Tom's Cabin* played in the abolitionist movement." The writer added, "EPA today may be said without exaggeration to be the extended shadow of Rachel Carson." The EPA was an administrative response to growing popular fears that the quality of human life and perhaps survival itself was being compromised by oil spills, smokestacks, auto emissions, and toxic chemicals. Through centralization, it sought to better coordinate the activities of other agencies, set standards, and deploy technology. In 1970, its budget was slightly more than $1 billion; by 1979, that figure had risen to $5.4 billion, and over the same period the EPA workforce grew from 4,000 to more than 12,000.[87]

Public support of environmental protection was evident both in opinion polls and through heightened involvement in environmental organizations. A poll in May 1971 showed 63 percent of Americans agreeing that "working to restore and enhance the natural environment" was a very important priority; 56 percent thought government spending for such programs should be increased. By the end of the decade, poll questions about the environment had become more numerous and included more detailed questions that revealed areas of disagreement, but general interest in protecting the environment remained high. A question asked in a January 1979 poll showed 68 percent of the public registering concern about "environmental issues," while only 12 percent indicated a lack of concern. In July of that year, 74 percent agreed that "economic policy should encourage growth in the economic areas which are less harmful to the environment and use up fewer natural resources. Opinions about environmentalists and leaders of environmental organizations were inevitably more divided, but showed considerable support. In a 1979 ABC News poll, 54 percent of the public said leaders of the environmental movement "genuinely want to help the public" and 40 percent thought these leaders were making "reasonable" criticisms and demands. Personal involvement in environmental organizations, through limited, had also grown, as had the number of such organizations. In 1969, membership in the Sierra Club was already ten times what it had been in 1952. By 1972, the twelve largest environmental organizations claimed more than one million members, compared with 100,000 in 1960. In 1974, one directory listed 1,130 private consulting firms and 322 professional associations actively working on environmental matters. At the end of the 1970s, there were approximately 3,000 organizations working for environmental causes, up from a few hundred in the 1960s. When asked in a 1980 poll if they were an "environmentalist," 18 percent of the public said they definitely were.[88]

The environmental movement succeeded in connecting fears about pollution and illness with practical problem-solving activities in which average citizens could engage at relatively little cost or, as Richard Nixon put it in the 1970 State of the Union address, "minimal demands" on themselves. "Each of us," Nixon explained, "must resolve that each day he will leave his home, his property, the public places of the city or town a little cleaner, a little better, a little more pleasant for himself and those around him." Earth Day (April 22—it began in 1970, the same year as the EPA) provided an occasion to engage in such activities. In cities and suburbs people gathered in parks to listen to earth-friendly music, drink Pepsi in "Keep America Beautiful" bottles, clean up litter, wash windows, and plant shrubs. In a 1971 survey, an overwhelming majority of the public—87 percent—claimed to have been personally involved in protecting the environment. This number included 54 percent who had taken empty bottles to a store, 35 percent who had tuned their automobile to reduce exhaust emissions, 33 percent who had stopped burning their trash, and 26 percent who had recycled newspapers and magazines. Other activities that qualified as ways of participating in the environmental movement included learning about the environment, limiting the size of one's family, planting a tree, and eating organic food.[89] Unlike the threat of nuclear annihilation, which enlisted relatively few citizens in building basement bomb shelters and stockpiling food, the peril identified by the environmental movement was thus one in which large numbers of people could take part in combating. Pollution was local and its effects more easily comprehended than those of an instantaneous megaton explosion.

As Rachel Carson had done, environmental organizations for the most part kept the scientific community on their side and thus benefited from the penumbra of legitimacy that science and scientific research provided for nearly all issues involving a perception of collective peril. The Environmental Defense Fund originated in 1967 through the work of a small group of scientists and over the next decade continued to support scientific research into the effects of pesticides and other environmental carcinogens. Barry Commoner's Committee for Environmental Information evolved from the earlier Committee for Nuclear Information, which set as its mission the task of bringing scientists together with civic activists. At the height of the antinuclear movement in the 1980s, scientists working on behalf of Environmental Action, the Environmental Policy Center, Friends of the Earth, the National Wildlife Association, and the Sierra Club frequently found themselves allied with one another in opposition to the Atomic Energy Commission. Tensions with the EPA over the pace and scope of regulatory activities were also evident, but scientists were enlisted routinely to review papers and proposals. Federal funding for environmental research rose significantly. From 1969 to 1973 alone, membership in the Ecological Society of America grew by 32 percent and funding for ecosystems research increased 123 percent.[90]

Despite widespread support in public opinion polls, environmentalism was nevertheless controversial from the start. The originator of Earth Day, Gaylord Nelson, a Democratic senator from Wisconsin and longtime supporter of wilderness protection legislation, envisioned it as a friendly event, like a picnic, but Denis Hayes, a Harvard student who did the organizing, gave it a more purposeful political edge. Although the celebration enlisted an estimated 20 million people nationwide and consisted largely of teach-ins and other peaceful activities, it included radical demonstrations of the kind frequenting campuses at the rate of two a day in conjunction with the Vietnam war. In San Francisco, demonstrators poured oil into the reflecting pool at the offices of Standard Oil. Students in Florida staged a mock trial and execution of the automobile. Critics charged that Earth Day had deliberately been staged to coincide with Lenin's birthday and accused its organizers of being communists. The latter accusation had little basis, other than the perception in some quarters that New Left "radicals" were instigating unrest about environmental issues for their own ends. Environmentalism *was* popularly associated with the *Whole Earth Catalog, Mother Jones,* "greens," hippies, organic foods, rural communes, and other publications and activities of the countercul-ture. The rift with industry over pesticides continued and deepened as environ-mentalists challenged the practices of oil and mining companies, automobile manufacturers, and nuclear power facilities. Spokespersons for U.S. Steel, Union Camp, Consolidated Edison, and other corporations told reporters that the eco-logical crusade would result in lost jobs. Environmentalists, economist Milton Friedman said, were guilty of casting corporate leaders as "evil devils."[91]

The notion that environmentalism was a special interest group instead of a goal to which all reasonable people could give assent took hold more firmly by the end of the 1970s. Barry Commoner, who had become a leading spokesman for environ-mental issues during the pesticide debate and as a result of his own research on strontium 90, was hailed in a 1970 *Time* cover story as the "Paul Revere of ecol-ogy," but by 1976 a writer for the *New York Times* noted that Commoner was "openly disliked by industry, mistrusted by labor and regarded with a mixture of envy and outrage by his peers." Commoner's views had evolved from his best-selling *Closing Circle* (1971), in which he emphasized the inherent interconnectedness of the nat-ural environment, to his 1976 *Poverty of Power*, in which he argued for an environ-mentally grounded socialism and the formation of a new political party. At about the same time, Edward Abbey's widely read *Monkey Wrench Gang*, featuring eco-anarchists who spike trees and sabotage earth-moving vehicles, and the subse-quent use of these tactics by Earth First! activists, contributed to the impression that the wilderness movement's "lunatic fringe" (as Theodore Roosevelt once described "the foolish fanatics" to be found in any reform movement) was making a comeback. Polls registered some of the public's misgivings. The same 1979 sur-vey in which a majority felt environmentalists were genuinely trying to help showed that 57 percent thought environmental movement leaders were making it more difficult to produce adequate energy for the country and 49 percent said these leaders were out of touch with the public.[92]

WHEN INTEREST IN GLOBAL WARMING BEGAN TO RISE in the late 1980s, environmental activists were among the earliest and most vocal proponents of taking aggressive measures. The World Resources Institute, formed in 1982 through a $15 million gift from the MacArthur Foundation and with staff who had been members of the Council on Environmental Quality and National Resources Defense Council, provided information about the implications of global warming for U.S. energy policy. The Safe Energy Communication Council, also organized in 1982, advocated the use of alternative energy sources as a way to combat global warming. Other organizations, including the National Resources Defense Council, Environmental Defense Fund, and American Council for an Energy-Efficient Economy, focused increasing attention on scientists' predictions about climate change. Yet the involvement of environmental organizations brought several distinctive and often contradictory understandings of how best to tackle the issue of global warming.

One idea was that environmental issues could be effectively addressed at the local level and through the grassroots involvement of ordinary citizens. Getting large segments of the public to use safer pesticides and dispose of trash in new ways, and even to join in efforts to protect lakes and lobby for clean air, had been a remarkable achievement, especially in contrast with the relatively sparse involvement of individuals in activities concerned with nuclear perils from the 1950s through the 1970s. There was an impulse to fight global warming the same way. People could make a difference by turning down their water heaters and furnaces, installing solar panels, and washing their clothes less often. From the start, though, critics and some environmentalists themselves questioned whether Earth Day festivals, recycling, and the occasional clean-up-litter campaign were sufficient to protect the environment from pollution. Finding appropriate ways to address global warming posed similar questions. Citizens who had participated in earlier environmental efforts in small ways could help by using more efficient light bulbs and driving less, and yet it was unclear how much these activities would help and to what extent they would need to be accompanied by other initiatives.

An idea that reflected continuity between earlier responses to nuclear weapons and more efforts to combat pollution was that science and technology were crucial to the success of any agenda-setting and problem-solving enterprise. This view had become so widely taken for granted during the twentieth century that to think in any other way was almost unimaginable. It made sense, as Rachel Carson had argued, to replace the pesticides produced by outmoded understandings of chemistry with better methods of insect control based on the latest scientific discoveries. Similarly, the way to reduce pollution was to invent smokestack scrubbers and invest in methods to reduce lead in gasoline. The same logic seemed inevitable when it came to global warming. Greenhouse gases could best be reduced by inventing automobiles that were more fuel-efficient and focusing more research on sustainable energy. Technical problems required technical solutions. However, the hopes society pinned on scientists and engineers to solve these technical problems also carried a cost that went beyond the expense of research itself. That was the authority to define the problem in the first place. Different scientists and bodies of scientists became the voices that articulated varying conceptions of what the problem was and what needed to be done. As long as scientists disagreed, the task was not to do anything drastic but to conduct more research. An additional cost of reliance on scientists and technocrats was that some contributing factors and solutions were ruled out of consideration. In efforts during the 1970s to think holistically about environmental protection, *social* aspects of the problem, such as those emphasized by Barry Commoner and others who regarded the basic organization of modern society as a contributing factor, were increasingly marginalized. The legacy inherited by environmental activists concerned with global warming was largely one of technical solutions, such as pollution controls and higher vehicle mileage standards. "Environmental leaders are like generals fighting the last war," environmentalists Michael Shellenberger and Ted Nordhaus wrote in a controversial 2005 essay, "using science to define the problem as 'environmental' and crafting technical policy proposals as solutions." Despite the fact that nothing much had yet worked to combat global warming, they charged, "there is nothing about the behavior of environmental groups [and] environmental leaders that indicates that we as a community are ready to think differently about our work."[93]

Another idea that grew out of the earlier struggles was that the leading enemy of better climate control was corporate America. Long scrutinized by environmentalists for its role in producing pesticides and other pollutants, industry came under increasing suspicion of obscuring scientific findings and downplaying predictions of climate change to sell oil and automobiles and bolster profits. By the 1980s, it was already far more common to find environmentalists and industry spokespersons depicting each other as the enemy than as potential collaborators. Environmentalists were engaged in lawsuits to impede offshore oil drilling, halt construction of the Trans-Alaska Pipeline, reduce emissions from coal-fired plants, and protect endangered wildlife. Business publications, such as the *Wall Street Journal* and *Business Week*, seldom had anything good to say about the organizations pressing these efforts. As one *Wall Street Journal* editorial put it, "environmentalist sanctimoniousness" and "the depredations of the environmentalists" were doing everything they could to bring "domestic energy production to a stop." Business leaders who thought this way about earlier environmental campaigns were prepared to resist claims about global warming. Insofar as there was evidence to support environmentalists' arguments that oil companies were funding efforts to obfuscate scientific evidence, an "anti-business ethic," as one environmental researcher put it, nevertheless made it more difficult to establish a broad consensus about global warming.[94]

The response to global warming that seemed to many observers at the end of the twentieth century to have been painfully slow and remarkably resistant to scientific evidence was not the result of grassroots Americans being too little afraid of its consequences to take more concerted action or so fearful that denial kept them from fully facing the dangers. In the absence of a single dramatic event capable of focusing public attention as the bombing of Hiroshima and the 9/11 attacks had done, global warming became an issue that waxed and waned with larger questions about national energy policy and was shaped by the preconceived ways in which policy makers, activists, and scientists had dealt with previous environmental issues. The dominant view among experts on climate change was that it was an issue grounded in firm scientific evidence and yet best addressed in conventional ways. If technology had solved the nation's problems in the past, it would surely do so again, and there was a century or perhaps much more in which to invest in new technology. If only a new book like *Silent Spring* could be written, many believed, policy makers might take the issue more seriously. Meanwhile, something like Earth Day or a recycling campaign might help to mobilize ordinary people. Those were the inherited schemas from previous perils. They persuaded most of the public that the new challenges would be easily managed. It would be a few more years before a new response would be attempted.

EIGHT

SETTING A NEW AGENDA

IN NOVEMBER 2006, DEMOCRATIC CANDIDATES succeeded in winning a majority in both the House and Senate, ending an era of Republican dominance of Congress that began in 1994. The election reflected the unpopularity of George W. Bush's faltering war in Iraq more than anything else, but it provided new hope to environmentalists and scientists who were pressing for stronger measures against global warming. There was indeed much to encourage such hope. Polls taken in preceding months showed widespread public concern about global warming and a clear sense that something should be done about it. Scientific evidence was demonstrating more conclusively than ever that mean temperatures were in fact rising and that carbon dioxide emissions were a contributing factor. In 2005, President Bush acknowledged that humans were partly to blame for global warming, and in his January 2007 State of the Union address he described global climate change as a "serious challenge."

Yet the task of putting climate change on the national agenda as a significant societal problem was far more complicated than simply declaring it so. Like the peril of nuclear weapons and the threat of terrorism, global warming was subject to numerous competing interpretations even among those who agreed it was serious. Facing up to the reality of humanity's impact on the environment brought forth proposals that inevitably reflected the nation's values and revealed the divisions in these values. The struggle showed leaders' continuing faith in science and technology, but also demonstrated wariness in the public about trusting scientists too much. Coming as it did in the aftermath of 9/11 and during an unpopular war, questions about fearmongering and the manipulation of emotions for political purposes became a significant part of the debate. The earlier environmentalist legacy continued to inform arguments about the responsibilities of individual citizens. Only from a much longer historical vantage point would it be clear whether a workable agenda had indeed been achieved. In the short term, the process itself of debating an agenda served as the dominant cultural response.

FORMER VICE PRESIDENT AL GORE'S MOTION PICTURE *An Inconvenient Truth* and companion book by the same title were the most highly publicized attempt in the years after 9/11 to draw public attention to global warming and set a new agenda for combating it. The film opened in New York and Los Angeles on May 24, 2006, and by August 4 it had grossed over $20 million. In February 2007 it received Oscars for best documentary feature and best original song. Compared with such 2006 box office hits as *Pirates of the Caribbean*, which grossed $423 million, and *Ice Age: The Meltdown*, which grossed $195 million, the film's return was modest, and yet among documentaries, it was the fourth-highest-grossing production in film history. A national poll showed that 4 percent of the adult public claimed to have seen it. Three quarters said it presented an accurate picture of global warming. The companion volume stayed on the *New York Times* best-seller list for thirty-one weeks. Every major news source—CNN, CBS, NBC, *Newsweek*, *Time*, national newspapers, and countless web sites—carried reviews, interviews, and commentary. "We talk about global warming," a viewer in Indiana said, "but when you see the footage of those glaciers disappearing, well, it just made it much more real."[1]

Textbook treatments of agenda-setting argue that attention to public issues is at best ephemeral and, for this reason, is significantly shaped by mass media publicity. As journalism professors Maxwell E. McCombs and Donald L. Shaw wrote in an essay on the topic in 1972, "the press may not be successful much of the time in telling people what to think, but it [may be] stunningly successful in telling its readers what to think about." Once researchers delved into the topic, the relation between media attention and public interest naturally proved to be complex. For instance, detailed examination of news coverage and interest in the energy crisis from 1972 to 1982 showed sharp peaks in both around 1974 and 1979; however, the media responded first in 1974, while public opinion reacted independent of media cues between 1976 and 1978. Sociologist W. Russell Neuman, the study's author, argued that *crises* are more likely than other events to exhibit a close relation between media coverage and public attention. The energy crisis, race riots, and street protests against the Vietnam war had definite beginnings, middles, and ends. Each showed a surge of concern that overshadowed all other issues and then faded as the concern was resolved. In contrast, concerns about pollution, drugs, and poverty have less distinct beginnings and are seldom fully resolved. Public interest is driven less by any singular event, such as an oil shortage or riot, than by the release of a policy statement or government report, the publication of a book, or a staged grassroots activity such as Earth Day. These *symbolic crises*, according to Neuman, typically attract widespread public attention only when significant media coverage occurs first. The issue itself persists unresolved but public interest wanes until another report or event attracts media interest. Neither media attention nor public interest ensures that policy decisions will follow. Nor is it clear what exactly spurs media coverage in the first place. This framework nevertheless underscores again the differences between global warming and sudden events like the 9/11 attacks. Interest in global warming rose and fell with discussions of energy policy, concerns about energy prices, and the release of major scientific reports.[2]

An Inconvenient Truth sought to fill an agenda-setting role much as Silent Spring had in the 1960s—and in the final analysis experienced similar success and limitations. Like Carson, Gore emphasized scientific research, presenting it in easy-to-understand language, and coloring it with aesthetic imagery. Where Silent Spring included a fable about a hypothetical community with which anyone could identify, An Inconvenient Truth opened with a quiet, almost nostalgic view of a small river in Tennessee. Carson's credentials as a scientist and science writer were already well established and further demonstrated in the book's extensive bibliography. Gore attributed his interest to a college class taught by Roger Revelle, a leading climate scientist and an early voice of concern about global warming. Silent Spring included pen drawings of scenic landscapes, flowering trees, deer, microscopic organisms, insects, sprayers, crop dusters, and dark clouds. An Inconvenient Truth included spectacular close-ups of melting ice, dramatic time-lapse images of receding glaciers, images from outer space, and temperature charts. It also included footage of Gore recalling his son almost dying, his family's reaction to his sister's death from smoking, a discussion of the tobacco lobby, a computer simulation of the former World Trade Center site being flooded because of rising sea levels, and an image of a mushroom cloud.

The film's reach was arguably much greater than Silent Spring's. As the almost-elected presidential candidate in 2000, an outspoken critic of George W. Bush in 2004, and possible contender in 2008, Gore was never far from the limelight. His appearance at the January 2006 Sundance Film Festival in the company of Ralph Nader and Jennifer Aniston drew instant attention to the forthcoming documentary. Further interest developed a few weeks later when a school board in Yakima, Washington, banned the film from being shown in classrooms after a distraught parent—who believed global warming was the result of natural causes predicted in the Bible—complained that the film's perspective was biased. Media reviews prior to the film's official release over Memorial Day weekend, though, were overwhelmingly favorable. "You will be captivated, and then riveted and then scared out of your wits," Richard Cohen wrote in the Washington Post. "Our earth is going to hell in a handbasket." Laurie David, the film's producer, publicized it in appearances on The Oprah Winfrey Show, Fox News, HBO, and an episode of the popular soap opera The Bold and the Beautiful. When the film finally appeared, reviewers touted it as a singular achievement. "You owe it to yourself to see this film," wrote movie critic Roger Ebert. "If you do not, and you have grandchildren, you should explain to them why you decided not to."[3]

However, like *Silent Spring, An Inconvenient Truth* faced significant barriers. Carson's message was dismissed by some of her critics because she was a woman; Gore's, because he was a failed presidential candidate who came off as a wooden figure at the podium and was an exuberant champion of environmental causes. Critics said he was a scaremonger promoting hysteria. Whereas Carson's popular appeal was limited by the fact that she was a private person who seldom appeared in public, Gore was accused of being too much in the public eye and of exploiting the issue for another presidential bid. Carson's book was at least deadly serious, offering a sobering account of dying birds and impending cancer; Gore attempted to overcome his image of stodginess by straining to be humorous. Even without these attempts, global warming conjured up the same lightheartedness with which newscasters typically reported the weather. Editors had a field day with headlines reporting that Gore was "steamed about the warm weather" and "turning up the heat." The White House was failing to "feel the heat," and thus a "storm over warming" was brewing that might result in a "hot case" before the Supreme Court with environmentalists singing "bye bye birdies."

As had been the case during the crusade against pesticides, a series of loosely related events stirred additional interest in global warming. Speculation continued from the previous fall about the possible relation of climate change to Hurricane Katrina, as warmer seas were known to intensify hurricanes' force (though not necessarily to spawn more of them). As James Hansen, NASA's top climate scientist, offered new warnings about global warming, a low-level political appointee, George Deutsch, who had falsely claimed to have a college degree, sparked controversy by attempting to censor Hansen's remarks. The furor continued when the White House Office of Management and Budget deleted references to global warming from official EPA reports. At the 2006 meeting of the American Association for the Advancement of Science, nine thousand scientists signed a petition denouncing the Bush administration's interference. A group calling itself the Evangelical Climate Initiative popularized the slogan "What would Jesus drive?" to draw churchgoers' attention to carbon dioxide emissions. The March 26 cover of *Time* magazine showed a polar bear on a melting ice floe and declared, "Be Worried. Be Very Worried." "Never mind what you've heard about global warming as a slow-motion emergency," the story began, "suddenly and unexpectedly, the crisis is upon us." President Bush's sinking popularity in opinion polls encouraged writers to challenge his views about global warming with greater vehemence. "Bush has been studiously antiscience," declared one editorial in the *Washington Post*, "a man of applied ignorance who has undernourished his mind with the empty calories of comfy dogma."[4]

Cumulative media coverage of global warming was significantly greater for the year than ever before. A database of national and local news sources showed that references to global warming—about a third more frequent in January 2006 as in January 2005—became more than twice as numerous by July than in the previous July and retained that margin through the remainder of the year. Besides its cover story in March, *Time* referenced global warming more than a hundred times and *Newsweek* did so nearly as often. In April, Earth Day organizers captured media attention through some 20,000 local events, double the previous year's number. In July, recently retired NBC News anchor Tom Brokaw produced a two-hour documentary on global warming for the Discovery Channel. Meteorologists reported that the previous six months were the hottest on record in over a century. Later in the summer, CNN presented a special program on global warming, hosted by actress Daryl Hannah, showing footage of dying polar bears, melting glaciers, and deteriorating coral reefs. In September, British billionaire Richard Branson made headlines by pledging to invest $3 billion in efforts to produce and promote alternative energy. News coverage also included a growing number of studies and events of local interest, such as an instructional program about global warming at a high school in Pennsylvania, a walk to call for government action in Vermont, a study of warming's effects on ski resorts in Oregon, and one about its effects on the wine industry in California.[5]

ON FEBRUARY 2, 2007, the Intergovernmental Panel on Climate Change held a news conference in Paris to announce the results of its latest assessment of global warming. The IPCC report capped a year of new scientific reports from other groups and government hearings which, coming amid discussions of *An Inconvenient Truth* and articles and interviews in the popular media, attracted more interest than usual. In February 2006, the Pew Center on Global Climate Change released its *Agenda for Climate Action*, a set of fifteen recommendations for reducing carbon dioxide emissions and promoting sustainable technology. In March, climate scientists issued results of a study showing significant warming of the Antarctic troposphere over the past three decades. A technical report released in June by the Environment Michigan Research and Policy Center showed that carbon dioxide emissions in the state had risen 46 percent since 1960. A month later a report expressing the views of fifty experts concluded that greenhouse gases were making the oceans more acidic and thus endangering coral reefs. In August, California legislators approved a bill to curb carbon dioxide emissions and encourage the production of alternative energy–powered automobiles and solar electricity and heating. In September, the White House released a 244-page report about its own plans to address the problem. In October, the National Center for Atmospheric Research published a report predicting that "precipitation-related extremes" such as heavy rainfall and flooding would result in "significant economic losses and fatalities." In November, the U.S. Supreme Court heard arguments brought by municipal and state governments suing the Environmental Protection Agency to regulate greenhouse gas emissions from new automobiles. More than a hundred bills, resolutions, and amendments addressing climate change and greenhouse gas emissions were introduced to the 109th Congress during 2005 and 2006. In 2006 alone, *Science* carried more than two hundred articles about climate change.[6] To anyone who may have been paying attention (and many Americans were), the response to global warming had clearly moved into a new phase. From denying that there was anything to worry about, the official position was rapidly turning to the question of what should be done.

The IPCC report was again the most definitive statement. It reflected the latest consensus of hundreds of scientists who had spent the past six years collecting and analyzing additional data. Whereas earlier IPCC reports spoke of likely danger and probable causes, this one offered simple declarative conclusions. "Global atmospheric concentrations of carbon dioxide, methane and nitrous oxide have increased markedly as a result of human activities since 1750," the report stated, and these concentrations "now far exceed pre-industrial values." No longer was it possible, the scientists argued, to believe that recent climate change was only the result of naturally occurring cycles. Increased use of fossil fuels was the main culprit. There was "very high confidence"—meaning nine chances out of ten of being correct—that human activities since 1750 were warming the planet. "Warming of the climate system is unequivocal." Over the past century and a half, the average temperature was estimated to have risen by 0.76 degrees centigrade. The increase over the past fifty years had been twice that of the previous half century.

The report noted that eleven of the twelve hottest years on record since 1850 had occurred between 1995 and 2006. The report also noted that mountain glaciers and snow cover had declined in both the northern and southern hemispheres and that sea levels had risen faster during the most recent decade than in previous decades. Besides these trends, there was also evidence of erratic weather patterns that the scientists thought were probably associated with global warming. Increased precipitation was observed in eastern parts of North and South America, northern Europe, and northern and central Asia, while drier weather was evident in the Mediterranean, southern Africa, and parts of southern Asia. Changes in wind patterns, extreme temperature fluctuations, and tropical cyclone activity was also evident.

Based on the available evidence, the IPCC scientists predicted that fewer cold days and nights and more frequent hot days and nights over most land areas during the twenty-first century were virtually certain. More heat waves were very likely, with average temperatures rising by two to twelve degrees Fahrenheit by 2100. Increases in total rainfall were very likely. At the same time, more areas were likely to be affected by drought, more tropical cyclones would occur, and sea levels would increase anywhere from seven to twenty-three inches by the end of the century. All of these changes, the report concluded, were likely or "more likely than not" the result of human activity.[7]

The panel's conclusions led to commentary from every major news outlet. "Humans Faulted for Global Warming: International Panel of Scientists Sounds Dire Alarm," the *Washington Post* headlined, noting that the consequences "could soon take decades" to reverse. The *New York Times* described the report as a "grim and powerful assessment" of global warming, but offered hope that the danger could be "substantially blunted by prompt action." "The debate on global warming is over," *Time* declared. *USA Today*'s coverage included comments from environmentalists and policy makers who described the conclusions as "scary," "bleak," and "dire." Some sections of the report, one observer remarked, "read like the Book of Revelations." The newspaper's web site asked readers, "What's your biggest fear about global warming?" Forty percent selected rising sea levels, floods, and droughts, and a quarter chose heat waves and hurricanes, while only a third said they were not worried. CNN.com offered its visitors a chance to watch IPCC scientist Susan Solomon "deliver the grim news on global warming" and view an animation of rising water engulfing San Francisco.[8]

Polling continued to show widespread consensus that global warming was a reality. A CBS News survey in January 2007 found 70 percent of Americans agreeing that global warming is "an environmental problem that is causing a serious impact now." Three-quarters of respondents in an Associated Press poll thought global warming would continue to worsen. Pew surveys showed that 77 percent of those polled thought "the earth is getting warmer" and 47 attributed the problem mostly to "human activity such as burning fossil fuels," while only 20 percent regarded it mostly because of "natural patterns in the earth's environment." An ACNielsen survey of Internet users concluded that 84 percent of U.S. users were aware of global warming, with 90 percent of these regarding it as a serious problem, although the study noted that this level of concern was lower than in Europe and Latin America. Even Fox News, which had long emphasized doubt about global warming, concluded from a poll it conducted just prior to the IPCC report that 82 percent of registered U.S. voters "believe global warming exists," up from 77 percent in 2005, and that only 14 percent regarded it as an entirely natural occurrence.[9]

The emerging consensus was not unanimous. The *Wall Street Journal* termed the IPCC report "typically breathless," likened it to the words of a "fervent religious evangelical," noted that "crystal balls are notoriously inaccurate," and called on readers to "keep one's head when everyone else is predicting the Apocalypse." J. R. Dunn wrote in the *American Thinker*, "The debate's over, you say? It seems to depend on which scientists you talk to. It's easy to achieve 'consensus' if you only consult people who agree with you." As in the past, the divide ran along partisan lines. A *National Journal* poll of members of Congress found that 95 percent of

Democrats regarded it "proven beyond a reasonable doubt that the Earth is warming because of man-made problems," compared with only 13 percent of Republicans.[10]

Yet the terms of disagreement were notably different than in the past. Naysayers notwithstanding, the new debate was less about whether global warming was happening and more about alternative methods of combating it. Once again, the response to danger was not to sit back, hamstrung by fear, but to focus on what could be done. The options fell into two broad categories: mitigation and adaptation. Mitigation—taking measures to reduce carbon dioxide emissions—was widely favored by those who regarded global warming as a deadly threat to the environment. Adaptation—finding ways to adjust—appeared to suggest that climate change was not as serious as mitigationists argued, and perhaps for this reason was less popular among analysts of the problem. Mitigation had the advantage of being a solution that would solve the possible ramifications of greenhouse gases worldwide. Progress could be monitored relatively easily. It meant that polluters—the most industrialized countries and people who drove the most fuel-inefficient cars—would shoulder most of the burden, thus giving the idea a sense of justice. Adaptation, though, was being discussed with increasing interest among experts in risk management and hazard preparedness. Scholars in these fields focused growing attention on differences in vulnerability among people living in coastal cities, in rich and poor countries, and with different access to services and support.[11]

ANOTHER SIGNIFICANT DEVELOPMENT involved new appeals to and from business. While the *Wall Street Journal* continued to question the veracity of IPCC findings, a growing number of business leaders embraced the view that global warming was a reality. Profits would be affected, they argued, either by climate change itself or by policies aimed at curbing greenhouse gas emissions. As Cinergy CEO James E. Rogers observed at a meeting of utility executives in November 2005, "The regulations will change someday. And if we're not ready, we're in trouble."[12]

If nothing else, risk factors needed to be recalibrated. Lloyds issued a widely discussed report entitled "Adapt or Bust" that advised the insurance industry to improve its capacity to understand and actively manage climate change risk. Erratic windstorm and precipitation patterns, the report warned, would require insurers to adjust underwriting practices and, indeed, to anticipate an increase in liability suits. JPMorgan Chase and other leading banks initiated programs to help model the impact of climate change on clients' portfolios. The need to adapt was especially evident in businesses dependent on particular climate conditions. Diavik, a diamond mining operation in Alaska that depended on a 200-mile ice highway to transport supplies and equipment overland, experienced dramatically higher costs when thin ice necessitated shifting to air transportation. Warmer temperatures adversely affected cold-climate forestry and fishing operations by creating a more hospitable climate for pine beetles and disease among salmon. Faced with possible stiffening of carbon dioxide regulations, petroleum and automobile companies responded to protect or enhance market shares. California's initiative to reduce greenhouse gas pollution, for example, drew support from British Petroleum and Shell (based in the Netherlands), while generating resistance from U.S.-owned Chevron and ExxonMobil. Threats of regulation led also to coalitions, such as Ceres, an environmental network founded in 1987 that grew to sixty companies promoting green investment practices and discussions about regulatory and voluntary initiatives to reduce carbon emissions.[13]

The decades-old rift between business and environmentalists remained, but activists increasingly sought help from business leaders to mitigate and adapt to global warming. *An Inconvenient Truth* observed that "one of the keys to solving the climate crisis involves finding ways to use the powerful force of market capitalism as an ally." *Red Sky at Morning*, by National Resources Defense Council cofounder James Gustave Speth, argued that "corporations are at the planetary controls [and] have the technology, access to capital, and managerial discipline essential to the transition to sustainability." The Pew Center on Global Climate Change assembled information from Alcoa, DuPont, Whirlpool, and several other companies to help businesses monitor carbon emissions and track emissions reductions. The program helped businesses think about new product lines, such as alternative energy, waste management, and recycled materials.[14]

When the IPCC released its 2007 report, a number of prominent business leaders were already voicing support for a more aggressive approach to global warming. In a letter to President Bush a few weeks before the report, chief executives of ten major corporations argued that mandatory reductions in greenhouse gases were necessary. The signatories represented utilities, aluminum and chemical companies, and financial institutions, including Alcoa, BP America, DuPont, Caterpillar, General Electric, and Duke Energy Corporation. Such controls, they argued, would encourage rather than stifle a market-driven approach to climate protection. That approach, known as "cap and trade," had been used successfully in Europe, where companies that beat emissions targets sold surplus allowances to other companies. The favorable publicity the CEOs' letter received contrasted sharply with news coverage at the same time of alleged efforts by ExxonMobil to pay scientists to question the IPCC's conclusions. The company, according to accusations by the Union of Concerned Scientists, spent $16 million between 1998 and 2004 to cultivate uncertainty about global warming. A few weeks later, Exxon's chairman and CEO Rex W. Tillerson made a widely publicized speech in which the company appeared to be modifying its earlier position. "The risks to society and ecosystems from climate change could prove to be significant," he said. "So, despite the uncertainties, it is prudent to develop and implement sensible strategies that address these risks."[15]

The shifting attitude among business leaders was further evidenced in February 2007 when Texas energy giant TXU Corporation agreed to a purchase offer from Kohlberg Kravis Roberts & Co. and Texas Pacific Group, two large private equity firms. The deal put TXU, long criticized by environmentalists, into the hands of executives with a different outlook on greenhouse gases. Texas Pacific's top management included two members of the World Wildlife Fund. Goldman Sachs, a strong proponent of reducing carbon emissions, played an important advisory role. With input from the Environmental Defense Fund and the Natural Resource Defense Council, and encouraged by predictions that carbon emissions would sooner or later be regulated and taxed, the new owners laid out a plan to scale back construction of new coal-burning plants and return emissions to 1990 levels by 2020.[16]

Broader assessments of what might actually work to reduce carbon emissions were sobering. A study by the Electric Power Research Institute showed that electric power companies could contribute significantly to emission reductions, but that it would take at least twenty years to do it. Meeting that goal, the authors argued, would require increasing the number of nuclear power plants from ten to fifty and tripling the output of wind and solar energy projects. Neither increase seemed likely. Another report lauded Toyota for aggressive investment in hybrid engines, but revealed that only 263,000 of the company's 8.45 million recent vehicles—a mere 3 percent—were hybrids.[17]

There was nevertheless a growing sense that climate change posed new opportunities for profitable product development. "Regardless if there is a basis for linking global warming to CO_2 emissions or not, this is a huge potential market," a blogger observed. "If regulators and conservation activists convince people that they need the environmentally friendly economy, it will be a big feast for everybody from biotech companies to the car industry for years to come." It may not have been a feast for everybody, but it was for some. Airtricity, founded in 2000, was operating sixteen wind farms, generating as much electricity as fourteen coal-fired plants, and earning more than $600 million a year. Westport Innovations was earning $40 million annually selling spark-ignited natural gas engines to bus companies. Others used the growing interest in climate change to redesign marketing campaigns. Hertz, for instance, offered drivers a chance to rent cars with EPA ratings of at least 28 miles per gallon for an extra $3 to $5 a day. Wal-Mart made headlines by launching a campaign to sell ultraefficient compact fluorescent bulbs to 100 million homes.[18]

JUST AS IT HAD DURING THE COLD WAR, fiction now played an important role in telling the public what to think. Global warming was grist for the imagination as much as it was a topic for scientific panels and corporate executives. Books and movies depicted environmental catastrophes of all kinds. Humans battled scorching heat, drought, and disease; braved tidal waves and extreme cold; endured food shortages; and faced the limits of their courage and ingenuity. Like their counterparts in earlier epics, the protagonists in these accounts struggled heroically to adapt, to carry on in search of loved ones and friends, and to solve the daily problems of existence with which they were confronted.

Fanciful characterizations of environmental destruction were common well before scientific discussions converged on global warming. In *Noah's Castle*, published in 1978, science fiction writer John Rowe Townsend described a family living in a postapocalyptic world in which food had become scarce and struggling with the moral question of whether or not to share the supplies they had the foresight to stockpile in their basement. Andre Norton's *No Night Without Stars* (1979) followed the journey of two young adults three centuries after an environmental catastrophe as they searched for remnants of civilization before the catastrophe. Both novels resembled Cold War science fiction in which destruction occurs from nuclear explosions, although the emphasis was more on floods, heat, and disease. In each, the catastrophe is irreversible and nothing the protagonists learn instructs readers how one could be prevented. The moral is to be courageous and honorable in the face of adversity.[19]

Depictions of environmental catastrophes in these years mostly featured nuclear radiation. *Damnation Alley* (1977) traced the adventures of four survivors of a nuclear war as they try to escape radiation and mutant killer cockroaches. *The China Syndrome* (1979) focused on a conspiracy at a nuclear plant to cover up its faulty safety mechanisms. *Silkwood* (1983) told the true story of radiation-contaminated, would-be whistleblower Karen Silkwood. *The Day After* (1983) and *Testament* (1983) dealt with family life following a nuclear holocaust. By the 1990s, other themes were being explored. *The Airzone Solution* (1993) depicted a future in which pollution has become so severe that people have to wear filtration masks and a powerful company earns huge profits offering to solve the problem. *On Deadly Ground* (1994) showed Steven Seagal fighting an Alaskan oil company's destruction of plankton. *Chain Reaction* (1996), starring Keanu Reeves and Morgan Freeman, portrayed an oil conglomerate plotting to hinder the search for cheaper and cleaner energy. In *A Civil Action* (1998), John Travolta played a personal-injury lawyer litigating on behalf of families whose children have died or suffered birth defects as a result of chemical dumping. *12 Monkeys* (1995) starred Bruce Willis struggling to save humanity from a deadly plague.

Imaginative renderings of climate-related catastrophes followed suit. In *A Friend of the Earth* (2000), T. C. Boyle's protagonists—involved in environmentalist causes for years and suffering personal tragedies of their own—struggled to find love and happiness amid deforestation, extreme wind and rain, and dying animals. Alistair Beaton's novel *A Planet for the President* (2004) satirized the Bush administration's failures to respond when global warming caused a large section of England to be submerged, destroyed the North Sea fishing industry, flooded valleys in Nepal, and set off a killer hurricane over New Orleans. Janet McNaughton's *Secret Under My Skin* (2005) chronicled the lives of homeless children living in concentration camps after an environmental disaster. Kim Stanley Robinson's trilogy—*Forty Signs of Rain* (2004), *Fifty Degrees Below* (2005), and *Sixty Days and Counting* (2007)—graphically depicted crop failures, flooding, a stalled Gulf Stream, greedy multinational corporations, nonresponsive government officials, and dedicated scientists.[20]

The Day After Tomorrow (2004), based on Art Bell and Whitley Strieber's novel *The Coming Global Superstorm*, entertained movie audiences with a story about a severe storm set off by climate change that shuts down the Gulf Stream and covers the northern hemisphere in hundreds of feet of snow and ice. Produced at a cost of $125 million, the film grossed more than $542 million worldwide. Extensive media coverage sparked speculation about how realistic the story might be. Critics described the science, as one blogger put it, as "pretty much loony," while others reported that a secret Pentagon memo predicted events almost identical to those in the movie. The *New York Times* revealed that government climatologists had been instructed not to comment on the film. The Pew Center on Global Climate Change created an informational web site that asked, "If *The Day After Tomorrow* is fiction, what is the truth about global warming?" The truth, it answered, is that "global warming is happening and that it is already too late to avoid some of the effects. Even under the most optimistic circumstances, atmospheric scientists expect global climate change to result in increased flooding and droughts, more severe storms, and a loss of plant and animal species." Center for Equal Opportunity president Linda Chavez offered a different perspective. "If Hollywood isn't drenching its audience in blood or titillating it with naked bodies," she wrote, "it is propagandizing us with left-wing paranoia."[21]

The various fictional accounts differed in particulars but conveyed common themes. The devastation from climate change would be massive and probably abrupt. Whole cities would be destroyed. Hundreds of thousands of people have died and millions more are likely to die. The world is largely unprepared. Government officials have failed to heed warning signs and the vast majority of humanity has become victimized by this indifference or by its own inattention. Once an official response is organized, it is usually ineffective, if not a source of additional suffering. Powerful administrators and greedy captains of industry scheme to protect themselves and boost profits. In the end, only a few survive: renegades who live outside of organized society and find ingenious ways to keep hope and their loved ones alive or visionary leaders who struggle against huge odds to save the world. The fears portrayed motivate protagonists' activity and in turn let readers and viewers imagine that danger can be overcome or at least endured. Protagonists not only survive, but typically solve problems and scale heights of heroism that few mortals can hope to achieve. The lead characters are united with true

objects of their dreams, miraculously locate and save loved ones, and forge unlikely bonds of new friendship. Their lives take on deep meaning as they unflinch-
ingly risk all to save themselves and the world.

Ecocatastrophe narratives also reveal tensions in the real world and show characters struggling with these tensions. Beaton and Robinson stay close enough to
real life to highlight conflicting desires to trust those in authority and to rebel
against them. *The Day After Tomorrow* pits individual responsibility against corporate action. Lonna Lisa Williams' *Like a Tree Planted* (2003) portrays the ambiguity
of making a living while preserving the environment through a romantic relationship between a logger and an environmentalist. In Octavia E. Butler's *Parable of the
Sower* (1993) and *Parable of the Talents* (1998), protagonist Lauren Oya Olamina, a
young woman with empathic sensitivities, tries to establish a utopian homestead-
ing enclave and after discovering its limitations sets off on a journey to create a
diffuse network of activists spreading new ideas about the environment.[22]

While fear was prominent enough in these depictions, by far the most controversial rendition took the topic in a different direction. Best-selling author Michael
Crichton's *State of Fear* (2004), with an initial print run of 1.5 million copies,
described a Ralph Nader–type activist who heads a radical environmental organization called the National Environmental Resource Fund (NERF), committing
murders and intentionally falsifying claims about global warming. The central
theme is that fear about climate change is being manufactured by environmentalists to bulk up their power base and fatten their pocketbooks. In detailing coun-
terevidence suggesting that neither temperatures nor sea levels are rising,
Crichton elaborated ideas originally given in a 2003 lecture at Cal Tech in which
he argued that "a belief in extraterrestrials has paved the way, in a progression of
steps, to a belief in global warming." Recalling how he had as a child "dutifully
crawled under my desk in preparation for a nuclear attack," the writer explained
that science was, in his view, the "great hope for our troubled and restless world,"
capable of extending life, feeding the hungry, and curing disease, and yet still
subject to manipulation by the demons of "prejudice and superstition, irrational
beliefs and false fears." In short, the world had nothing to fear as long as it trusted
in science. The danger was in being fooled by activists and politicians instead of
listening to scientists. Unsurprisingly, scientists responded by vigorously defending the accumulated evidence about global warming and by arguing that Crichton
had cherry-picked and misinterpreted the studies featured in his novel, but at the
same time agreeing that dissent among scientists was healthy and fearmongering
inappropriate.[23]

Literary and cinematic works of these kinds could be interpreted as fantasies
through which repressed fears are brought to the surface, experienced, and dis-
pelled through the heroic actions of protagonists or the exposés of skeptics. The
catastrophes portrayed do play on fear, often positing death and destruction on a

larger and more immediate scale than even the grimmest scientific projections would suggest. Yet this is not all they do. Apocalyptic and utopian scenarios make us more aware of the realities of our own situation. They do not show us how to resolve global warming and other threats. Rather, they reveal that life as we know it is good, if imperfect, and that meaning lies in the immediate tasks of daily existence and in the warmth of human relationships more than in hopes of an imperishable tomorrow.

IF THERE WAS A GROWING CONSENSUS about climate change among scientists, this sentiment was by no means universal, nor did it sufficiently express the passion that had welled up among large segments of the public and even among specialists. An issue that had been debated so long and in such partisan terms could hardly be settled by cold facts. In the debate about global warming fear played a different role, but in some ways as central a role as it did in the war on terror. The possibility that a millennia-old balance in nature had been disturbed was frightening to contemplate, no matter how far in the future the predicted consequences might be.[24] People wondered too if the news was really as alarming as newscasters made it seem. Were their friends as alarmed as they were? There was also the inevitable wrangling among policy makers about how much or how little to say about the impending dangers. With little in the way of an immediate catastrophe to fear, people worried that their fears were possibly being manipulated, as advocacy groups encouraged the public to be concerned about climate change, and just as easy to conclude that a bit more fear might be a good thing.

Polls registered some of the public's fears, although they were frequently as inadequate for gauging the depth of these feelings as they were about nuclear weapons and terrorism. A Gallup poll in 1998 showed that almost four of every ten Americans (39 percent) thought it "very likely" or "somewhat likely" that "Earth will be destroyed by an asteroid, ozone layer problem, or other environmental disaster within the next century." Most striking was the fact that 49 percent of 18-to-29-year-olds thought this, compared with fewer than a third of those 50 and older. And among those who anticipated an earth-ending environmental disaster, fully two-thirds thought it would happen in the next twenty-five years.[25]

Belief that the world might end this soon was widely popularized in conservative religious circles. Interpretations of biblical prophecies asserted that conditions would worsen and Jesus would return to rescue believers and punish the wicked. *Left Behind* books, a series of novels loosely based on these prophecies, sold 65 million copies and were said to have been read by at least twice that many adults.[26] In one poll, two-thirds of the public agreed that "Jesus Christ will return to earth sometime in the future," and among these, a third thought it would happen in the "next one hundred years." Another survey showed that about one person in five thought Jesus would return during his or her lifetime; of these, nearly everyone thought that "natural disasters like earthquakes and floods" were evidence that Jesus was coming soon.[27]

Conservative Christians who thought they would be lifted to heaven when Jesus came had no reason to fear environmental destruction. They did have reason to talk about it, though, and this interest spilled easily into heated debates about the significance of global warming. One side, publicized in the 1980s by Reagan administration Interior Secretary James Watt, held that Christians need not be concerned about environmental problems because the end was coming anyway. That view, even if taken seriously by few on the Christian right, inevitably fueled concerns among those who disagreed. As one environmentalist observed, "I'm scared to death. These radical evangelical Christians actually believe that the faster we destroy the earth and our environment, the faster the 'second coming of Christ' will happen."[28]

The alternative view, which became more widely held among evangelicals by century's end, urged Christians to be good stewards of the planet by advocating against global warming. "I've been attending church for most of my life," said one, "and I have never, ever, been preached to about not needing to care for the environment because of the second coming of Christ." Observed another: "I believe it is my God-given duty to be not only environmentally conscious, but also open to the needs of the socially downtrodden the world over."[29] There was enough to be worried about that conservative Christians of this persuasion increasingly voiced concern about climate change. *The Great Warming* (2006), an evangelical film similar to Gore's *Inconvenient Truth*, showed a young mother being rushed to the hospital with an asthma attack, a child in Peru suffering from cholera, and a New Orleans tarot-reader predicting a violent hurricane. "To deplete our resources, to harm our world by environmental degradation," evangelical leader Richard Cizik said in promoting the film, "is an offense against God."[30]

Whether they thought of it in apocalyptic terms or not, global warming evoked worry among a sizable share of the American public. In a CBS News poll conducted in 2006, thirty-six percent of the public admitted that global warming worried them "a great deal." A Pew survey about the same time showed that 77 percent of the public was convinced that the average temperature of the earth had been getting warmer over the past few decades, and among this number, 45 percent regarded the change as a "very serious" problem.[31]

Other research suggested that global warming probably was not at the top of Americans' list of worries. In fact, one survey in 2006 suggested it might be near the bottom—at least fewer said it was "the most important problem facing the United States" than did the war in Iraq, the economy, immigration, terrorism, health care, and poverty. And yet, the poll showed that people worried about global warming as part of a larger cluster of environmental concerns, including pollution of lakes and drinking water, contamination of soil and water by toxic waste, air pollution, the availability of fresh water, deforestation, and extinction of plant and animal species.[32] A woman in South Carolina who said global warming would be a "seven" if she had to put it on a ten-point scale of serious concerns put it well. "It means we're not being good stewards of the environment," she said. "We're just depleting natural resources and not using things wisely."[33] If temperature change itself was not an immediate threat, it was an added indication that the planet was fragile.

What might be driving these worries was not always clear. The scientific reports gave reason for concern, but generally stopped short of associating current weather hazards with long-term climate change. Few Americans actually became ill from contaminated water or went hungry because of drought. It was more that reasonable people worried aloud about impending danger and wrote or spoke of their concerns. They did not fear only in private or deny their fears. "For a long time, we feared that we would destroy ourselves by a sudden spasm of bomb-dropping," writer Chad Harbach observed, arguing that global warming was worse because then we believed nobody would willingly push the button whereas now there was no button to push. "Like Oedipus, we flout the warning, and we'll act surprised, even outraged, when we find out what we've done." The real danger from global warming, others contended, was that there were subtle tipping points—thresholds— that might be crossed through a seemingly innocent rise in temperature and then initiate catastrophic changes across the planet. "Odds are you've never heard of most of these tipping points," one commentator cautioned, "even though your entire genetic legacy—your children, your grandchildren, and beyond—may survive or not depending on their status."[34]

Exposure to such fears, expressed by writers venturing to interpret the human significance of climate change, left many people worried. "ALL of FL will be under water in the not so distant future," a young woman wrote after watching a program about global warming on the Discovery Channel. "We here in the Northeast don't fare any better. They theorize that NY CITY and Boston will be under water too!"[35] It was easy to imagine that nature, so long personified, was responding to humans' neglect of it and perhaps even to well-intentioned efforts to manipulate it. "When the earth is ready she will do what she wants," an older woman who had lived through hurricanes observed. "It is terrible with all the things that scientists are doing to nature, including cloning humans, test tube babies, picking the sex of your next child, etc. Life was intended to be this way and I think God is showing us how wrong we are to do these things!"[36]

Had they been given a test about the science of global warming, few people would have passed. They had heard the term but were unsure what exactly it meant or why it was happening. What they knew was that there was a problem, perhaps not an immediate one, but a concern nonetheless, and what they could recall were pictures. A man in Minnesota who had several years of college training, worked at a school, and thought of himself as a wilderness person, was fairly knowledgeable about global warming, but faltered when asked to explain it. He wasn't sure what we were putting into the atmosphere that was causing the trouble, but he was quite concerned about it. "I've seen the pictures of the ice cap melt," he said. "Polar bears, my favorite animal, aren't going to have an iceberg to float around on. They're going to be drowning at sea." And he was especially worried that a nearby lake was becoming polluted.[37]

Worries about global warming connected readily to a wider array of frustrations. The proximate cause, as scientists said, might be greenhouse gases, but for ordinary people, a problem this big prompted larger thoughts about what might be wrong with society and even the human race. The real trouble, they said, was big government, fat oil guys, a country run by the rich, self-serving scientists, not knowing whom to trust, human stupidity, greed. Asked if global warming could be stopped, a woman in Indiana said yes; asked why nothing more was being done about it, she replied, "Because some people are getting rich selling us the fuels that cause the problem."[38] Another woman mused that nature was paying us back for our sins. "Maybe God is just cleaning house," she said.[39]

The more people heard about climate change, the more they brought their concerns about it down to a personal level, not necessarily connecting it to troubles in their own family, but interpreting it in ways that resonated with their values and experiences—their preexisting "mental models," as one scholar observed.[40] A woman in Michigan nicely illustrated the thought processes involved. She had a reasonably accurate sense of what was causing climate change, but after a few sentences asserted, "I don't understand exactly how it works, but I know it is not a good thing." What stuck in her mind was a story she had read about a community near Alaska that was "losing their homes inch by inch, foot by foot." This was the human dimension that drove home the meaning of global warming. "We in this country don't care about community. We don't even speak to our neighbor. For them, their community is their life, and here they are losing it completely."[41] A cabinetmaker in Illinois had a rather different view. He attributed global warming to people in underdeveloped countries cutting down too many trees. The solution: developing new materials that could be produced locally.

There was also the loathing-tinged fear that rose from so many years of partisan wrangling about environmental protection. Those who doubted global warming cautioned against fearmongers, while those who thought climate change was being undersold feared the power of their opponents almost as much as the environmental threat itself. Fear was a currency for trading jabs, a commodity thrown about in editorials and on talk shows. Few denied that global warming was a scary topic; they reveled in disagreeing about which aspect was scariest. Was it what would happen as the planet warmed? Or was it sleepless nights, the overweening power of environmentalists, and the possibility of lost jobs and rising taxes? Probably the latter, Fred Smith of the Competitive Enterprise Institute explained to MSNBC's Tucker Carlson. "It's essentially a plot by which rich guilty people allow poor people to stay poor," he said, adding that coal miners would lose their jobs and the world would be starved for energy. Prudent minds, critic William Rusher argued, should recognize the easily exploited "human impulse to fear" and further understand that left-liberal media liked to play on these fears and that scientists not only hated corporations but also used billions of taxpayers' money to study what might not be a serious danger at all. "Global warming is real," the Cleveland *Plain Dealer*'s Kevin O'Brien acknowledged, cautioning that the reason children might be worried was "because their little heads have been filled with overblown fears by people who ought to know better."[42]

The fears engendered by global warming were, in these ways, fundamentally similar to the anxieties that Americans had learned to experience about nuclear weapons and weapons of mass destruction. Fear was an emotion, felt viscerally as any reasonable person contemplated the day's news and worried where humanity was headed. But it was also a product of debate, the lingua franca through which the public made sense of what they were experiencing. People read and listened and watched, drew connections among the hard facts that came from scientists by way of the media, and imagined how all of this coincided with their views of human nature and society. Environmental change came into their lives both as images of a warmer planet and as a story about whom to trust, what lessons should be drawn, and how much to be concerned. Being human still meant taking charge, exercising control, dividing the big challenge of saving the planet into manageable tasks. The basic existential question of how to think of ourselves as one species among many on a planet that might be in peril was largely unasked, at least in broad philosophical terms. The question was rather addressed by assuming that what we had done in the past would work well in the future.

WHILE MUCH OF THE PUBLIC DEBATE focused on what to do next and at what cost, the threat of environmental chaos wore on the minds of many ordinary citizens, homemakers, and consumers. The problem might be so huge that nothing short of an international treaty or radical technological innovation could solve it. And yet to do nothing in one's daily life struck many Americans as being profoundly irresponsible. Fear of the worst was to be overcome by doing a little. Whatever it amounted to, doing something was morally better than doing nothing at all. This sentiment was clearly evident in a survey conducted in 2007 in which two-thirds of those who thought global warming was a problem at all (nearly everyone) felt "people like yourself [should] be doing more to help reduce global warming," while only 29 percent thought there was "not much that individuals like yourself can do."[43]

What could be done? There was a laundry list of useful activities, just as there had been decades earlier when environmentalists first urged people to pick up litter and recycle old bottles. "Here's what you personally can do to help solve the climate crisis," Gore said at the end of *An Inconvenient Truth*. Begin by replacing incandescent bulbs with fluorescent lights. Purchase more energy-efficient gas or electrical appliances. Turn down the thermostat. Use less hot water. The list went on. Walk, bike, and carpool. Avoid rush-hour traffic so as not to waste fuel in snarled traffic. Work from home. Purchase less. Recycle. Take your own bag to the grocery store. Become a vegetarian. Everyone, Gore said, had a moral imperative to act. These were simple, largely cost-free ways of fulfilling that imperative and many people agreed. Nearly six in ten in one study said it was possible for them "as an individual" to do something about global warming. In another study, 71 percent agreed that it was patriotic to "drive a more fuel-efficient vehicle."[44]

Sales of fluorescent lights and energy saving appliances edged up, and some organized projects attracted publicity (such as a tree-planting program in Sacramento), but the mental turmoil people experienced over these activities was almost more interesting than the activities themselves. So much attention focused on carbon dioxide emissions that people familiar with the issue thought instinctively about their driving habits and their automobiles—and often concluded that not much could be done. "The first thing we did," evangelical leader Richard Cizik told an interviewer, "was sell our recreational vehicle," a "gas-guzzler," and buy a hybrid.[45] People in less fortunate circumstances probably did not have a recreational vehicle to begin with, so it was easy for them to condemn SUVs. "Those things have just multiplied like lemmings," a man in Ohio said. But it was much harder to cut back on one's own driving. "I'm not prepared to make radical changes in my lifestyle," a man in Maryland admitted, explaining that he just wasn't ready for that and couldn't exactly say why.[46] When they thought of their automobiles, Americans recognized that drastic reductions in miles driven and perhaps a wholesale shift to public transportation would curb greenhouse gases, but just as strongly realized that they were unlikely to make these changes. "I've got a giant car that sucks gas," a man in California acknowledged, but "am I going to get rid of it; probably not." They often drew on the language of addiction—seemingly the common currency to describe all troubles. "We have a serious problem," President Bush said in his 2006 State of the Union address; "America is addicted to oil."[47] But, as with other addictions, the ability to change was not as strong as the desire. "We will have to change our habits," said the man in Maryland, "but I'm not ready."

These arguments played against the same background assumptions that had prevailed during the early years of the nuclear era. One assumption was that the issue was so large that there was very little the average person could do about it. In the nuclear era, this fatalistic assumption sometimes took the form of a near–fait accompli; for instance, if the Russians decided to strike, there was little hope that the average citizen would be spared. There was also the assumption that technological change was inevitable and at least beyond being guided very much by human decisions. Having been discovered, atomic power was simply a reality that would follow its own course, for good or ill, as though the technology had a will of its own. The same views surfaced repeatedly in discussions of global warming. The problem was so vast that individual Americans could do nothing about it. It would do no good for Americans to turn down their thermostats or drive more fuel-efficient cars because pollution from China and other developing countries, it was assumed, would more than make up for these savings. Besides the perceived scope of the problem, an awareness of the social complexity of scientific innovation and of society itself was significant. It took thousands of scientists and engineers to produce the atomic bomb. It had taken a century or more for society to become dependent on oil. Too many jobs were now at stake, the social infrastructure was too completely organized around highways and electricity grids, and the American way of life itself required that people drive and consume energy. It would take some massive innovation to change all that. The best hope lay in new technology. As columnist Robert J. Samuelson opined in a *Newsweek* editorial, "We don't know how to cut greenhouse gases in politically and economically acceptable ways." The only hope, he said, was new technology. "Unless we develop cost-effective technologies that break the link between carbon-dioxide emissions and energy use, we can't do much."[48]

The other assumption that resembled rhetoric of the early nuclear era was that the changes facing the world were actually beneficial. Discussions of atomic energy ranged from stoic acceptance to outright exuberance about the prospects of inexpensive power and new labor saving devices. Global warming less often found supporters saying it was an unabashed boon. It was harder to argue that when so many of the predictions described coastal flooding, violent hurricanes, drought, and disease. It may have also been more difficult to argue that something as unintended as global warming could be beneficial in the way that atomic energy and other inventions of science had been. The more common way of finding the silver lining in global warming was to leave the links unspecified. Weather forecasters, whose role on television news typically included light banter and a sunny personal outlook, encouraged viewers to enjoy mild winter days and visit beaches and swimming pools in summer. And it was not hard for Americans quietly to appreciate the daily forecasts. For more than a generation, Americans had been moving in droves from colder climates in the Northeast and Midwest to the Sun Belt. Now the Sun Belt was coming to them. They could remain in Chicago and Milwaukee and New York and worry less about snowstorms and ice. Climate change meant being able to save money on heating bills. In one national study, 28 percent of Americans actually said they had "positive feelings" about global warming.[49] It mattered little if oranges now came from the Carolinas instead of Florida, or if corn were grown increasingly in Canada. Balmy winter days and earlier spring flowers were hardly a problem. As one editorial in a New Jersey newspaper advised, "Most of us cannot control these forces of economics and nature, so perhaps we should just take our cue from the crocuses and try to enjoy the warm winter weather."[50]

Having lived for as long as they had with nuclear weapons, Americans had learned to focus on practical problems that they—or more likely, scientists—could actually solve. If we were to invest tax dollars in environmental programs, we wanted to know that there would be immediate results. Clearer reception on televisions, microwave ovens, heart stents—these were the kinds of innovations that could spark one's imagination. These were how we measured progress, how we convinced ourselves we were doing the right thing. In contrast, climate change had been happening for quite a while and would probably have really serious effects only in the distant future, people said. As one man explained, "I'm more of an immediate person. I want to see change happen and see things affected right now. With global warming, I don't know that anything we're doing today is going to affect me or my children even fifty years from now."[51]

NINE

THE CALL FOR ACTION

AT THE START OF THE PAST CENTURY, a German expert on agrarian economics put forth a bold argument about the dynamism of modern business. The enormous progress embodied in the industrial revolution, he argued, could not be explained simply as a technological feat. It could be understood only partly as the result of steam power, improved communication, better methods of keeping ledgers and organizing workers, and even of a conducive political climate. All these were necessary but insufficient conditions for economic growth. Entrepreneurs and the people who worked for them also needed to be motivated. They needed reasons to work long hours, to save and invest their money, and to plan for the future. Those reasons, he argued, could be found in the profound uncertainty they faced about the fundamental realities of life.

The writer was Max Weber, a forty-year-old economist trained in legal history at the University of Berlin, who had recently resigned a teaching post because of severe nervousness and insomnia. The essay, which appeared in a German social science journal, was later published as *The Protestant Ethic and the Spirit of Capitalism*. It gained instant attention among leading thinkers in Germany and soon sparked debates among scholars in England and France. After 1930, when the first English translation was published, it acquired prominence in the United States as well. Today, brief summaries of the book's main argument appear in numerous social science texts and the book itself is required reading in many college courses.[1]

What made Weber's work so interesting was his argument about the psychological effects of uncertainty. Humans have a fundamental desire for meaning, Weber believed, a need to think that life makes sense and is basically good and that a person who lives rightly can at least reduce the likelihood of experiencing the consequences of evil. Religions in their various ways, he argued, provide answers to questions about the meaning and purpose of life, and about why evil exists and how it can be avoided. Some religions encourage people to do good deeds to counteract the bad things that may happen. Other religions tell people to meditate, pray, or withdraw from a world that is inevitably filled with evil. What intrigued Weber was the way one offshoot of the Protestant Reformation—the Puritans who flourished in seventeenth-century England and America—answered these questions. Puritans taught that a person was destined to spend eternity in heaven with God or in hell with the devil. No difficulty that a person experienced in this life, including death itself, was as frightening as the possibility of endless torment in hell. To make matters worse, there was little a person could do to escape this dreadful fate. God alone decided who were among the chosen few to be blessed with eternal glory and who would be forever damned. Further, it was impossible to know which of these fates was waiting.

Faced with that kind of uncertainty, the logical course of action surely would have been to sit back and do nothing. Or to say, what the hell, let's enjoy life while we can. But the Puritans did just the opposite. They worked morning to night and did hardly anything that truly amounted to having fun. Weber saw that this was actually because of the radical uncertainty they lived with as a result of their religious beliefs. If a person was unable ultimately to control his or her fate, at least the responsible thing to do was to be a good steward. Working hard was no guarantee of escaping the fires of hell. But there was hope that if one did work hard, the work would be blessed—and surely being rewarded was a sign of divine favor.

Weber's thesis has much to tell us about the crises the world currently faces. The radical danger people now fear is no longer that of roasting eternally in hell (the many who believe in an afterlife for the most part believe they are going to heaven). It is the threat of life being cut off prematurely and on a massive scale that brings social chaos and perhaps destroys the planet or makes it unlivable for future generations. The road to perdition cannot be avoided with 100 percent certainty, any more than the Puritans could escape theirs. Nor is it possible to know for sure if the right decisions are being made—if the scientists who serve as high priests of our time are as wise as we hope they are. It is simply impossible to know for sure whether some hideous threat will become reality on a normal, blue-sky Tuesday morning or whether the dangers public officials warn about are exaggerated and long in the future. Yet the dominant response is action, just as it was for the Puritans. Action is driven by uncertainty. The possibility of danger is a motivating force. Taking action is a way of assuring ourselves that we are doing something— doing what we can, hoping that the search for knowledge will be rewarded.

The contemporary perils that threaten to kill hundreds of millions of people have been a strong motivating force for action, just as the theological uncertainties were for the Puritans. To be sure, there are other reasons to plan, to work hard, and to organize large-scale social projects. Weber himself recognized this. Once established, modern business is a self-sustaining dynamo. People work hard because their jobs require it and because their lifestyle benefits from it. In some ways, the frenetic pace of modern life is an escape from having to think much about the possibility of mass peril. Nevertheless, it is hard to exaggerate the extent to which modern society has also been shaped by efforts to anticipate, divert, and manage these potential dangers. The world has hardly sat back and waited for devastation to arrive. The threats, moreover, have been impossible to eradicate. Like the Puritans, the contemporary world lives in perpetual anxiety, never knowing with certainty whether it is on the path to salvation or destruction.

ON JANUARY 11, 2006, POPE BENEDICT XVI spoke to an audience of eight thousand at St. Peter's in Rome about the uncertainties of the human condition. Basing his remarks on the psalmist's lament in the Hebrew scriptures, Benedict observed that life is like a breath, a passing shadow, always limited, always subject to the flux of time. Humans are nothing, decrepit, weak, fragile. As knowledge of life and of the world has increased, he said, the possible uses of this knowledge have become increasingly dangerous, menacing. He exhorted his listeners to be aware of the continuing reality of divine action in the world.[2]

Fragility was a theme to which the Pope turned often. At a meeting a few days before Christmas 2006 with a group of young Catholics from Italy, he spoke of divine revelation to humankind coming not through force or power, but "in weakness and the fragile constitution of a child." Humanity being made in the image of God meant that acknowledging one's own fragility was to be "more human, more true, more beautiful."[3] On other occasions, he spoke about the fragility of life experienced by refugees, the persecuted, and those with disabilities. They were weak, easily broken. Similarly, he described democracy, freedom, and faith as fragile aspects of contemporary life. They could easily be subverted if not cared for properly. Fragility was a theme he had undoubtedly thought of many times when, as Cardinal Joseph Ratzinger, he served as close advisor to Pope John Paul II and witnessed the pontiff's long struggle with declining health. As one observer remarked, it was John Paul's fragility on the verge of death, struggling to speak and seeking to embody transcendence, that was perhaps his most memorable legacy.[4] For both popes, fragility linked closely to the belief that human life is a divine gift to be graciously received and carefully guarded. It connoted the very old and the very young, the dying and the unborn, the vulnerability of love in a world of self-interest, the faint voice of hope in a world of fear.

Yet fragility was an odd word to characterize the spiritual condition of humankind. A more likely choice would have been fallibility. Throughout its history, the church's leaders emphasized fallenness, denoting sinfulness, imperfection, and separation from God. Saint Augustine had an overpowering sense of human fallibility, especially his own in matters of fleshly temptation. Puritan children learned their ABCs from the New England Primer, beginning with the letter A, for which they memorized, "In Adam's fall, we sinned all." In theological terms, a fallible person has fallen away from God and for this reason is sinful, blameworthy, subject to divine punishment, and in need of redemption. In general usage, fallibility means making mistakes, committing errors of judgment, deriving or purveying falsehoods, and being untrustworthy, irresponsible, and unreliable. Fallibility is not pretty. It may be human to err, but error that involves being untrustworthy and dishonest is morally reprehensible.

Fragility does not imply the same sense of culpability. It is morally neutral. Fragility is merely a state of being. It implies no failure of moral judgment, no lack of purity, no ungodliness. A fallible person is the antithesis of holiness; a fragile person can still be likened to the incarnate God. People who are elderly, weak, frail, ill, or dying are not at fault. They cannot be blamed for their condition. A kind of innocence is implied. Babies are fragile and innocent. Fragility pertains to the nonhuman and the inanimate in a way that fallibility cannot. A delicate flower can be fragile, but not fallible. The moral implication for the unfragile and fragile alike is to be caring. Action must be taken to protect the innocent, the weak, and the vulnerable. Fragile families need support. Fragile communities require protection. Benedict's emphasis on the fragility of life is meant to call the faithful to action on behalf of the unborn, the poor, and the church.

Aside from religious contexts, writers increasingly describe fragility as the situation in which humans now find themselves as they face threats of nuclear annihilation, terrorism, destruction of the environment, and possibilities of unstoppable disease. "Whether we like one another or not, it is essential to learn to coexist, to live in peace on this tiny and fragile planet," Mikhail Gorbachev said in a 1987 New Year's message to the United States.[5] The Soviet leader's reference to a fragile planet echoed words that antinuclear activists and environmentalists used with increasing frequency since the early 1970s. In views from outer space, the earth took on new meaning as an island home, brilliantly blue against a sea of blackness, but also delicate and endangered. "It looks fragile," astronaut Kathy Sullivan said after her spacewalk in 1984. "It gave me the feeling of really wanting us all to take care of the earth."[6] The fragile planet was like a precious garden in danger of being overrun with people and pollutants. The imagery was reminiscent of Rachel Carson's portrait of jays and wrens, laurel and viburnum precariously balanced against the onslaught of dangerous pesticides.

An awareness of fragility can be a powerful incentive for action. A fragile ecosystem demands efforts to preserve it. A fragile planet requires special care. In accepting the 1985 Nobel Peace Prize on behalf of International Physicians for the Prevention of Nuclear War, Bernard Lown described an "extraordinary energizing strength" kindled from the realization that atomic warfare would have catastrophic consequences for humanity.[7] There was a sense of urgency, he said, to warn people and to work for a moratorium on the nuclear arms race. The opposite of fragility is robustness. A robust planet may also be an occasion for action. No harm will be done. It is simply a matter of taking advantage of opportunities. When danger is present, it becomes necessary to think harder and work more diligently. Survival itself may depend on it.

Vulnerability—the term more commonly used in discussions of terrorism— carries similar connotations. Like fragility, it suggests a need for action—a need to protect, care for, and otherwise reduce the possibility of damage. In some instances, the need for action may be even more urgent. Being fragile does not necessarily imply a condition that needs to be corrected. Babies are fragile, but they are expected to be fragile. Vulnerability suggests that something is askew—that the ordinary or past state of affairs was one of strength, which has now been weakened, or is threatened, and must be strengthened again. The actual or imminent presence of a hazard is implied. A hurricane is approaching. Terrorists may strike. The atmosphere is polluted. The action that results from vulnerability is consequently more aggressive. If weakness is to be overcome, more must be done than simply making sure things do not get worse. Some show of strength—some added commitment of resources—is required.

IN EACH OF THE PRECEDING CHAPTERS, the evidence examined showed that the response to an impending crisis was action. The threat of atomic weapons evoked action well before the bombing of Hiroshima, when in 1939 physicists Leo Szilard, Albert Einstein, and other scientists became concerned about the possibility of Nazi Germany using nuclear fission as a weapon. The Manhattan Project that produced the Allies' atomic bomb was a feat of both social organization and technical innovation. Research and production took place at thirty different sites. The largest, at Oak Ridge in Tennessee, appeared on no maps, but spread over 60,000 acres, included 75,000 employees, and used as much electricity as New York or Chicago. People knew they were working on something important, even though they did not know what it was. When news came of the devastation at Hiroshima and Nagasaki, the world was hardly silent. The intense commentary that filled newspapers was a form of action. It satisfied the public's curiosity about how a weapon of such power had been developed and what its implications for the future might be. Americans soberly consumed the information about conditions in Japan and mentally related it to what they knew about military casualties and the costs of war. As the war ended, the Atomic Energy Commission became the nation's response to the opportunities and dangers of nuclear energy. There was plenty of debate about how the AEC should be organized, but there was little disagreement that some such regulatory agency was needed. In later years, antinuclear activists would charge that the public had not taken sufficient action to halt the proliferation of nuclear weapons. Yet the lack of activism was not inaction. The public had responded by investing in the construction of weapons designed to counter other weapons and by electing leaders who promised vigilance and bold action in the event of a Soviet attack. That had seemed sufficient at the time. Eventually the public did begin to mobilize against further proliferation and especially against nuclear power plants being built near their communities.

The response to 9/11 consisted of a strong call to action fueled by shock, rage, and fear of further attacks. Clearer evidence cannot be found that the response to life-endangering threats is to take action, not to sit back and do nothing. Feeling itself vulnerable, the nation wanted to show strength. The immediate perpetrators were dead, so their coconspirators needed to be hunted down, whether they were in Afghanistan, in sixty other countries, or in sleeper cells hidden in Paterson, New Jersey, or Buffalo, New York. If coconspirators could not be found, regimes harboring them had to be punished. The logic was decisively one of problem solving—of rooting out terrorists and making America safe. It was also a matter of overcoming weakness by exercising the nation's military might. The time proved right to mobilize public opinion for a war that in quieter times would have received little support.

The intermittent threats of swine flu, avian flu, and other viruses—as well as the threat of a massive meltdown of the nation's computers—were similarly responded to with a can-do and (literally) roll-up-your-sleeves attitude. People installed updates on their computers and lined up for vaccinations. Panic was rare. A few people quit their jobs and fled to the hills or barricaded themselves in their basements. But the majority responded by supporting the efforts being waged on their behalf by doctors, scientists, and public health officials. These were costly efforts and there was no guarantee that they would be effective. It was possible to imagine that millions of people would die. Yet the projections of worst-case scenarios were part of the information being produced and distributed by organizations charged with monitoring infectious diseases and anticipating alternative possibilities. For the average citizen, problem solving consisted not only of knowing what precautions to take, but also of determining how to think about the information these organizations supplied. Taking action, however limited, affirmed something basic about the human condition. It assured us that we were responding appropriately.

The possibility of environmental chaos from climate change is quite different from the danger Americans experienced and feared from the 9/11 attacks or avian flu. It has been much harder for the public to feel a sense of urgency about global warming. Few were losing jobs or homes because of rising temperatures. Oil and coal generally remained cheaper than alternative sources of energy. The mobilization that did occur was largely an effort, on one side, to demonstrate that a problem existed, and on the other side, to show that it did not. The former accused the latter of being in denial. But if they were, it was not the kind of denial born of abject fear. It was rather based on information they believed to be credible. It came from articles and advertisements in newspapers and from debates on television and at congressional hearings. As public opinion gradually tilted toward accepting the evidence that climate change was real and caused by humans, the reason was that investments in research were providing more convincing evidence. The costs of failure and the benefits of taking judicious steps toward reducing carbon dioxide emissions were also becoming clearer.

If the response to perceived dangers is actually one of taking aggressive action, why is it so easy to assume that just the opposite is the case? Because promoters of action try to mobilize the public by accusing it of inaction. Writers who saw the potential horror of atomic weapons told the public that it should rise up in support of a ban on the production of such weapons. The problem, they said, was public apathy. The same was true of environmentalists who counseled the public to be more concerned about banning pesticides, combating acid rain and toxins, and lobbying for legislation against greenhouse gases. Public officials, they said, were not paying attention and were unwilling to invest more in efforts to pass laws and promote imaginative research. Health officials said the public should pay more attention to the threat of a pandemic. Paying more attention meant supporting appropriation bills and helping monitor the spread of infectious disease. Preppers—people who prided themselves on being prepared for all contingencies—warned that individual citizens should stockpile food and medical supplies.

Another reason why concerted action could seem like inaction is the ambiguity over officials' and citizens' responsibilities. People who pay attention to news about impending crises—and not everyone does—know that scientists and public officials are working on possible solutions, but people also feel that they themselves should be doing something. In most aspects of life, the way to protect oneself and one's family is to take personal responsibility—purchase insurance, see the doctor, eat healthy. Trusting a faceless organization to solve the problem runs counter to these inclinations. Surely an individual should also take action. And admonitions to do something are abundant. A schoolchild should be prepared to "duck and cover." Her parents should have a bomb shelter in the basement. The prudent person will stockpile food and water. Despite the fact that few people actually do these things, many feel they should. They feel guilty for not doing more to protect their families, or apathetic because they have not participated in a protest march—whereas in fact, they have as taxpayers and citizens been part of a massive, organized effort to support scientific research and to enlist the nation's experts in programs to anticipate the worst.

BUSINESS CONSULTANTS THOMAS J. PETERS and Robert H. Waterman Jr. popularized the phrase "a bias for action" in their 1982 best seller *In Search of Excellence*. The leaders of highly successful companies, they argued, seldom sat around wondering what to do. They instead took action. Inaction stemmed from being overwhelmed by complexity, wading knee-deep in ideas, and forming committees that prevented anything from being done. A bias (or inclination) in favor of action characterized companies that pieced together practical information to solve problems. The process was partly mental, involving what the authors called "chunking"—breaking large problems into smaller ones and thus making them manageable. Instead of feeling stymied by a seemingly intractable situation, managers with an action bias created ad hoc teams and linked them informally into networks that got the job done.[8]

The writers acknowledged that it was difficult to articulate exactly what a bias for action was—and Peters later confessed (and then retracted his confession) that he and Waterman faked the data from which they claimed to have drawn their conclusions about excellent companies.[9] The notion of a bias for action nevertheless resonated. Motivational speakers included it among the marks of great leaders. Companies mentioned it among the characteristics they were seeking in new employees. CEOs assured board members that their companies were indeed being led by executives with a bias for action.[10] Research seldom offered definitive evidence, but suggested that effective entrepreneurs frequently did embody a disposition to act. They took risks, played hunches, and trusted their instincts.[11] More important, the research also suggested that everyone has a propensity to take action. It is simply facilitated in some circumstances and hindered in others. As social scientists Anthony Patt and Richard Zeckhauser observed, nature itself has "equipped us with a desire to do something," noting that fight-or-flight responses basically consist of physiological preparations for action and that humans seem inclined to escape boredom by seeking stimulation in new activities.[12]

If there is a basic propensity for action, it is not surprising that the human response to peril follows suit. Against the view that danger is immobilizing, the bias for action suggests that people are programmed to seek solutions, even if there are no guarantees of success. Peters and Waterman suggest, moreover, that organizations thrive on this bias. They succeed by encouraging it. Business leaders are recruited to take action and rewarded for it. It is not in their interest to wait around and do nothing. The same is true of experts paid to anticipate and guard against large catastrophes. It is their job to do something. When terror and disease threaten, they are entrusted with the responsibility of anticipating the worst and figuring out how to avoid it. They have a built-in bias for action.

This is to say, again, that crises have essentially become institutionalized. By their nature, crises are unexpected, and do indeed occur unexpectedly, as 9/11 so clearly demonstrated. Yet the recurrence of small and large catastrophes—and the ongoing possibility of even larger-scale perils—creates a demand for preparation. The refrain of society being "overdue" for a catastrophe—the "not if, but when" language—encourages preparation for action. To institutionalize peril is to set in motion a process of always being slightly on edge. It is like posting warning signs on a highway. The signs are meant to reduce danger, but do so by evoking anxiety—at least enough that drivers will be vigilant. The experts society hires to protect it perform a similar role.

The bias for action observed in business contexts is instructive for what it reveals about the psychology associated with action in the face of danger. Taking action in an uncertain business environment is necessarily an act of faith. There are no guarantees that the action taken will result in success. A person nevertheless moves forward trusting that things will work out. "The most important and visible outcropping of the action bias in excellent companies," Peters and Waterman write, "is their willingness to try things out, to experiment."[13] An action bias is a combination of old-fashioned ingenuity with the best information available about new methods and techniques. It is pragmatically relevant to the task at hand, not action for its own sake, but action oriented toward flourishing. Or, in the worst case, surviving.

An action bias is nearly the opposite of the response predicted by theorists of fear. In their view, the ultimate dangers the world has faced for more than two generations should have weighed it down with emotional gravity. Inaction would have replaced action. A malaise of passivity would have overtaken the world. Alternatively, some frenetic response may have occurred that would have offered nothing more than a distraction. Instead, efforts large and small have clearly been directed toward diagnosing and resolving the dangers faced.

The large efforts, organized through massive investments in science and technology, are obvious enough. But the bias for action is also evident in small ways among ordinary people who lack the capacity to do very much individually and yet feel they can do something. Consider this remark by a computer programmer in Maryland; "I think you can put a little drop in the bucket and everybody putting a little drop in the bucket can really make a difference." He was talking about the car pool he belonged to. That was better, he said, than imagining some grandiose plan that he couldn't actually make work. Like Peters and Waterman's entrepreneurs, he was chunking the problem.

Or consider the remark of a nurse in Pennsylvania who said something like the 1918 pandemic could happen again. "It would be a very sad thing to cope with, but we have a very resilient population, and we would move on." She understands that vaccines are important, even though they are not always effective. She works in a hospital and will be there if an outbreak occurs. And she supports the CDC's efforts to monitor infectious disease as the nation's first line of defense.

SOME OF THE MOST INSIGHTFUL WORK on responses to fear has come from an approach called *terror management*. This approach was inspired by cultural anthropologist

Ernest Becker's Pulitzer Prize–winning book, *The Denial of Death* (1973). The starting point for Becker was Freud's belief that people are driven by a deeply repressed fear of their own death. Becker argued that this fear was so profoundly disturbing as to warrant being called a kind of "terror." People did not like to think about death, but were nevertheless guided by an awareness of their mortality. Much of his argument focused on human activity resulting from this repressed fear, rather than on inaction or passivity. In a particularly revealing passage, he wrote: "On the most elemental level the organism works actively against its own fragility by seeking to expand and perpetuate itself in living experience; instead of shrinking, it moves toward more life." Becker was pointing to the same bias for action that Peters and Waterman were to write about a decade later. Action, he felt, was motivated by the repressed fear of death. It kept a person mentally focused and emotionally anchored. In another passage, he observed a process similar to Peters and Waterman's notion of chunking. People cut out for themselves a "manageable world," he wrote, adding, a person "doesn't bite the world off in one piece as a giant would, but in small manageable pieces, as a beaver does."[14]

The psychological research that came to be known as terror management theory focused on the mechanisms that enabled activity, rather than withdrawal, to be an individual's response to anxiety about death. In a series of experiments, psychologists Tom Pyszczynski, Jeff Greenberg, and Sheldon Solomon showed that people consciously defend themselves against fears of death by imagining their own death to be in the distant future. However, less conscious concerns about mortality are typically dealt with by affirming a worldview that imbues life with order, permanence, and stability, and by viewing oneself as an upholder of these values. In short, people see themselves as valuable participants in a meaningful world.[15] Other research confirmed Becker's hunch about the desire for manageable pieces of information. Laboratory subjects forced to contemplate their mortality often engaged in thought processes characterized by an emphasis on consistency, structure, and order.[16]

The terror management literature adds an important caveat to the more impressionistic discussions of an action bias. The human response to fear—whether of death or uncertainty—is activity. But this activity is not a knee-jerk reaction that consists of doing something merely for the sake of being active. There is a heavy dose of mental engagement as well. Anxiety invokes a cognitive map of the world—a map that imposes order, defines values, and associates a person with those values. The process is nicely illustrated by research among patients suffering from obsessive-compulsive disorder (OCD), an extreme form of anxiety. Whereas it has long been assumed that these patients' ritualistic behavior (repetitive hand washing, locking and unlocking doors, and so on) is routine activity that shuts down mental functioning, researchers using functional magnetic resonance imaging (fMRI) find that this behavior involves heightened cognitive activity. Counting the number of times a door has been locked or performing a regimented ritual of hand washing engages the brain. This response occurs because OCD syndrome interferes with ordinary feedback in the processing of perceived threats. In normal adults a "hazard precaution system" calibrates detection and response to inferred threats. The resulting actions are attention grabbing. They result from anxiety, but also reduce it, and they often eventuate in rituals, such as scanning newspapers for information about new threats, reviewing the history of past crises, debating what should and should not be done, and discussing which authorities are most reliable. Terror management studies suggest that these precaution systems consist of mental activity and behavior that affirms the basic order of one's world.[17]

This literature holds important implications for understanding the broader cultural responses to imagined and actual threats. When serious threats occur, people react with fear and disbelief. Expressions of shock and horror, accompanied by feeling stunned or disoriented, are typical. These reactions were abundantly evident in real-time responses to 9/11. When the initial shock subsides or when a threat is only anticipated or distant, a different reaction is more common. This reaction consists of sense-making activities, such as absorbing and sharing information and engaging in preventive or ameliorative behavior. A study of students at a university in the Midwest two weeks after 9/11 illustrated this second pattern. Most of the students reported having performed charitable activities and talking with friends about the event. A few had made bigoted remarks about Muslims. According to the study's authors, these activities reduced anxiety, affirmed values, and gave students opportunities to interact with others and compare their responses.[18] Pyszczynski and his colleagues noted other responses indicative of Americans' need to do something: going to church in record numbers, purchasing Bibles and inspirational books, flying flags, registering approval of the president's handling of the crisis, stigmatizing foreigners, donating blood, doing volunteer work, and looking for enemies to retaliate against.[19]

Stigmatizing foreigners? Looking for enemies? Terror management theory emphasizes that people respond mentally as well as emotionally, and the mental responses help create meaning and reinstate order. But these mental maps do not arise wholly from some hardwired process in the brain. They are shaped by the society in which people live—by the cultural messages to which they have been exposed. This is why it is crucial to understand how peril has been interpreted in the past. The bias for action encourages people to act, but does not dictate exactly how they will act. That part is shaped more by what they have heard and learned about previous crises. If they learned that a big nuclear buildup during the Cold War was what saved the nation from annihilation, they are likely to imagine that a huge military budget will be the best way to deter terrorists. If they saw the Cold War as unnecessary bellicosity, maybe donating blood would seem the better response.

ALTHOUGH TERROR MANAGEMENT STUDIES EMPHASIZE the psychological and mental responses of individuals, the theory strongly predicts the occurrence of socially organized activities as well. People not only attend religious services in reaction to crises but also encourage religious organizations to staff these events. They expect the money and time they give to voluntary organizations to be used for the relief of disaster victims. The time they spend talking with friends and watching television together strengthens social ties and boosts viewer ratings. The high approval they accord the president encourages public officials to launch otherwise unlikely legislative agendas. These are not random activities engaged in merely to fill the time. There is a need to connect with others who share one's values. A threat to a society encourages expressions of loyalty to that society. This was especially true during the Cold War, when patriotic fervor ran high. The desire for order in the face of possible enemy attacks provides a reason to hunt down "reds" or "radical Muslims." A bit of collective fear raises the chances of passing appropriation bills for national security. As H. L. Mencken observed, "The whole aim of practical politics is to keep the populace alarmed—and hence clamorous to be led to safety."[20]

It is easy to see that a surge of public-spirited activity might follow a terrorist attack, only to wane a few weeks later when anxiety fades. However, that view attaches too much importance to psychological factors. What I have called the "institutionalization of peril" means that whole systems of self-perpetuating organizations have come into being to prepare us for danger and protect us from it. The threat of nuclear annihilation, accidental or otherwise, resulted in the Atomic Energy Commission, and after 1975, the Nuclear Regulatory Commission. The research begun under the Manhattan Project during World War II has continued at Oak Ridge National Laboratory in Tennessee, Lawrence Livermore National Laboratory in California, through the Department of Energy, and at dozens of universities. The response to terrorism, before and after 9/11, was largely managed by the White House, the National Security Council, the CIA, and the military, and eventually by the new Department of Homeland Security. Climate change predictions and research grew from efforts by the Environmental Protection Agency, private watchdog groups such as the Natural Resources Defense Council and the Environmental Defense Fund, and the United Nations–sponsored Intergovernmental Panel on Climate Change. Information about pandemics came largely from the World Health Organization and the Centers for Disease Control and Prevention.[21]

Institutionalization means that organizations are shielded from constantly having to win popular support. Stable organizations are quite different from fads, crazes, and social movements that ebb and flow as public interest rises and falls. Institutionalized organizations persist despite the vicissitudes of public opinion. To be sure, it may help them to have good public relations campaigns or to drum up fear. But they have other ways of securing resources. They provide services that the public needs. Their finances are often built into the tax system and their activities are mandated by law. Organizations specializing in protection against peril are no exception. They are staffed by professionals who enjoy a certain degree of autonomy either from public scrutiny or from political favoritism—which is why accusations of cronyism and instances of incompetence by political appointees are roundly criticized by insiders as well as by the public. Professional autonomy encourages the technical and scientific specialization needed to guard against major crises.

The bias for action is magnified by the existence of these organizations. They make it possible for the public to engage in activities that individual citizens could not possibly accomplish alone—build bombs, hunt terrorists, conduct studies of climate change, develop vaccines. Organizations are systems for extracting small, almost imperceptible commitments of resources—usually in tax dollars—from individuals and then orienting those resources toward specific goals. They also encourage an action bias in subtler ways. The personnel employed in these organizations are paid to do things. Whether a threat is imminent or not, these employees' jobs, pay raises, and promotions reward them for being active. They act not only on their own behalf, but as agents of the public. As agents, they do things that show how active they are. They file reports, issue warnings, and hold press conferences.[22]

The institutionalization of peril significantly shapes what is known about threats to public safety and how these threats are perceived. Information about possible worst-case scenarios is constantly available. Alarmists can always find a credible expert or report warning that terrible things could happen. One of the roles of these experts and reports is to monitor danger and keep the public informed. Institutionalization leads to the nearly continuous release of new studies and research findings. The fact that these organizations are publicly funded and publicly accountable means that lawmakers frequently hold hearings at which officials testify. Journalists interested in telling the public that a new warning has been issued do not have to look far to find stories. It is no accident that on any given day an informed person can hear about five ways in which the world might come crashing to an end.

Terror management theory distinguishes between proximal and distal threats. Proximal threats are close by, real, as in the case of a person being confronted by a poisonous snake. Distal threats are further removed spatially and temporally. They must be inferred from hearsay or general knowledge, such as knowing that snakes live in a particular climate zone. The institutionalization of peril means that most threats are distal. The Department of Homeland Security reports that it thinks a terrorist strike will happen sometime, but it does not know when or where. The Intergovernmental Panel on Climate Change predicts that there will be serious consequences from rising temperatures in fifty or a hundred years. The World Health Organization reports that a death has occurred from avian flu somewhere in Thailand. Distal threats are easier to ignore than proximal danger. Consequently, the organizations involved find it useful to establish gradients against which to compare inferred dangers and to evaluate progress in reducing these dangers. Examples include counting the number of top al Qaeda operatives captured or killed, raising the threat level to "orange," and reporting the proportion of flu victims who have died.

Risk managers at disaster prevention organizations refer to these practices as the "bright lines" phenomenon. The mental processing—the chunking—that precedes action organizes perceptions of reality into meaningful categories. These categories include lines that, when crossed, tell us that the time for action has come. In so many words, the message is, "Okay, now you've crossed the line. We're going to strike back." Many of these lines are instinctual or so deeply programmed that little thought is required. A physical blow to one's body and an intruder entering one's home are examples. A terrorist strike on the "homeland" is another. (See discussion of the term "homeland" in Chapter 5.) Other lines are more arbitrary and for this reason are defined by authorities or though public debate. Soviet missiles in Cuba were quickly viewed as having crossed the line. Raising a threat level to "orange" was a way of signaling that surveillance was picking up chatter deemed to be ominous. Bright lines of this kind are the markers that tell when action is needed and when it has been successful. The disaster prevention industry devotes considerable energy to defining these bright lines. Water is contaminated if it contains so many pollutants per liter. A cancer risk is excessive if it is likely to occur in one person per 100,000, and so on. It is up to the experts to define these lines and to inform policy makers and the public about them.[23]

The public is not unmindful of the fact that these organizations are self-perpetuating. The result is a mixture of trust and mistrust. We expect scientific and technical expertise to give us better weapons than our enemies have and to warn us of terrorist plots. Technology is widely viewed as the solution to greenhouse gases and biomedical research is regarded as the world's best hope against avian flu. These expectations give the disaster prevention industry a high level of legitimacy. At the same time, misgivings are common. People worry that not enough is being done or that particular leaders and organizations are functioning below par. Polls have shown this repeatedly. A poll in 1947 showed that 73 percent of the public had heard about the appointment of David E. Lilienthal to head the Atomic Energy Commission, and, of these, 84 percent said this was a very important job. Two years later, 59 percent of the public said they had heard criticisms of Lilienthal. By 1976, when the AEC was dissolved, only 19 percent said they had a great deal of confidence in the people running it.[24] Views of health organizations are similarly mixed. A 2006 survey asked respondents how much they would trust the Centers for Disease Control and Prevention to give them useful and correct information about a possible outbreak of pandemic flu. Sixty percent said a lot, but 38 percent said only a little or some. A second study asked how much people would trust the CDC director to provide reliable information about prevention and treatment of avian flu. Forty-five percent said they would trust her a great deal, 28 percent said a good amount, and 25 percent said only some or very little.[25]

A significant source of misgiving about organizations such as the AEC and CDC is the fact that they are centralized bureaucracies. As such, they are the subject of many longstanding criticisms. Bureaucracies are said to be inefficient, cumbersome, rule bound, authoritarian, burdened with red tape. They are the antithesis of Peters and Waterman's action-biased companies. Bureaucracies are not nimble enough to anticipate new dangers. They fail to respond because of weighty decision-making processes. A closed circle sets the tone, rather than facilitating open and dynamic communication among a wider range of people. These were the criticisms widely heard after 9/11. The various agencies were guarding their turf instead of communicating with one another. Similar criticisms were voiced again as the Bush administration's war in Iraq became mired in controversy. The president, critics said, listened only to a few of his closest advisors instead of entertaining frank discussion among advisors with dissimilar views.

With response agencies fully institutionalized, attitudes toward peril necessarily focus on organizations as well as on the threat itself. A vivid example occurred in 2006 as part of the debate about global warming. On July 14, the *Wall Street Journal* carried an editorial entitled "Hockey Stick Hokum," charging that warnings about global warming could not be trusted because the research was produced by an "insular coterie" of experts who shared the same views.[26] The accusation was markedly similar to criticisms at the time about the Bush administration's decision to invade Iraq. The difference—besides this one being made by conservatives—was that it was based on a statistical analysis of social networks. The impetus for the study was the view held by many conservatives that climate change was merely the result of natural cycles rather than a trend associated with the recent rise in carbon dioxide emissions. The hockey stick had become a visual symbol of this rise, almost in the same way that the mushroom cloud had become symbolic of nuclear warfare. Al Gore had included the image in "An Inconvenient Truth." The long handle of the hockey stick represented stable temperatures over a 900-year period. The sharp upward curve at the end of the stick showed the rise in global warming. If it could be shown that the hockey stick was invalid, significant doubt could be cast on arguments about the ill effects of greenhouse gases. The network study was commissioned by the House Energy and Commerce Committee, the leaders of which doubted the validity of the hockey stick research. The study itself was conducted by three statisticians who also reanalyzed the original data from which the hockey stick graph had been produced. In testimony before the House committee, the lead author, Edward J. Wegman, stated that at least forty-two paleoclimatologists had direct ties to the author of the hockey stick study, and that because of these connections, "independent studies may not be as independent as they might appear on the surface." In the full report, Wegman presented the network analysis in detail and touted open networks' capacity to generate new ideas and opportunities.[27] Although the criticism in this instance was roundly refuted by other scientists who confirmed the hockey stick pattern, the exchange was instructive. It illustrated that crises must be understood in organizational as well as in technical terms.

The good thing about skepticism toward emergency-response bureaucracies is that questions are being raised about the knee-jerk propensity to engage in action, any action, as a way of demonstrating the bureaucracy's vigilance. Bureaucracies are like individuals in responding to situations on the basis of what they learned from the last crisis. Being nimble does not mean launching a new program just to have one. As Peters and Waterman caution, it requires willingness to abandon old ways and experiment with new ideas. The danger in focusing too much criticism on bureaucracies is that bureaucracy itself becomes the scapegoat for everything that goes wrong.

THE PERIL-INDUCED BIAS FOR ACTION has had significant economic implications. It would overstate the case to argue, as Weber did, that existential anxiety has been the motor of economic growth. Yet it is important to reckon with the fact that vast sums have been spent over the past half century protecting ourselves from large-scale catastrophes. Writers who think the world has been too much in denial to focus on these possible dangers do well to be reminded of these expenditures. The nuclear-haunted era was a time of huge investments in self-protection. Physical capital outlays for defense-related atomic energy programs are particularly revealing. In 1947, when the United States was the sole nuclear power, the nation invested a mere $51 million in these programs. Two years later, as the Soviet threat appeared, this figure rose more than ninefold to $471 million. Over the next decade, it grew steadily, reaching $1.7 billion in 1959. In 1962, the year of the Cuban missile crisis, all defense-related atomic energy programs cost more than $2 billion. They fell gradually over the next decade, only to rise again in the 1980s. In 1989, the nation spent more than $8 billion on these activities; in 1993, more than $11 billion. During the course of the Cold War, total expenditures on national defense never fell below 20 percent of all federal outlays and were always at least 4 percent of gross domestic product. In the decade leading up to the Cuban missile crisis, they averaged more than 10 percent of GDP.[28]

Other threats have also led to considerable expenditures. The war on terror, for instance, resulted in significantly increased military expenditures. From an annual average of $317 billion between 1998 and 2001, military expenditures rose to $500 billion in 2002 and reached nearly $644 billion in 2008.[29] Rising concerns about avian flu caused federal appropriations to rise from $50 million in 2004 to $182 million in 2005, and then to nearly $5.7 billion in 2006.[30] Expenditures on climate change programs have come from both private and public sources, making them harder to estimate, but amount to hundreds of millions of dollars or more.

In absolute terms, these were large amounts. In relative terms, they were small compared to the potential costs of terror, disease, and other catastrophes. After 9/11, the New York Stock Exchange fell 684 points when it reopened after being closed for nearly a week. In 1918, influenza resulted in an 11 percent decline in the U.S. economy. The minor epidemic of 1958 led to a 3 percent downturn. Defense contractors probably benefited from the Cold War, but scholars still debate whether there was a tradeoff between "guns" and "butter." The point is not that anxiety spurred the economy. It is rather that significant sums have been directed specifically toward the monitoring and prevention of peril. Those expenditures show that action, rather than inaction, is society's way of responding. They also show, though, that getting it right is extremely important. Is society willing to spend a trillion dollars finding a way to repair the nation's feelings of vulnerability? Are citizens capable of investing appropriate amounts in protecting the planet even though it feels better to drive a big SUV and tell oneself that recycling the newspaper is actually doing quite a lot?

TERROR MANAGEMENT THEORISTS ARGUE that we respond to danger not only by seeking protection but also by reaffirming our self-worth. What they mean is that we are consoled somewhat in facing our mortality if we know our life has not been in vain. Soldiers who die in battle give up their lives for a cause. Innocent victims who die in terrorist attacks or from influenza also need to be viewed by their loved ones as having lived worthy lives. They worked hard, loved their families, parented well. Anticipating the possibility of death from a nuclear explosion or pandemic sets in motion the same desire for meaning. This is the reason for some of the churchgoing and volunteering observed in times of national crisis. It explains the compulsion to purchase duct tape, even when duct tape provides no real protection. Having done something demonstrates that a person was responsible.

There is some evidence that people want to show not only that they were responsible but also that they were *better* than others at whatever they did. The bias is not only to act, but also to excel and to show off. Survivalists' newsletters and blogs are full of remarks about dumb, apathetic, irresponsible neighbors who someday will be sorry. National pride sometimes kicks in, as it does when Americans feel especially wounded by a terrorist strike on the homeland, or when residents of rich countries figure the death toll from a pandemic will be lower than in poor countries. Affirming one's status within a society's pecking order is evident as well. An interesting study of college students showed how this interest in status affirmation might be affected by concerns about one's death. The subjects were first divided randomly into two groups, with one given materials to read that prompted thoughts about mortality and the other serving as a control group. Each group was then shown advertisements for four products and asked to rate the products in terms of the ads' effectiveness, their interest in the product, and their likelihood of purchasing each. Two of the products were high-status: a Lexus and a Rolex watch. Two were low-status: a Chevy Metro and Pringles. The students whose concerns about mortality had been stimulated consistently rated the high-status products higher than students in the control group, whereas there were no differences in the two groups' ratings of low-status products. "Marketers of luxury products," the authors concluded, "should advertise during program content such as 'When Animals Attack' [a terror film], while those who market low- or non-status items should steer clear of these programs."[31]

THE BIAS FOR ACTION IN FACE OF POTENTIAL DANGER carries costs—beyond expenditures for research, vaccines, and the like—as well as obvious benefits. One cost is the tendency to overreact, resulting in excessive expenditures or additional damage. The huge expenses involved in preparing for the Y2K crisis were widely regarded in retrospect as an overreaction, at least by critics. Research among action-oriented business leaders shows a pattern of "over trust." Thinking they know best and that things will work out, they sometimes move too quickly. Having more information would serve them better. Other research shows that investors sometimes act too often, apparently thinking they can control the market, whereas a better strategy would have been to let stock prices gradually rise.[32] America's war on terror may be the clearest example on a larger scale. History will judge, but hundreds of thousands of casualties among Iraqis and the displacement of millions more—not to mention the thousands of American and allies' soldiers killed and wounded—left many observers with serious doubts.[33]

Another cost is typically less evident to people living in rich countries. Expenditures on protection against peril frequently benefit the rich more than the poor, and sometimes exacerbate differences between the two. The rich simply have more resources to expend on protecting themselves, and these efforts sometimes fall most heavily on other parts of the world. The World Health Organization estimated the total cost of the SARS outbreak to be $30 billion, falling heaviest on low-wage populations in Asia.[34] The slaughter of hundreds of millions of chickens and ducks to curb avian flu was devastating to farmers throughout the region. Education and medical treatment for HIV/AIDS has been far more extensive and effective in the United States than in Africa. Within the United States, fears affect rich and poor in different ways. For instance, worries about crime led to a massive increase in the incarcerated population, resulting in more than 2 million

Americans being incarcerated by 2003—a 500 percent increase since 1980. The majority of inmates were from low-income families and had not graduated from high school. The impact on crime was negligible.[35]

Costs such as these notwithstanding, the benefits of taking action are considerable. During the twentieth century, between 300 and 500 million people worldwide died of smallpox. As recently as 1967, 2 million people succumbed from the disease. By 1977, smallpox was virtually eradicated. In 1952, 58,000 Americans contracted polio, more than 3,000 died and 21,000 were left with paralysis. Following the development of the Salk vaccine in 1955 and a mass immunization campaign promoted by the March of Dimes, the number of cases fell by 90 percent. The relatively small number of deaths from swine flu and SARS was partly attributable to the aggressive efforts of health officials.

Besides the raw benefit of lives saved and disasters averted, the bias for action drives experimentation and innovation. In a world of potential peril, risk is managed less by retreating into shells of safety and more by diversifying our options. We figure out multiple ways of solving problems. In the free market of ideas, some prove helpful while others fail. Good planners consider a range of possible solutions. Being fully human means chunking large problems into manageable strategies.

The peril that poses an undeniable threat to the quality of life that humans can expect in the twenty-first century and beyond is global warming. While terrorist strikes and pandemics may well occur, there is no question that climate change has become a reality, possibly inexorable. The call for action in this regard is not simply to do something—indeed the danger is compounded by imagining that the debate generated by Y2K, 9/11, Katrina, and other threats constitutes an appropriate response. Some social scientists who think they have cleverly shown that organizations matter have also argued that risks are being hyped by self-interested personnel at these organizations. That may be so in some instances, but it is no reason to ignore what we're being told by the experts employed to identify danger and seek solutions. In the case of climate change, the call for action requires doing more than performing random acts of individual good citizenship, such as recycling and lowering the thermostat. It requires supporting green initiatives and electing public officials who understand the significance of climate change and are willing to address the problem.

There are no guarantees. The 9/11 attacks happened even though security analysts warned that they would. The flu epidemic of 1918 was devastating. Scientists who predict that another pandemic will happen could well be right. The exact consequences of global warming remain unknown. Anxieties about these possibilities cannot be escaped or fully denied. They can be reduced. In many instances, it makes sense to pay attention to the warnings of impending doom, and then to get on with life, working at what is already known to be of personal and collective benefit. In others, prudence requires pitching in and doing much more, working together and through the organizations we have created to find and implement solutions. Action not only affirms our humanity. It is our way of fighting back against the fragility of our lives and our planet. It is our best effort to preserve what we hold most dear.

NOTES

INTRODUCTION

1. The evidence I draw on consists of published and unpublished materials. I pay particular attention to widely read books (such as Rachel Carson's *Silent Spring*) and popular films (such as Al Gore's *An Inconvenient Truth*) that have played an agenda-setting function in public debates about the threats under consideration. In addition, I have examined hundreds of newspaper articles, blogs, scientific studies, government reports, novels and films, and analyses by historians, cultural critics, and social scientists. Numerous polls and surveys provide an indication of public sentiment at various times about the relevant issues, and several qualitative and experimental studies have been especially rich. To supplement these materials, my research team and I also conducted more than a hundred in-depth interviews to ask people from a variety of occupations, backgrounds, and locations about their perceptions and interpretations.

CHAPTER 1

1. Works featuring scientific information about peril include Tony Hallam, *Catastrophes and Lesser Calamities: The Causes of Mass Extinctions* (New York: Oxford University Press, 2004), Elizabeth Kolbert, *Field Notes from a Catastrophe: Man, Nature, and Climate Change* (New York: Bloomsbury, 2006), John Leslie, *The End of the World: The Science and Ethics of Human Extinction* (New York: Routledge, 1996), and Richard A. Posner, *Catastrophe: Risk and Response* (New York: Oxford University Press, 2004); see also Alvin M. Weinberg, "Scientific Millenarianism," *Proceedings of the American Philosophical Society* 143 (1999): 531–39.

2. On the cognitive blocking of mirror neuron responses, see Pascal Boyer and Pierre Lienard, "Why Ritualized Behavior? Precaution Systems and Action Parsing in Developmental, Pathological and Cultural Rituals," Washington University, Department of Psychology, July 2005. The cultural repertoire's cognitive roots and constraints are valuably examined in Karen A. Cerulo, *Never Saw It Coming: Cultural Challenges to Envisioning the Worst* (Chicago: University of Chicago Press, 2006).

3. Guy Stecklov and Joshua R. Goldstein, "Terror Attacks Influence Driving Behavior in Israel," *Proceedings of the National Academy of Sciences* 101 (October 5, 2004): 14551–56.

4. Stanley Cohen, *States of Denial: Knowing about Atrocities and Suffering* (Cambridge, U.K.: Polity Press, and Malden, Mass.: Blackwell, 2001), 1.

5. On denial, see especially Anna Freud, *The Ego and the Mechanisms of Defense* (New York: International Universities Press, 1946); see also Robert Coles, *Anna Freud: The Dream of Psychoanalysis* (Reading, Mass.: Addison-Wesley, 1992).

6. The original experiments were reported in Daniel M. Wegner, David J. Schneider, Samuel R. Carter III, and Teri L. White, "Paradoxical Effects of Thought Suppression," *Journal of Personality and Social Psychology* 53 (1987): 5–13; a popular version of the research was presented in Daniel M. Wegner, *White Bears and Other Unwanted Thoughts: Suppression, Obsession, and the Psychology of Mental Control* (New York: Viking, 1989); and for a retrospective account of the research and its impact, see Daniel M. Wegner and David J. Schneider, "The White Bear Story," *Psychological Inquiry* 14 (2003): 326–29.

7. Jorge L. Armony and Raymond J. Dolan, "Modulation of Spatial Attention by Fear-Conditioned Stimuli: An Event-Related fMRI Study," *Neuropsychologia* 40 (2002): 817–26; Ernst H. W. Koster, Geert Crombez, Stefaan Van Damme, Bruno Verschuere, and Jan De Houwer, "Does Imminent Threat Capture and Hold Attention?" *Emotion* 4 (2004): 312–17.

8. This point has been elaborated in Eviatar Zerubavel, *The Elephant in the Room: Silence and Denial in Everyday Life* (New York: Oxford University Press, 2006).

9. Fantasy and fiction as a response to terror are usefully discussed in Margot A. Henriksen, *Dr. Strangelove's America: Society and Culture in the Atomic Age* (Berkeley: University of California Press, 1997).

10. Two of the most popular renditions of this argument are Ernest Becker, *The Denial of Death* (New York: Free Press, 1973), and Elisabeth Kübler-Ross, *On Death and Dying* (New York: Macmillan, 1969).

11. Roxane Cohen Silver, E. Alison Holman, Daniel N. McIntosh, Michael Poulin, and Virginia Gil-Rivas, "Nationwide Longitudinal Study of Psychological Responses to September 11," *Journal of the American Medical Association* 288 (September 11, 2002): 1235–44; other studies of responses to 9/11 are discussed in Chapter 4 and to nuclear threats in Chapters 2 and 3.

12. Katrina Carlsson, Karl Magnus Petersson, Daniel Lundqvist, Andreas Karlsson, Martin Ingvar, and Arne Ohman, "Fear and the Amygdala: Manipulation of Awareness Generates Differential Cerebral Responses to Phobic and Fear-Relevant (but Nonfeared) Stimuli," *Emotion* 4 (2004): 340–53; E. K. Miller, "An Integrative Theory of Prefrontal Cortex Function," *Annual Review of Neuroscience* 24 (2001): 167–202; Maurizio Corbetta and Gordon L. Shulman, "Control of Goal-Directed and Stimulus-Driven Attention in the Brain," *Nature Reviews: Neuroscience* 3 (2002): 201–15; Susan Mineka and Arne Ohman, "Learning and Unlearning Fears: Preparedness, Neural Pathways, and Patients," *Biological Psychiatry* 52 (2002): 927–37.

13. These alternative interpretations have been discussed especially in the sociological and anthropological literature on funerary rites; for example, see Glennys Howarth, *Last Rites: The Work of the Modern Funeral Director* (Amityville, N.Y.: Baywood, 1996); James J. Farrell, *Inventing the American Way of Death, 1830–1920* (Philadelphia: Temple University Press, 1980); and Richard Huntington and Peter Metcalf, *Celebrations of Death: The Anthropology of Mortuary Ritual* (New York: Cambridge University Press, 1979).

14. This cognitive aspect of crises is emphasized in Lee Clarke, *Worst Cases: Terror and Catastrophe in the Popular Imagination* (Chicago: University of Chicago Press, 2006): 99–128.

15. Thomas F. Hack, Harvey Max Chochinov, Thomas Hassard, Linda J. Kristjanson, Susan McClement, and Mike Harlos, "Defining Dignity in Terminally Ill Cancer Patients: A Factor-Analytic Approach," *Psycho-Oncology* 13 (2004): 700–708; Hubert R. Jocham, Theo Dassen, Guy Widdershoven, and Ruud Halfens, "Quality of Life in Palliative Care Cancer Patients: A Literature Review," *Journal of Clinical Nursing* 15 (2006): 1188–95.

16. Agnes Noble and Colin Jones, "Benefits of Narrative Therapy: Holistic Interventions at the End of Life," *British Journal of Nursing* 14 (2005): 330–33; Elizabeth K. Vig and Robert A. Pearlman, "Quality of Life While Dying: A Qualitative Study of Terminally Ill Older Men," *Journal of the American Geriatrics Society* 51 (2003): 1595–1601.

17. Karl Duncker, *On Problem Solving* (Washington, D.C.: American Psychological Association, 1945), which summarizes theoretical and experimental work begun in 1926.

18. Clifford Geertz, *The Interpretation of Cultures: Selected Essays* (New York: Basic Books, 1973), 5.

19. Discussed in Allen Newell and Herbert A. Simon, *Human Problem Solving* (Englewood Cliffs, N.J.: Prentice-Hall, 1972); Mihaly Czikszentmihalyi, *Creativity: Flow and the Psychology of Discovery and Invention* (New York: HarperCollins, 1996); and Alan H. Schoenfeld, "Beyond the Purely Cognitive: Belief Systems, Social Cognitions, and Metacognitions as Driving Forces in Intellectual Performance," *Cognitive Science* 7 (1983): 329–63.

20. Lewis Thomas, "Dying as Failure," *Annals of the American Academy of Political and Social Science* 447 (1980): 1–4; quotation is on 4.

21. For an interesting treatment of the power relations involved in responding to contemporary hazards, see Ulrich Beck, *Risk Society: Towards a New Modernity*, trans. by Mark Ritter (London: Sage, 1992), especially 51–84.

22. One of the more readable discussions of schemata is Roy D'Andrade, *The Development of Cognitive Anthropology* (New York: Cambridge University Press, 1995).

23. George Lakoff and Mark Johnson, *Metaphors We Live By* (Chicago: University of Chicago Press, 1980).

24. Frank Neuner, Margarete Schauer, Unni Karunakara, and Christine Klaschik, "A Comparison of Narrative Exposure Therapy, Supportive Counseling, and Psychoeducation for Treating Posttraumatic Stress Disorder in an African Refugee Settlement," *Journal of Counseling and Clinical Psychology* 72 (2004): 579–87.

25. Gerard Genette, *Narrative Discourse: An Essay in Method* (Ithaca, N.Y.: Cornell University Press, 1980).

CHAPTER 2

1. Toyofumi Ogura, *Letters from the End of the World: A Firsthand Account of the Bombing of Hiroshima* (Tokyo: Kodansha International, 1997), 158, notes that a week after the bombing the death toll was set at 30,000 but rose to more than 92,000 by September 1946, with another 37,000 wounded.

2. Jeffrey C. Alexander, "Toward a Theory of Cultural Trauma," in *Cultural Trauma and Collective Identity*, edited by Jeffrey C. Alexander, Ron Eyerman, Bernhard Giesen, Neil J. Smelser, and Piotr Sztompka (Berkeley: University of California Press, 2004), 1.

3. Paul S. Boyer, *By the Bomb's Early Light: American Thought and Culture at the Dawn of the Atomic Age*, rev. ed. (New York: Pantheon, 1985).

4. An important precursor of this interest was Joseph R. Gusfield, *Symbolic Crusade: Status Politics and the American Temperance Movement* (Urbana: University of Illinois Press, 1963).

5. Joseph R. Gusfield, *The Culture of Public Problems: Drinking-Driving and the Symbolic Order* (Chicago: University of Chicago Press, 1981).

6. Elizabeth M. Armstrong, *Conceiving Risk, Bearing Responsibility: Fetal Alcohol Syndrome and the Diagnosis of Moral Disorder* (Baltimore: Johns Hopkins University Press, 2003).

7. Kai T. Erikson, *Wayward Puritans: A Study in the Sociology of Deviance*, rev. ed., with a new foreword and afterword (Boston: Allyn and Bacon, 2005).

8. Harry Truman, "Statement by the President of the United States," White House (August 6, 1945); on file at the Truman Presidential Museum and Library.

9. William L. Laurence, "Is Atomic Energy the Key to Our Dreams?" *Saturday Evening Post* (August 13, 1946): 9–10, 36–39; quote is on pp. 9–10.

10. "Energy in U-235 Termed Force to Remake Life," *Chicago Tribune* (August 7, 1945), 2.

11. Hanson W. Baldwin, "Atom Bomb Wins Victory, but Sows Whirlwind," *New York Times* (August 9, 1945), 1.

12. Norman Cousins, "Modern Man is Obsolete," *Saturday Review* (August 18, 1945), 5.

13. This argument about culture in unsettled times is developed in Ann Swidler, "Culture in Action: Symbols and Strategies," *American Sociological Review* 51 (1986): 273–86; see also Ann Swidler, "Cultural Power and Social Movements," in *Social Movements and Culture*, edited by Hank Johnston and Bert Klandermans (Minneapolis: University of Minnesota Press, 1995), 25–40.

14. James Reston, "Dawn of the Atom Era Perplexes Washington," *New York Times* (August 12, 1945), E6.

15. Arnold Toynbee, "The Present Point in History," *Foreign Affairs* 26 (1947): 187–95; quote is on 195.

16. George Bernard Shaw, "The Atomic Bomb," London *Times* (August 20, 1945), 5.

17. Reinhold Niebuhr, "The Atomic Issue," *Christianity and Crisis* 5 (October 15, 1945): 6; and for background on Niebuhr's thinking, see also Campbell Craig, "The New Meaning of Modern War in the Thought of Reinhold Niebuhr," *Journal of the History of Ideas* 53 (1992): 687–701.

18. "Big Peace Role for Atom," *New York Times* (August 7, 1945), 7.

19. Arthur C. Compton, "The Atomic Crusade and Its Social Implications," *Annals of the American Academy of Political and Social Science* 249 (1947): 9–19; quote is on 19.

20. William Faulkner, "Banquet Speech," Stockholm, December 10, 1950; online at Nobelprize.org.

21. Hazel Gaudet Erskine, "The Polls: Atomic Weapons and Nuclear Energy," *Public Opinion Quarterly* 27 (1963): 155–190; quote is on 155.

22. Orville Prescott, "Books of the Times," *New York Times* (January 28, 1946), 17.

23. Yoshio D. Kishi, "What It Means to Me to Be Growing Up with Nuclear Energy," *Journal of Educational Sociology* 22 (1949): 336–37.

24. Barbara Schiff, "What It Means to Me to Be Growing Up with Nuclear Energy," *Journal of Educational Sociology* 22 (1949): 338–39.

25. "Heard Round the World," *New York Times* (August 7, 1945), 22.

26. "Report to Federal Council on 'The Churches and World Order,'" *New York Times* (March 8, 1946), 4.

27. Leon Whipple, "Culture Repositories," *New York Times* (January 19, 1947), E8.

28. "Atomic Warfare Peril Told by the Presidential Council," *New York Times* (June 2, 1947), 1.

29. "Heard Round the World," *New York Times* (August 7, 1945), 22.

30. Hanson W. Baldwin, "Atomic Bomb Responsibilities: Resolving of Problem in Relation to Peace Is Linked to Moral Leadership of America," *New York Times* (September 12, 1945), 4.

31. Ibid.

32. William S. White, "Congress Passes Bill to Rule Atom," *New York Times* (July 27, 1946), 3.

33. Robert A. Dahl, "Atomic Energy and the Democratic Process," *Annals of the American Academy of Political and Social Science* 290 (1953): 1–6; quote is on 1.

34. R. L. Meier and E. Rabinowitch, "Scientists Before and After the Bomb," *Annals of the American Academy of Political and Social Science* 290 (1953): 118–26. This essay is also the source of the figures for numbers of scientists and research expenditures.

35. Benjamin Fine, "Hutchins Demands Adult Education," *New York Times* (May 4, 1946), 30.

36. William Fielding Ogburn, "Sociology and the Atom," *American Journal of Sociology* 51 (1946): 267–75; quote is on 267–68.

37. Ansley J. Coale, "The Problem of Reducing Vulnerability to Atomic Bombs," *American Economic Review* 37 (1947): 87–97; quote is on 94.

38. "Industry Opposes Strict Atom Curb," *New York Times* (February 9, 1946), 8.

39. "Editorial Comment," *Journal of Clinical Psychology* 22 (1947): 399.

40. Compton, "The Atomic Crusade," 10.

41. Ibid., 18.

42. David E. Lilienthal, 'We Must Grasp the Facts about the Atom,' *New York Times* (May 4, 1947), SM7.

43. Robert M. Hutchins, "Great Books Foundation Sponsors a Campaign for Adult Re-education in America," *New York Times* (August 24, 1947), E9.

44. These local examples are described in George L. Glasheen, Michael Amrine, Richard C. Robin, and Richard C. Hitchcock, "The Adult Meets and Tries to Understand the Atom," *Journal of Educational Sociology* 22 (1949): 339–56.

45. Anna C. Williams, "We Exposed Our Students to Atomic Energy," *School Review* 57 (1949): 295–99.

46. Boyer, *By the Bomb's Early Light*, 276–77.

47. Elizabeth Douvan and Stephen B. Withey, "Some Attitudinal Consequences of Atomic Energy," *Annals of the American Academy of Political and Social Science* 290 (1953): 108–17; quotes are on 115. The primary studies were Social Science Research Council Committee on Social and Economic Aspects of Atomic Energy, *Public Reaction to the Atomic Bomb and World Affairs* (Ithaca, N.Y.: Cornell University, 1947); *Public Thinking about Atomic Warfare and Civil Defense* (Ann Arbor: Survey Research Center, University of Michigan, 1951); *The Public and Civil Defense* (Ann Arbor: Survey Research Center, University of Michigan, 1952); and *The Impact of Atomic Energy on Society* (Ann Arbor: Survey Research Center, University of Michigan, 1953).

48. Robert F. Kennedy, *Thirteen Days: A Memoir of the Cuban Missile Crisis* (New York: W. W. Norton, 1969).

49. Ernest R. May and Philip D. Zelikow, eds., *The Kennedy Tapes* (Cambridge, Mass.: Harvard University Press, 1997).

50. "Text of Kennedy's Address on Moves to Meet the Soviet Build-Up in Cuba," *New York Times* (October 23, 1962), 18.

51. "Cuba Action Gets Public Backing," *New York Times* (October 23, 1962), 21; Nan Robertson, "Anxiety Coupled with Support Here on U.S. Move," *New York Times* (October 24, 1962), 26; Claude Sitton, "Measures Taken in Civil Defense," *New York Times* (October 26, 1962), 18.

52. Alice L. George, *Awaiting Armageddon: How Americans Faced the Cuban Missile Crisis* (Chapel Hill: University of North Carolina Press, 2003), 6.

53. Gallup Poll (November 16, 1962), available online through Lexis-Nexis.

54. "70-Year Effect of Bombs Denied," *New York Times* (August 9, 1945), 8; in Japan this report was widely publicized in newspapers on August 24, 1945; Ogura, *Letters from the End of the World*, 152.

55. David Bradley, *No Place to Hide: What the Atomic Bomb Can Do to Ships, or Water, or Land, and Thereby to Human Beings* (Boston: Little, Brown, 1948).

56. Steven M. Spencer, "Fallout: The Silent Killer," *Saturday Evening Post* (August 29, 1959), 26–27, 88–90, and (September 6, 1959), 83–86.

57. U.S. Department of Agriculture, "Defense Against Radioactive Fallout on the Farm," Bulletin No. 2107 (1957).

58. Philip Benjamin, "Steep Drop in Milk Consumption Stirs Government and Dairymen," *New York Times* (February 18, 1962), 1; Donald Janson, "Minnesota Acts on Iodine in Milk," *New York Times* (August 26, 1962), 56.

59. *Duck and Cover* and other civil defense materials can be viewed at conelrad.com.

60. These quotes are from short reviews of *Duck and Cover* posted at www.archive.org/details/DuckandC1951.

61. Katherine D'Evelyn, Marion E. Wiles, and John L. Miller, "What to Do about Air Raid Drills," *Child Study* 28 (Spring 1951): 21; quoted in JoAnne Brown, "'A is for Atom, B is for Bomb': Civil Defense in American Public Education, 1948–1963," *Journal of American History* 75 (1988): 68–90; quote is on 78. Numerous accounts of the organization of civil defense in this period exist; for example, Guy Oakes, *The Imaginary War: Civil Defense and American Cold War Culture* (New York: Oxford University Press, 1994), and Lee Clarke, *Mission Improbable: Using Fantasy Documents to Tame Disaster* (Chicago: University of Chicago Press, 1999).

62. Kristina Zarlengo, "Civilian Threat, the Suburban Citadel, and Atomic Age American Women," *Signs* 24 (1999): 925–58; quote is on 943.

63. U.S. Department of Defense, "Fallout Protection, What to Know and Do about Nuclear Attack" (December 30, 1961).

64. Thomas P. Ronan, "Homeowners Get Fallout Advice," *New York Times* (October 25, 1962), 14.

65. Elizabeth Ford, "Role is Assigned Women," *Washington Post* (September 30, 1959), D2.

66. Zarlengo, "Civilian Threat," 939.

67. Gallup Polls conducted between July 1961 and June 1962, available online through Lexis-Nexis. See also Tom W. Smith, "The Cuban Missile Crisis and U.S. Public Opinion," *Public Opinion Quarterly* 67 (2003): 265–93, which mentions the Illinois poll.

68. Nevil Shute, *On the Beach* (New York: William Morrow, 1957), 10.

69. Ibid., 34.

70. Ibid., 56.

71. Ibid., 270.

72. Helen Caldicott, an Australian physician and antinuclear activist who played a key role in founding Physicians for Social Responsibility and providing major impetus for the antinuclear

movement in the early 1980s, credited *On the Beach* with having prompted her first activities against nuclear weapons; "Interview with Helen Caldicott," online at www.abc.net.au/btn/australians/caldicott.htm.

73. Robert Torry, "Apocalypse Then: Benefits of the Bomb in Fifties Science Fiction Films," *Cinema Journal* 31 (1991): 7–21; Bryan Fruth, Alicia Germer, Keiko Kikuchi, and Anamarie Mihalega, "The Atomic Age: Facts and Films from 1945–1965," *Journal of Popular Film and Television* 23 (1996): 154–60.

74. Smith, "The Cuban Missile Crisis and U.S. Public Opinion," 275.

75. "Cuban Action Gets Public Backing."

76. Donald Janson, "In Corn Belt Community Only a Few Express Isolationist Views," *New York Times* (October 5, 1962), 14.

77. Clayton Knowles, "8,000 Conservatives at Rally Jeer Cuba Action as Too Timid," *New York Times* (October 23, 1962), 28.

78. Smith, "The Cuban Missile Crisis and U.S. Public Opinion," 270.

79. John H. Fenton, "Campuses Voice Some Opposition," *New York Times* (October 24, 1962), 25.

80. "Campus Opinion in the West," *New York Times* (October 24, 1962), 25.

81. "Concern is Voiced by Church Council," *New York Times* (October 24, 1962), 24.

82. "Women March to Demand that Cuban Crisis Be Settled Within the U.N.," *New York Times* (October 24, 1962), 24.

83. Kennedy, *Thirteen Days*, 98.

84. Quoted in James G. Blight, Joseph S. Nye Jr., and David A. Welch, "The Cuban Missile Crisis Revisited," *Foreign Affairs* 66 (1987): 177.

85. Ibid., 186.

CHAPTER 3

1. Robert Kleidman, *Organizing for Peace: Neutrality, the Test Ban, and the Freeze* (Syracuse: Syracuse University Press, 1993), 93–96.

2. Alvin Shuster, "Close-up of a 'Peace Striker,'" *New York Times* (May 6, 1962), 251.

3. Amy Swerdlow, *Women Strike for Peace: Traditional Motherhood and Radical Politics in the 1960s* (Chicago: University of Chicago Press, 1993).

4. Shuster, "Close-up of a 'Peace Striker.'"

5. Swerdlow, *Women Strike for Peace*, 235.

6. Port Huron Statement of the Students for a Democratic Society, 1962; online at http://coursesa.matrix.msu.edu/~hst306/documents/huron.html. Also in paperback: Tom Hayden, *The Port Huron Statement: The Visionary Call of the 1960s Revolution*. New York: Thunder's Mouth Press, 2005.

7. Todd Gitlin, *The Whole World Is Watching: Mass Media in the Making and Unmaking of the New Left* (Berkeley: University of California Press, 1980), 103–4.

8. Peter J. Schuyten, "Scientists and Society's Fears," *New York Times* (April 9, 1979), A1.

9. Laurie Johnston, "New York Syndrome: Fear and Unconcern," *New York Times* (April 1, 1979), 28.

10. D. R. Wernette, "The Freeze Movement on the Local Level," in *Peace Action in the Eighties: Social Science Perspectives*, edited by Sam Marullo and John Lofland (New Brunswick, N.J.: Rutgers University Press, 1990), 140–51.

11. The psychological literature is reviewed in Susan T. Fiske, "People's Reactions to Nuclear War: Implications for Psychologists," *American Psychologist* 42 (1987): 207–17; quotation is on 215.

12. Michael Useem, "Apocalypse Tomorrow," *Contemporary Sociology* 11 (1982): 610–11; quotation is on 610.

13. John Leonard, "Review of *The Fate of the Earth* by Jonathan Schell," *New York Times* (April 8, 1982), section C.

14. Jonathan Schell, *The Fate of the Earth and the Abolition* (Stanford: Stanford University Press, 2000), quotation is on 96.

15. Ibid., 173.

16. Ibid., 175.

17. John Lofland, *Polite Protestors: The American Peace Movement of the 1980s* (Syracuse: Syracuse University Press, 1993), 233–72; Jerome Price, *The Antinuclear Movement*, rev. ed. (Boston: Twayne, 1990), 24–27.

18. For instance, a Harris Poll showed 80 percent in favor of "a reduction in the number of nuclear weapons each country has" and 76 in favor of "a freeze on all nuclear weapons each country can build and keep on hand." Survey by Louis Harris & Associates, November 23–November 28, 1982. Retrieved July 26, 2006 from the iPOLL Databank, Roper Center for Public Opinion Research, University of Connecticut. www.ropercenter.uconn.edu/ipoll.html.

19. CBS News/New York Times poll (May 1982), online from the Roper Center for Public Opinion Research.

20. Robert D. McFadden, "A Spectrum of Humanity Represented at the Rally," *New York Times* (June 13, 1982), 42.

21. Interpretive histories include John Lewis Gaddis, *The Cold War: A New History* (New York: Penguin, 2005), John Lewis Gaddis, *We Now Know: Rethinking Cold War History* (New York: Oxford University Press, 1998), Walter Lafeber, *America, Russia, and the Cold War, 1945–2002* (New York: McGraw-Hill, 2002), and Martin Walker, *The Cold War: A History* (New York: Henry Holt, 1994).

22. Robert S. Norris and William M. Arkin, "U.S. Nuclear Weapon Locations, 1995," *Bulletin of the Atomic Scientists* 51 (November/December, 1995): 74–75.

23. Kerry G. Herron and Hank C. Jenkins-Smith, *Public Perspectives on Nuclear Security: U.S. National Security Surveys 1993–1997* (Albuquerque: University of New Mexico, Institute for Public Policy, 1998), 29–34.

24. Mick Broderick, "Is This the Sum of Our Fears? Nuclear Imagery in Post–Cold War Cinema," in *Atomic Culture: How We Learned to Stop Worrying and Love the Bomb*, edited by Scott C. Zeman and Michael A. Amundson (Boulder: University Press of Colorado, 2004), 125–48.

25. Daniel Deudney and G. John Ikenberry, "Who Won the Cold War?" *Foreign Policy* 87 (1992): 123–38; quotation is on 123. Opinions about the Soviet Union and about U.S. defense spending changed among elites and more knowledgeable members of the public, but public opinion more generally showed considerable resistance to change; Bruce Russett, Thomas Hartley, and Shoon Murray, "The End of the Cold War, Attitude Change, and the Politics of Defense Spending," *PS, Political Science and Politics* 27 (1994): 17–22.

26. "A Look Back at the Polls," CBS News Polls, online at www.cbsnews.com; compared with Reagan's 68 percent approval rating, the end-of-term approvals of other presidents were: Roosevelt, 66 percent; Truman, 31 percent; Eisenhower, 59 percent; Kennedy, 58 percent; Johnson, 49 percent; Nixon, 24 percent; Ford, 53 percent; Carter, 34 percent.

27. John Tirman, "How We Ended the Cold War," *Nation* 269 (1999): 13–21; quotation is on 15.

28. David C. Morrison, "Like, You Know, the Bomb Thing," *National Journal* 26 (October 15, 1994): 24–27; quotation is on 24.

29. Ronald Reagan, "Address Before the Japanese Diet in Tokyo," November 11, 1983, online at www.reagan.utexas.edu.

30. Quoted in Tirman, "How We Ended the Cold War," 16.

31. George Weigel, "Shultz, Reagan, and the Revisionists," *Commentary* 96 (August 1993): 50–53; quotation is on 50.

32. Bob Edwards and Sam Marullo, "Organizational Mortality in a Declining Social Movement: The Demise of Peace Movement Organizations in the End of the Cold War Era," *American Sociological Review* 60 (1995): 908–27.

33. Bob Ortega, "Ban the Bargains: Aging Activists Turn, Turn, Turn Attention to Wal-Mart Protests," *Wall Street Journal* (October 11, 1994), A1.

34. A useful overview is provided in John K. Glenn III, *Framing Democracy: Civil Society and Civic Movements in Eastern Europe* (Stanford: Stanford University Press, 2001); see also Janine Wedel, *Collision and Collusion: The Strange Case of Western Aid to Eastern Europe* (New York: St. Martin's Press, 1998).

35. Robert D. Putnam, "Bowling Alone: America's Declining Social Capital," *Journal of Democracy* 6 (1995): 65–78.

36. Robert D. Putnam, *Bowling Alone: The Collapse and Revival of American Community* (New York: Simon & Schuster, 2000).

37. Robert S. Norris and Hans M. Kristensen, "Global Nuclear Stockpiles, 1945–2006," *Bulletin of the Atomic Scientists* 62 (July/August 2006): 64–66.

38. Survey by Civil Society Institute and Opinion Research Corporation, May 18–May 21, 2006. Retrieved July 24, 2006 from the iPOLL Databank, Roper Center for Public Opinion Research, University of Connecticut. www.ropercenter.uconn.edu/ipoll.html.

39. The quotes included here are from in-depth qualitative interviews conducted in 2006 and 2007.

40. Survey by German Marshall Fund of the US and the Compagnia di San Paolo, Italy, with additional support from the Luso-American Foundation, and Fundacion BBVA and TNS Opinion and Social Institutes, May 30–June 17, 2005. Retrieved July 24, 2006 from the iPOLL Databank, Roper Center for Public Opinion Research, University of Connecticut. www.ropercenter.uconn.edu/ipoll.html.

41. Survey by Associated Press and Ipsos-Public Affairs, March 21–March 23, 2005. Retrieved July 24, 2006 from the iPOLL Databank, Roper Center for Public Opinion Research, University of Connecticut. www.ropercenter.uconn.edu/ipoll.html.

42. Survey by CBS News/New York Times, February 24–February 28, 2005. Retrieved July 24, 2006 from the iPOLL Databank, Roper Center for Public Opinion Research, University of Connecticut. www.ropercenter.uconn.edu/ipoll.html.

43. Survey by Fox News and Opinion Dynamics, June 13–June 14, 2006. Retrieved July 24, 2006 from the iPOLL Databank, Roper Center for Public Opinion Research, University of Connecticut. www.ropercenter.uconn.edu/ipoll.html.

44. Survey by Pew Research Center and Princeton Survey Research Associates International, May 2–May 14, 2006. Retrieved July 24, 2006 from the iPOLL Databank, Roper Center for Public Opinion Research, University of Connecticut. www.ropercenter.uconn.edu/ipoll.html.

45. Survey by Public Agenda Foundation, January 10–January 22, 2006. Retrieved July 24, 2006 from the iPOLL Databank, Roper Center for Public Opinion Research, University of Connecticut. www.ropercenter.uconn.edu/ipoll.html.

46. Claudia Rowe, "Communities: A Grassroots Fight," *New York Times* (December 16, 2001), WE7.

47. "Thousands Back Nuclear Treaty in U.N.," *Los Angeles Times* (May 2, 2005), A12.

48. Randal C. Archibold, "In Shadow of Reactors, Parents Seek Peace of Mind in a Pill," *New York Times* (January 21, 2002), B1.

49. Figures included in this paragraph are from Internal Revenue Service Form 990 reports for the organizations listed as reported in 2004, retrieved from www.guidestar.org.

50. Letter from James L. Caldwell, NRC Regional Administrator to Ms. Sandy Buchanan, Executive Director, Ohio Citizen Action, October 21, 2004.

51. Eliot Marshall, "Is the Friendly Atom Poised for a Comeback?" *Science* 309 (2005): 1168–69; Jon Palfreman, "A Tale of Two Fears: Exploring Media Depictions of Nuclear Power and Global Warming," *Review of Policy Research* 23 (2006): 23–43.

52. Smith, "The Cuban Missile Crisis and U.S. Public Opinion," 274.

53. Fiske, "People's Reactions to Nuclear War."

54. On family, a widely read book is Elaine Tyler May, *Homeward Bound: American Families in the Cold War Era* (New York: Basic Books, 1988); the criticisms mentioned are also raised in Beth L. Bailey, "Review of *Homeward Bound: American Families in the Cold War Era*," *American Historical Review* 95 (1990): 620–21; Joan Aldous, "Review of *Homeward Bound: American Families in the Cold War Era*," *Contemporary Sociology* 19 (1990): 458–59; and Anne M. Boylan, "Containment on the Home Front: American Families During the Cold War," *Reviews in American History* 17 (1989): 301–5. Richard V. Wagner, "Psychology and the Threat of Nuclear War," *American Psychologist* 40 (1985): 531–35, discusses evidence that nuclear fear may result in not having children or in family disruption. On religion in the 1950s see Robert Wuthnow, *After Heaven: Spirituality in America Since the 1950s* (Berkeley: University of California Press, 1998). On irrational behavior and panics, see Boyer, *By the Bomb's Early Light* and Spencer R. Weart, *Nuclear Fear: A History of Images* (Cambridge, Mass.: Harvard University Press, 1988). On Orson Welles's broadcast, see Hadley Cantril, *The Invasion from Mars: A Study in the Psychology of Panic* (Princeton, N.J.: Princeton University Press, 1947). Also of interest is Stephen J. Whitfield, *The Culture of the Cold War*, 2nd ed. (Baltimore: Johns Hopkins University Press, 1996).

55. George, *Awaiting Armageddon*, 163.

56. "A Civil Defense Program for Parent-Teacher Associations," *National Parent-Teacher* 45 (June 1951): 34–35.

57. An interesting overview of these developments is presented in E. Brooks Holifield, *A History of Pastoral Care in America: From Salvation to Self-Realization* (Eugene, Ore.: Wipf and Stock, 2005).

58. Anna Freud and Dorothy T. Burlingham, *War and Children: A Message to American Parents* (New York: Medical War Books, 1943).

59. Robert Jay Lifton, *Death in Life: Survivors of Hiroshima*, rev. ed. (Chapel Hill: University of North Carolina Press, 1991), 479, 500, 541.

60. John H. Moehle, "Civil Defense Begins with You," *New York State Education* 39 (December 1951): 210.

61. A survey of SANE/Freeze board members in 1987 found that 81 percent had bachelor's degrees and 40 percent had graduate degrees; H. Edward Price Jr., "Historical Generations in Freeze

Member Mobilization," in *Peace Action in the Eighties: Social Science Perspectives*, edited by Sam Marullo and John Lofland, 207–16; see especially 214.

62. Nahum Z. Medalia and Otto N. Larsen, "Diffusion and Belief in a Collective Delusion: The Seattle Windshield Pitting Epidemic," *American Sociological Review* 23 (1958): 180–86.

63. "Shelter Is 'Family Room,'" *Washington Post* (December 31, 1959), B3.

64. "ColoradoRuss" at www.archive.org/details/DuckandC1951 (July 3, 2004).

CHAPTER 4

1. Descriptive accounts of the day's events include Richard B. Bernstein, *Out of the Blue: A Narrative of September 11, 2001* (New York: Times Books, 2003), and Nafeez Mosaddeq Ahmed, *The War on Freedom: How and Why America Was Attacked, September 11th, 2001*, with a Backword by John Leonard (New York: Media Messenger Books, 2002); numerous Internet sites provide timelines and other summaries; for instance, cnn.com, cooperativeresearch.org, and patriotresource.com.

2. John West, "It's Time for U.S. to Fight Fire with Fire," *Buffalo News* (September 19, 2001), B9.

3. Jacqueline Darvin, "Teaching in the Days after September 11, 2001," *The English Journal* 91 (2002): 18–19; quotation is on 18.

4. Eric Lichtblau and James Gerstenzang, "Anti-Muslim Violence Up, Officials Say," *Los Angeles Times* (September 18, 2001), A3; Thomas B. Edsall, "Anti-Muslim Violence Assailed," *Washington Post* (September 15, 2001), A9.

5. Lexis-Nexis keywords "terrorism," "September 11," or "9/11" for the dates indicated.

6. These covers can be viewed at September11news.com.

7. Television News Archive, Vanderbilt University, online at tvnews.vanderbilt.edu.

8. Mark A. Schuster, Bradley D. Stein, Lisa H. Jaycox, Rebecca L. Collins, Grant N. Marshall, Marc N. Elliott, Annie J. Zhou, David E. Kanouse, Janina L. Morrison, and Sandra H. Berry, "A National Survey of Stress Reactions After the September 11, 2001, Terrorist Attacks," *New England Journal of Medicine* 345 (November 15, 2001): 1507–12; "American Psyche Reeling from Terror Attacks," *Pew Research Center for the People and the Press Survey Reports* (September 19, 2001), online at people-press.org.

9. Richard Wiggins, "The Effects of September 11 on the Leading Search Engine," *First Monday* 7 (October 2001), online at firstmonday.org.

10. A. M. Homes, "We All Saw It, or The View from Home," in *110 Stories: New York Writes After September 11*, edited by Ulrich Baer (New York: New York University Press, 2002), 151–53; quotation is on 151.

11. Quoted in "World Trade Center Stories—Day One," online at www.stinky.com.

12. David Friend, *Watching the World Change: The Stories Behind the Images of 9/11* (New York: Farrar, Straus & Giroux, 2006).

13. Homes, "We All Saw It," 152.

14. Phillip Lopate, "Altering the World We Thought Would Outlast Us," in *110 Stories*, 189–91; quotation is on 191.

15. "Bush: U.S. Military on 'High Alert,'" *CNN* (September 11, 2001), online at archives.cnn.com.

16. Anthony Lewis, "A Different World," *New York Times* (September 12, 2001), A27.

17. Quoted in Carl M. Cannon, "America's Challenge," *National Journal* (September 15, 2001), 2810–21; quotes are on 2011 and 2015.

18. Congressional Record (September 11, 2001), H5501.

19. "The Day the World Changed," *The Economist* (September 15, 2001), 13–16.

20. Quoted in Peter Grier, "A Changed World," *Christian Science Monitor* (September 17, 2001).

21. David M. Kennedy, "Fighting an Elusive Enemy," *New York Times* (September 16, 2001), section 4, 11.

22. President George W. Bush, "President Discusses War on Terrorism in Address to the Nation," White House, Office of the Press Secretary (November 8, 2001), online at www.whitehouse.gov.

23. "A Nation and a World, Changed," *CNN News* (September 21, 2002), online at cnnstudentnews.cnn.com.

24. Quoted in Giovanna Borradori, *Philosophy in a Time of Terror: Dialogues with Jurgen Habermas and Jacques Derrida* (Chicago: University of Chicago Press, 2003), 102.

25. Quoted in Ibid., 26.

26. Theda Skocpol, "Will 9/11 and the War on Terror Revitalize American Civic Democracy?" *PS: Political Science and Politics* 35 (2002): 537–40.

27. Robert MacNeil, "Culture after September 11," *NewsHour* (January 1, 2002), online at www.pbs.org.

28. Time Magazine/SRBI Survey (August 22–24, 2006), online at www.srbi.com.

29. Matt Adams and Penny Jane Burke, "Recollections of September 11 in Three English Villages: Identifications and Self-Narrations," *Journal of Ethnic and Migration Studies* 32 (2006): 983–1003; Dennis Bruce, "Focusing on September 11: Observations from Focus Groups Conducted Since the Terror Attacks," *Marketing Magazine* (October 22, 2001), 11–13.

30. Andrew Sullivan, "Yes, America Has Changed," *Time* (September 11, 2002), online at www.time.com.

31. Conrad C. Lautenbacher Jr., "Remarks at NOAA Auditorium," Unpublished lecture, Silver Spring, Maryland, September 11, 2002.

32. Quoted in Adam Clymer, "In the Day's Attacks and Explosioons, Official Washington Hears the Echoes of Earlier Ones," *New York Times* (September 12, 2001), A20.

33. Robert Keith, "Initial Federal Budget Response to the 1941 Attack on Pearl Harbor," *CRS Report for Congress* (September 13, 2001), Order Code RS21010.

34. Fred L. Borch, "Comparing Pearl Harbor and '9/11': Intelligence Failure? American Unpreparedness? Military Responsibility?" *Journal of Military History* 67 (2003): 845–60.

35. Both are quoted in Cannon, "America's Challenge," 2817.

36. Quoted in Cannon, "America's Challenge," 2821.

37. Amitav Ghosh, "Neighbors," in *110 Stories*, 102–105; quotation is on p. 104.

38. "Visions of the 9/11 Attack," online at paranormal.about.com.

39. Wendy Wasserstein, "Under a Desk on Prospect Park West," *New York Times* (September 16, 2001), CY8.

40. James Carroll, "The Nagasaki Principle," *Boston Globe* (August 7, 2006), online at www.boston.com.

41. Erica Jong, "New York at War," in *September 11, 2001: American Writers Respond*, edited by William Heyen (Silver Spring, Md.: Etruscan Press, 2002), 217–220; quotation is on p. 220.

42. Diana Taylor, "Ground Zero," *Signs* 28 (2002): 448–50.

43. Robert Polito, "Last Seen," in 110 Stories, 238–39; quotation is on p. 239.

44. Richard Rodriguez, "Zero Times One," *News Hour* (August 15, 2002), online at www.pbs.org.

45. Alicia Ostriker, "The Window, at the Moment of Flame," in *September 11, 2001*, 294.

46. Dean E. Murphy, "A Wounded City Struggles to Discover How to Carry On," *New York Times* (September 16, 2001), 12.

47. Galway Kinnell, "When the Towers Fell," *New Yorker* (September 16, 2002), online at www.newyorker.com.

48. Toni Morrison, "The Dead of September 11," *Vanity Fair* (November 2001), 48–49; online at www.legacy-project.org.

49. Walker Percy, *Lost in the Cosmos: The Last Self-Help Book* (New York: Washington Square Press, 1983), 68.

50. Jessica Hagedorn, "Notes from a New York Diary," in *110 Stories*, 134–37; quotations are on pp. 134 and 135.

51. Quoted in "In Memoriam: 9/11/01 List Archive," online.

52. James Gibbons, "The Death of a Painter," in *110 Stories*, 106–109, quotation is on p. 106.

53. NBC News/Wall Street Journal poll (September 15, 2001), available online through Lexis-Nexis.

54. People and the Press Post-Terrorist Attack Poll (September 17, 2001), available online through Lexis-Nexis.

55. "Public Remains Steady in Face of Anthrax Scare," *Pew Research Center for the People and the Press Survey Reports* (October 15, 2001), online at people-press.org.

56. "American Psyche Reeling from Terror Attacks."

57. Harris Interactive Poll (September 14, 2001), available online through Lexis-Nexis.

58. Roger Rosenblatt, "Fear Itself," *NewsHour* (October 22, 2001), online at www.pbs.org.

59. W. Frederick Wooden, "American Myths Reconsidered" (August 15, 2006), online at www.uuworld.org.

60. Interview, Steven Mufson, "For Bush's Veteran Team, What Lessons to Apply?" *Washington Post* (September 15, 2001), A5.

61. Similarities between red scares during the Cold War and red alerts after 9/11 are discussed in David L. Altheide, "Consuming Terrorism," *Symbolic Interaction* 27 (2004): 389–408.

62. NBC News poll (September 12, 2001), available online through Lexis-Nexis.

63. Survey by Pew Research Center and Princeton Survey Research Associates, October 1–October 3, 2001. Survey by National Opinion Research Center, September 13–September 27, 2001. Both available online at www.ropercenter.uconn.edu/ipoll.html. The latter study also showed that 65 percent nationally and 71 percent in New York City "felt angry" about the "terrible deed" of September 11; Kenneth A. Rasinski, Jennifer Berktold, Tom W. Smith, and Bethany L. Albertson, *America Recovers: A Follow-Up to a National Study of Public Response to the September 11th Terrorist Attacks* (Chicago: National Opinion Research Center, 2002), 9.

64. Emily Borenstein, "From 'Twelve Meditations,'" in *September 11, 2001: American Writers Respond*, 58–60; quotation is on p. 58.

65. Gallup Poll (September 15, 2001), available online through Lexis-Nexis.

66. People and the Press Post-Terrorist Attack Poll (September 17, 2001), available online through Lexis-Nexis.

67. Nova Spivack, "Facing South," September 16, 2001, online at www.stinky.com

68. "Public Remains Steady." These symptoms subsided rather dramatically after the initial shock but remained evident in a minority of the public. By mid-October, the percentage who said they felt depressed dropped from 71 percent to 29 percent and the proportion reporting trouble sleeping fell from 33 percent to 12 percent.

69. Kate Stone Lombardi, "On the Lookout for High Anxiety," *New York Times* (December 30, 2001), WE5; Erica Goode, "Stress from Attacks Will Chase Some Into the Depths of Their Minds, and Stay," *New York Times* (September 18, 2001), B1.

70. Alison Hawthorne Deming, "Waking to the World's Pain," in *September 11, 2001: American Writers Respond*, 90–91; quotation is on p. 90.

71. Alex Kuczynski, "What, Me Worry?" *New York Times* (July 28, 2002), H1.

72. Erica Goode, "Lessons from Abroad on Dealing with Anxiety," *New York Times* (October 28, 2001), B10.

73. Sandro Galea, Jennifer Ahern, Heidi Resnick, Dean Kilpatrick, Michael Bucuvalas, Joel Gold, and David Vlahov, "Psychological Sequelae of the September 11 Terrorist Attacks in New York City," *New England Journal of Medicine* 346 (2002): 982–87.

74. Rasinski et al., *America Recovers*, 19.

75. National Opinion Research Center, *National Tragedy Survey* (2002), electronic datafile; my analysis of the New York and national samples with appropriate sampling weights applied.

76. Homes, "We All Saw It," 152.

77. Ronald Steel, "The Weak at War With the Strong," *New York Times* (September 14, 2001), A27. Similar themes were emphasized in John F. Burns, "America the Vulnerable Meets a Ruthless Enemy," *New York Times* (September 12, 2001), A23.

78. James W. Fernandez, "Mutual Vulnerability," *Anthropological Quarterly* 75 (2001): 152–54.

79. Robert Jay Lifton and Charles B. Strozier, "We Were Exposed and Raw," *New York Times* (September 16, 2001), CY7.

80. Murphy, "A Wounded City Struggles to Discover How to Carry On."

81. Ericka White, quoted in "Readers Put Fear, Sorrow into Words," *Washington Post* (September 20, 2001), T6.

82. Quoted in Clyde Haberman, "Agonized, New York Bends, But It Doesn't Break," *New York Times* (September 16, 2001), WK5.

83. Jessie Kindig, quoted in Karen W. Arenson, "A Generation Unfamiliar with Feeling Vulnerable," *New York Times* (September 14, 2001), A22.

84. Darvin, "Teaching in the Days after September 11, 2001."

85. Justin Hudnall, quoted in David Von Drehle, "World War, Cold War Won, the Gray War," *Washington Post* (September 12, 2001), A9.

86. Michael Cervieri, from an online listserve, "In Memoriam: 9/13/01 List Archive," online at wwwac.org.

87. Karen Blomain, "Sisters," in *September 11, 2001: American Writers Respond*, 51–53; quotation is on p. 53.

88. Chen-Jih Chen, in "World Trade Center Stories—Day Five and Following," online at www.stinky.com.

89. Quoted in Vedantam Shankar, "Finding Personal Ways to Cope with National Trauma," *Washington Post* (September 14, 2001), C4.

90. "Editorial," *Washington Post* (September 11, 2001), A30.

91. Diane Glancy, "Lamentations," in *September 11, 2001: American Writers Respond*, 145–48; quotation is on 147.

92. Von Drehle, "World War, Cold War Won, Now, the Gray War."

93. Mary Marshall Clark, "The September 11, 2001, Oral History Narrative and Memory Project: A First Report," *Journal of American History* 89 (2002): 569–79; quotation is on 571.

94. Dan Eggen and Vernon Loeb, "U.S. Intelligence Points to Bin Laden Network," *Washington Post* (September 12, 2001), A1.

95. Joel Achenbach, "The Enemies May Change, But the Hate Lives On," *Washington Post* (September 13, 2001), C4.

96. Quoted in Steven Mufson, "U.S. Urged to Target Nations that Aid Terrorism," *Washington Post* (September 12, 2001), A12.

97. President George W. Bush, "Address to a Joint Session of Congress and the American People," Office of the Press Secretary (October 20, 2001), online at www.whitehouse.gov.

98. Wwwac.org/wtc/911archive.html.

99. "Retaliation Should Be America's Response," *Plain Dealer* (September 20, 2001), B8.

100. Blaine Harden, "After the Attacks, the Reaction," *New York Times* (September 14, 2001), 15.

101. Peter Carey, "Union Square," in *110 Stories*, 54–56; quotation is on 56.

102. "Terrorists Attacked All Americans," *Dayton Daily News* (September 12, 2001), 23A.

103. Brian Witte, "Delegation Says Government Committed to Retaliate," *Associated Press* (September 11, 2001).

104. John Tierney, "Fantasies of Vengeance," *New York Times* (September 18, 2001), 24.

105. Dan Giancola, "The Ruin," in *September 11, 2001: American Writers Respond*, 132–33; quotation is on p. 133.

106. George F. Will, "War Without Catharsis," *Washington Post* (September 20, 2001), A35.

107. Quoted in "World Trade Center Stories—Day Three," online at www.stinky.org.

108. Larry Legman-Miller, quoted in Harden, "After the Attacks."

109. Quoted in "World Trade Center Stories—Day One," online at www.stinky.org.

110. Valerie Strauss, "'Eye for an Eye' Has Its Detractors," *Washington Post* (September 17, 2001), B7.

111. Wwwac.org/wtc/911archive.html.

112. "World Trade Center Stories—Day Three," online at www.stinky.org.

113. Bob Woodward, *Bush at War* (New York: Simon & Schuster, 2002), 15, 37, 38.

114. Richard A. Clarke, *Against All Enemies: Inside America's War on Terror* (New York: Free Press, 2004), 24.

115. President George W. Bush, "Remarks by the President in Photo Opportunity with the National Security Team," Office of the Press Secretary (September 12, 2001), online at www.whitehouse.gov.

116. D. T. Max, "The Making of the Speech," *New York Times* (October 7, 2001), 32. President George W. Bush, "Address to a Joint Session of Congress and the American People," Office of the Press Secretary (September 20, 2001).

117. Discussions of the rhetoric used include Sandra Silberstein (ed.), *War of Words: Language, Politics and 9/11* (London and New York: Routledge, 2002) and George Lakoff, *Whose Freedom? The Battle over America's Most Important Idea* (New York: Farrar, Straus & Giroux, 2006).

118. Congressional Record (September 12, 2001), S9302.

119. Eric Andrew, "Under Attack," *Washington Post* (September 12, 2001), A30.

120. Woodward, *Bush at War*, 84.

121. Jim Hoagland, "How to Respond," *Washington Post* (September 18, 2001), A31.

122. Bush, "Address to a Joint Session of Congress and the American People," September 20, 2001.

123. A particularly interesting discussion of the earlier meanings of retaliation is found in Samuel F. Wells Jr., "The Origins of Massive Retaliation," *Political Science Quarterly* 96 (1981): 31–52; see also Robert Powell, "Nuclear Deterrence and the Strategy of Limited Retaliation," *American Political Science Review* 83 (1989): 503–19, and Timothy J. Van Gelder, "Credible Threats and Usable Weapons: Some Dilemmas of Deterrence," *Philosophy and Public Affairs* 18 (1989): 158–83.

124. Bryan Brophy-Baermann and John A. C. Conybeare, "Retaliating against Terrorism: Rational Expectations and the Optimality of Rules versus Discretion," *American Journal of Political Science* 38 (1994): 196–210.

125. The connection between fear and fighting back is insightfully examined in Neta C. Crawford, "The Passion of World Politics: Propositions on Emotion and Emotional Relationships," *International Security* 24 (2000): 116–56.

126. For example, the *New York Times* carried 172 articles referring to Afghanistan during the seven days prior to the October 7, 2001, invasion, up from 86 during the seven days after 9/11.

127. Woodward, *Bush at War*, 153.

128. John J. Mearsheimer, "Guns Won't Win the Afghan War," *New York Times* (November 4, 2001), WK13.

129. Ibid. "War on Terrorism," PollingReport.com.

130. Time/CNN poll (January 30, 2002), online at web.lexis-nexis.com.

131. "President, General Franks Discuss War Effort," Office of the Press Secretary (December 28, 2001).

132. Time/CNN poll (September 28, 2001), online at web.lexis-nexis.com.

133. ABC News poll (January 4, 2002), online at web.lexis-nexis.com.

134. CBS News polls, online at www.cbsnews.com.

CHAPTER 5

1. Personal interview, April 10, 2006.

2. Allison Macfarlane, "All Weapons of Mass Destruction Are Not Equal" (February 8, 2006), online at www.alternet.org.

3. A count of *New York Times* articles shows only two mentions of "weapons of mass destruction" in 1987, fluctuating patterns during the 1990s, 61 mentions in 2000, 167 in 2001, 548 in 2002, and 880 in 2003.

4. News programs available at the Television News Archive, Vanderbilt University, included 2 in 2000 that referred to "weapons of mass destruction," rising to 30 mentions in 2001, 115 in 2002, and 235 in 2003.

5. George F. Will, "The End of Our Holiday from History," *Washington Post* (September 12, 2001), A31.

6. Bob Woodward, *Plan of Attack* (New York: Simon & Schuster, 2004), 29–30; Michael Dobbs, "Plotters Found the Flaw in Nation's Defense Plans," *Washington Post* (September 12, 2001), A4.

7. U.S. Congress, Office of Technology Assessment, *Proliferation of Weapons of Mass Destruction: Assessing the Risks* (Washington, D.C.: U.S. Government Printing Office, 1993), 54.

8. Ibid., 15.

9. "Archbishop's Appeal," *The Times* (December 28, 1937), 1.

10. Ulrich Trumpener, "The Road to Ypres: The Beginnings of Gas Warfare in World War I," *Journal of Modern History* 47 (1975): 460–80, is an especially useful overview.

11. Gavin Cameron, Jason Pate, and Kathleen Vogel, "Planting Fear," *Bulletin of the Atomic Scientists* 57 (2001): 38–44.

12. F. Stansbury Haydon, "A Proposed Gas Shell, 1862," *Journal of the American Military History Foundation* 2 (1938): 52–54; Wyndham D. Miles, "The Idea of Chemical Warfare in Modern Times," *Journal of the History of Ideas* 31 (1970): 297–304.

13. Keith Schneider, "U.S. Plan to Burn Chemical Weapons Stirs Public Fear," *New York Times* (April 29, 1991), A1.

14. Times Mirror Poll (September 15, 1993), online at web.lexis-nexis.com. The comparable figure in 1995 was 68 percent; Times Mirror Poll (June 11, 1995), online at web.lexis-nexis.com. And in 1997, the figure was 70 percent; Pew Research Center Poll (September 11, 1997), online at web.lexis-nexis.com.

15. NBC News poll (December 14, 1993), online at roperweb.ropercenter.uconn.edu.

16. Pew Research Center Poll (September 23, 1997), online at roperweb.ropercenter.uconn.edu.

17. William J. Broad and Judith Miller, "Iraq Said to Hide Deadly Germ Agents," *New York Times* (December 17, 1998), A15.

18. Harris Interactive Poll (September 14, 2001), online at web.lexis-nexis.com.

19. Gallup Poll (September 15, 2001), online at web.lexis-nexis.com.

20. Woodward, *Bush at War*, 46; *The 9/11 Commission Report*, 334–35.

21. Woodward, *Plan of Attack*, 10, 286–95.

22. NBC News polls conducted during 2002, online at www.pollingreport.com.

23. CBS News polls conducted in late 2002 and early 2003, online at www.pollingreport.com.

24. Fox News poll (January 30, 2003), online at web.lexis-nexis.com.

25. ABC News poll (April 21, 2003), online at www.pollingreport.com.

26. Peter Steinfels, "Beliefs: The Just-War Tradition," *New York Times* (March 1, 2003), A16.

27. Fox News poll (February 12, 2003), online at web.lexis-nexis.com.

28. Pew Research Center Survey (February 18, 2003), online at web.lexis-nexis.com.

29. David Frum, *The Right Man: The Surprise Presidency of George W. Bush* (New York: Random House, 2003).

30. Woodward, *Plan of Attack*, 86–87.

31. Bush, "State of the Union Address" (January 29, 2002), online at www.whitehouse.gov.

32. Democracy Corps Survey (March 3, 2002), online at web.lexis-nexis.com.

33. Gallup Poll (February 10, 2002), online at web.lexis.nexis.com.

34. John R. Bolton, "Beyond the Axis of Evil: Additional Threats from Weapons of Mass Destruction," Heritage Lecture #743 (May 6, 2002), online at www.heritage.org.

35. "Powell, Rice Defend Bush's 'Axis of Evil' Speech," CNN (February 18, 2002), online at archives.cnn.com.

36. Joseph Montville of the Center for Strategic and International Studies, quoted in Maura Reynolds, "'Axis of Evil' Rhetoric Said to Heighten Dangers," *Common Dreams News Center* (January 21, 2003), online at www.commondreams.org.

37. Quoted in Bob Woodward, *State of Denial: Bush at War*, Part III (New York: Simon & Schuster, 2006), 408.

38. President George W. Bush, "Operation Iraqi Freedom" (March 19, 2003), online at www.whitehouse.gov.

39. Jeffrey Folks, "A Burkean Argument Against Saddam," *Washington Times* (February 26, 2003), A20.

40. Jodi Wilgoren, "U.S. Terror Alert Led to No Change in States' Security," *New York Times* (May 25, 2002), A1.

41. "New Terror Alert," *New York Times* (October 20, 2002), C2.

42. President George W. Bush, "State of the Union" (January 28, 2003), online at www.whitehouse.gov.

43. Randal C. Archibold, "Cheney, Invoking the Specter of a Nuclear Attack, Questions Kerry's Strength," *New York Times* (October 20, 2004), A20.

44. Alexis Simendinger, "The Angst Approach," *National Journal* (October 6, 2001), 3092.

45. Bill Keller, "Fear Factor," *New York Times* (June 15, 2002), A17.

46. Maureen Dowd, "Scaring Up Votes," *New York Times* (November 23, 2003), A11.

47. David Ropeik, "We're Being Scared to Death," *Los Angeles Times* (September 22, 2004), B11.

48. Geoffrey R. Stone, "America's New McCarthyism," *Chicago Tribune* (October 17, 2004), 11.

49. Al Gore, "The Politics of Fear," *Social Research* 71 (2004): 779–98; quotation is on 779.

50. Kenneth Prewitt, "The Politics of Fear After 9/11," *Social Research* 71 (2004): 1129–46; quotation is on 1131.

51. Marist Poll (August 2003), Marist College Institute for Public Opinion, online at www.maristpoll.marist.edu.

52. Irwin Redlener and David A. Berman, "National Preparedness Planning: The Historical Context and Current State of the U.S. Public's Readiness, 1940–2005," *Journal of International Affairs* 59 (2006): 87–103; quotation is on 88.

53. James Jay Carafano, "Beyond Duct Tape: The Federal Government's Role in Public Preparedness," Heritage Foundation Executive Memorandum 971 (June 3, 2005), online at www.heritage.org.

54. *The 9/11 Commission Report*, 317, 398.

55. Casey Cavanaugh Grant, "The Birth of the NFPA," *NFPA Journal* (1996): online at www.nfpa.org.

56. Richard E. Vernor, "Developments in the Field of Fire Prevention," *Annals of the American Academy of Political and Social Science* 161 (1932): 152–58; quotation is on 153.

57. *NFPA 1600 Standard on Disaster/Emergency Management and Business Continuity Programs 2004 Edition* (Quincy, Mass.: National Fire Protection Association, 2004).

58. For instance, the 2003 Marist Poll (www.maristpoll.marist.edu) of New York City found only 23 percent thought their community "has an adequate emergency response plan currently in place."

59. President George W. Bush, "Homeland Security: Creation of a New Agency" *Vital Speeches of the Day* (June 6, 2002), 517–19.

60. Further information at www.dhs.gov.

61. "The National Defense," *New York Times* (September 12, 2001), A26.

62. Ismar Schorsch, "A Message from the Jewish Theological Seminary," *New York Times* (September 12, 2001), B17.

63. Gary Hart and Warren Rudman, *Road Map for National Security: Imperative for Change, Phase III Report* (Washington, D.C.: United States Commission on National Security/21st Century, February 15, 2001); quotation is on viii.

64. For an imaginative meditation on the meanings of home, see Jennifer Bajorek, "The Offices of Homeland Security, or, Holderlin's Terrorism," *Critical Inquiry* 31 (2005): 874–902; I have explored the meanings of home in my book *After Heaven: Spirituality in America Since the 1950s* (Berkeley: University of California Press, 1998).

65. Elizabeth Becker, "Prickly Roots of 'Homeland Security,'" *New York Times* (August 31, 2002), A10.

66. Woodward, *Bush at War*, 89.

67. Hart and Rudman, *Road Map for National Security*, vi.

68. On the precedents involved in creating the Department of Homeland Security, see Harold C. Relyea, "Organizing for Homeland Security," *Presidential Studies Quarterly* 33 (2003): 602–24.

69. Ibid., iv and viii.

70. U.S. Congress, Public Law 107–296 (November 25, 2002), 2163–64.

71. Office of the Press Secretary, "Remarks by the President on Signing Homeland Security Appropriations Act" (October 1, 2003).

72. "Fiscal Year 2007 Department of Homeland Security Appropriations Bill–H.R. 5441," *Appropriations Update* 6 (May 24, 2006): 1–2.

73. *Science and Technology: A Foundation for Homeland Security* (Washington, D.C.: Office of Science and Technology Policy, 2005), 32.

74. "News from NASFAA," National Association of Student Financial Aid Administrators (January 22, 2004), online at www.nasfaa.org.

75. "Bioterror Tester Kits Trouble Federal Agencies," *Nature* 428 (April 1, 2004): 454.

76. Robert Popp, Thomas Armour, Ted Senator, and Kristen Numrych, "Countering Terrorism with Information Technology," *Communications of the ACM* 47 (2004): 41–43.

77. Thomas J. Badey, *Annual Editions: Homeland Security* (New York: McGraw-Hill, 2007).

78. Richard H. Minear, "Homeland Security," *Review of Politics* 66 (2004): 330–33; Elizabeth Duquette, "Homeland Security: Writing the American Civil War," *Southern Literary Journal* 35 (2002): 160–63.

79. Lee Herring, "How Would Sociologists Design a Homeland Security Alert System?" *ASA Footnotes* (April 2003): 2–4; online at www.asanet.org.

80. Jeremy Cohen, "Homeland Security," *Journalism and Mass Communication Educator* 59 (2004): 119–20.

81. *Are You Ready? An In-depth Guide to Citizen Preparedness*, rev. ed. (Washington, D.C.: Federal Emergency Management Agency, 2004); online at www.fema.gov/areyouready.

82. Ibid., 165.

83. *Preparing Makes Sense: Get Ready Now* (Washington, D.C.: Department of Homeland Security, 2003), online at www.ready.gov; quotation is on 1.

84. Vanessa O'Connell and Nicholas Kulish, "Government Ads Bring More News of Duct Tape and Plastic," *Wall Street Journal* (February 19, 2003), B1.

85. Peter Amacher, "You're on Your Own—Again," *Bulletin of the Atomic Scientists* 59 (2003): 34–43.

86. Matt Nannery, "Duck . . . At Least I Warned You," *Home Channel News* (March 3, 2003), 11.

87. Jeffrey Selingo, "For Some, the Jitters Help the Bottom Line," *New York Times* (February 20, 2003), G5.

88. "Personal Toxic-Gas Monitor," *Journal of Environmental Health* 67 (September 2004): 45; see also www.raesystems.com.

89. Online at www.iac-online.com.

90. Li Ding, Pranam Kolari, Tim Finin, Anupam Joshi, Yun Peng, Yelena Yesha, "On Homeland Security and the Semantic Web: A Provenance and Trust Aware Inference Framework," paper presented to the American Association for Artificial Intelligence (August 2005), online at www. aaai.org.

91. "Small Business Expo Highlights Homeland Security Products," Public Forum Institute Newsroom (July 11, 2002), online at www.publicforuminstitute.org.

92. Vermont Summit on Homeland Security (December 15, 2003), online at www.vtsbdc.org.

93. These and other examples can be found at politicalhumor.about.com; www.humorgazette. com; and www.topplebush.com. See also Gail Diane Cox, "You'd Hope This One Would Be a Parody," *National Law Journal* 25 (March 17, 2003): A14.

94. CBS News poll (June 20, 2002), online at web.lexis-nexis.com.

95. *Time* CNN Harris Interactive Poll (June 20, 2002), online at web.lexis-nexis.com.

96. *Los Angeles Times* Poll (August 25, 2002), online at web.lexis-nexis.com.

97. Gallup Poll (November 24, 2002), online at web.lexis-nexis.com.

98. Fox News poll (December 4, 2002), online at web.lexis-nexis.com.

99. The quotes in this paragraph are from Frank James, "Critics Unglued by Government's Advice to Buy Duct Tape," *Chicago Tribune* (February 13, 2003), 1.

100. D. C. Montague, "Letter to the Editor," *New York Times* (February 14, 2003), A30.

101. On the policy history of FEMA, see Patrick S. Roberts, "FEMA After Katrina," *Policy Review* 137 (2006): 15–33.

102. Time SRBI Poll (September 8, 2005), online at web.lexis-nexis.com.

103. Forty-five percent said safer, 49 percent said not safer, and 6 percent were unsure; Newsweek Poll (September 30, 2005), online at web.lexis-nexis.com.

104. Anthony Ramirez, "Polls Show Drop in Assurance Since the Attacks of September 11," *New York Times* (September 8, 2006), online at select.nytimes.com; a subsequent poll in 2006 showed a slight increase to 44 percent who expressed confidence.

105. Irwin Redlener, quoted in ibid.

106. *The National Security Strategy of the United States of America* (Washington, D.C.: The White House, 2006), 1.

107. Office of the Press Secretary, "'Islam Is Peace' Says President" (September 17, 2001), online at www.whitehouse.gov.

108. Office of the Press Secretary, "Address to a Joint Session of Congress and the American People" (September 20, 2001), online at www.whitehouse.gov.

109. Laurie Goodstein, "Relations," *New York Times* (September 12, 2001), A12; Thomas L. Friedman, "Foreign Affairs," *New York Times* (September 13, 2001), A27; Richard Boudreaux, "A Superpower's Sorrow, Comeuppance," *Los Angeles Times* (September 13, 2001), A12.

110. The study described in this paragraph was the basis for my book *America and the Challenges of Religious Diversity* (Princeton, N.J.: Princeton University Press, 2005), which reports fully on the results.

111. Michael Kilian, "Terror Calls for New Strategies, Experts Say," *Chicago Tribune* (September 13, 2001), 6; Amos Oz, "Struggling Against Fanaticism," *New York Times* (September 14, 2001), A27; Jodi Wilgoren, "The Hijackers," *New York Times* (September 15, 2001), A2; Judith Miller, "The Organizer," *New York Times* (September 14, 2001), A4.

112. Office of the Press Secretary, "International Campaign Against Terror Grows" (September 25, 2001), online at www.whitehouse.gov "New York Author E. L. Doctorow on Religious Fundamentalism," *NPR Weekend Edition* (September 15, 2001; John F. Burns, "America Inspires Both Longing and Loathing in Muslim World," *New York Times* (September 16, 2001), 4; Thomas L. Friedman, "Smoking or Non-Smoking?" *New York Times* (September 14, 2001), A27.

113. Nadine Gurr and Benjamin Cole, *The New Face of Terrorism: Threats from Weapons of Mass Destruction* (London and New York: I. B. Tauris, 2000), 187; Fareed Zakaria, "The End of the End of History," *Newsweek* (September 24, 2001), 70; Donna Britt, "Seeing the Us in Them," *Washington Post* (September 14, 2001), B1; William Safire, "Of Human Missiles," *New York Times* (September 17, 2001), A15.

114. Edward W. Said, *Orientalism* (New York: Vintage, 1979).

115. Edward W. Said, "The Phony Islamic Threat," *New York Times* (November 21, 1993), A1.

116. Samuel P. Huntington, "The Clash of Civilizations?" *Foreign Affairs* (Summer 1993): online at www.foreignaffairs.org; Samuel P. Huntington, *The Clash of Civilizations and the Remaking of World Order* (New York: Simon & Schuster, 1996).

117. Quoted in "Words to a Hurt World: Action, Not Deliberation," *New York Times* (October 2, 2001), B5.

118. Ronald Brownstein, "War on Terror Will Test U.S. in Terrible Ways," *Los Angeles Times* (September 17, 2001), A3.

119. Arthur Schlesinger Jr., "Sand Trap," *Los Angeles Times* (September 23, 2001), M1.

120. Michael Kelley, quoted in "Readers Put Fear, Sorrow Into Words"; Jessica Carter, quoted in "The Terrorists Cannot Kill Our Spirit," *Washington Post* (September 20, 2001), T16; Gustav Niebuhr, "Excerpts from Sermons across the Nation," *New York Times* (September 17, 2001), A1.

121. Gustav Niebuhr, "U.S. 'Secular' Groups Set Tone for Terror Attacks, Falwell Says," *New York Times* (September 14, 2001), A18; Laurie Goodstein, "Falwell's Finger-Pointing Inappropriate, Bush Says," *New York Times* (September 15, 2001), A15.

122. Wayne Visser, "9/11: The Day the World Changed," October 28, 2001, online at www.waynevisser.com.

123. Katharine Winans, "Wrong-Headed Warmongering," *Washington Post* (September 15, 2001), online at washingtonpost.com.

124. Anne Taylor Fleming, "Living with Grief," *NewsHour* (December 24, 2001), online at www.pbs.org.

125. Wilbur J. Scott, "PTSD in DSM-III: A Case in the Politics of Diagnosis and Disease," *Social Problems* 37 (1990): 294–310; Leslie Roberts, "Study Raises Estimate of Vietnam War Stress," *Science* 241 (August 12, 1988): 788.

126. R. C. Kessler, A. Sonnega, E. Bromet, M. Hughes, and C. B. Nelson, "Posttraumatic Stress Disorder in the National Comorbidity Survey," *Archives of General Psychiatry* 52 (1996): 1048–60.

127. *Improving Care for Our Nation's Veterans with PTSD* (Washington, D.C.: U.S. Department of Veterans Affairs National Center for PTSD, 2006), 3.

128. William E. Schlenger, Juesta M. Caddell, Lori Ebert, B. Kathleen Jordan, Kathryn M. Rourke, David Wilson, Lisa Thalji, J. Michael Dennis, John A. Fairbank, and Richard A. Kulka, "Psychological

Reactions to Terrorist Attacks: Findings from the National Study of Americans' Reactions to September 11," *Journal of the American Medical Association* 288 (August 7, 2002): 581–88; Sandro Galea, "Mental Health in New York City after the September 11 Terrorist Attacks: Results from Two Population Surveys," in *Mental Health, United States, 2002*, edited by Ronald W. Manderscheid and Marilyn J. Henderson (Washington, D.C.: U.S. Government Printing Office, 2003), 83–91.

129. Gerry Fairbrother and Sandro Galea, *Terrorism, Mental Health, and September 11: Lessons Learned about Providing Mental Health Services to a Traumatized Population* (New York: The Century Foundation, 2005), 13. In the one extensive psychological assessment that did examine fear, 65 percent of respondents nationally who were interviewed two months after the attack said they feared future terrorism and 60 percent said they feared harm to their family from terrorism; at six months, 38 and 41 percent, respectively, registered these fears; Roxane Cohen Silver, "Nationwide Longitudinal Study of Psychological Responses to September 11," *Journal of the American Medical Association* 288 (September 11, 2002): 1235–44.

130. "Views of Terrorism," *New York Times* (September 7, 2006), A1. A national poll conducted for *Time* showed that 18 percent "still think about the September 11th attacks" every day and another 35 percent think about them a few times a week; *Time Magazine/SRBI Survey* (August 22–24, 2006), online at www.srbi.com.

131. "Echoes of 9/11 Define Life 5 Years Later," *New York Times* (September 8, 2006); online reader's comments posted at news.blogs.nytimes.com.

132. *Time* Magazine/SRBI Survey (August 22–24, 2006), online at www.srbi.com. When asked how much the "September 11th attacks and the terrorist threats that followed" had changed their "own life personally," 27 percent replied "a great deal" and another 39 percent said "some." Other questions showed similar proportions saying they travel less by airplane, avoid large crowds, and avoid traveling to certain cities.

133. "Echoes of 9/11 Define Life 5 Years Later."

134. Woodward, *Bush at War*, 79, writes of a meeting on September 15, 2001: "Not used to the company, intimidated by the presence of the nation's top leadership, Mueller gave a routine summary of the investigation into the hijackings. He realized he was almost babbling and quickly yielded the floor."

135. Keyword count of mentions in citation and document texts for "Iraq" (1,092 in 2001, 3,295 in 2002, and 10,377 in 2003) and for "World Trade Center" (4,040 in 2001, 2,973 in 2002, and 1,538 in 2003).

136. Figures are through 2006, online at www.the-numbers.com.

137. Jesse McKinley, "9/11 Miniseries Is Criticized as Inaccurate and Biased," *New York Times* (September 6, 2006), online at www.nytimes.com.

138. President George W. Bush, "The National Security Strategy" (March 16, 2006), online at www.whitehouse.gov.

CHAPTER 6

1. Sigmund Freud, *Group Psychology and the Analysis of the Ego* (New York: W. W. Norton, 1959), 36–37. The eyewitness account of the Iroquois Theater fire is from actor Eddie Foy in Eddie Foy and Alvin F. Harlow, *Clowning Through Life* (New York: E. P. Dutton, 1928), 113.

2. Account closings during the 1857 bank crisis are analyzed in Cormac O'Grada and Eugene N. White, "Who Panics During Panics? Evidence from a Nineteenth Century Savings Bank," *National*

Bureau of Economic Research Working Papers (April 2002), No. 8856; on Depression era bank panics, see Charles W. Calomiris and Joseph R. Mason, "Contagion and Bank Failures During the Great Depression: The June 1932 Chicago Banking Panic," *National Bureau of Economic Research Working Papers* (November 1994), No. 4934. See also Charles W. Calomiris and Gary Gorton, "The Origins of Banking Panics: Models, Facts, and Bank Regulation," in *Financial Markets and Financial Crises*, edited by R. Glenn Hubbard (Chicago: University of Chicago Press, 1991), 109–74.

3. Hadley Cantril, *The Invasion from Mars: A Study in the Psychology of Panic* (Princeton: Princeton University Press, 1947); my information about the wooden water tower is from Spencer and Elise Bruno, friends who owned the property in the 1970s.

4. "City Held Unable to Flee an Attack," *New York Times* (July 1, 1954), 7; Federal Civil Defense Administration, "The Problem of Panic," *Civil Defense Technical Bulletin*, TB-19-2 (June 1955): 1–2.

5. Ralph H. Turner and Lewis M. Killian, *Collective Behavior* (Englewood Cliffs, N.J.: Prentice-Hall, 1957), 94; a similar point is made in Neil J. Smelser, *Theory of Collective Behavior* (New York: Free Press, 1962), 131. A more recent approach which is more consistent with the one taken here is Lee Clarke and Caron Chess, "Elites and Panic: More to Fear than Fear Itself," *Social Forces* 87 (2008): 993–1014.

6. Peter de Jager, quoted in Beverly Orndorff, "Year 2000 May Send Computer Back 100 Years," *Richmond Times-Dispatch* (February 2, 1995), E1.

7. Stephanie D. Esters, "Y2K Bug Bites E&O Policies," *National Underwriter* (November 10, 1997): 9. N. Ben Fairweather, "Not Facing the Future: Computing Chaos in the New Century," a widely circulated 1997 paper discussed studies, e-mails, newsletters, and web site advice.

8. Bruce D. Berkowitz, "'Y2K' Is Scarier Than the Alarmists Think," *Wall Street Journal* (June 18, 1998), 1.

9. "Panic in the Year 2000," *Business Week* (March 2, 1998), 154; Elisa Williams, "Firms of All Size Warned about Sting of Y2K Bug," *Chicago Tribune* (May 2, 1998), 1.

10. Gary North, "Y2K," October 6, 1998, online at cypherpunks.venoma.com.

11. "The Millennium Bug: How It Will Change Civilization," *Countryside and Small Stock Journal* (July/August 1998): 8–12.

12. Elisa Williams, "The Bills Come in for the Y2K Bug," *Chicago Tribune* (May 4, 1998), 1.

13. Americans Talk Issues Survey (August 9, 1998), online at roperweb.ropercenter.uconn.edu.

14. Gallup National Science Foundation Survey (December 13, 1998), online at roperweb.ropercenter.uconn.edu.

15. Michael Logan, "Preparing for the End of the World as We Know It," *Pittsburgh Post-Gazette* (January 3, 1999), A1; John McCormick, "Glitch-leery Iowans Are Stocking Their Shelves," *Des Moines Register* (January 6, 1999), 1A.

16. Barnaby J. Feder, "Fear of the Year 2000 Bug Is a Problem, Too," *New York Times* (February 9, 1999), A1.

17. Quoted in "Residents Are Quietly Stockpiling Supplies in the Event of National Chaos," *Atlanta Journal-Constitution* (January 31, 1999), D5.

18. CBS News poll (January 2, 2000), online at roperweb.ropercenter.uconn.edu.

19. Lynne Gomez, "Annals of Y2K: Ants and Grasshoppers," Letter to the Editor, *New York Times* (January 2, 2000), CT17.

20. Gayle Willman, "What Should the MIT Community Do to Prepare for Y2K?" *I/S News* (September/October 1999), online at web.mit.edu. "Preparations for Naught as Y2K Bug Bypasses

MIT" (January 5, 2000), online at www-tech.mit.edu. "I/T Delivery President's Report for FY2000," online at web.mit.edu.

21. "University Outlines Y2K Contingency Plans," *Princeton Weekly Bulletin* (November 22, 1999); Andrew Pollack, "For Year 2000 Fix-It Crew, New Tasks or No Jobs," *New York Times* (January 3, 2000), A1; C. J. Chivers, "The Word from the Bunker," *New York Times* (January 3, 2000), B3.

22. A count of articles in Proquest journals and media showed nearly as many mentioning Y2K in January 2000 (226) as in December 1999 (230). By March 2000, the number fell to 29, reached a low of 11 in August, and then climbed to 45 in December and 38 in January 2001, after which there was a steady decline to only 6 in June 2001.

23. Steven Levy, "The Bug That Didn't Bite," *Newsweek* (January 10, 2000), 41.

24. "This Is Not a Test," *Wired News* (April 1999), online at www.wired.com.

25. "The Wisdom of Y2K Planning," *New York Times* (January 3, 2000), A18.

26. Ellen Ullman, "The Myth of Order," *Wired News* (April 1999), online at www.wired.com.

27. "National Security Agency Lost Computers for Days," *New York Times* (January 31, 2000), A14.

28. Gail Collins, "Overkilling Y2K," *New York Times* (January 4, 2000), A4.

29. Quoted in Steve Lohr, "Computers Prevail in First Hours of '00," *New York Times* (January 1, 2000), A1; Marcia Stepanek, "The Y2K Bug Repellent Wasn't a Waste," *Business Week* (January 17, 2000), 35.

30. "Y2K: Risk Management Triumph or Much Ado about Nothing?" *National Underwriter* (February 14, 2000): 22.

31. Fox News poll (January 13, 2000), online at roperweb.ropercenter.uconn.edu.

32. W. H. McNeill, *Plagues and Peoples* (Oxford: Oxford University Press, 1977); Christine A. Smith, "Plague in the Ancient World: A Study from Thucydides to Justinian," *Student Historical Journal* 28 (1996–97), online at www.loyno.edu/~history/journal; J. C. F. Poole and J. Holladay, "Thucydides and the Plague of Athens," *Classical Quarterly* 29 (1979): 282–300; Patrick Olson, "The Thucydides Syndrome: Ebola Déjà vu? (or Ebola Reemergent?)," *Emerging Infectious Diseases* 2 (1996): 1–23.

33. Smith, "Plague in the Ancient World."

34. J. R. Maddicott, "Plague in Seventh-Century England," *Past and Present* 156 (1997): 7–54.

35. Ole J. Benedictow, *The Black Death, 1346–1353: The Complete History* (Woodbridge, U.K.: Boydell Press, 2004).

36. Michael Platiensis, quoted in Johannes Nohl, *The Black Death* (London: George Allen & Unwin, 1926), 18–19.

37. J. M. W. Bean, "Plague, Population and Economic Decline in England in the Later Middle Ages," *Economic History Review* 15 (1963): 423–37.

38. Gilles Li Muisis, quoted in Louise Marshall, "Manipulating the Sacred: Image and Plague in Renaissance Italy," *Renaissance Quarterly* 47 (1994): 485–532.

39. Ibid.

40. John Hatcher, "England in the Aftermath of the Black Death," *Past and Present* 144 (1994): 3–35.

41. John C. Caldwell and Pat Caldwell, "Toward an Epidemiological Model of AIDS in Sub-Saharan Africa," *Social Science History* 20 (1996): 559–91.

42. Phillip Ziegler, *The Black Death* (London: Collins, 1969), 17.

43. For example, see the study plans provided for high school students by the National Endowment for the Humanities, online at edsitement.neh.gov.

44. John Duffy, *Epidemics in Colonial America* (Baton Rouge: Louisiana State University Press, 1953), 184–88.

45. John R. Mote, *Virus and Rickettsial Diseases* (Cambridge, Mass.: Harvard University Press, 1940), 433.

46. John M. Barry, *The Great Influenza: The Story of the Deadliest Pandemic in History* (New York: Viking, 2005), 96.

47. Alfred W. Crosby, *America's Forgotten Pandemic: The Influenza of 1918*, 2nd ed. (New York: Cambridge University Press, 2003), 5–6.

48. "Ten Million Deaths in 'Flu' Plague a Year Ago," *New York Times* (February 1, 1920), 31.

49. "Quick Action Slowed Spread of 1918 Flu," *Scientific American* (April 3, 2007), online at www.sciam.com.

50. "Pandemics and Pandemic Scares in the 20th Century," United States Department of Health and Human Services, National Vaccine Program Office, online at www.hhs.gov/nvpo/pandemics.

51. Available online at http://publichealthlaw.law.lsu.edu/cphl/history/books/sw/documents.pdf.

52. Included online at http://publichealthlaw.law.lsu.edu/cphl/history/books/sw/documents.pdf.

53. Gallup Poll (August 23, 1976), Roper Poll (September 4, 1976, and December 11, 1976), online at web.lexis.nexis.com.

54. K. Michael Cummings, Alan M. Jette, Bruce M. Brock, and Don P. Haefner, "Psychosocial Determinants of Immunization Behavior in a Swine Influenza Campaign," *Medical Care* 17 (1979): 639–49. The swine flu episode has been examined in detail in Richard E. Neustadt and Harvey V. Fineberg, *The Swine Flu Affair: Decision-Making on a Slippery Disease* (Seattle: University Press of the Pacific, 2005).

55. Harris Survey (February 7, 1977), online at web.lexis.nexis.com.

56. "Swine Flu—Action" and other HEW and CDC memos written in March and April 1976 are online at online at http://publichealthlaw.law.lsu.edu/cphl/history/books/sw/documents.pdf.

57. Theodore Cooper, "Flu Vaccine: Better Safe Than Sorry," *Washington Post* (June 13, 1976), 29.

58. "Swine Flu," *60 Minutes* (November 4, 1979).

59. David J. Sencer and J. Donald Millar, "Reflections on the 1976 Swine Flu Vaccination Program," *Emerging Infectious Diseases* 12 (2006): 29–33; quotation is on 33.

60. Robert G. Webster, quoted in Rick Weiss, "Viruses: The Next Plague?" *Washington Post* (October 8, 1989), C1.

61. Richard Preston, *The Hot Zone* (New York: Random House, 1994); Frank Ryan, "Panic in the Laboratory," *New York Times* (October 30, 1994), A1.

62. Figures from CDC and other sources as summarized at www.aegis.com.

63. Peter Davis, "Exploring the Kingdom of AIDS," *New York Times* (May 31, 1987), SM32.

64. *Time* (September 19, 1985), online at web.lexis-nexis.com.

65. Joe Stein, "1986: Crack, AIDS and Then Some," *Evening Tribune* (December 31, 1986), D1.

66. Daniel Q. Haney, "Estimated 5 Million Americans at High Risk of Catching AIDS," *Associated Press* (July 9, 2000).

67. "World Health Organization Issues Emergency Travel Advisory," World Health Organization (March 15, 2003), and "Disease Outbreak Reported," World Health Organization (March 16, 2003),

online at www.who.int.; Daniel Yee, "CDC: Vigilance Against Flu Helped U.S. Officials Respond to Mysterious Outbreak in Asia," *Associated Press* (March 16, 2003), online at infoweb.newsbank.com.

68. Geoff Hiscock, "Virus Raises Asian Recession Fear," CNN (April 1, 2003), online at cnn.com/business; Megan Murray, quoted in Alvin Powell, "Unknown Feeds Public Fear of SARS," *Harvard University Gazette* (April 10, 2003); Amy Harmon, "Public Confronts New Virus on Laymen's Terms," *New York Times* (April 6, 2003), A16.

69. Elizabeth W. Etheridge, *Sentinel for Health: A History of the Centers for Disease Control* (Berkeley: University of California Press, 1992); Bindu Tharian, "Centers for Disease Control and Prevention," *New Georgia Encyclopedia* (Athens: University of Georgia Press, 2007), online at www.georgiaencyclopedia.org.

70. Cecilia Cheng, "To Be Paranoid Is the Standard? Panic Responses to SARS Outbreak in the Hong Kong Special Administrative Region," *Asian Perspective* 28 (2004): 67–98.

71. Archie Campbell, *Spring of Fear* (Ontario: The Sars Commission, 2006).

72. *Emerging Infectious Diseases: Asian SARS Outbreak Challenged International and National Responses* (Washington, D.C.: United States General Accountability Office, 2004); perhaps belying the precision implied in such figures, other reports suggest that the global toll may have been as high as 8,427 cases, with 916 deaths, and as many as 74 cases in the United States.

73. Oliver Razum, Heiko Beecher, Annette Kapaun, and Thomas Junghariss, "SARS, Lay Epidemiology, and Fear," *Lancet* (May 2, 2003), online at image.thelancet.com.

74. SARS Survey, Program on Biological Security and the Public, Harvard School of Public Health (April 15, 2003), ABC News poll (April 3, 2003), both online at roperweb.ropercenter.uconn.edu.

75. *Emerging Infectious Diseases.*

76. Campbell, *Spring of Fear*, 2.

77. Cheng, "To Be Paranoid Is the Standard?" Bobbie Person, Francisco Sy, Kelly Holton, Barbara Govert, and Arthur Liang, "Fear and Stigma: The Epidemic within the SARS Outbreak," *Emerging Infectious Diseases* 10 (February 2004): 358–63. Quoted in "Health Officials: SARS Could Come Back," CNN (September 26, 2003), online at www.cnn.com.

78. Campbell, *Spring of Fear*, 1.

79. "Angry Chinese Riot Over SARS," CNN (May 6, 2003), online at www.cnn.com.

80. Joshua Lederberg, "Infectious History," *Science* 288 (April 14, 2000): 287–93; quotation is on page 290; Gretchen Vogel, "Sequence Offers Clues to Deadly Flu," *Science* 279 (January 16, 1998): 324.

81. Martin Enserink, "Looking the Pandemic in the Eye," *Science* 306 (October 15, 2004): 392–94; quotation is on 392.

82. The countries were Cambodia, China, Croatia, Indonesia, Japan, Kuwait, Myanmar, Philippines, Romania, Sri Lanka, Thailand, Turkey, Ukraine, Vietnam, and Zimbabwe. Data are from the WAHID Interface at www.oie.int and WHO Avian Influenza Situation Updates at www.who.int.

83. The WHO situation updates are from the organization's Epidemic and Pandemic Alert and Response listings, online at www.who.int; transcripts of CNN coverage are from infoweb.newsbank.com.

84. Minor inconsistencies in CNN's coverage were evident: on February 2 Costello's introduction wrongly stated that the person who died was a man and on February 4 Costello said that a total of 14 people had died, only to be contradicted by Mintier's report that 11 had died in Vietnam and 4 in Thailand.

85. Keith Bradsher and Lawrence K. Altman, "As Bird Flu Persists, Global Leaders Prepare for the Worst," *New York Times* (July 9, 2004), A6.

86. Dr. Omi's statement was quoted in Keith Bradsher and Lawrence K. Altman, "W.H.O. Official Says Deadly Pandemic Is Likely if the Asian Bird Flu Spreads Among People," *New York Times* (November 30, 2004), A12; the transcript of CNN's "Paula Zahn Now" for December 7, 2004, written by Andrea Koppel, is from infoweb.newsbank.com.

87. David Brown, "HHS Calls for Plan to Counter Threat of Flu: Potential Strains Could Devastate Worldwide," *Washington Post* (August 26, 2004), A21; Alice Park, "Flu-Shot Anxiety," *Time* (October 18, 2004), 91; Julie L. Gerberding, "Flu Vaccine Supply," Testimony before the Health Subcommittee of the House Energy and Commerce Committee (November 18, 2004) and the Committee on House Government Reform (February 10, 2005), online at web.lexis-nexis.com.

88. Rob Stein, "Internal Dissension Grows as CDC Faces Big Threats to Public Health," *Washington Post* (March 6, 2005), A9; "Health System Preparedness to Handle Health Threats," Committee on House Government Reform (February 12, 2004), John M. Meenan, "Blocking Global Spread of Disease Facilitated by Air Travel," Committee on House Transportation and Infrastructure, Subcommittee on Aviation (April 6, 2005), "The Threat of and Planning for Pandemic Flu," Hearing of the Health Subcommittee of the House Energy and Commerce Committee (May 26, 2005), "Hearing on U.S. Flu Readiness," House Committee on Government Reform (June 30, 2005), online at web.lexis-nexis.com.

89. Fox News (October 12, 2005), Gallup Poll (October 23, 2005), New Models Survey (October 16, 2005), NBC News (November 7, 2005), online at roperweb.ropercenter.uconn.edu.

90. George Washington University Battleground 2006 Survey (October 12, 2005), online at roperweb.ropercenter.uconn.edu.

91. George W. Bush, "President Outlines Pandemic Influenza Preparations and Response," White House, Office of the Press Secretary (November 1, 2005), online at www.whitehouse.gov. Homeland Security Council, *National Strategy for Pandemic Influenza* (Washington, D.C.: White House, 2005).

92. Kagan, "President Outlines Flu Pandemic Strategy," CNN (November 1, 2005), Wolf Blitzer, "Bush Unveils $7 Billion Plan to Fight Possible Bird Flu Pandemic" (November 1, 2005), online at infoweb.newsbank.com.

93. Terrence M. Tumpey, Christopher F. Basler, Patricia V. Aguilar, Hui Zeng, Alicia Solorzano, David E. Swayne, Nancy J. Cox, Jacqueline M. Katz, Jeffery K. Taubenberger, Peter Palese, and Adolfo Garcia-Sastre, "Characterization of the Reconstructed 1918 Spanish Influenza Pandemic Virus," *Science* 310 (October 7, 2005): 77–80; Elodie Ghedin et al., "Large-Scale Sequencing of Human Influenza Reveals the Dynamic Nature of Viral Genome Evolution," *Nature* 437 (October 2005): 1162–66; and David Brown, "Changes Cited in Bird Flu Virus," *Washington Post* (October 6, 2005), A3.

94. Gallup Poll (December 11, 2005), online at roperweb.ropercenter.uconn.edu. Fox News (January 11, 2006), online at web.lexis-nexis.com. Health Poll Report (December 11, 2005), online at roperweb.ropercenter.uconn.edu.

95. Sanjay Gupta, "Flu Season Makes Bird Flu Fears Stronger," CNN (December 10, 2005), and Sanjay Gupta, "Killer Flu: A Breath Away," CNN (December 11, 2005), transcripts from infoweb.newsbank.com.

96. Daryn Kagan, "President Bush Outlines Flu Pandemic Strategy."

97. "What We Worry About," anonymous blog posted March 11, 2006 on europeanflu. blogspot.com.

98. One example was Mark Jenkins, "Is Bird Flu Really a Threat?" (January 2006), online at www.thetrumpet.com, in which Jenkins provided a thorough and informative overview of the recent evidence, and then by connecting bird flu with apocalyptic predictions, called on readers to repent and trust in God.

99. "Think Influenza Came in U-Boat," New York Times (September 18, 1918); on deaths and illnesses at the time, see Crosby, America's Forgotten Pandemic, 38–69.

100. Bradsher and Altman, "W.H.O. Official Says Deadly Pandemic Is Likely."

101. Steven Woloshin, Lisa M. Schwartz, and H. Gilbert Welch, "A Shot of Fear: Flu Death Risk Often Exaggerated," Washington Post (October 25, 2005), F1.

102. Mark J. Gibbs and Adrian J. Gibbs, "Was the 1918 Pandemic Caused by a Bird Flu?" Nature 440 (April 2006): E8–10.

103. Lisa Prososki, "Bird Flu: The Next Pandemic?" NewsHour (March 15, 2007), online at www.pbs.org.

CHAPTER 7

1. Mike Tidwell, "The End Is Near," Washington Post (September 9, 2001), A1 and E1.

2. Harris Poll (August 22, 2001), CBS News poll (June 18, 2001), online at web.lexis-nexis.com; the questions were: "Have you ever seen, heard or read about the theory of global warming—that average temperatures are rising slowly and will continue to mainly because of coal, oil, and other fuels?" and "Do you believe the theory that increased carbon dioxide and other gases released into the atmosphere will, if unchecked, lead to global warming and an increase in average temperatures?"

3. "Letters to the Editor," Dayton Daily News (August 31, 2001), 13A; "Greenhouse Gases Dadlier than Traffic Crashes," Telegraph Herald (August 19, 2001), A6; Kevin Van Genechten, quoted in "Vermont High School Student Congressional Town Meeting" Congressional Record (September 10, 2001), E1609; Scott Spoolman, "Bush is Full of Hot Air," Capital Times (August 8, 2001), 9A; Paul Rauber, "Life in a Warmer World," Sierra Magazine (May/June 2001), online at www.sierra-club.org.

4. Climate Change 2001: Synthesis Report Summary for Policymakers (Wembly, U.K.: Intergovernmental Panel on Climate Change, September 2001); quotation is on 9; see also Mark Schrope, "Consensus Science, or Consensus Politics?" Nature 412 (July 12, 2001): 112–14.

5. Andrew C. Revkin, "Warming's Likely Victims," New York Times (February 19, 2001), A4; Patrick J. Michaels, "Global Warming Warnings: A Lot of Hot Air," USA Today (January 2001), 18–20; Gary Cuneen, "It's Time to Wake Up and Smell the Carbon," U.S. Catholic (November 2001), 32–35; John Bellamy Foster, "Ecology Against Capitalism," Monthly Review 53 (October 2001): 1–15, quotation is on 15; Thomas H. Standing, "Climate Change Projections Hinge on Global CO_2 Temperature Data," Oil and Gas Journal 99 (November 12, 2001): 20–26.

6. Of particular interest is U.S. Senate, Committee on Energy and Natural Resources, "California's Electricity Crisis and Implications for the West" (January 31, 2001), S. Hrg. 107-27. Senator Murkowski's statement appears in U.S. Senate, Committee on Energy and Natural Resources, "Current U.S. Energy Trends and Recent Changes in Energy Markets" (March 21, 2001), S. Hrg.

107–90. President George W. Bush, "Text of a Letter from the President to Senators Hagel, Helms, Craig, and Roberts," Office of the Press Secretary (March 13, 2001), online at www.whitehouse.gov. "Mr. Bush Reverses Course," *New York Times* (March 15, 2001), A24. *Sierra Club v. Vice President Richard Cheney, et al.* (January 2002), online at findlaw.com. United States General Accounting Office, "Energy Task Force: Process Used to Develop the National Energy Policy" (August 2003), GAO-03–894.

7. U.S. Senate, Committee on Energy and Natural Resources, "Fiscal Year 2002 Budget Request for the Department of Energy" (May 10, 2001), S. Hrg. 107–107; Office of the Press Secretary, "Remarks by the President to Capital City Partnership" (May 17, 2001), online at www.whitehouse.gov; National Energy Policy Development Group, *National Energy Policy* (Washington, D.C.: The White House, May 2001); Robert L. Bamberger and Mark E. Holt, "Bush Energy Policy: Overview of Major Proposals and Legislative Action" (August 22, 2001), CRS Report for Congress, Order Code RL31096.

8. Committee on the Science of Climate Change, *Climate Change Science: An Analysis of Some Key Questions* (Washington, D.C.: National Academy of Sciences, 2001). Quotation is on 1.

9. Office of the Press Secretary, "President Bush Discusses Global Climate Change" (June 11, 2001), online at www.whitehouse.gov.

10. U.S. Senate, Committee on Energy and Natural Resources, "Climate Change and Balanced Energy Policy Act" (June 28, 2001), S. Hrg. 107–189; quotation is on 5.

11. Ross Gelbspan, "A Modest Proposal to Stop Global Warming," *Sierra* magazine (May/June 2001), online at www.sierraclub.org.

12. Eric J. Barron, testimony to the U.S. Senate, Committee on Energy and Natural Resources, "Climate Change and Balanced Energy Policy," 66.

13. Glenn Kelly quoted in Elizabeth Shogren, "Powerful Pact Formed in Senate on Global Warming," *Los Angeles Times* (August 4, 2001), A12.

14. Michael Catanzaro, "Senate Is Ratifying Liberal Concept of Global Warming," *Human Events* (September 10, 2001), 5.

15. Ross Gelbspan, "Bush's Climate Follies," *American Prospect* (July 30, 2001), 11–12; quotation is on 12.

16. Donald A. Brown, "The Ethical Dimensions of Global Environmental Issues," *Daedalus* (Fall 2001), 59–76; quotation is on 60.

17. *New York Times* full-text keyword search for "global warming" results: 303 from March 11, 2001, through September 10, 2001; 98 for the following six months; Eric Pianin, "War Effort Pushes 'Green' Issues Aside," *Washington Post* (October 21, 2001), A5; Eric Pianin, "Bush Unveils Global Warming Plan," *Washington Post* (February 15, 2002), A9; Global Engagement Survey (December 6, 2001), online at web.lexis-nexis.com.

18. Deputy Secretary of Commerce Sam Bodman, "Welcoming Remarks," Climate Change Science Program Workshop (December 3, 2002); an example of Pew Center research is John M. Reilly, Henry D. Jacoby, and Ronald G. Prinn, *Multi-Gas Contributors to Global Climate Change: Climate Impacts and Mitigation Costs of Non-CO2 Gases* (Arlington, Virginia: Pew Center on Global Climate Change, 2003); the figure for private foundations is from Foundation Center data analyzed by Professor Helmut Anheier at UCLA (personal communication); specific projects are described in annual reports entitled *Our Changing Planet: The U.S. Climate Change Science Program* (Washington, D.C.: Climate Change Science Program and Subcommittee on Global Change Research, 2002–2006), online at www.gcrio.org.

19. *Climate Change Impacts on the United States: The Potential Consequences of Climate Variability and Change* (Cambridge: Cambridge University Press, 2001), 22.

20. Quoted in Tekla S. Perry, "Capturing Climate Change," *IEEE Spectrum* (January 2002), 58–65; quotation is on 59.

21. R. Z. Poore, M. J. Pavich, and H. D. Grissino-Mayer, "Record of North American Southwest Monsoon from Gulf of Mexico Sediment Cores," *Geology* 33 (2005): 209–12.

22. H. N. Pollack and J. E. Smerdon, "Borehole Climate Reconstructions: Spatial Structure and Hemispheric Averages," *Journal of Geophysical Research* 109 (2004): D11106.

23. Richard A. Kerr, "No Doubt about It, the World Is Warming," *Science* 312 (May 2006): 825.

24. Committee on Surface Temperature Reconstructions for the Last 2,000 Years, *Surface Temperature Reconstructions for the Last 2,000 Years* (Washington, D.C.: National Academy of Sciences, 2006), 4.

25. National Academy of Sciences, *Understanding and Responding to Climate Change: Highlights of National Academies Reports* (Washington, D.C.: National Academy of Sciences, 2005), 2.

26. James Hansen, "Defusing the Global Warming Time Bomb," *Scientific American* 290 (2004): 68–77; and James Hansen, "A Slippery Slope: How Much Global Warming Constitutes 'Dangerous Anthropogenic Interference'?" *Climatic Change* 68 (2005): 269–79; quotation is on 270.

27. David Appell, "Behind the Hockey Stick," *Scientific American* (March 2005): 34–35.

28. United Nations Framework Convention on Climate Change, "National Greenhouse Gas Inventory Data for the Period 1990–2003 and Status of Reporting" (2005), GE 05–63835; online at unfeee.int.resource/docs.

29. Quoted in Paul McFedried, "Climate Change, Changing Language," *Spectrum Online* (August 2005), online at www.spectrum.ieee.org. See also National Academy of Sciences, *Understanding and Responding to Climate Change*.

30. Richard A. Kerr, "A Worrying Trend of Less Ice, Higher Seas," *Science* 311 (March 24, 2006): 1698–1701; J. Hansen and L. Nazarenko, "Soot Climate Forcing Via Snow and Ice Albedos," *Proceedings of the National Academy of Science* 101 (2004): 423–28.

31. D. Chen, M. A. Cane, A. Kaplan, S. E. Zebiak, and D. Huang, "Predictability of El Niño over the Past 148 Years," *Nature* 428 (2004): 733–36; A. Ruiz-Barradas and S. Nigam, "IPCC's Twentieth-Century Climate Simulations: Varied Representations of North American Hydroclimate Variability," *American Meteorological Society* 19 (2006): 4041–58.

32. E. R. Cook, C. W. Woodhouse, C. M. Eakin, D. M. Meko, and D. W. Stahle, "Long-Term Aridity Changes in the Western United States," *Science* 306 (2004): 1015–18.

33. National Academy of Sciences, *Abrupt Climate Change: Inevitable Surprises* (Washington, D.C.: National Academies Press, 2002).

34. For instance, S. Parkpoom, G. P. Harrison, and J. W. Bialek, "Climate Change Impacts on Electricity Demand," *Universities Power Engineering Conference* 3 (2004): 1342–46; G. P. Harrison, H. W. Whittington, and A. R. Wallace, "Climate Change Impacts on Financial Risk in Hydropower Projects," *IEEE Transactions on Power Systems* 18 (2003): 1324–30; B. K. Biswas, Y. M. Svirezhev, and B. K. Bala, "A Model to Predict Climate-Change Impact on Fish Catch in the World Oceans," *IEEE Transactions on Systems, Man and Cybernetics, Part A* 35 (2005): 773–83; Paul R. Epstein, "Is Global Warming Harmful to Health?" *Scientific American* (August 2000): 50–57.

35. Nicholas Stern, *The Economics of Climate Change: The Stern Review* (Cambridge: Cambridge University Press, 2006).

36. A convenient overview is given in Robert H. Socolow and Stephen W. Pacala, "A Plan to Keep Carbon in Check," *Scientific American* (September 2006): 50–57.

37. C. M. Barker, W. K. Reisen, and V. L. Kramer, "California State Mosquito-Borne Virus Surveillance and Response Plan," *Journal of Tropical Medicine and Hygiene* 68 (2003): 508–18; Western Governors' Association, *Creating a Drought Early Warning System for the 21st Century* (2004), online at www.westgov. org; and T. J. Brown, A. Barnston, J. O. Roads, R. Martin, and K. E. Wolter, "Seasonal Consensus Climate Forecasts for Wildland Fire Management," *Experimental Long-Lead Forecasts Bulletin* 12 (2003): 1–6.

38. Committee on the Science of Climate Change, *Climate Change Science: An Analysis of Some Key Questions*, 17.

39. National Academy of Sciences, *Understanding and Responding to Climate Change*, 25.

40. Kerr, "A Worrying Trend of Less Ice."

41. CBS News poll (August 21, 2006), online at web.lexis-nexis.com.

42. Center for a New American Dream Survey (June 20, 2006), online at web.lexis.nexis.com.

43. Pew Research Center (July 19, 2006), online at web.lexis-nexis.com.

44. The most engaging of these stories is Spencer R. Weart, *The Discovery of Global Warming* (Cambridge, Mass.: Harvard University Press, 2003); another readable account is Gale E. Christianson, *Greenhouse: The 200-Year Story of Global Warming* (New York: Walker, 1999).

45. Assembly of Mathematical and Physical Sciences, Geophysics Study Committee, *Energy and Climate* (Washington, D.C.: National Academy of Sciences, 1977).

46. See also Wallace S. Broecker, "Climate Change: Are We on the Brink of a Pronounced Global Warming?" *Science* 189 (August 8, 1975): 460–63; Paul E. Damon and Steven M. Kunen, "Global Cooling?" *Science* 193 (August 6, 1976): 447–53.

47. Walter Sullivan, "Scientists Fear Heavy Use of Coal May Bring Adverse Shift in Climate," *New York Times* (July 25, 1977), 45.

48. Philip H. Abelson, "Energy and Climate," *Science* 197 (September 2, 1977): 941.

49. "Coal and the Global Greenhouse," *Washington Post* (July 27, 1977), A22.

50. Dean B. Wheeler, "Disaster Seen if U.S. Relies on Fossil Fuels," *Los Angeles Times* (November 20, 1977), A3.

51. Oil prices are from the Department of Energy, online at www.eia.doe.gov; gasoline is from the Bureau of Labor Statistics figures at current prices; online at zfacts.com.

52. Jimmy Carter, "The President's Proposed Energy Policy," April 18, 1977, *Vital Speeches* 43 (May 1, 1977): 418–20; quotation is on 418.

53. "Researchers Renew Warning on Effects of Global Warming," *New York Times* (July 21, 1982), A14; "Waiting for the Greenhouse Effect," *New York Times* (August 3, 1982), A20; "Greenhouse Effect," CBS Evening News (March 25, 1982), Television News Archive, Vanderbilt University. The network news programs mentioned the greenhouse effect or global warming five times in late 1983, none in 1984 and 1985, and once each in 1986 and 1987.

54. "Environment: Future Shock, Deep Debate, Planting a Seed," CBS News Inside Sunday (June 26, 1988), Television News Archive, Vanderbilt University.

55. William J. Clinton and Albert Gore Jr., *The Climate Change Action Plan* (Washington, D.C.: Office of the President, 1993); U.S. Congress, Office of Technology Assessment, *Preparing for an Uncertain Climate*, 2 vols. (Washington, D.C.: U.S. Government Printing Office, 1993).

56. David E. Fisher, *Fire & Ice: The Greenhouse Effect, Ozone Depletion, and Nuclear Winter* (New York: Harper & Row, 1990); "The Truth about Global Warming," *Reader's Digest* (February 1990).

57. Philip Shabecoff, "Parley Urges Quick Action to Protect Atmosphere," *New York Times* (July 1, 1988), A3; Thomas Lovejoy in an August 1988 speech, quoted in Tom Wicker, "Decade of Decision," *New York Times* (February 28, 1989), A23; National Academy of Sciences, quoted in Philip Shabecoff, "Bush Is Urged to Fight Threat of Global Warming," *New York Times* (January 6, 1989), A16; Albert Gore Jr., "An Ecological Kristallnacht," *New York Times* (March 19, 1989), E27; Union of Concerned Scientists and Citizens and Scientists for Environmental Solutions, "World Scientists' Warning to Humanity" (November 1992), online at www.ucsusa.org.

58. Cambridge Reports National Omnibus Survey (July 1988), online at roperweb.ropercenter. uconn.edu; the question read: "To the extent that the ozone is being depleted, one cause is a group of chemicals known as chlorofluorocarbons, or CFCs. CFCs have a wide range of uses, including coolants in refrigerators and air conditioners, Styrofoam products and packaging, and foam cushions. CFCs are nontoxic and nonflammable, but when they rise high in the atmosphere they change character and deplete the ozone layer. The ozone layer partially screens ultraviolet rays and prevents skin cancer, cataracts, crop and fish damage, and global warming. Do you think the benefits of using CFCs outweigh the risks, or do the risks outweigh the benefits?" Analysis Group National Survey on Energy Policy (September 14, 1988), online at roperweb.ropercenter.uconn.edu; the question read: "There have been many reports in the last year, including those from a broad range of scientists, that the earth is warming up because of air pollution—what is normally called the 'greenhouse effect.' That could lead to a drying up of the central farming areas of the United States, the erosion of east coast beaches and the deterioration of forests. Do you view these reports as a truthful warning of a real and important danger or do you view these reports as probably exaggerated and too alarmist?"

59. Cambridge Reports National Omnibus Survey (October 1988); Times Mirror People, the Press and Politics Poll (January 1989); both online at roperweb.ropercenter.uconn.edu.

60. Cambridge Reports National Omnibus Survey (September 1992), "America at the Crossroads: A National Energy Strategy Poll" (December 1990); both online at roperweb.ropercenter. uconn.edu.

61. Bureau of Labor Statistics, current prices; online at zfacts.com.

62. "America at the Crossroads" (December 1990).

63. Americans Talk Security Foundation (December 15, 1991), online at roperweb.ropercenter. uconn.edu; Susan Yoachum, "Pols, Pols, and Populism," *Mother Jones* (January/February 1994), online at www.motherjones.com.

64. Cambridge Reports National Omnibus Survey (September 1992).

65. Many of the interim proposals are discussed in Stephen H. Schneider, "The Greenhouse Effect: Science and Policy," *Science* 243 (1989): 771–81.

66. "David Gardner, Testimony," U.S. House of Representatives, Committee on Science, Subcommittee on Energy and Environment (November 16, 1996).

67. Frank H. Murkowski, "Testimony," Hearing on U.S. Global Climate Change Policy," U.S. Senate, Committee on Energy and Natural Resources (September 17, 1996).

68. J. T. Houghton, ed., *Climate Change, 1994: Radiative Forcing of Climate Change and an Evaluation of the IPCC IS92 Emission Scenarios* (New York: Cambridge University Press, 1995); James P. Bruce, Hoesung Lee, and Erik F. Haites, eds., *Climate Change, 1995: Economic and Social Dimensions of Climate Change* (New York: Cambridge University Press, 1996).

69. Bureau of Labor Statistics, current prices; online at zfacts.com.

70. Network television news programs featured global warming 62 times in 1997, up from only 2 in 1993, 3 in 1994, 4 in 1995, and 9 in 1996; in 1998 the number fell to 26 and then receded to 12 in 1999.

71. Jim Talent, "Testimony," House Committee on Small Business (July 29, 1998).

72. In 1999, the *New York Times* mentioned global warming in 164 articles, down from 280 in 1997 and 214 in 1998; *Washington Post* coverage dropped from 227 in 1997 and 216 in 1998 to 127 in 1999. In public opinion polls, 174 questions about global warming were included in 1997, 23 in 1998, and only 7 in 1999.

73. Senator John McCain, "Reductions in Greenhouse Gases," Hearing of the Senate Commerce, Science and Transportation Committee (September 21, 2000).

74. Rachel Carson, *Silent Spring* (New York: Houghton Mifflin, 1962). On the publishing history of *Silent Spring*, see Paul Brooks, *The House of Life: Rachel Carson at Work* (Boston: Houghton Mifflin, 1972); see also "Transcript of the President's News Conference," *New York Times* (August 30, 1962), 10; and Val Adams, "'CBS Reports' Plans a Show on Rachel Carson's New Book," *New York Times* (August 30, 1962), 42.

75. Carson, *Silent Spring*, 6.

76. Brooks Atkinson, "Rachel Carson's 'Silent Spring' Is Called 'The Rights of Man' of Our Time," *New York Times* (April 2, 1963), 44; Harry Hansen, "A Book Not Out Yet Reaping Praise and Condemnation," *Chicago Tribune* (September 23, 1962), F7; I. L. Baldwin, "Chemicals and Pests," *Science* 137 (September 28, 1962): 1042–43; ESA statement cited in Garrett Hardin, "Not Peace, But Ecology," in Brookhaven National Laboratory, Diversity and Stability in Ecological Systems (Brookhaven Symposium, December 1969); F. R. Fosberg, "Pesticides and Ecology," *Ecology* 44 (1963): 624; Norman H. Dill, Elizabeth M. Haines, Joan Hellerman, and Robert A. Jervis, "The Spray Around Us," *Bulletin of the Torrey Botanical Club* 90 (March 1963): 149–52, quotation is on 152; Denzel E. Ferguson, "Review of *Silent Spring*," *Copeia* (March 1963): 207–8.

77. U.S. Senate, Committee on Commerce, "Pesticide Research and Controls" (June 5–6, 1962), 88 S1561–4; Jean White, "Author of 'Silent Spring' Urges Pesticide Controls," *New York Times* (June 5, 1963), A2.

78. Jean M. White, "Is Too Much of a Safe Pesticide Dangerous?" *Washington Post* (April 5, 1964), B13; Victor Cohn, "Environment Agency Acts Against DDT," *Washington Post* (January 16, 1971); "DDT Ban Takes Effect," EPA Press Release (December 31, 1972), online at www.epa.gov/history. Walter Cronkite, "Pesticide DDT Banned in Effort to Save Environment," CBS Evening News (June 14, 1972), online at tvnews.vanderbilt.edu. See also Thomas R. Dunlap, *DDT: Scientists, Citizens, and Public Policy* (Princeton, N.J.: Princeton University Press, 1981).

79. John George quoted in Jeannette Smyth, "Recalling Rachel Carson," *Washington Post* (September 28, 1972), B3; Barbara Walters, "Pesticides Safety," ABC Evening News (January 3, 1977), online at tvnews.vanderbilt.edu; Bill Moyers, "Commentary," CBS Evening News (September 22, 1982), online at tvnews.vanderbilt.edu; Peter Jennings, "Special Assignment: *Silent Spring* 25 Years later," ABC Evening News, online at tvnews.vanderbilt.edu; Peter Singer, *Animal Liberation* (New York: Random House, 1975); Fred A. Wilcox, *Waiting for an Army to Die: The Tragedy of Agent Orange* (New York: Seven Locks Press, 1989); Edward O. Wilson, *The Diversity of Life* (Cambridge, Mass.: Harvard University Press, 1992); Albert Gore Jr., *Earth in the Balance: Ecology and the Human Spirit* (Boston: Houghton Mifflin, 1992); Bill McKibben, *The End of Nature* (New York: Anchor, 1990); David S. Reay, "A *Silent Spring* for Climate Change?" *Nature* 440 (March 2, 2006): 27.

80. Ralph Nader, *Unsafe at Any Speed: The Designed-In Dangers of the American Automobile* (New York: Grossman, 1965); Eric Schlosser, *Fast Food Nation: The Dark Side of the All-American Meal* (Boston: Houghton Mifflin, 2001); Murray Bookchin, *Our Synthetic Environment* (New York: Alfred A. Knopf, 1962); Theron G. Randolph, *Human Ecology and Susceptibility to the Chemical Environment* (Springfield, Ill.: C. C. Thomas, 1962); Robert Rudd, *Pesticides and the Living Landscape* (Madison: University of Wisconsin Press, 1964); on these books, see Craig Waddell, "The Reception of *Silent Spring*," in *And No Birds Sing: Rhetorical Analyses of Rachel Carson's* Silent Spring, edited by Craig Waddell (Carbondale, Ill.: Southern Illinois University Press, 2000), 1–16, quotation is on 11.

81. These factors in *Silent Spring*'s success are extensively developed in the essays in Waddell, *And No Birds Sing*, and in Priscilla Coit Murphy, *What a Book Can Do: The Publication and Reception of Silent Spring* (Springfield, Mass.: University of Massachusetts Press, 2005) and Linda Lear, *Rachel Carson: Witness for Nature* (New York: Owl Books, 1998).

82. Rob Nixon, "Not-So-Silent Spring" (April 3, 2006), online at www.slate.com; Ralph H. Lutts, "Chemical Fallout: *Silent Spring*, Radioactive Fallout, and the Environmental Movement," *Environmental Review* 9 (1985): 210–25 and revised in Waddell, *And No Birds Sing*, 17–41; White, "Author of 'Silent Spring' Urges Pesticide Controls."

83. Bess Furman, "Role of Chemicals in Food Is Studied," *New York Times* (May 16, 1949), 24; Harry Fox, "Insecticide Report," *New York Times* (September 14, 1949), 59; "DDT Sprays Called a Cancer Menace," *New York Times* (February 14, 1958), 25; Dunlap, *DDT*.

84. Al Gore, *An Inconvenient Truth: The Planetary Emergency of Global Warming and What We Can Do About It* (New York: Rodale Books, 2006); Elizabeth Kolbert, *Field Notes from a Catastrophe: Man, Nature, and Climate Change* (New York: Bloomsbury, 2006); Tim Flannery, *The Weather Makers: How Man Is Changing the Climate and What It Means for Life on Earth* (New York: Atlantic Monthly Press, 2006).

85. George Thayer, "The Full Range of Man's Stupidity," *Washington Post* (February 18, 1970), B6. President Richard Nixon, "State of the Union Address," January 22, 1970, online at www.whitehouse.gov; "Issue of the Year: The Environment," *Time* (January 4, 1971), online at www.time.com;

86. Robert Gottlieb, *Forcing the Spring: The Transformation of the American Environmental Movement*, rev. ed. (Washington, D.C.: Island Press, 2005), 151; Stacy J. Silveira, "The American Environmental Movement: Surviving Through Diversity," *Boston College Environmental Affairs Law Review* 28 (2001): 497–532; Bill Shaw, "Economics and the Environment: A 'Land Ethic' Critique of Economic Policy," *Journal of Business Ethics* 33 (2001): 51–57.

87. Jack Lewis, "The Birth of EPA," *EPA Journal* (November 1985), online at www.epa.gov/history; annual budget and workforce figures are also online at www.epa.gov.

88. Opinion Research Corporation, "Nixon Poll" (May 7–25, 1971), online at roperweb.ropercenter.uconn.edu; Cambridge Reports National Omnibus Survey (July 1979), online at roperweb.ropercenter.uconn.edu; ABC News Survey (July 1979), online at roperweb.ropercenter.uconn.edu; Jacqueline Vaughn and Gary C. Bryner, *Environmental Politics: Domestic and Global Dimensions* (New York: St. Martin's Press, 1998), 10; Mary Graham, *The Morning after Earth Day: Practical Environmental Politics* (Washington, D.C.: Brookings Institution, 1999), 37; Kirkpatrick Sale, *The Green Revolution: The American Environmental Movement, 1962–1992* (New York: Hill and Wang, 1993), 32; Council for Environmental Quality, "Public Opinion on Environmental Issues" (January 1980).

89. Nixon, "State of the Union Address, 1970"; Opinion Research Corporation Poll (July 16–August 2, 1971), online at roperweb.ropercenter.uconn.edu.

90. Martin L. Perl, "The Scientific Advisory System: Some Observations," *Science* 173 (September 24, 1971): 1211–15; Dorothy Nelkin, "Scientists and Professional Responsibility: The Experience of American Ecologists," *Social Studies of Science* 7 (1977): 75–95; Dorothy Nelkin, "Ecologists and the Public Interest," *Hastings Center Report* 6 (1976): 38–44; Nelkin observes that the rapid growth of applied ecology research was also a source of some misgiving within the discipline.

91. Patricia Sullivan, "Progressive Wisconsin Senator Was Founder of Earth Day," *Washington Post* (July 4, 2005), A1; Cary Coglianese, "Social Movements, Law, and Society: The Institutionalization of the Environmental Movement," *University of Pennsylvania Law Review* 150 (2001): 85–118; William K. Stevens, "First Signs of a Backlash Emerge in Ecology Drive," *New York Times* (May 4, 1970), 1.

92. "Paul Revere of Ecology," *Time* (February 2, 1970), online at www.time.com; Alan Anderson Jr., "Scientist at Large," *New York Times* (November 7, 1976), SM15; Gottlieb, *Forcing the Spring*, 231; ABC News Survey (July 1979), online at roperweb.ropercenter.uconn.edu.

93. Michael Shellenberger and Ted Nordhaus, "The Death of Environmentalism: Global Warming Politics in a Post-Environmental World," *Grist* (January 13, 2005), online at www.grist.org.

94. "Environmentalist Nerve," *Wall Street Journal* (February 20, 1980); Lisa Newton, quoted in Andi Rierden, "'We've Got to Stop the Pollution Now,'" *New York Times* (December 11, 1988), CN3.

CHAPTER 8

1. Interview conducted on August 23, 2006; Los Angeles Times/Bloomberg Poll (August 3, 2006), online at web.lexis-nexis.com.

2. Maxwell E. McCombs and Donald L. Shaw, "The Agenda-Setting Function of the Mass Media," *Public Opinion Quarterly* 36 (1972): 176–87; W. Russell Neuman, "The Threshold of Public Attention," *Public Opinion Quarterly* 54 (1990): 159–76.

3. Richard Cohen, "A Campaign Gore Can't Lose," *Washington Post* (April 18, 2006), A19; Felicia R. Lee, "Scared of Global Warming and Eager to Spread the Fright," *New York Times* (April 22, 2006), B12; Roger Ebert, quoted in Rob Zaleski, "Gore Finds Believers Here on Global Warming," *Capital Times* (July 3, 2006), C1.

4. "Pursuing Ignorance," *St. Louis Post-Dispatch* (February 28, 2006), B6; "Be Worried, Be Very Worried," *Time* (March 26, 2006); Cohen, "A Campaign Gore Can't Lose."

5. Newsbank Database of United States Newspapers, in which 1,215 and 1,655 references to "global warming" appeared in January 2005 and January 2006, respectively; 2,189 and 4,434 in July, respectively; and 1,917 and 3,949 in December, respectively.

6. J. Turner, T. A. Lachlan-Cope, S. Colwell, G. J. Marshall, and W. M. Connolley, "Significant Warming of the Antarctic Winter Troposphere," *Science* 311 (March 31, 2006): 1914; Mark Hicks, "Report Cites Jump in Emissions in State and Nation," *Detroit News* (June 21, 2006), 2B; Pew Center on Global Climate Change, "2006 Year in Review," online at www.pewclimate.org; Marla Cone, "Forecast for 2080 Is a Study in Extremes: A New Method Predicts More Storms, Drought and Heat Waves This Century, But Offers Hope," *Los Angeles Times* (October 20, 2006), A14; Stephen Leahy, "Ailing Reefs Face New Climate-Change Threat," *Global Information Network* (July 6, 2006), 1.

7. Intergovernmental Panel on Climate Change, *Climate Change 2007: The Physical Science Basis, Summary for Policymakers* (Geneva, Switzerland: IPCC Secretariat, 2007), online at www.ipcc.ch.

8. Juliet Eilperin, "Humans Faulted for Global Warming: International Panel of Scientists Sounds Dire Alarm," *Washington Post* (February 3, 2007), A1; Elisabeth Rosenthal and Andrew C.

Revkin, "Science Panel Calls Global Warming 'Unequivocal,'" *New York Times* (February 3, 2007), online at www.nytimes.com; Bryan Walsh, "Climate Change: Case Closed," *Time* (February 2, 2007), online at www.time.com; "Report Says Global Warming Very Likely Man-Made, to Continue "For Centuries," *USA Today* (February 2, 2007), online at www.usatoday.com; "Scientists: Humans 'Very Likely' Cause Global Warming," CNN.com (February 3, 2007).

9. CBS News, "Global Warming Serious for 70 Percent of Americans," *Angus Reid Global Monitor* (January 25, 2007), online at www.angus-reid.com; Seth Borenstein, "Global Warming to Continue for Centuries," *Miami Herald* (February 2, 2007), online at www.miami.com; "Final Topline," *January 2007 News Interest Index* (January 22, 2007), online at people-press.org; "Global Warming," ACNielsen News Release (January 29, 2007), online at www2.acnielsen.com; Dana Rohinsky, "Fox News Poll: Most Americans Believe in Global Warming" Fox News (February 2, 2007), online at www.foxnews.com.

10. "Climate of Opinion: The Latest U.N. Report Shows the "Warming" Debate Is Far from Settled," *Wall Street Journal* (February 5, 2007), online at www.opinionjournal.com; J. R. Dunn, "Scientific Consensus—Except for Those Other Scientists," *American Thinker* (February 15, 2007), online at www.americanthinker.com; Noel Sheppard, "Congressional Global Warming Poll," *NewsBusters* (February 6, 2007), online at newsbusters.org.

11. Hans-Martin Fussel and Richard J. T. Klein, "Climate Change Vulnerability Assessments: An Evolution of Conceptual Thinking," *Climate Change* 75 (2006): 301–29.

12. Quoted in Adam Aston and Burt Helm, "The Race Against Climate Change," *Business Week* (December 12, 2005), online at www.businessweek.com.

13. "360 Climate Change: Adapt or Bust" (2006), online at www.lloyds.com/360; John Carey, "Business on a Warmer Planet," *Business Week* (July 17, 2006), 26; Marc Lifsher, "Big Oil Divided Over Initiative," *Houston Chronicle* (March 21, 2006), 6.

14. Gore, *An Inconvenient Truth*, 270; James Gustave Speth, *Red Sky at Morning: America and the Crisis of the Global Environment* (New Haven, Conn.: Yale University Press, 2005), 217; Andrew J. Hoffman, *Getting Ahead of the Curve: Corporate Strategies that Address Climate Change* (Washington, D.C.: Pew Center on Global Climate Change, 2006).

15. H. Josef Hebert, "CEOs Urge Bush on Climate Change," *Associated Press* (January 22, 2007); Fred Krupp, "Grab the Green Brass Ring," *Business Week* (February 5, 2007), 104; Clifford Krauss, "Exxon Accused of Trying to Mislead Public," *New York Times* (January 4, 2007), A1; Clifford Krauss and Jad Mouawad, "Exxon Chief Cautions Against Rapid Action to Cut Carbon Emissions," *New York Times* (February 14, 2007), C3.

16. Andrew Ross Sorkin, "A Buyout Deal That Has Many Shades of Green," *New York Times* (February 26, 2007), A19; Landon Thomas Jr., "For TXU, One of the Street's Fabled Barbarians Is Back in the Hunt," *New York Times* (February 26, 2007), C1.

17. Matthew L. Wald, "Study Questions Prospects for Much Lower Emissions," *New York Times* (February 15, 2007), C2; Martin Fackler, "With $12 Billion in Profit, Toyota Has G.M. in Sight," *New York Times* (May 11, 2006), C4.

18. Posted by "NB," January 14, 2007, at www.businessweek.com; Chris Taylor, "Go Green, Get Rich," *Business 2.0* (January/February 2007), 68–82; Claudia H. Deutsch, "Selling Fuel Efficiency the Green Way," *New York Times* (December 11, 2006), online at select.nytimes.com.

19. John Rowe Townsend, *Noah's Castle* (New York: Dell, 1978); Andre Norton, *No Night Without Stars* (New York: Fawcett, 1979).

20. T. Coraghessan Boyle, *A Friend of the Earth* (New York: Penguin, 2000); Alistair Beaton, *A Planet for the President* (New York: Weidenfeld & Nicolson, 2004); Janet McNaughton, *The Secret Under My Skin* (New York: Eos, 2005); Kim Stanley Robinson, *Forty Signs of Rain* (New York: Bantam, 2004); Kim Stanley Robinson, *Fifty Degrees Below* (New York: Bantam, 2005); Kim Stanley Robinson, *Sixty Days and Counting* (New York: Bantam, 2007).

21. Andrew C. Revkin, "The Sky Is Falling! Say Hollywood and, Yes, the Pentagon," *New York Times* (February 29, 2004), 4; Richard C. Hoagland and David Wilcock, "Interplanetary 'Day After Tomorrow'?" *Enterprise Mission* (May 14, 2004), online at www.enterprisemission.com; "The Day After Tomorrow: Could It Really Happen?" (May 28, 2004), online at www.pewclimate.org/dayaftertomorrow. Linda Chavez, "Social Propaganda Films Sent from Hollywood," *Human Events* 1 (2004): 26.

22. Lonna Lisa Williams, *Like a Tree Planted* (New York: BookSurge, 2003); Octavia E. Butler, *Parable of the Sower* (New York: Warner Books, 1993); Octavia E. Butler, *Parable of the Talents* (New York: Warner Books, 1998); Jerry Phillips, "The Intuition of the Future: Utopia and Catastrophe in Octavia Butler's *Parable of the Sower*," in *Novel: A Forum on Fiction* (Fall 2002), online at www.findarticles.com; Lawrence Buell, *The Future of Environmental Criticism: Environmental Crisis and Literary Imagination* (Oxford: Blackwell, 2005), 91–92.

23. Michael Crichton, *State of Fear* (New York: HarperCollins, 2004); Michael Crichton, "Aliens Cause Global Warming," Lecture at California Institute of Technology (January 17, 2003), online at www.crichton-official.com. "Global Warming: Crichton's Thriller State of Fear: Separating Fact from Fiction," Union of Concerned Scientists (August 11, 2005), online at www.ucsusa.org; Gavin Schmidt, "Distort Reform," *Grist* (February 1, 2005), online at www.grist.org; Hans von Storch, "Climate Change Assessments," Committee on House Energy and Commerce Subcommittee on Oversight and Investigations (July 19, 2006).

24. The view that nature is delicately balanced and thus precarious is sometimes described as a "nature ephemeral" perspective and depicted as a ball perched atop an inverted semicircle; although the research is sparse, it suggests that this view is commonly held; see Linda Steg and Inge Sievers, "Cultural Theory and Individual Perceptions of Environmental Risks," *Environment and Behavior* 32 (2000): 250–69.

25. Gallup/USA Today Poll (October 1, 1998), online at web.lexis-nexis.com.

26. For a thoughtful examination of these books see especially Bruce David Forbes and Jeanne Halgren Kilde, eds., *Rapture, Revelation, and the End Times: Exploring the Left Behind Series* (New York: Palgrave Macmillan, 2004), and Amy Johnson Frykholm, *Rapture Culture: Left Behind in Evangelical America* (New York: Oxford University Press, 2004).

27. Newsweek polls (February 27, 1998, and October 22, 1999), available from roperweb. ropercenter.uconn.edu. A Newsweek poll in May 13–14, 2004, found that 12 percent of the public claimed to have read at least one of the Left Behind books.

28. Glenn Scherer, "The Godly Must Be Crazy," *Grist* (October 27, 2004), online at www.grist.com; Janet Lehr, quoted in "The Christians Write," *Grist* (January 21, 2005), online at www.grist.com.

29. Janet Lehr and Peter Bakken, quoted in Ibid.

30. *The Great Warming* (2006), www.greatwarming.com; Kate Sheppard, "The Moral of the Story," *Grist* (October 30, 2006), online at www.grist.com.

31. CBS News poll (March 2006), online at www.nytimes.com; an ABS News poll (January 2007), however, showed only 26 percent giving a similar response; Pew Research Center News Interest Poll (January 2007), online at roperweb.ropercenter.uconn.edu.

32. CBS News poll (March 2006), between 34 and 54 percent said they worried a great deal about each of these problems.

33. Interview conducted on August 22, 2006.

34. Chad Harbach, "On Global Warming," *Science Creative Quarterly* 2 (January–March 2007), online at www.scq.ubc.ca. Julia Whitty, "The Thirteenth Tipping Point," *Mother Jones* (November/December 2006), online at motherjones.com.

35. Lisa Allen posted May 2006 on www.city-data.com/forum.

36. Bamboosmom posted May 2006 on www.city-data.com/forum.

37. Interview conducted on April 21, 2006.

38. Interview conducted August 23, 2006.

39. Interview conducted August 18, 2006.

40. Anthony Allen Leiserowitz, *Global Warming in the American Mind: The Roles of Affect, Imagery, and Worldviews in Risk Perception, Policy Preferences and Behavior* (Eugene: University of Oregon, Environmental Studies Program, PhD diss., 2003).

41. Interview conducted August 24, 2006, and July 11, 2006.

42. Fred Smith, quoted on "Tucker" (MSNBC, February 27, 2008); William Rusher, "The Global Warming Hysterics Strike Again," *The World* (February 28, 2007), 3; Kevin O'Brien, "Half-Baked Climate Fears," *Plain Dealer* (February 28, 2007), B9.

43. Pew Research Center News Interest Poll (January 2007), online at roperweb.ropercenter.uconn.edu.

44. Environmental Issues Survey (March 2, 2006) and Global Warming and Alternative Energy Survey (February 26, 2006), online at web.lexis-nexis.com.

45. "Interview with Rev. Richard Cizik," online at www.thegreatwarming.com.

46. Interviews conducted July 27, 2006, and August 1, 2006.

47. President George W. Bush, "State of the Union Address" (January 31, 2006), online at www.whitehouse.gov.

48. Robert J. Samuelson, "The Worst of Both Worlds," *Newsweek* (November 13, 2006), 50.

49. Leiserowitz, *Global Warming in the American Mind*, 122.

50. "Forces Beyond Our Control," *The Jersey Journal* (January 5, 2007), A14.

51. Interview conducted July 12, 2006.

CHAPTER 9

1. Weber's treatise appeared as essays in 1904 and 1905 in the *Archiv für Sozialwissenschaft und Sozialpolitik*. Primary and secondary sources in English include Max Weber, *The Protestant Ethic and the Spirit of Capitalism* (Oxford: Blackwell, 2002), Max Weber, *Sociology of Religion* (Boston: Beacon, 1993), and William H. Swatos and Lutz Kaelber, eds., *The Protestant Ethic Turns 100: Essays on the Centenary of the Weber Thesis* (New York: Paradigm, 2005).

2. Pope Benedict XVI, "Human Fragility Points Up God's Grandeur: Comments on Psalm 143 at General Audience" (January 11, 2006), available at www.zenit.org.

3. Pope Benedict XVI, "God Comes Among Man in Weakness" (December 21, 2006), available at www.catholic.org.

4. Rudiger Safranski, quoted in "The Pope Was the Message," *Der Spiegel* (April 11, 2005), online at www.spiegel.de.

5. Mikhail Gorbachev, quoted in "Gorbachev Sends New Year's Message," *Seattle Times* (December 31, 1986), A5.

6. Quoted in Seth Borenstein, "Astronauts Recall View Before Earth Day," *Houston Chronicle* (April 20, 2007), online at www.chron.com.

7. From text reprinted in "Speeches by Two in Oslo," *New York Times* (December 11, 1985), A10.

8. Thomas J. Peters and Robert H. Waterman Jr., *In Search of Excellence: Lessons from America's Best-Run Companies* (New York: Warner, 1982), especially 119–55.

9. John A. Byrne, "The Real Confessions of Tom Peters," *Business Week* (December 3, 2001), online at www.businessweek.com.

10. Examples can be found in Abby Brach, "Author Defines Traits that Build Leaders," *Columbus Ledger-Enquirer* (March 11, 1999), B7; Helen Brand and Adam Taylor, "What Is Corporate Finance?" Lehman Brothers, unpublished slide show; and "Q3 2006 Aetna Inc. Earnings Conference Call," *Congressional Quarterly Transcriptions* (October 26, 2006).

11. A useful review of this literature can be found in Sanjay Goel and Ranjan Karri, "Entrepreneurs, Effectual Logic, and Over-Trust," *Entrepreneurship Theory and Practice* 30 (2006): 477–93.

12. Anthony Patt and Richard Zeckhauser, "Action Bias and Environmental Decisions," *Journal of Risk and Uncertainty* 21 (2000): 45–72.

13. Peters and Waterman, *In Search of Excellence*, 134.

14. Ernest Becker, *The Denial of Death* (New York: Free Press, 1973), 21, 23.

15. See especially Tom Pyszczynski, Jeff Greenberg, and Sheldon Solomon, "A Dual-Process Model of Defense Against Conscious and Unconscious Death-Related Thoughts: An Extension of Terror Management Theory," *Psychological Review* 106 (1999): 835–45. The references in this article include many of the authors' earlier studies.

16. Mark J. Landau, Michael Johns, Jeff Greenberg, Tom Pyszczynski, Andy Martens, Jamie L. Goldenberg, and Sheldon Solomon, "A Function of Form: Terror Management and Structuring the Social World," *Journal of Personality and Social Psychology* 87 (2004): 190–210.

17. Pierre Lienard and Pascal Boyer, "Whence Collective Rituals? A Cultural Selection Model of Ritualized Behavior," *American Anthropologist* 108 (2006): 814–27.

18. Young-Ok Yum and William Schenck-Hamlin, "Reactions to 9/11 as a Function of Terror Management and Perspective Taking," *Journal of Social Psychology* 145 (2005): 265–86.

19. Tom Pyszczynski, Sheldon Solomon, and Jeff Greenberg, *In the Wake of 9/11: The Psychology of Terror* (Washington, D.C.: American Psychological Association, 2003), 93–113.

20. H. L. Mencken, *In Defense of Women* (New York: Alfred A. Knopf, 1922).

21. Other examples of the institutionalization of peril include organizations monitoring earthquake threats, as discussed in Robert A. Stallings, *Promoting Risk: Constructing the Earthquake Threat* (Hawthorne, N.Y.: Aldine de Gruyter, 1995), and governmental emergency management agencies, as discussed in Charles Perrow, *The Next Catastrophe: Reducing Our Vulnerabilities to Natural, Industrial, and Terrorist Disasters* (Princeton, N.J.: Princeton University Press, 2007).

22. Patt and Zeckhauser, "Action Bias and Environmental Decisions," 63, write, "Since our principals can not observe what we have done, we must do something to show our impact. From the waiter who stops by the table to ask whether everything is okay, to the politician who files a bill he can report to this constituency even though it is sure to lose, agents are continually trying to make their actions evident."

23. A useful discussion of bright lines is included in the Commission on Risk Assessment and Risk Management, *Risk Assessment and Risk Management in Regulatory Decision-Making* (February 5, 1997), 74-76.

24. Gallup Poll (March 4, 1947), Gallup Poll (June 16, 1949), Harris Poll (July 18, 1976), available at roperweb.ropercenter.uconn.edu.

25. Pandemic Influenza Survey (October 5, 2006) and Avian Flu Survey (January 25, 2006), both conducted by the Harvard School of Public Health Project on the Public and Biological Security, online at roperweb.ropercenter.uconn.edu.

26. "Hockey Stick Hokum," *Wall Street Journal* (July 14, 2006), A12.

27. Edward J. Wegman, "Climate Change Assessments," Testimony before the House Energy and Commerce Committee, Oversight and Investigations Subcommittee (July 19, 2006) and "Ad Hoc Committee Report on the 'Hockey Stick' Global Climate Reconstruction," available at web.lexis-nexis.com.

28. Historical Tables, Budget of the United States Government, Fiscal Year 2005 (Washington, D.C.: Government Printing Office, 2005).

29. Washington Newsletter, Friends Committee on National Legislation (March 2006).

30. Sarah A. Lister, "Pandemic Influenza: Appropriations for Public Health Preparedness and Response," *CRS Report for Congress* (January 23, 2007).

31. Naomi Mandel and Steven J. Heine, "Terror Management and Marketing: He Who Dies With the Most Toys Wins," unpublished paper, Wharton School of Management, University of Pennsylvania, 2006.

32. Goel and Karri, "Entrepreneurs, Effectual Logic, and Over-Trust." Terrence Odean, "Volume, Volatility, Price, and Profit When All Traders are Above Average," *Journal of Finance* 53 (1998): 1887-1934.

33. The official death toll on September 11, 2001, was 2,973, not counting the hijackers; that number was exceeded among U.S. soldiers deployed in Afghanistan and Iraq on September 22, 2006. In 2006 alone, 34,000 Iraqis—more than ten times the number of 9/11 casualties—were killed. Four million fled to other countries.

34. "The Cost of SARS" (April 18, 2003), online at www.emsnow.com; an independent analysis put the figure at $60 billion ("Assessing the Impact and Cost of SARS in Developing Asia," *Asian Development Outlook: 2003 Update*, Hong Kong: Asian Development Bank, 2003).

35. Bruce Western, *Punishment and Inequality in America* (New York: Russell Sage Foundation, 2006).

SELECTED BIBLIOGRAPHY

Adams, Matt, and Penny Jane Burke. "Recollections of September 11 in Three English Villages: Iden-tifications and Self-Narrations." *Journal of Ethnic and Migration Studies* 32 (2006): 983–1003.

Ahmed, Nafeez Mosaddeq. *The War on Freedom: How and Why America Was Attacked, September 11th, 2001.* Backword by John Leonard. New York: Media Messenger Books, 2002.

Alexander, Jeffrey C. "Toward a Theory of Cultural Trauma." In *Cultural Trauma and Collective Iden-tity,* edited by Jeffrey C. Alexander, Ron Eyerman, Bernhard Giesen, Neil J. Smelser, and Piotr Sztompka, pp. 1–33. Berkeley: University of California Press, 2004.

Altheide, David L. "Consuming Terrorism." *Symbolic Interaction* 27 (2004): 389–408.

Armoney, Jorge L., and Raymond J. Dolan. "Modulation of Spatial Attention by Fear-Conditioned Stimuli: An Event-Related fMRI Study." *Neuropsychologia* 40 (2002): 817–26.

Armstrong, Elizabeth M. *Conceiving Risk, Bearing Responsibility: Fetal Alcohol Syndrome and the Diag-nosis of Moral Disorder.* Baltimore: Johns Hopkins University Press, 2003.

Arndt, J., S. Solomon, T. Kasser, and K. M. Sheldon. "The Urge to Splurge: A Terror Management Account of Materialism and Consumer Behavior." *Journal of Consumer Psychology* 14, no. 3 (2004): 198–212.

Atran, S., and A. Norenzayan. "Religion's Evolutionary Landscape: Counterintuition, Commitment, Compassion, Communion." *Behavioral and Brain Sciences* 27, no. 6 (2004): 713ff

Badey, Thomas J. *Annual Editions: Homeland Security.* New York: McGraw-Hill, 2007.

Baer, Ulrich, ed. *110 Stories: New York Writes after September 11.* New York: New York University Press, 2002.

Barry, John M. *The Great Influenza: The Story of the Deadliest Pandemic in History.* New York: Viking, 2005.

Bean, J. M. W. "Plague, Population and Economic Decline in England in the Later Middle Ages." *Economic History Review* 15 (1963): 423–37.

Beaton, Alistair. *A Planet for the President.* New York: Weidenfeld & Nicolson, 2004.

Beck, Ulrich. *Risk Society: Towards a New Modernity.* Translated by Mark Ritter. London: Sage, 1992.

Becker, Ernest. *The Denial of Death.* New York: Free Press, 1973.

Benedictow, Ole J. *The Black Death, 1346–1353: The Complete History.* Woodbridge, U.K.: Boydell Press, 2004.

Bernstein, Richard B. *Out of the Blue: A Narrative of September 11, 2001.* New York: Times Books, 2003.

Blomain, Karen. "Sisters." In *September 11, 2001*, edited by William Heyen, pp. 51–53. Silver Spring, Md.: Etruscan Press, 2002.

Bookchin, Murray. *Our Synthetic Environment.* New York: Alfred A. Knopf, 1962.

Borch, Fred L. "Comparing Pearl Harbor and '9/11': Intelligence Failure? American Unpreparedness? Military Responsibility?" *Journal of Military History* 67 (2003): 845–60.

Borenstein, Emily. "From 'Twelve Meditations.'" In *September 11, 2001*, edited by William Heyen, pp. 58–60. Silver Spring, Md.: Etruscan Press, 2002.

Borradori, Giovanna. *Philosophy in a Time of Terror: Dialogues with Jürgen Habermas and Jacques Derrida.* Chicago: University of Chicago Press, 2003.

Boyer, Paul. *When Time Shall Be No More: Prophecy Belief in Modern America.* Cambridge, Mass.: Harvard University Press, 1994.

Boyer, Paul S. *By the Bomb's Early Light: American Thought and Culture at the Dawn of the Atomic Age.* 1st ed. New York: Pantheon, 1985.

Boyle, T. Coraghessan. *A Friend of the Earth.* New York: Penguin, 2000.

Bradley, David. *No Place to Hide: What the Atomic Bomb Can Do to Ships, or Water, or Land, and Thereby to Human Beings.* Boston: Little, Brown, 1948.

Broderick, Mick. "Is This the Sum of Our Fears? Nuclear Imagery in Post–Cold War Cinema." In *Atomic Culture: How We Learned to Stop Worrying and Love the Bomb*, edited by Scott C. Zeman and Michael A. Amundson, pp. 125–48. Boulder: University Press of Colorado, 2004.

Brophy-Baermann, Bryan, and John A. C. Conybeare. "Retaliating against Terrorism: Rational Expectations and the Optimality of Rules Versus Discretion." *American Journal of Political Science* 38 (1994): 196–210.

Brown, JoAnne. "'A Is for Atom, B Is for Bomb': Civil Defense in American Public Education, 1948–1963." *Journal of American History* 75 (1988): 68–90.

Brownlee, Donald, and Peter D. Ward. *The Life and Death of Planet Earth: How the New Science of Astrobiology Charts the Ultimate Fate of Our World.* New York: Henry Holt, 2004.

Buell, Lawrence. *The Future of Environmental Criticism: Environmental Crisis and Literary Imagination.* Oxford: Blackwell, 2005.

Burris, C. T., and J. K. Rempel. "'It's the End of the World as We Know It': Threat and the Spatial-Symbolic Self." *Journal of Personality and Social Psychology* 86, no. 1 (2004): 19–42.

Butler, Octavia E. *Parable of the Sower.* New York: Warner Books, 1993.

———. *Parable of the Talents.* New York: Warner Books, 1998.

Caldwell, John C., and Pat Caldwell. "Toward an Epidemiological Model of AIDS in Sub-Saharan Africa." *Social Science History* 20 (1996): 559–91.

Calomiris, Charles W., and Gary Gorton. "The Origins of Banking Panics: Models, Facts, and Bank Regulation." In *Financial Markets and Financial Crises*, edited by R. Glenn Hubbard, pp. 109–74. Chicago: University of Chicago Press, 1991.

Calomiris, Charles W., and Joseph R. Mason. "Contagion and Bank Failures During the Great Depression: The June 1932 Chicago Banking Panic." *National Bureau of Economic Research Working Papers* (1994): No. 4934.

Cameron, Gavin, Jason Pate, and Kathleen Vogel. "Planting Fear." *Bulletin of the Atomic Scientists* 57 (2001): 38–44.

Campbell, Archie. *Spring of Fear*. Ontario: The SARS Commission, 2006.

Cantril, Hadley. *The Invasion from Mars: A Study in the Psychology of Panic*. Princeton, N.J.: Princeton University Press, 1947. Reprint, New York: Transaction, 2005.

Carey, Peter. "Union Square." In *110 Stories: New York Writes after September 11*, edited by Ulrich Baer, pp. 54–56. New York: New York University Press, 2002.

Carlsson, Katrina, Karl Magnus Petersson, Daniel Lundqvist, Andreas Karlsson, Martin Ingvar, and Arne Ohman. "Fear and the Amygdala: Manipulation of Awareness Generates Differential Cerebral Responses to Phobic and Fear-Relevant (but Nonfeared) Stimuli." *Emotion* 4 (2004): 340–53.

Carson, Rachel. *Silent Spring*. New York: Houghton Mifflin, 1962.

Cerulo, Karen A. *Never Saw It Coming: Cultural Challenges to Envisioning the Worst*. Chicago: University of Chicago Press, 2006.

Cheng, Cecilia. "To Be Paranoid Is the Standard? Panic Responses to SARS Outbreak in the Hong Kong Special Administrative Region." *Asian Perspective* 28 (2004): 67–98.

Christianson, Gale E. *Greenhouse: The 200-Year Story of Global Warming*. New York: Walker, 1999.

Clark, Mary Marshall. "The September 11, 2001, Oral History Narrative and Memory Project: A First Report." *Journal of American History* 89 (2002): 569–79.

Clarke, Lee. *Mission Improbable: Using Fantasy Documents to Tame Disaster*. Chicago: University of Chicago Press, 1999.

———. *Worst Cases: Terror and Catastrophe in the Popular Imagination*. Chicago: University of Chicago Press, 2006.

Clarke, Lee, and Caron Chess. "Elites and Panic: More to Fear Than Fear Itself." *Social Forces* 87 (2008): 993–1014.

Clarke, Richard A. *Against All Enemies: Inside America's War on Terror*. New York: Free Press, 2004.

Clinton, William J., and Albert Gore Jr. *The Climate Change Action Plan*. Washington, D.C.: Office of the President, 1993.

Coale, Ansley J. "The Problem of Reducing Vulnerability to Atomic Bombs." *American Economic Review* 37 (1947): 87–97.

Coglianese, Cary. "Social Movements, Law, and Society: The Institutionalization of the Environmental Movement." *University of Pennsylvania Law Review* 150 (2001): 85–118.

Cohen, Jeremy. "Homeland Security." *Journalism and Mass Communication Educator* 59 (2004): 119–20.

Cohen, Stanley. *States of Denial: Knowing About Atrocities and Suffering*. Cambridge, U.K.: Polity Press, and Malden, Mass.: Blackwell, 2001.

Coles, Robert. *Anna Freud: The Dream of Psychoanalysis*. Reading, Mass.: Addison-Wesley, 1992.

Compton, Arthur C. "The Atomic Crusade and Its Social Implications." *Annals of the American Academy of Political and Social Science* 249 (1947): 9–19.

Corbetta, Maurizio, and Gordon L. Shulman. "Control of Goal-Directed and Stimulus-Driven Attention in the Brain." *Nature Reviews: Neuroscience* 3 (2002): 201–15.

Couchman, Judith. *Encouragement for Your Heart: Reflections from Psalm 103*. Grand Rapids, Mich.: Zondervan, 2000.

Cozzolino, P. J., A. D. Staples, L. S. Meyers, and J. Samboceti. "Greed, Death, and Values: From Terror Management to Transcendence Management Theory." *Personality and Social Psychology Bulletin* 30, no. 3 (2004): 278–92.

Craig, Campbell. "The New Meaning of Modern War in the Thought of Reinhold Niebuhr." *Journal of the History of Ideas* 53 (1992): 687–701.

Crawford, Neta C. "The Passion of World Politics: Propositions on Emotion and Emotional Relationships." *International Security* 24 (2000): 116–56.

Crichton, Michael. *State of Fear*. New York: HarperCollins, 2004.

Crosby, Alfred W. *America's Forgotten Pandemic: The Influenza of 1918*. 2nd ed. Cambridge and New York: Cambridge University Press, 2003.

Czikszentmihalyi, Mihaly. *Creativity: Flow and the Psychology of Discovery and Invention*. New York: HarperCollins, 1996.

Dahl, Robert A. "Atomic Energy and the Democratic Process." *Annals of the American Academy of Political and Social Science* 290 (1953): 1–6.

D'Andrade, Roy. *The Development of Cognitive Anthropology*. New York: Cambridge University Press, 1995.

Darvin, Jacqueline. "Teaching in the Days after September 11, 2001." *The English Journal* 9 (2002): 18–19.

Dechesne, M., T. Pyszczynski, J. Arndt, S. Ransom, K. M. Sheldon, A. van Knippenberg, and J. Janssen. "Literal and Symbolic Immortality: The Effect of Evidence of Literal Immortality of Self-Esteem Striving in Response to Mortality Salience." *Journal of Personality and Social Psychology* 84, no. 4 (2003): 722–37.

Deming, Alison Hawthorne. "Waking to the World's Pain." In *September 11, 2001*, edited by William Heyen, pp. 90–91. Silver Spring, Md.: Etruscan Press, 2002.

Deudney, Daniel, and John Ikenberry. "Who Won the Cold War?" *Foreign Policy* 87 (1992): 123–38.

Douvan, Elizabeth, and Stephen B. Withey. "Some Attitudinal Consequences of Atomic Energy." *Annals of the American Academy of Political and Social Science* 290 (1953): 108–17.

Duffy, John. *Epidemics in Colonial America*. Baton Rouge: Louisiana State University Press, 1953.

Duncker, Karl. *On Problem Solving*. Washington, D.C.: American Psychological Association, 1945.

Edwards, Bob, and Sam Marullo. "Organizational Mortality in a Declining Social Movement: The Demise of Peace Movement Organizations in the End of the Cold War Era." *American Sociological Review* 60 (1995): 908–27.

Erikson, Kai T. *Wayward Puritans: A Study in the Sociology of Deviance*. Rev. ed, with a new foreword and afterword. Boston: Allyn and Bacon, 2005.

Erskine, Hazel Gaudet. "The Polls: Atomic Weapons and Nuclear Energy." *Public Opinion Quarterly* 27 (1963): 155–90.

Etheridge, Elizabeth W. *Sentinel for Health: A History of the Centers for Disease Control*. Berkeley: University of California Press, 1992.

Fairbrother, Gerry, and Sandro Galea. *Terrorism, Mental Health, and September 11: Lessons Learned About Providing Mental Health Services to a Traumatized Population*. New York: Century Foundation, 2005.

Farrell, James J. *Inventing the American Way of Death, 1830–1920*. Philadelphia: Temple University Press, 1980.

Fernandez, James W. "Mutual Vulnerability." *Anthropological Quarterly* 75 (2001): 152–54.

Ferraro, R., B. Shiv, and J. R. Bettman. "Let Us Eat and Drink, for Tomorrow We Shall Die: Effects of Mortality Salience and Self-Esteem on Self-Regulation in Consumer Choice." *Journal of Consumer Research* 32, no. 1 (2005): 65–75.

Fisher, David E. *Fire & Ice: The Greenhouse Effect, Ozone Depletion, and Nuclear Winter*. New York: Harper & Row, 1990.

Fiske, Susan T. "People's Reactions to Nuclear War: Implications for Psychologists." *American Psychologist* 42 (1987): 207–17.

Flannery, Tim. *The Weather Makers: How Man Is Changing the Climate and What It Means for Life on Earth*. New York: Atlantic Monthly Press, 2006.

Forbes, Bruce David, and Jeanne Halgren Kilde, eds. *Rapture, Revelation, and the End Times: Exploring the Left Behind Series*. New York: Palgrave Macmillan, 2004.

Foy, Eddie, and Alvin F. Harlow. *Clowning Through Life*. New York: E. P. Dutton, 1928.

Freud, Anna. *The Ego and the Mechanisms of Defense*. New York: International Universities Press, 1946.

Freud, Anna, and Dorothy T. Burlingham. *War and Children: A Message to American Parents*. New York: Medical War Books, 1943.

Freud, Sigmund. *Group Psychology and the Analysis of the Ego*. New York: W. W. Norton, 1959.

Friend, David. *Watching the World Change: The Stories Behind the Images of 9/11*. New York: Farrar, Straus and Giroux, 2006.

Frum, David. *The Right Man: The Surprise Presidency of George W. Bush*. New York: Random House, 2003.

Fruth, Bryan, Alicia Germer, Keiko Kikuchi, and Anamarie Mihalega. "The Atomic Age: Facts and Films from 1945–1965." *Journal of Popular Film and Television* 23 (1996): 154–60.

Frykholm, Amy Johnson. *Rapture Culture: Left Behind in Evangelical America*. New York: Oxford University Press, 2004.

Fussel, Hans-Martin, and Richard J. T. Klein. "Climate Change Vulnerability Assessments: An Evolution of Conceptual Thinking." *Climate Change* 75 (2006): 301–29.

Gaddis, John Lewis. *The Cold War: A New History*. New York: Penguin, 2005.

———. *We Now Know: Rethinking Cold War History*. New York: Oxford University Press, 1997.

Galea, Sandro. "Mental Health in New York City after the September 11 Terrorist Attacks: Results from Two Population Surveys." In *Mental Health, United States, 2002*, edited by Ronald W. Manderscheid and Marilyn J. Henderson, pp. 83–91. Washington, D.C.: U.S. Government Printing Office, 2003.

Galea, Sandro, Jennifer Ahern, Heidi Resnick, Dean Kilpatrick, Michael Bucuvalas, Joel Gold, and David Vlahov. "Psychological Sequelae of the September 11 Terrorist Attacks in New York City." *New England Journal of Medicine* 346 (2002): 982–87.

Geertz, Clifford. *The Interpretation of Cultures: Selected Essays*. New York: Basic Books, 1973.

George, Alice L. *Awaiting Armageddon: How Americans Faced the Cuban Missile Crisis*. Chapel Hill: University of North Carolina Press, 2003.

Ghosh, Amitav. "Neighbors." In *110 Stories: New York Writes after September 11*, edited by Ulrich Baer, pp. 102–05. New York: New York University Press, 2002.

Giancola, Dan. "The Ruin." In *September 11, 2001*, edited by William Heyen, pp. 132–33. Silver Spring, Md.: Etruscan Press, 2002.

Gibbons, James. "The Death of a Painter." In *110 Stories: New York Writes after September 11*, edited by Ulrich Baer, pp. 106–09. New York: New York University Press, 2002.

Gitlin, Todd. *The Whole World Is Watching: Mass Media in the Making and Unmaking of the New Left*. Berkeley: University of California Press, 1980.

Glancy, Diane. "Lamentations." In *September 11, 2001*, edited by William Heyen, pp. 145–48. Silver Spring, Md.: Etruscan Press, 2002.

Glasheen, George L., Michael Amrine, Richard C. Robin, and Richard C. Hitchcock. "The Adult Meets and Tries to Understand the Atom." *Journal of Educational Sociology* 22 (1949): 339–56.

Glenn, John K., III. *Framing Democracy: Civil Society and Civic Movements in Eastern Europe.* Stanford: Stanford University Press, 2001.

Goel, Sanjay, and Ranjan Karri. "Entrepreneurs, Effectual Logic, and Over-Trust." *Entrepreneurship Theory and Practice* 30 (2006): 477–93.

Goldenberg, J. L. "The Body Stripped Down: An Existential Account of the Threat Posed by the Physical Body." *Current Directions in Psychological Science* 14, no. 4 (2005): 224–28.

Goldenberg, J. L., T. Pyszczynski, J. Greenberg, and S. Solomon. "Fleeing the Body: A Terror Management Perspective on the Problem of Human Corporeality." *Personality and Social Psychology Review* 4, no. 3 (2000): 200–18.

Goldenberg, J. L., T. Pyszczynski, J. Greenberg, S. Solomon, B. Kluck, and R. Cornwell. "I Am Not an Animal: Mortality Salience, Disgust, and the Denial of Human Creatureliness." *Journal of Experimental Psychology-General* 130, no. 3 (2001): 427–35.

Gore, Albert, Jr. *Earth in the Balance: Ecology and the Human Spirit.* Boston: Houghton Mifflin, 1992.

Gore, Al. *An Inconvenient Truth: The Planetary Emergency of Global Warming and What We Can Do About It.* New York: Rodale Books, 2006.

Gottlieb, Robert. *Forcing the Spring: The Transformation of the American Environmental Movement.* Rev. ed. Washington, D.C.: Island Press, 2005.

Grabe, S., C. Routledge, A. Cook, C. Andersen, and J. Arndt. "In Defense of the Body: The Effect of Mortality Salience on Female Body Objectification." *Psychology of Women Quarterly* 29, no. 1 (2005): 33–37.

Graham, Mary. *The Morning after Earth Day: Practical Environmental Politics.* Washington, D.C.: Brookings Institution, 1999.

Greenberg, J., J. Arndt, L. Simon, T. Pyszczynski, and S. Solomon. "Proximal and Distal Defenses in Response to Reminders of One's Mortality: Evidence of a Temporal Sequence." *Personality and Social Psychology Bulletin* 26, no. 1 (2000): 91–99.

Greenberg, J., S. Solomon, and T. Pyszczynski. "Terror Management Theory of Self-Esteem and Cultural Worldviews: Empirical Assessments and Conceptual Refinements." *Advances in Experimental Social Psychology* 29 (1997): 61–139.

Gurr, Nadine, and Benjamin Cole. *The New Face of Terrorism: Threats from Weapons of Mass Destruction.* London and New York: I. B. Tauris, 2000.

Gusfield, Joseph. *Symbolic Crusade: Status Politics and the American Temperance Movement.* Urbana: University of Illinois Press, 1963.

Hack, Thojmas, Harvey Max Chochinov, Thomas Hassard, Linda J. Kristjanson, Susan McClement, and Mike Harlos. "Defining Dignity in Terminally Ill Cancer Patients: A Factor-Analytic Approach." *Psycho-Oncology* 13 (2004): 700–08.

Hagedorn, Jessica. "Notes from a New York Diary." In *110 Stories: New York Writes after September 11,* edited by Ulrich Baer, pp. 134–37. New York: New York University Press, 2002.

Hallam, Tony. *Catastrophes and Lesser Calamities: The Causes of Mass Extinctions.* New York: Oxford University Press, 2004.

Hansen, James. "Defusing the Global Warming Time Bomb." *Scientific American* 290 (2004): 68–77.

———. "A Slippery Slope: How Much Global Warming Constitutes 'Dangerous Anthropogenic Interference'?" *Climatic Change* 68 (2005): 269–79.

Hatcher, John. "England in the Aftermath of the Black Death." *Past and Present* 144 (1994): 3–35.

Hayden, Tom. *The Port Huron Statement: The Visionary Call of the 1960s Revolution.* New York: Thunder's Mouth Press, 2005.

Haydon, F. Stansbury. "A Proposed Gas Shell, 1862." *Journal of the American Military History Foundation* 2 (1938): 52–54.

Henriksen, Margot A. *Dr. Strangelove's America: Society and Culture in the Atomic Age.* Berkeley: University of California Press, 1997.

Herron, Kerry G., and Hank C. Jenkins-Smith. *Public Perspectives on Nuclear Security: U.S. National Security Surveys 1993–1997.* Albuquerque: University of New Mexico, Institute for Public Policy, 1998.

Heyen, William, ed. *September 11, 2001: American Writers Respond.* Silver Spring, Md.: Etruscan Press, 2002.

Hoffman, Andrew J. *Getting Ahead of the Curve: Corporate Strategies That Address Climate Change.* Washington, D.C.: Pew Center on Global Climate Change, 2006.

Holifield, E. Brooks. *A History of Pastoral Care in America: From Salvation to Self-Realization.* Eugene, Oregon: Wipf and Stock, 2005.

Homes, A. M. "We All Saw It, or the View from Home." In *110 Stories: New York Writes after September 11,* edited by Ulrich Baer, pp. 151–53. New York: New York University Press, 2002.

Howarth, Glennys. *Last Rites: The Work of the Modern Funeral Director.* Amityville, N.Y.: Baywood, 1996.

Huntington, Richard, and Peter Metcalf. *Celebrations of Death: The Anthropology of Mortuary Ritual.* New York: Cambridge University Press, 1979.

Huntington, Samuel P. *The Clash of Civilizations and the Remaking of World Order.* New York: Simon & Schuster, 1996.

Jocham, Hubert R., Theo Dassen, Guy Widdershove, and Ruud Halfens. "Quality of Life in Palliative Care Cancer Patients: A Literature Review." *Journal of Clinical Nursing* 15 (2006): 1188–95.

Jonas, E., J. Schimel, J. Greenberg, and T. Pyszczynski. "The Scrooge Effect: Evidence That Mortality Salience Increases Prosocial Attitudes and Behavior." *Personality and Social Psychology Bulletin* 28, no. 10 (2002): 1342–53.

Jones, Kaylie. *Speak Now.* New York: Akashic Books, 2005.

Jong, Erica. "New York at War." In *September 11, 2001: American Writers Respond,* edited by William Heyen, pp. 217–20. Silver Spring, Md.: Etruscan Press, 2002.

Kennedy, David M. "Fighting an Elusive Enemy." *New York Times,* September 16, 2001, 11.

Kennedy, Robert F. *Thirteen Days: A Memoir of the Cuban Missile Crisis.* New York: McCall, 1968.

Kessler, R. C., A. Sonnega, E. Bromet, M. Hughes, and C. B. Nelson. "Posttraumatic Stress Disorder in the National Comorbidity Survey." *Archives of General Psychiatry* 52 (1996): 1048–60.

Kishi, Yoshio D. "What It Means to Me to Be Growing up with Nuclear Energy." *Journal of Educational Sociology* 22 (1949): 338–39.

Kleidman, Robert. *Organizing for Peace: Neutrality, the Test Ban, and the Freeze.* Syracuse, N.Y.: Syracuse University Press, 1993.

Kolbert, Elizabeth. *Field Notes from a Catastrophe: Man, Nature, and Climate Change.* New York: Bloomsbury, 2006.

———. "Human Nature." "Comment" in *The New Yorker*'s "Talk of the Town" on the centenary of Rachel Carson's birth, p. 23. *The New Yorker*, May 28, 2007.

Koltko-Rivera, M. E. "The Psychology of Worldviews." *Review of General Psychology* 8, no. 1 (2004): 3–58.

Koster, Ernst H., Geert Crombez, Stefaan Van Damme, Bruno Verschuere, and Jan De Houwer. "Does Imminent Threat Capture and Hold Attention?" *Emotion* 4 (2004): 312–17.

Kübler-Ross, Elisabeth. *On Death and Dying.* New York: Macmillan, 1969.

Lafeber, Walter. *America, Russia, and the Cold War, 1945–2002.* New York: McGraw-Hill, 2002.

Lakoff, George. *Whose Freedom? The Battle over America's Most Important Idea.* New York: Farrar, Straus and Giroux, 2006.

Lakoff, George, and Mark Johnson. *Metaphors We Live By.* Chicago: University of Chicago Press, 1980.

Landau, M. J., J. Greenberg, and S. Solomon. "The Motivational Underpinnings of Religion." *Behavioral and Brain Sciences* 27, no. 6 (2004): 743ff.

Landau, M. J., M. Johns, J. Greenberg, T. Pyszczynski, A. Martens, J. L. Goldenberg, and S. Solomon. "A Function of Form: Terror Management and Structuring the Social World." *Journal of Personality and Social Psychology* 87, no. 2 (2004): 190–210.

Landau, M. J., S. Solomon, J. Greenberg, F. Cohen, and T. Pyszczynski. "Deliver Us from Evil: The Effects of Mortality Salience and Reminders of 9/11 on Support for President George W. Bush." *Personality and Social Psychology Bulletin* 30, no. 9 (2004): 1136–50.

Lear, Linda. *Rachel Carson: Witness for Nature.* New York: Owl Books, 1998.

Leslie, John. *The End of the World: The Science and Ethics of Human Extinction.* New York: Routledge, 1996.

Lewis, Anthony. "A Different World." *New York Times*, September 12, 2001, A27.

Lieberman, J. D., J. Arndt, J. Personius, and A. Cook. "Vicarious Annihilation: The Effect of Mortality Salience on Perceptions of Hate Crimes." *Law and Human Behavior* 25, no. 6 (2001): 547–66.

Lienard, Pierre, and Pascal Boyer. "Whence Collective Rituals? A Cultural Selection Model of Ritualized Behavior." *American Anthropologist* 108 (2006): 814–27.

Lifton, Robert Jay. *Death in Life: Survivors of Hiroshima.* Rev. ed. Chapel Hill: University of North Carolina Press, 1991.

Lofland, John. *Polite Protestors: The American Peace Movement of the 1980s.* Syracuse: Syracuse University Press, 1993.

Lopate, Phillip. "Altering the World We Thought Would Outlast Us." In *110 Stories: New York Writes after September 11*, edited by Ulrich Baer, pp. 189–91. New York: New York University Press, 2002.

Maddicott, J. R. "Plague in Seventh-Century England." *Past and Present* 156 (1997): 7–54.

Marshall, Eliot. "Is the Friendly Atom Poised for a Comeback?" *Science* 309 (2005): 1168–69.

Marshall, Louise. "Manipulating the Sacred: Image and Plague in Renaissance Italy." *Renaissance Quarterly* 47 (1994): 485–32.

May, Ernest R., and Philip Zelikow, eds. *The Kennedy Tapes.* Cambridge, Mass.: Harvard University Press, 1997.

May, Elaine Tyler. *Homeward Bound: American Families in the Cold War Era.* New York: Basic Books, 1988.

McCombs, Maxwell E., and Donald L. Shaw. "The Agenda-Setting Function of the Mass Media." *Public Opinion Quarterly* 36 (1972): 176–87.

McKibben, Bill. *The End of Nature.* New York: Anchor, 1990.

McNaughton, Janet. *The Secret under My Skin.* New York: Eos, 2005.

McNeill, W. H. *Plagues and Peoples.* Oxford: Oxford University Press, 1977.

Medalia, Nahum Z., and Otto N. Larsen. "Diffusion and Belief in a Collective Delusion: The Seattle Windshield Pitting Epidemic." *American Sociological Review* 23 (1958): 180–86.

Meier, R. L., and E. Rabinowitch. "Scientists Before and After the Bomb." *Annals of the American Academy of Political and Social Science* 290 (1953): 118–26.

Mencken, H. L. *In Defense of Women.* New York: Alfred A. Knopf, 1922.

Miles, Wyndham D. "The Idea of Chemical Warfare in Modern Times." *Journal of the History of Ideas* 31 (1970): 297–304.

Miller, E. D. "Imagining Partner Loss and Mortality Salience: Consequences for Romantic-Relationship Satisfaction." *Social Behavior and Personality* 31, no. 2 (2003): 167–80.

Miller, E. K. "An Integrative Theory of Prefrontal Cortex Function." *Annual Review of Neuroscience* 24, no. 167–202 (2001).

Minear, Richard H. "Homeland Security." *Review of Politics* 66 (2004): 330–33.

Mineka, Susan, and Arne Ohman. "Learning and Unlearning Fears: Preparedness, Neural Pathways, and Patients." *Biological Psychiatry* 52 (2002): 927–37.

Morrison, David C. "Like, You Know, the Bomb Thing." *National Journal* 26 (1994): 24–27.

Moskalenko, S., C. McCauley, and P. Rozin. "Group Identification under Conditions of Threat: College Students' Attachment to Country, Family, Ethnicity, Religion, and University before and after September 11, 2001." *Political Psychology* 27, no. 1 (2006): 77–97.

Mote, John R. *Virus and Rickettsial Diseases.* Cambridge, Mass.: Harvard University Press, 1940.

Murphy, Priscilla Coit. *What a Book Can Do: The Publication and Reception of* Silent Spring. Springfield: University of Massachusetts Press, 2005.

Nader, Ralph. *Unsafe at Any Speed: The Designed-In Dangers of the American Automobile.* New York: Grossman, 1965.

National Academy of Sciences. *Understanding and Responding to Climate Change: Highlights of National Academies Reports.* Washington, D.C.: National Academy of Sciences, 2005.

Nelkin, Dorothy. "Ecologists and the Public Interest." *Hastings Center Report* 6 (1976): 38–44.

———. "Scientists and Professional Responsibility: The Experience of American Ecologists." *Social Studies of Science* 7 (1977): 75–95.

Neuman, W. Russell. "The Threshold of Public Attention." *Public Opinion Quarterly* 54 (1990): 159–76.

Neuner, Frank, Margarete Schauer, Unni Karunakara, and Christine Klaschik. "A Comparison of Narrative Exposure Therapy, Supportive Counseling, and Psychoeducation for Treating Posttraumatic Stress Disorder in an African Refugee Settlement." *Journal of Counseling and Clinical Psychology* 72 (2004): 597–87.

Neustadt, Richard E., and Harvey V. Fineberg. *The Swine Flu Affair: Decision-Making on a Slippery Disease.* Seattle: University Press of the Pacific, 2005.

Newell, Allen, and Herbert A. Simon. *Human Problem Solving.* Englewood Cliffs, N.J.: Prentice-Hall, 1972.

Noble, Agnes, and Colin Jones. "Benefits of Narrative Therapy: Holistic Interventions at the End of Life." *British Journal of Nursing* 14 (2005): 330–33.

Nohl, Johannes. *The Black Death*. London: George Allen & Unwin, 1926.

Norton, Andre. *No Night without Stars*. New York: Fawcett, 1979.

Oakes, Guy. *The Imaginary War: Civil Defense and American Cold War Culture*. New York: Oxford University Press, 1994.

Odean, Terrence. "Volume, Volatility, Price, and Profit When All Traders Are above Average." *Journal of Finance* 53 (1998): 1887–934.

Office of Technology Assessment. *Proliferation of Weapons of Mass Destruction: Assessing the Risks*. Washington, D.C.: U.S. Government Printing Office, 1993.

Ogburn, William Fielding. "Sociology and the Atom." *American Journal of Sociology* 51 (1946): 267–75.

O'Grada, Cormac, and Eugene N. White. "Who Panics During Panics? Evidence from a Nineteenth Century Savings Bank." *National Bureau of Economic Research Working Papers* (2002): No. 8856.

Ogura, Toyofumi. *Letters from the End of the World: A Firsthand Account of the Bombing of Hiroshima*. Tokyo: Kodansha International, 1997.

Olson, Patrick. "The Thucydides Syndrome: Ebola Déjà Vu? (or Ebola Reemergent?)." *Emerging Infectious Diseases* 2 (1996): 1–23.

Ostriker, Alicia. "The Window, at the Moment of Flame." In *September 11, 2001*, edited by William Heyen, p. 294. Silver Spring, Md.: Etruscan Press, 2002.

Palfreman, Jon. "A Tale of Two Fears: Exploring Media Depictions of Nuclear Power and Global Warming." *Review of Policy Research* 23 (2006): 23–43.

Patt, Anthony, and Richard Zeckhauser. "Action Bias and Environmental Decisions." *Journal of Risk and Uncertainty* 21 (2000): 45–72.

Percy, Walker. *Lost in the Cosmos: The Last Self-Help Book*. New York: Washington Square Press, 1983.

Perrow, Charles. *Normal Accidents: Living with High-Risk Technologies*. Princeton, N.J.: Princeton University Press, 1999.

———. *The Next Catastrophe: Reducing Our Vulnerabilities to Natural, Industrial, and Terrorist Disasters*. Princeton, N.J.: Princeton University Press, 2007.

Peters, Thomas J., and Robert H. Waterman Jr. *In Search of Excellence: Lessons from America's Best-Run Companies*. New York: Warner, 1982.

Polito, Robert. "Last Seen." In *110 Stories: New York Writes after September 11*, edited by Ulrich Baer, pp. 238–39. New York: New York University Press, 2002.

Poole, J. C. F. "Thucydides and the Plague of Athens." *Classical Quarterly* 29 (1979): 282–300.

Posner, Richard A. *Catastrophe: Risk and Response*. New York: Oxford University Press, 2004.

Powell, Robert. "Nuclear Deterrence and the Strategy of Limited Retaliation." *American Political Science Review* 83 (1989): 503–19.

Preston, Richard. *The Hot Zone*. New York: Random House, 1994.

Prewitt, Kenneth. "The Politics of Fear after 9/11." *Social Research* 71 (2004): 1129–46.

Price, Edward, Jr. "Historical Generations in Freeze Member Mobilization." In *Peace Action in the Eighties: Social Science Perspectives*, edited by Sam Marullo and John Lofland, pp. 24–27. New Brunswick, N.J.: Rutgers University Press, 1990.

Price, Jerome. *The Antinuclear Movement*. Boston: Twayne, 1990.

Putnam, Robert D. "Bowling Alone: America's Declining Social Capital." *Journal of Democracy* 6 (1995): 65–78.

———. *Bowling Alone: The Collapse and Revival of American Community*. New York: Simon & Schuster, 2000.

Pyszczynski, T. "What Are We So Afraid Of? A Terror Management Theory Perspective on the Politics of Fear." *Social Research* 71, no. 4 (2004): 827–48.

Pyszczynski, Tom, Jeff Greenberg, and Sheldon Solomon. "A Dual-Process Model of Defense against Conscious and Unconscious Death-Related Thoughts: An Extension of Terror Management Theory." *Psychological Review* 106 (1999): 835–45.

Pyszczynski, T., J. Greenberg, and S. Solomon. "Why Do We Need What We Need? A Terror Management Perspective on the Roots of Human Social Motivation." *Psychological Inquiry* 8, no. 1 (1997): 1–20.

Pyszczynski, T., S. Solomon, J. Greenberg, J. Arndt, and J. Schimel. "Why Do People Need Self-Esteem? A Theoretical and Empirical Review." *Psychological Bulletin* 130, no. 3 (2004): 435–68.

Pyszczynski, Thomas A., Sheldon Solomon, and Jeff Greenberg. *In the Wake of 9/11: The Psychology of Terror*. Washington, D.C.: American Psychological Association, 2002.

Randolph, Theron G. *Human Ecology and Susceptibility to the Chemical Environment*. Springfield, Ill.: C. C. Thomas, 1962.

Rasinski, Kenneth A., Jennifer Berktold, Tom W. Smith, and Bethany L. Albertson. *America Recovers: A Follow-up to a National Study of Public Response to the September 11th Terrorist Attacks*. Chicago: National Opinion Research Center, 2002.

Redlener, Irwin, and David A. Berman. "National Preparedness Planning: The Historical Context and Current State of the U.S. Public's Readiness, 1940–2005." *Journal of International Affairs* 59 (2006): 87–103.

Relyea, Harold C. "Organizing for Homeland Security." *Presidential Studies Quarterly* 33 (2003): 602–24.

Rindfleisch, A., and J. E. Burroughs. "Terrifying Thoughts, Terrible Materialism? Contemplations on a Terror Management Account of Materialism and Consumer Behavior." *Journal of Consumer Psychology* 14, no. 3 (2004): 219–24.

Roberts, Leslie. "Study Raises Estimate of Vietnam War Stress." *Science* 241 (1988): 788.

Roberts, Patrick S. "Fema after Katrina." *Policy Review* 137 (2006): 15–33.

Robinson, Kim Stanley. *Fifty Degrees Below*. New York: Bantam, 2005.

———. *Forty Signs of Rain*. New York: Bantam, 2004.

———. *Sixty Days and Counting*. New York: Bantam, 2007.

Rodgers, J. L., C. A. St John, and R. Coleman. "Did Fertility Go up after the Oklahoma City Bombing? An Analysis of Births in Metropolitan Counties in Oklahoma, 1990–1999." *Demography* 42, no. 4 (2005): 675–92.

Rudd, Robert. *Pesticides and the Living Landscape*. Madison: University of Wisconsin Press, 1964.

Russett, Bruce, Thomas Hartley, and Shoon Murray. "The End of the Cold War, Attitude Change, and the Politics of Defense Spending." *PS: Political Science and Politics* 27 (1994): 17–22.

Said, Edward W. *Orientalism*. New York: Vintage, 1979.

Sale, Kirkpatrick. *The Green Revolution: The American Environmental Movement, 1962–1992*. New York: Hill and Wang, 1993.

Salzman, M. B. "Globalization, Culture, and Anxiety: Perspectives and Predictions from Terror Management Theory." *Journal of Social Distress and the Homeless* 10, no. 4 (2001): 337–52.

Schell, Jonathan. *The Fate of the Earth*. New York: Alfred A. Knopf, 1982.

Schlenger, William E., Juesta M. Caddell, Lori Ebert, B. Kathleen Jordan, Kathryn M. Rourke, David Wilson, Lisa Thalji, J. Michael Dennis, John A. Fairbank, and Richard A. Kulka. "Psychological Reactions to Terrorist Attacks: Findings from the National Study of Americans' Reactions to September 11." *Journal of the American Medical Association* 288, no. 2002 (2002): 518–88.

Schlosser, Eric. *Fast Food Nation: The Dark Side of the All-American Meal.* Boston: Houghton Mifflin, 2001.

Schoenfeld, Alan H. "Beyond the Purely Cognitive: Belief Systems, Social Cognitions, and Metacognitions as Driving Forces in Intellectual Performance." *Cognitive Science* 7 (1983): 329–63.

Scott, Wilbur J. "PTSD in DSM-III: A Case in the Politics of Diagnosis and Disease." *Social Problems* 37 (1990): 294–310.

Sencer, David J., and J. Donald Millar. "Reflections on the 1976 Swine Flu Vaccination Program." *Emerging Infectious Diseases* 12 (2006): 29–33.

Shapiro, Jerome. *Atomic Bomb Cinema: The Apocalyptic Imagination on Film.* New York: Routledge, 2001.

Sharrett, Christopher. *Crisis Cinema: The Apocalyptic Idea in Postmodern Narrative Film.* Washington, D.C.: Maisonneuve Press, 1993.

Shaw, Bill. "Economics and Environment: A 'Land Ethic' Critique of Economic Policy." *Journal of Business Ethics* 33 (2001): 51–57.

Shute, Nevil. *On the Beach.* New York: William Morrow, 1957.

Silberstein, Sandra, ed. *War of Words: Language, Politics and 9/11.* London and New York: Routledge, 2002.

Silveira, Stacy J. "The American Environmental Movement: Surviving through Diversity." *Boston College Environmental Affairs Law Review* 28 (2001): 497–532.

Singer, Peter. *Animal Liberation.* New York: Random House, 1975.

Skocpol, Theda. "Will 9/11 and the War on Terror Revitalize American Civic Democracy?" *PS: Political Science and Politics* 35 (2002): 537–40.

Smelser, Neil J. *Theory of Collective Behavior.* New York: Free Press, 1962.

Smith, Tom W. "The Cuban Missile Crisis and U.S. Public Opinion." *Public Opinion Quarterly* 67 (2003): 265–93.

Sontag, Susan. "The Imagination of Disaster." In *Against Interpretation and Other Essays,* edited by Susan Sontag, pp. 209–25. New York: Noonday Press, 1966.

Speth, James Gustave. *Red Sky at Morning: America and the Crisis of the Global Environment.* New Haven, Conn.: Yale University Press, 2005.

Stallings, Robert A. *Promoting Risk: Constructing the Earthquake Threat.* Hawthorne, N.Y.: Aldine de Gruyter, 1995.

Steg, Linds, and Inge Sievers. "Cultural Theory and Individual Perceptions of Environmental Risks." *Environment and Behavior* 32 (2000): 250–69.

Stern, Nicholas. *The Economics of Climate Change: The Stern Review.* Cambridge: Cambridge University Press, 2006.

Swatos, William H., and Lutz Kaelber, eds. *The Protestant Ethic Turns 100: Essays on the Centenary of the Weber Thesis.* New York: Paradigm, 2005.

Swerdlow, Amy. *Women Strike for Peace: Traditional Motherhood and Radical Politics in the 1960s.* Chicago: University of Chicago Press, 1993.

Swidler, Ann. "Cultural Power and Social Movements." In *Social Movements and Culture,* edited by Hank Johnston and Bert Klandermans, pp. 25–40. Minneapolis: University of Minnesota Press, 1995.

———. "Culture in Action: Symbols and Strategies." *American Sociological Review* 51 (1986): 273–86.

Taubman-Ben-Ari, O. "Intimacy and Risky Sexual Behavior—What Does It Have to Do with Death?" *Death Studies* 28, no. 9 (2004): 865–87.

Taubman-Ben-Ari, O., and L. Findler. "Reckless Driving and Gender: An Examination of a Terror Management Theory Explanation." *Death Studies* 27, no. 7 (2003): 603–18.

Taylor, Diana. "Ground Zero." *Signs* 28 (2002): 448–50.

Thomas, Lewis. "Dying as Failure." *Annals of the American Academy of Political and Social Science* 447 (1980): 1–4.

Tirman, John. "How We Ended the Cold War." *Nation* 269 (1999): 13–21.

Torry, Robert. "Apocalypse Then: Benefits of the Bomb in Fifties Science Fiction Films." *Cinema Journal* 31 (1991): 7–21.

Townsend, John Rowe. *Noah's Castle*. New York: Dell, 1978.

Toynbee, Arnold. "The Present Point in History." *Foreign Affairs* 26 (1947): 187–95.

Trumpener, Ulrich. "The Road to Ypres: The Beginnings of Gas Warfare in World War I." *Journal of Modern History* 47 (1975): 460–80.

Turner, Ralph H., and Lewis M. Killian. *Collective Behavior*. Englewood Cliffs, N.J.: Prentice-Hall, 1957.

Twenge, Jean M. "The Age of Anxiety? Birth Cohort Change in Anxiety and Neuroticism, 1952–1993." *Journal of Personality and Social Psychology* 79, no. 6 (2000): 1007–21.

Useem, Michael. "Apocalypse Tomorrow." *Contemporary Sociology* 11 (1982): 610–11.

Van Gelder, Timothy J. "Credible Threats and Usable Weapons: Some Dilemmas of Deterrance." *Philosophy and Public Affairs* 18 (1989): 158–83.

Vaughn, Jacqueline, and Gary C. Bryner. *Environmental Politics: Domestic and Global Dimensions*. New York: St. Martin's Press, 1998.

Vernor, Richard E. "Developments in the Field of Fire Prevention." *Annals of the American Academy of Political and Social Science* 161 (1932): 152–58.

Vig, Elizabeth K., and Robert A. Pearlman. "Quality of Life While Dying: A Qualitative Study of Terminally Ill Older Men." *Journal of the American Geriatrics Society* 51 (2003): 1959–601.

Waddell, Craig, ed. *And No Birds Sing: Rhetorical Analyses of Rachel Carson's* Silent Spring. Carbondale, Ill.: Southern Illinois University Press, 2000.

Wagner, Richard V. "Psychology and the Threat of Nuclear War." *American Psychologist* 40 (1985): 531–35.

Walker, Martin. *The Cold War: A History*. New York: Henry Holt, 1994.

Weart, Spencer R. *The Discovery of Global Warming*. Cambridge, Mass.: Harvard University Press, 2003.

———. *Nuclear Fear: A History of Images*. Cambridge, Mass.: Harvard University Press, 1988.

Webb, E. "Ernest Becker and the Psychology of Worldviews." *Zygon* 33, no. 1 (1998): 71–86.

Weber, Eugen. *Apocalypses: Prophecies, Cults, and Millennial Beliefs through the Ages*. Cambridge, Mass.: Harvard University Press, 2000.

Weber, Max. *The Protestant Ethic and the Spirit of Capitalism*. Oxford: Blackwell, 2002.

———. *Sociology of Religion*. Boston: Beacon, 1993.

Wedel, Janine. *Collision and Collusion: The Strange Case of Western Aid to Eastern Europe*. New York: St. Martin's Press, 1998.

Wegner, Daniel M. *White Bears and Other Unwanted Thoughts: Suppression, Obsession, and the Psychology of Mental Control*. New York: Viking, 1989.

Wegner, Daniel M., and David J. Schneider. "The White Bear Story." *Psychological Inquiry* 14 (2003): 326–29.

Wegner, Daniel M., David J. Schneider, Samuel R. III Carter, and Teri L. White. "Paradoxical Effects of Thought Suppression." *Journal of Personality and Social Psychology* 53 (1987): 5–13.

Weigel, George. "Schultz, Reagan, and the Revisionists." *Commentary* 96 (1993): 50–53.

Weinberg, Alvin M. "Scientific Millenarianism." *Proceedings of the American Philosophical Society* 143 (1999): 531–39.

Wells, Samuel F. Jr. "The Origins of Massive Retaliation." *Political Science Quarterly* 96 (1981): 31–52.

Wernette, D. R. "The Freeze Movement on the Local Level." In *Peace Action in the Eighties: Social Science Perspectives*, edited by Sam Marullo and John Lofland, pp. 140–51. New Brunswick, N.J.: Rutgers University Press, 1990.

Western, Bruce. *Punishment and Inequality in America*. New York: Russell Sage Foundation, 2006.

Whitfield, Stephen J. *The Culture of the Cold War*. 2nd ed. Baltimore: Johns Hopkins University Press, 1996.

Wilcox, Fred A. *Waiting for an Army to Die: The Tragedy of Agent Orange*. New York: Seven Locks Press, 1989.

Williams, Anna C. "We Exposed Our Students to Atomic Energy." *School Review* 57 (1949): 295–99.

Williams, Lonna Lisa. *Like a Tree Planted*. New York: BookSurge, 2003.

Wilson, Edward O. *The Diversity of Life*. Cambridge, Mass.: Harvard University Press, 1992.

Wisman, A., and J. L. Goldenberg. "From the Grave to the Cradle: Evidence That Mortality Salience Engenders a Desire for Offspring." *Journal of Personality and Social Psychology* 89 (2005): 46–61.

Woodward, Bob. *Bush at War*. New York: Simon & Schuster, 2002.

———. *Plan of Attack. Bush at War*, Part II. New York: Simon & Schuster, 2004.

———. *State of Denial. Bush at War*, Part III. New York: Simon & Schuster, 2006.

Wuthnow, Robert. *America and the Challenges of Religious Diversity*. Princeton, N.J.: Princeton University Press, 2005.

Yum, Y. O., and W. Schenck-Hamlin. "Reactions to 9/11 as a Function of Terror Management and Perspective Taking." *Journal of Social Psychology* 145 (2005): 265–86.

Zarlengo, Kristina. "Civilian Threat, the Suburban Citadel, and Atomic Age American Women." *Signs* 24 (1999): 925–58.

Zerubavel, Eviatar. *The Elephant in the Room: Silence and Denial in Everyday Life*. New York: Oxford University Press, 2006.

Ziegler, Phillip. *The Black Death*. London: Collins, 1969.

INDEX